Justice, Luck, and Knowledge

Justice, Luck, and Knowledge

S. L. Hurley

Harvard University Press

Cambridge, Massachusetts, and London, England | 2003

Copyright © 2003 by the President and Fellows of Harvard College

All rights reserved

Printed in the United States of America

Library of Congress Cataloging-in-Publication Data

Hurley, S. L. (Susan L.)
  Justice, luck, and knowledge / S. L. Hurley.
    p. cm.
  Includes bibliographical references (p.   ) and index.
  ISBN 0-674-01029-9 (alk. paper)
  1. Responsibility. 2. Distributive justice. 3. Fortune—Moral and ethical
aspects. I. Title.

BJ1451.H87 2003
172—dc21   2002038824

For Alasdair and Merryn

Acknowledgments

Many thanks to the Nuffield Foundation for its support of this work in the form of a Social Science Senior Research Fellowship, and to the University of Warwick for giving me leave to take up this fellowship. The time it provided was crucial in bringing this project to fruition. I am also grateful to All Souls College for providing a serene and congenial environment in which to produce the final draft of this book.

For helpful comments on earlier drafts of various chapters and discussion of related ideas, thanks also to Karin Boxer, Bill Brewer, Ruth Chang, Gerald Cohen, Joshua Cohen, Roger Crisp, Martin Davies, Ronald Dworkin, John Martin Fischer, Harry Frankfurt, Mark Greenberg, Stephen Hartkamp, Brad Hooker, Shelly Kagan, Martha Klein, Liam Murphy, Michael Otsuka, David Papineau, Derek Parfit, Thomas Pogge, Joseph Raz, John Roemer, Gideon Rosen, Paul Seabright, Michael Smith, Hillel Steiner, Steven Stich, Galen Strawson, Larry Temkin, Peter Vallentyne, Frank Vandenbroucke, Philippe Van Parijs, Andrew Williams, Bernard Williams, Susan Wolf, Christopher Woodard, various anonymous referees, and members of audiences on various occasions on which I've presented this material, including those at several seminars at All Souls College, Oxford. Very many thanks to Lindsay Waters for his excellent editorial advice and his patience. I am also especially grateful to Gerald Cohen for his generous interest in and encouragement of this project, and for providing an inimitably marvelous combination of inspiration, criticism, and jokes.

I am grateful for permission to use revised material from previously published articles in this book. Chapters 1 and 2 revise material from "Responsibility, Reason, and Irrelevant Alternatives," *Philosophy and Public Affairs*, 28 (2000) 205–241, copyright © 2000 Princeton University Press, by permission of Princeton University Press. Chapter 3 revises "Is Responsibility Essentially Impossible?," *Philosophical Studies*, 99 (2000)

229–268, by permission of Kluwer Academic Publishers, copyright © 2000. Chapter 4 uses revised material from "Luck, Responsibility, and the 'Natural Lottery,'" *Journal of Political Philosophy* 10(1) (2002), 79–94, copyright © S. L. Hurley, 2002. Chapter 6 revises "Luck and Equality," *Proceedings of the Aristotelian Society*, Supp. Volume LXXV (2001), 51–72, by courtesy of the editor of the Aristotelian Society, copyright © 2001. Chapter 7 uses revised material from "Roemer on Responsibility and Equality," *Law and Philosophy* 21 (2002), 39–64, by permission of Kluwer Academic Publishers, copyright © 2002. Chapter 10 is based on "Cognitivism in Political Philosophy," in *Well-Being and Morality: Essays in Honour of James Griffin,* Roger Crisp and Brad Hooker, eds., Oxford, Oxford University Press, 2000, 177–208, by permission of Oxford University Press, copyright © 2000.

Contents

Contents

Introduction:
Responsibility and Justice

1. Recent Advances in Two Areas

The recent past has seen striking advances in our understanding of two related topics in normative philosophy: moral responsibility and distributive justice. The advances are striking in part because the debates and their battle lines have been long established. Distinctive new insights on such well-worn topics may take us by surprise. Yet distinctive new insights there are, and traditional battle lines have been altered.

The new understanding of distributive justice sees the deep structure of issues about egalitarianism in terms of responsibility. It is associated especially with work by Cohen, Arneson, and Roemer (who gives it a canonical statement in his 1996 book *Theories of Distributive Justice*). This new body of work sheds much light on the preceding debate about whether justice requires equality of welfare, of resources, or of something else, by analyzing this debate in terms of an underlying egalitarian aim, the *luck-neutralizing aim*. This is held to require that distributive justice should respect differences between people's positions for which they are responsible but should neutralize differences that are a matter of luck. It is arguable that the motivation for the luck-neutralizing account of justice is the broadly Kantian view that justice, along with rationality and autonomy, cannot depend on mere luck. The Kantian seeds of the fully blossomed luck-neutralizing account we now have were already present in Rawls's 1971 book *A Theory of Justice*, with its use of the veil of ignorance to avoid the influence of "morally arbitrary" differences between people.

While the luck-neutralizing account gives responsibility a central role in distributive justice, it has not focused much analysis on responsibility itself or on how its structure or character might constrain its role within distributive justice. "Responsibility" is a term that provides considerable scope for equivocation. The central program of the luck-neutralizing approach

1

to distributive justice puts moral responsibility in play, yet at times "responsibility" seems to be used instead to mean something closer to deservingness, to fairness, or to institutional accountability. Moral responsibility is not the same thing as deservingness or fairness, nor is it entailed by institutional accountability. Indeed, moral responsibility itself is a contested concept. Appeals are often made to choice and control in this context, but with little differentiation or explanation. Roemer makes the frank assumption that issues about responsibility are to be bracketed and determined exogenously to the theory of distributive justice. Yet at times he makes moves that implicitly commit him to specific and disputed requirements for responsibility (see discussion in Chapters 6 and 7).

Meanwhile, the rumblings of change in our understanding of responsibility had begun with Harry Frankfurt's articles challenging the principle that responsibility for an act requires that you could have done otherwise. The traditional opponents, compatibilists and incompatibilists, shared this principle, and differed over whether you could indeed do otherwise in any relevant sense given causal determinism. But in what have become known as *Frankfurt Cases* the agent could not have done otherwise, yet intuitively may still be responsible.

For example, Sam confides his plan to murder the mayor, and his political reasons for this plan, to his friend Jack. Jack likes this plan, but to ensure that Sam carries it out he installs a monitoring device in Sam's brain that would intervene, should Sam's resolve waver, to cause him to act as planned. As it turns out, Sam's resolve does not waver. He assassinates the mayor for his own reasons and the fail-safe device has no causal influence on what happens. Sam is intuitively morally responsible, even though he could not have done otherwise (Fischer and Ravizza 1991).

From this point the debate about responsibility proceeded in various fruitful directions. Frankfurt's position has been challenged but also extensively and subtly defended (Fischer 1994; Klein 1990; Shatz 1986; Van Inwagen 1983; Watson 1982). The moral importance of Frankfurt's cases can be questioned; in view of the role of the science-fiction fail-safe device in such cases, they may be seen as special or quirky cases, not central to morality. I here dispute this view, and argue that a central intuition behind Frankfurt Cases generalizes and has a wide and significant range of application. But even setting this claim aside, these cases have important taxonomic implications. The salient consequence for present purposes is the emergence of a distinction between two principles of responsibility that the traditional debate ran together (Fischer 1994; Klein 1990). One is the *ability-to-do-otherwise requirement*. It claims that responsibility requires the possibility of acting otherwise than you do. The other is what I here call the *regression requirement*.[1] It claims that to be responsible for something you must be responsible for its causes.

These two requirements turn out to be independent of one another, at least at a very general level. The regression requirement concerns the character of the actual sequence of causes that leads to an act. The ability-to-do-otherwise requirement, by contrast, requires the possibility of an alternate sequence leading to some other possible act (Fischer 1994). In principle someone might be responsible for all the actual causes of an act, and all their causes, and so on, even though no other acts were possible, given determinism. Conversely, it might be possible for someone to have acted otherwise, given indeterminism, even though he was not responsible for all the actual causes of his actual act, their causes, and so on. Once these two conditions of responsibility are distinguished, they can be better evaluated. Moreover, these two requirements illustrate a more general distinction between alternate-sequence and actual-sequence requirements for responsibility (Fischer 1994). Within each category there are other, rival requirements. For example, a rival alternate-sequence requirement is the requirement of ability to avoid blame. Various dispositional reason-responsiveness requirements are rival actual-sequence principles.

2. Opening the Black Box

This book has a modest aim. It is not to offer a full theory or comprehensive survey or general evaluation of developments in the area of responsibility or justice. Rather, it brings some of the developments in these two areas into contact with one another. It entertains positions in each area for the sake of argument and considers relations between them. It examines, in a piecemeal way and by no means exhaustively, some of the ways in which the articulation of responsibility can affect or constrain its potential roles within theories of distributive justice.

The black box of responsibility that luck-neutralizing accounts build into the heart of egalitarian distributive justice turns out, when opened, to be something of a Pandora's box. Must egalitarianism be so burdened? We can accept that the luck-neutralizing aim provides an illuminating and uni-

---

1. There are various related formulations in the literature, not all equivalent, but what I call "the regression requirement" represents their central tendency.

fying account of the motivations underlying recent debate about egalitarianism. But having identified this aim, we can step back from it, consider the further issues it raises and whether on reflection it provides the best basis for an egalitarian account of distributive justice. I do this by distinguishing various roles that responsibility might play in a theory of distributive justice. I emphasize the distinction between the question of *what* to distribute and the question of *how* to distribute. I argue that responsibility cannot tell us how to distribute at all, let alone to distribute in an egalitarian manner. It can, however, play other important roles in a theory of justice.

Can a stronger case for egalitarianism be made by assuming a fundamental aim other than the aim to neutralize luck? In Chapter 10 I suggest an alternative: the *bias-neutralizing aim*. Instead of aiming to neutralize luck, we could aim to neutralize bias—that is, to neutralize influences that distort beliefs about what should be done, such as the influence of personal desires to believe that something is true. Responsibility would still play essential if indirect roles in distributive justice, in relation to the personality structures that set the parameters of incentive-seeking behavior and as a component of our well-being. But in these less demanding roles responsibility may not be as problematic as when it is centerstage, as in luck-neutralizing accounts of justice. I argue that aiming to neutralize bias instead of luck in fact supports egalitarianism, and does so in a way that avoids the difficulties about responsibility faced by luck-neutralizing egalitarianism.

Throughout this book, "responsibility" is intended in the full-blooded sense that licenses praise, blame, and reactive attitudes and that implies accountability in principle. Sometimes I will distinguish between moral responsibility and causal responsibility. But when I speak simply of "responsibility" I mean moral responsibility in this full-blooded sense. On the one hand, accountability does not entail moral responsibility. Perhaps in some situations there can be good institutional or pragmatic or other reasons to hold people accountable, even if they are not morally responsible for what they do. But responsibility in the sense of institutional accountability cannot provide a basis for designing the institutions of distributive justice in the first place, which is what responsibility is supposed to do in luck-neutralizing approaches to distributive justice. So institutional accountability cannot play the role that responsibility is supposed to play in this approach. On the other hand, I use "responsibility" in a sense such that moral responsibility does entail accountability in principle (even if this is overridden for pragmatic or institutional reasons). Those who are morally responsible for what they do are by the same token accountable, in principle, for what they do even if there are good practical reasons not to hold them institutionally accountable. If there is some weaker sense of "responsibility" that does not have this implication of accountability in principle, it is not mine, nor do I think it is a sense that has been central to the literature on moral responsibility.

3. Survey

Part I of the book, Chapters 1 through 4, focuses on responsibility and its inverse correlate, luck. Part II, Chapters 5 through 10, goes on to assess responsibility-based approaches to justice, in the light of arguments about responsibility from Part I. A brief description of each chapter is given below.

Chapter 1 provides a philosophical landscape, a background against which the arguments of subsequent chapters is developed.[2] It lays out a view of how issues about responsibility are reconfigured in light of the distinction between actual-sequence and alternate-sequence conditions of responsibility. In the wake of Frankfurt's work, this important distinction has been further articulated by others and has influenced in particular the development of reason-based views of responsibility. The interacting arguments of three philosophers, Martha Klein, Susan Wolf, and John Martin Fischer, are used as reference points in laying out the new articulation of responsibility. In the course of exploring this territory, I explain why the ability-to-do-otherwise requirement is independent of the regression requirement. I distinguish causal conceptions of moral responsibility, such as those involving actual choice or control, from noncausal conceptions, such as a hypothetical choice conception. I explain why the latter leaves responsibility indeterminate. I distinguish a regression requirement from other actual-sequence requirements, such as various requirements of reason-responsiveness. I explain why the combination of a regression requirement with a requirement of choice or control makes responsibility impossible. The major threat to responsibility now looks to be the regression requirement rather than determinism, and I consider how reason-based accounts of responsibility can respond to this threat.

---

2. The view it provides is strongly influenced by Fischer's work and general conception of the territory.

Chapter 2 argues that alternate sequences are irrelevant to responsibility. It gives an argument that is tangentially related to but more general in certain respects than Frankfurt's argument. A recipe is developed for eliciting the *irrelevant-alternative intuition*. According to this intuition, the outright possibility of doing otherwise, all else constant, is not what matters for responsibility. If the agent *wouldn't* have done otherwise whether or not she could have, then it is irrelevant whether or not she could have. This intuition is a significant generalization of the intuition evoked by Frankfurt Cases, and applies to a wider range of cases. The irrelevant-alternative intuition is illustrated by various cases involving weakness of will, evil, and medical problems. It is explained in terms of the possibility of variable realization of a disposition across deterministic and indeterministic worlds.

Chapter 3 pursues the question of whether responsibility is essentially impossible because it requires regressive choice or control. It briefly canvasses the general issue of when elimination of an entity or property is warranted, as opposed to revision of our view of it, and the connections of this issue with the distinction between context-driven and theory-driven accounts of reference and essence. Context-driven accounts tend to be less hospitable to eliminativism than theory-driven accounts, but this tendency should not be overstated. Since both types of account give essences explanatory depth, eliminativist claims associated with supposed impossible essences are problematic on both types of account.

These considerations are then applied to responsibility in particular. I argue that the impossibility of regressive choice or control does not support eliminativism about responsibility, on either context-driven or theory-driven accounts of responsibility. To avoid indeterminacy problems, responsibility needs a causal component that is incompatible with a regression requirement. From this we should conclude not that responsibility is impossible, but rather that responsibility is not regressive.

Chapter 4 probes the concept of luck as it features in moral and political philosophy. I distinguish a thin concept of luck from various thick conceptions. On the thin concept, luck is simply the inverse correlate of responsibility, so that what is a matter of luck for someone is what he is not responsible for. On alternative thick readings, luck has more specific implications; for example, it may be associated with luck in lotteries, or lack of control, or lack of choice. I argue that we should adopt the thin usage of "luck" for purposes of moral and political philosophy. In particular, I apply the distinction to constitutive luck, and use it to criticize the thick conception of constitutive luck expressed by the idea of a "natural lottery." This metaphor does no work in helping to understand constitutive luck. The concept of a lottery does have independent implications, first about the identity of the agent who enters the lottery, and second about the role of chance in lotteries. But both of these implications are misleading and confusing when applied to constitutive luck. The identity-dependence of lotteries gives rise to a bare self problem, and the relationship of chance to responsibility is not what the lottery metaphor suggests, whether chance is understood metaphysically or epistemically. The natural lottery metaphor is positively unhelpful in understanding constitutive luck, and is better avoided.

At the end of Chapter 4 I briefly draw together and highlight arguments from Part I that are used in Part II, which brings the discussion of responsibility to bear on theories of justice.

Egalitarians believe that distributive justice favors equality across persons. But equality of what? The answers to that question that have evolved over the past three decades have given concepts of luck and responsibility an increasingly explicit and central role. Even so, these concepts operate for many purposes as black boxes within accounts of justice. I argue that when we open the black box, the role of responsibility in justice is reconfigured and relocated. The luck-neutralizing account of justice backs into the role of responsibility from a focus on intuitions about distributive justice. My complementary approach is to articulate and distinguish various conditions of responsibility and their relations to control, to choice, and so on, and then to work forward to consider the possible roles of these conceptions of responsibility in an account of justice.

Part II begins with a survey of luck-neutralizing views of distributive justice. Chapter 5 again provides a philosophical landscape.[3] (It can be skimmed over by those already familiar with the territory.) It briefly and selectively describes the development of the luck-neutralizing approach from Rawls, through Sen and Dworkin, to Cohen and Roemer. Though I go on to criticize the luck-neutralizing approach to justice, my arguments are especially indebted to the seminal articulations of luck-neutralizing egalitarianism by Cohen and Roemer.

Gerald Cohen has expressed the view that the aim to neutralize luck provides the fundamental motivation of egalitarianism. In Chapter 6 I ar-

---

3. The view it provides is strongly influenced by Roemer's conception of the territory, especially in his 1996 book.

gue that the luck-neutralizing aim cannot provide a basis for egalitarianism. It can neither specify nor justify an egalitarian pattern of distribution. Luck and responsibility can play a role in determining *what* justice requires to be redistributed, but from this we cannot derive *how* to distribute: we cannot derive a pattern of distribution from the currency of distributive justice, let alone an equal pattern in particular. Nor does responsibility provide a basis for taking equality as a default position, departures from which must be justified. I also set out the *luck-neutralizer's dilemma*. We can understand bad luck in either interpersonal or counterfactual terms. On the one hand, the aim to neutralize interpersonal bad luck specifies an egalitarian pattern of distribution only trivially, since interpersonal inequality is used to define bad luck and does nothing to justify it. On the other hand, the aim to neutralize counterfactual bad luck neither specifies nor justifies an egalitarian pattern of distribution. Responsibility judgments cannot in general tell us how to distribute, because they are not primarily about interpersonal relations and because they often do not extend in any determinate way to counterfactual situations.

It may be tempting to think that, at least if everything were a matter of luck and no one were responsible for anything, then egalitarianism would be supported. Aiming to neutralize the effects on something of luck that occurs anywhere back among that thing's causes leads to treating everything as among the effects of luck. Aiming to neutralize *the effects of luck on X* just is aiming to neutralize the effects *of luck in X's causes*. In effect, this aim operationalizes the regression requirement, which threatens to make responsibility impossible. But even if everything turns out to be among the effects of luck, this still gives us no reason to think that equality would neutralize the effects of luck. And if responsibility is impossible, then it is also impossible to neutralize the effects of luck. It might also be thought that we can argue for equality from the supposition of identical autonomous bare selves, which are supposedly what is left when everything that is a matter of luck is stripped away from the self. However, there are powerful reasons to doubt there are any such selves.

Chapter 6 does not argue against egalitarianism, or even against the view that equality should be taken as a default position when people are not responsible for what they have. Rather, it argues that considerations of responsibility and luck do not provide a basis for these views. But there may well be some other basis for them.

John Roemer gives an ingenious and illuminating account of what it would be to neutralize luck. Chapter 7 examines Roemer's account to see whether it can be used to show how the luck-neutralizing aim could provide a basis for egalitarianism (though this may not have been Roemer's intention). I argue that it cannot do this work. What it does do is show how to reward people equally who make equal efforts to behave in ways we regard as deserving. But giving people what they deserve on account of their efforts is not the same as giving them what they are responsible for. Nor is equalizing what people are not responsible for the same as giving them what they are responsible for. Moreover, depending on what behavior we regard as deserving, a Roemerian system of rewards may or may not favor equal patterns of distribution. Treating like cases alike in the way Roemer spells out is not enough to guarantee that relatively equal patterns of distribution are favored over relatively unequal ones, other things equal. However, if Roemer's scheme for rewarding merit is properly limited to specific, democratically adopted policies, it may well be a valuable and effective tool of policy implementation.

The arguments of Chapters 6 and 7 emphasize the distinction between *what* to distribute and *how* to distribute. They focus on why responsibility cannot tell us how to distribute, or to distribute equally in particular. For responsibility to play this role, it would have to tell us, when the level of goods someone actually enjoys is a matter of luck for him, what other, counterfactual level of goods would not be a matter of luck for him. But I argue that such issues of counterfactual responsibility are often indeterminate.

My arguments up to this point, however, leave it open for responsibility to tell us what goods to redistribute. It can contribute to defining the currency of distributive justice within a theory according to which goods are exempt from redistribution to the extent people are responsible for them, so that distributive justice is only concerned with redistributing goods that are a matter of luck for people. In this way, responsibility can act as a filter on some independently specified category of goods (such as welfare or resources). Chapters 8 and 9 assess this goods-filtering, currency-defining role of responsibility in accounts of distributive justice.

Chapter 8 explores issues raised by Cohen's arguments about incentive inequality. Cohen considers whether the normative and supposedly descriptive premises of the standard maximin argument for incentive inequality are inconsistent. That is, is it inconsistent for the talented to aim to make the worst off as well off as possible, while also choosing to demand incentives and thus refusing to work harder without getting extra return? By making the latter choices, the talented fail to do what they could do to make the worst off still better off. But I uncover a danger of a different inconsistency. Is it inconsistent to aim to redistribute to the worst off only what is not down to choice while also holding that the talented can and should choose to work harder for less, to benefit the worst off? If goods for which people are responsible as a result of the choices they make are (at least partly) exempt from redistribution, why aren't the extra goods that result from the choices of the talented to work harder (at least partly) exempt?

My general strategy in Chapter 8 is to ask how Cohen's views about the currency of distributive justice can be combined with his separate arguments against incentive inequality. I consider various possible responses to this question, and how it interacts with various different views about the nature of responsibility (canvassed in Part I).

So far I have argued that responsibility cannot play a patterning role, telling us *how* to distribute, and have raised some issues about how it could be given a currency role, telling us *what* to distribute. Chapter 9 brings into focus two further roles that responsibility can play in accounts of distributive justice, the incentive-parameter role and the well-being role. These, I argue, are really the most important roles for responsibility in justice. When their relations to a currency role are examined, further problems emerge for the currency role, which I conclude is problematic and better dispensed with.

Facts and beliefs about responsibility can play an important role in motivating productive activity, including by acting as parameters on which the range of possible incentive-seeking behavior depends. Cohen suggests that whether the talented can work harder for less can depend on alterable normative expectations. Such normative expectations would include expectations based on the prevalent conception of responsibility and corresponding beliefs by the talented about how responsible they are for what they do. Such expectations, and hence the range of possible levels of incentive seeking, might be altered by altering conceptions of and beliefs about responsibility. If so, such conceptions and beliefs have a role as parameters on which the range of possible incentive-seeking behavior by the talented depends. From the perspective of a luck-neutralizing egalitarian social engineer, on what basis should such parameters be fixed? As Cohen points out, until this range is determined, the implications of a maximin principle of justice are indeterminate.

Moreover, facts and beliefs about responsibility can constitute and influence people's well-being in important ways. How should the egalitarian social engineer factor this well-being role into the parameter-setting and currency-filtering issues? I consider how the incentive-parameter and well-being roles of responsibility are related to the currency role. How do these three distinct roles interact: do they conflict, or constrain one another, or create unstable interdependencies, or admit of stable equilibria?

The final section of Chapter 9 considers briefly how these issues about incentive inequality look from an alternative, cognitive point of view, which adopts the aim to neutralize bias rather than luck. Aiming at knowledge provides a reason to adopt a perspective of ignorance in thinking about how goods should be distributed: because ignorance of ourselves would rule out many biasing influences, such as those deriving from self-interest. Thus a veil of ignorance may help to address the issue of what it is possible for the talented to do, while avoiding biasing influences. An approach to distributive justice based on the aim to neutralize bias rather than luck dispenses with the currency role of responsibility, but retains the incentive-parameter and well-being roles. While responsibility has an essential position in a cognitive approach, it is a different, less demanding position.

The bias-neutralizing alternative is pursued in the final chapter, Chapter 10. A bias-neutralizing account of distributive justice illustrates a cognitivist approach to political philosophy. As such, it must be sensitive to the concerns that prompt political liberals such as Rawls to deny that aiming at knowledge can provide a basis for justice in a pluralistic democratic society. I argue that political cognitivism can provide an account of distributive justice that does not threaten the liberal values of pluralist democracies.

Moreover, the bias-neutralizing aim can provide a stronger basis for egalitarianism than the luck-neutralizing aim. The latter puts responsibility in roles that it is not suited to play, while the former does not. The bias-neutralizing aim provides an argument for a maximin principle of distribution that avoids standard objections to luck-related arguments for maximin. I tease apart the luck-neutralizing and the bias-neutralizing strands in familiar arguments for maximin, and relate them to the decision-theoretic distinction between risk aversion and uncertainty aversion. The normative significance of a veil of ignorance is found in the aim to avoid the biasing influences that inevitably go with information, even probabilistic information, about who you are and what you are like, your talents and handicaps. And weak aversion to uncertainty can be justified as part of the minimal rationality required for intentional agency. By giving a cognitive slant to the perspective of justice, and dissociating it from the luck-neutralizing aim and related ideas, we can reclaim egalitarian results. In this way we can take a lead as egalitarians from Rawls even if we do not share his Kantian, luck-neutralizing sympathies.

This book aims to demonstrate some of the ways in which issues about responsibility interact with issues about distributive justice and with the roles responsibility can play in distributive justice. I hope to show why it is important for work on distributive justice to distinguish responsibility from other values, such as deservingness or fairness, to distinguish different conceptions of responsibility, and to distinguish different roles responsibility might play in distributive justice.

I

RESPONSIBILITY

1

Philosophical Landscape:
The New Articulation
of Responsibility

Seminal work on responsibility by Harry Frankfurt has had a deep influence on subsequent philosophical thinking about responsibility. In particular, Frankfurt's arguments highlight a certain distinction. Some conditions for responsibility are conditions on the *actual sequence* of causes leading up to the action, responsibility for which is in question. Other conditions for responsibility instead concern what might have happened in other possible sequences of events, or *alternate sequences*. In the wake of Frankfurt's work, this important distinction has been further articulated by others and has influenced in particular the development of reason-based views of responsibility.

This chapter provides a philosophical landscape, a background against which the arguments of subsequent chapters will be developed. It lays out a view of how issues about responsibility are reconfigured in light of the distinction between actual-sequence and alternate-sequence conditions of responsibility. The arguments of three philosophers—Martha Klein, Susan Wolf, and John Martin Fischer—will be used as reference points in my survey of the new articulation of responsibility. We learn something important about responsibility from each of them, and also from comparisons between them.[1]

In the course of exploring this territory, I explain why the *ability-to-do-otherwise requirement* (an alternate-sequence requirement) is independent of the *regression requirement* (an actual-sequence requirement). I distinguish causal conceptions of moral responsibility from noncausal concep-

---

1. There are other philosophers who have made closely related arguments. By concentrating on these three, I make the discussion more wieldy, though I do not do justice to the literature as a whole.

tions, and the regression requirement from various other actual-sequence requirements, such as various requirements of *reason-responsiveness*.

In Chapter 2 I go on to argue that alternate sequences are irrelevant to responsibility. My argument is tangentially related to but more general in certain respects than Frankfurt's arguments. In Chapter 3 I argue against the actual-sequence regression requirement for responsibility. Reason-responsiveness conditions will be prominent among the actual-sequence conditions of responsibility that are left in play after the ground has been cleared in these ways.

1. Conditional Analyses, the Distinction between Actual and Alternate Sequences, and Frankfurt Cases

The traditional debate about free will and determinism presupposes that responsibility for what you do requires the ability to do otherwise. Compatibilists argue that the ability to do otherwise is compatible with determinism, and incompatibilists deny this.

Some compatibilists have defended their thesis by giving a *conditional analysis* of "could have done otherwise." On this account, to say that you could have done otherwise is just to say that you would have done otherwise if you had chosen to. For example, if the reasons for acting had been different, you might have chosen to act differently, and so have done otherwise. Your having such a conditional disposition, to act otherwise under counterfactual suppositions, is compatible with its being causally determined that you act as you do under actual conditions.

Incompatibilists hold that the conditional analysis is incorrect. They insist that the ability to do otherwise entails the outright possibility of acting otherwise: it entails that there is a causal possibility of acting otherwise, as things are. A counterfactually conditioned disposition to act otherwise is not the same as an outright possibility of acting otherwise, all else constant. That the former is compatible with determinism does not entail that the latter is. It might not be possible for you to choose to do otherwise, hence not be possible for you to do otherwise, holding all else constant, yet still be true that if you had chosen to do otherwise, you would have done otherwise.

The essential point against the conditional analysis turns on the contrast between an outright possibility of an alternate sequence of events, and the dispositional features of the actual sequence of events leading to your action (Fischer 1994, chaps. 7, 8; see also Klein 1990). The ability to do otherwise requires the outright possibility of an alternate sequence of events. By contrast, your acting on the basis of a disposition that would have led you to act differently under counterfactual suppositions is a feature of the actual sequence of causes that leads to your act. The actual causes of your act, in the actual sequence of events leading to your act, may involve dispositional properties such that if certain counterfactual conditions were to obtain, then you would act differently, as the conditional analysis specifies. But your having a disposition to act otherwise under different conditions does not entail the unconditioned possibility of your acting otherwise as things are (see and cf. Fischer and Ravizza 1998, pp. 53, 144n).

Conditions of responsibility can be categorized as alternate-sequence conditions or as actual-sequence conditions, depending on whether they require the outright possibility of an alternate sequence of events with certain features or rather require the actual sequence of events to have certain features.[2] The alternate sequence / actual sequence distinction helps to get and keep clear distinctions between different principles of responsibility that have too often been run together. For example, the alternate-sequence ability-to-do-otherwise requirement for responsibility should be distinguished from the actual-sequence regression requirement (see and cf. Klein 1990). The latter says, roughly, that to be responsible for something you must be responsible for its causes. Regression is a structural requirement, which does not itself specify what substantive conception of responsibility it is applied to. Applied recursively, regression requires that responsibility reach back through the actual sequence of causes. This is incompatible with some substantive conceptions of responsibility. A regressive conception of responsibility may be incompatible with determinism even if ability to do otherwise is not required.

There are other candidate principles in each category to consider as well, which will be examined in what follows. The *ability-to-avoid-blame requirement* is an alternate-sequence condition that may be more plausible than the ability-to-do-otherwise requirement (Otsuka 1998). And some version of a reason-responsiveness requirement may provide an actual-sequence dispositional conception of responsibility that is more attractive than regressive conceptions (Fischer 1994; Fischer and Ravizza, 1998; cf. Wallace 1996; Wolf 1990).

Suppose conditional analyses of "could have done otherwise" are cor-

---

2. No specific level of description of events is required by this distinction.

rect. That would be to suppose that ability-to-do-otherwise requirements are actual-sequence, dispositional requirements, that they do not impose alternate-sequence requirements. So even if responsibility does require that someone could have done otherwise, that does not require the outright possibility of an alternate sequence, and so is compatible with determinism.

Next, suppose instead we agree for the sake of argument that incompatibilists are correct to reject conditional analyses and to insist that ability to do otherwise is incompatible with determinism. This is to admit that ability to do otherwise requirements are indeed alternate-sequence requirements.

But how far does this concession get the incompatibilist? On this supposition, the distinction between alternate and actual sequences cuts against compatibilists, so far as the traditional debate goes. This distinction, however, is a double-edged sword. It also makes available challenges to the presupposition of the traditional debate, namely, that responsibility does require the outright possibility of acting otherwise.

Harry Frankfurt broke ranks by denying this presupposition in an influential series of articles (1969, 1971, etc.). His essential insight was, in effect, that responsibility turns on the character of the actual sequence of events leading to an act, not on the possibility of alternate sequences. This opens up the possibility that determinism may be compatible with responsibility even if it is incompatible with the ability to do otherwise. Even if conditional analyses do not give correct accounts of the ability to do otherwise, some conditional actual-sequence account of responsibility may be correct. If so, then whether or not conditional analyses give the correct account of the ability to do otherwise, responsibility does not require alternate sequences.

In Frankfurt's well-known example (1969, p. 835), Black wants Jones to perform a certain action, and is prepared to go to considerable lengths to ensure this. But Black also wants to avoid showing his hand unnecessarily. Black waits until Jones is about to make up his mind and does nothing unless Black, who is an excellent judge of such things, judges that Jones is not going to do what Black wants him to do. Only if Black so judges does he intervene and take effective steps to ensure that Jones decides to do, and indeed does, what Black wants him to do. Perhaps Black manipulates Jones's brain processes, for example. Whatever conditions are needed for it to be the case that Jones cannot do otherwise, Black makes it the case that those conditions prevail. But Black never actually has to show his hand, because Jones, for reasons of his own, decides to do and does do the very thing Black wants him to do. Frankfurt claims that in this case the fact that Jones could not have done otherwise is irrelevant to his responsibility for what he does. What matters is the actual sequence of events leading to his act.

Various cases that illustrate Frankfurt's point have a certain common structure. Suppose someone acts in a prima facie blameworthy way, for bad reasons but for reasons that are *her* reasons (Fischer and Ravizza 1991, p. 258). Standing by is a counterfactual intervenor who wants her to act just as she acts, but who is prepared, in case he predicts she will waver, to intervene to bring it about that she goes ahead. The counterfactual intervenor is usually personified, but it could be an impersonal force that acts as a fail-safe device. In fact no intervention is needed and none occurs; the agent does not waver but acts of her own initiative. In a case with this structure, the agent could not have done otherwise—though not because of determinism but because of the counterfactual intervenor in the alternate sequence. There is an alternate possible sequence, but in it she does the same thing. Despite that, the character of the actual sequence of events leading to her act is such that she is responsible. The parallel point can be made for praiseworthiness. Cases with this structure can be called "Frankfurt Cases."

Various attempts have been made to avoid these conclusions: by distinguishing act tokens from act types, by appealing to a "flicker of freedom" in the possibility of wavering, and so on. These avoidance possibilities have been widely and ably discussed in the literature, and are not rehearsed or assessed here. In Chapter 2, however, I present a different strategy of argument for a conclusion similar to Frankfurt's, that alternate sequences are irrelevant to responsibility.

So far, I have sketched the context in which the actual sequence/alternate sequence distinction emerges. It operates as the pivot between the pre- and post-Frankfurt stages of debate about responsibility. It both undermines conditional analyses in the traditional debate and underwrites Frankfurt's rejection of the ability-to-do-otherwise requirement, which the traditional debate assumed.

It is helpful to distinguish two readings of the deep point of Frankfurt issues. On my interpretation the most important and fundamental point of Frankfurt's arguments is the insight that responsibility turns on the character of the actual sequence, not that of the alternate sequence. Frankfurt can be regarded as arguing against the requirement of ability to do otherwise, whether this is interpreted as an alternate sequence or as a dispositional actual-sequence requirement, along the lines of conditional analyses. But my reading sees the deeper lesson of Frankfurt Cases to be the irrelevance of the alternate sequence.[3] My own argument in the following chapter focuses on and generalizes the latter point.

Unless otherwise indicated, I hereinafter use the phrases "could have done otherwise" and "ability to do otherwise" to signal a requirement of an outright possibility of an alternate sequence, as opposed to a dispositional actual-sequence requirement. My arguments in Chapter 2 are directed specifically against alternate-sequence requirements, not against dispositional actual-sequence requirements such as those suggested by conditional analyses of ability to do otherwise. The latter, in my view, should be relabelled to distinguish them clearly from alternate-sequence requirements. Using the phrase "ability to do otherwise" to express an alternate-sequence requirement, which I reject, begs no substantive questions, and for present purposes avoids ambiguity and makes what is at stake clearer.

In the next several sections I explain why the ability to do otherwise, understood in alternate-sequence terms, is logically independent of the actual-sequence regression requirement, from which it is often not distinguished.

2. Klein on Regression and Ability to Do Otherwise

The regression requirement for responsibility holds that to be responsible for X you must also be responsible for its causes. It applies recursively, giving rise to a regress. This is an actual-sequence requirement: it requires responsibility for the actual sequence of causes leading to X.

As already indicated, regression is a structural requirement, which could be combined with various different substantive conceptions of responsibility. It requires that responsibility extends backward through the actual sequence of causes of X. But it does not itself specify how such responsibility is to be substantively understood.

The alternate-sequence ability-to-do-otherwise requirement and the actual-sequence regression requirement are mutually independent, or doubly dissociable. This is important, since these conditions have not traditionally been distinguished in the debate between compatibilists and

---

3. My view here is strongly influenced by Fischer's work. I'm grateful for discussion of these points to Harry Frankfurt and Gideon Rosen.

incompatibilists. Martha Klein has emphasized this point, though I draw the distinction and make the point in a somewhat different way than she does. ("Regression" is my terminology, not hers.) I first explain her position, then explain how I want to go beyond her position.

In Klein's view, the incompatibilist's anxieties about determinism have two distinct sources: a regressive conception of responsibility, and a requirement that the agent could have done otherwise:

> [One] worry can be put like this: if agents' acts are caused by factors for which they are not responsible, then how can they be morally responsible for acting as a result of those factors? This is obviously different from the thought: if agents' acts are causally determined, then how can they act otherwise than they do? But although these worries can be distinguished, they are often spoken of as if they were inseparable. (Klein 1990, p. 50; see also pp. 64–65)

Klein also argues that Frankfurt Cases show convincingly that the second of these worries does not generate an independent condition for blameworthiness, once it is distinguished from the first:

> The intuition to which Frankfurt is appealing is this: what matters for blameworthiness is why the agent did what he did. It is irrelevant that other options were closed to him unless their non-availability *explains* his action. (Klein 1990, p. 34)

So, the position Klein suggests is this. A regression requirement for responsibility is distinct from an ability-to-do-otherwise requirement. Frankfurt shows that responsibility does not require the ability to do otherwise. So the incompatibility of the ability to do otherwise with determinism does not make responsibility incompatible with determinism.

The old debate about determinism took compatibilist and incompatibilist to agree that responsibility in some sense requires the ability to do otherwise, but to disagree about whether this requirement could be satisfied if determinism is true. Following Frankfurt, Klein rejects this conception of the territory. She holds that both compatibilists and incompatibilists are wrong to take themselves to be committed to an ability-to-do-otherwise requirement. Rather, they disagree over whether responsibility must be regressive (1990, pp. 7, 63).

Klein supports the regression requirement by considering reprehensible motivations that result in wrongdoing. Some such motivations can be traced to causes for which the wrongdoers are not responsible, such as early deprivation. According to Klein, our intuitions about such cases commit us to the view that for a wrongdoer to be blameworthy, it must not be the case that his motivations were caused by factors for which he is not responsible (1990, pp. 1–2). This condition is satisfied "when an agent's (morally reprehensible) decision or choice has not been caused by anything for which he is not responsible" (1990, p. 57). That is, blame for wrongdoing requires that the wrongdoer be responsible for any causes of the motivation that leads to it; responsibility must follow causes, as far back as they go. This requirement makes responsibility incompatible with determinism, on the assumption that we are not responsible for the causes of our acts, all the way back.

Klein argues that we are intuitively committed to such a regressive conception of responsibility, on the ground that we lack any other plausible explanation of our intuitions about why people are not responsible when brainwashing, brain tumors, emotional deprivation, and so on are among the causes of their motivations and hence of their actions (1990, pp. 70, 73–75). A regressive conception of responsibility explains these intuitions, and at the same time extends the excusing condition from these special cases to any offender who is not responsible for the causes of his motivations as a result of normal genetic and environmental influences.[4]

In Klein's view there are in principle two different ways in which the condition for blameworthiness could be met: either the motivation is uncaused, or the agent is responsible for its causes. Klein regards it as impossible that the relevant motivations might be caused but the wrongdoer be responsible for those causes, all the way back. Thus she focuses instead on the possibility that uncaused motivations might satisfy the condition for blameworthiness (so she calls her condition "U" for "uncaused") (1990, p. 57 ff).[5]

---

4. Wallace (1996) brilliantly argues that the truth of determinism would not generalize the sound reasons we have for excusing or exempting from responsibility in specific cases, such as physical coercion, coercion, youth, mental illness, hypnosis, etc. (see, e.g., p. 181 and passim). Many of his points could be adapted to argue that the failure to satisfy a regression requirement would not generalize these reasons either.

5. For this reason, the regression condition can be regarded as a generalization of Klein's U-condition, though she does not use the term "regressive." Her condition says: blame for an act requires responsibility for any causes there may be of the motivations that cause the act. The regression condition says: responsibility (in the blame-licensing sense) for something requires responsibility for any causes there may be of it.

Klein concedes that if regressive responsibility could be shown to be logically incoherent, that would provide conclusive grounds for saying we should not be committed to it. But in her view regressive responsibility for reasonless choices is logically possible, if not empirically possible. While reasons are causes, a reasonless choice might be uncaused. So she understands how regressive responsibility is even logically possible in terms of uncaused choice, given indeterminism.[6]

3. The Double Dissociability of Regression and Ability to Do Otherwise

I take a stronger position than Klein does about the mutual independence of ability to do otherwise and regression: they are doubly dissociable. Neither entails the other. And I have a different understanding of how regressive responsibility is even possible: not in terms of indeterministic, uncaused choice, but rather in the combination of regression with a noncausal conception of responsibility, for example, in terms of hypothetical choice (rather than actual choice or control).[7]

Ability to do otherwise does not entail regression. If the world is indeterministic there can be alternate possible sequences, so that an agent could have done otherwise (outright, all else constant, not just conditionally). Then it is the case not just that she would have done otherwise if some other mechanism leading to choice had operated, but also that some other mechanism could have operated. But from this it does not follow that the agent is responsible for all the causes in the actual sequence leading to what she does. That is, it does not follow that regression is satisfied.

Conversely, regression does not entail ability to do otherwise. In my view this point does not depend on the possibility of uncaused choice. An agent might in principle be responsible for all the causes in the actual sequence leading to what she does, even though the world is deterministic

---

6. Klein suggests this asymmetry: while praiseworthy choices must be choices made for reasons, blameworthy choices need not be (1990, pp. 130–131, 162; cf. pp. 170–171).

7. Neither Klein nor I advocate a hypothetical-choice account of responsibility. See and cf. Klein 1990, pp. 56–58, on the possibility of an agent with an infinite history; compare also pp. 64–65, on whether satisfaction of her U-condition implies satisfaction of her C-condition, that is, whether an uncaused choice of future motivations implies that the agent could have done otherwise, unconditionally, on subsequent occasions.

and there are no alternate sequences, so that she could not have done otherwise than she did. This might be the case if responsibility is substantively understood in terms of hypothetical choice. I explain how in the following section.

4. Causal versus Noncausal Conceptions of Moral Responsibility, and How Regressive Responsibility Is Even Possible

In order to make good my claim that ability to do otherwise and regression are doubly dissociable without relying on the idea of uncaused choice, I need to show that someone could in principle be regressively responsible even though he could not have done otherwise. Thus I need to explain how regressive responsibility is even possible, although I do not advocate a regressive account of responsibility. I do this by distinguishing causal and noncausal conceptions of responsibility. In a nutshell, regression is coherently compatible with noncausal (for example, hypothetical choice) conceptions of responsibility, but not with causal (for example, choice or control) conceptions of responsibility.

I have explained that Klein understands how regressive responsibility is possible in terms of uncaused choice. If you are responsible for a choice, but it has no causes, then the regression requirement is trivially satisfied.

I am not happy with this strategy, however, because I find it hard to make sense of the idea of events, including choices, that have no causes at all. As Klein recognizes, the fact that reasons are causes does not mean that reasonless choices are uncaused (1990, p. 148). The causes of certain choices may not be reasons, but what would it be for a choice to have no causes at all? If causation has to be deterministic, then choice in an indeterministic world might be uncaused. But Klein seems not to hold that causation must be deterministic (1990, pp. 62; cf. p. 64), and surely she is right not to. We should allow that causation could operate statistically or probabilistically, so that even in an indeterministic world choices have causes, and causal mechanisms and dispositions can make counterfactuals about action true (see also Scanlon 1998, pp. 250, 256; and see Chapter 2, note 15). But when we allow this, the notion of being completely uncaused becomes mysterious.

There is another way to show how regressive responsibility is possible that does not depend on the mysterious idea of uncaused choice. I explain this in two stages. First, responsibility for X in the full-blooded blame-licensing sense can be understood to require forms of causal responsibility for X, such as actual choice or control of X. Causal conceptions of moral responsibility are, I argue, incompatible with regression. Second, responsibility for X can instead be understood in terms of hypothetical, counterfactual choice of X, which does not require any sort of causal responsibility for X. Such a noncausal conception of responsibility, by contrast, is compatible with regression. Thus, regressive responsibility is possible, if responsibility is conceived in noncausal terms.

Now I also think that there are serious objections to purely noncausal conceptions of responsibility. So, even if it is possible for responsibility to be regressive, we have good reasons to reject accounts of responsibility that allow it to be regressive. But my aim at present is to establish the double dissociability in principle of ability to do otherwise and regression, and to do this I merely need to show that certain logical spaces are occupied, not to accept or defend the accounts that occupy them. Moreover, hypothetical choice requirements for responsibility have been appealed to in the literature; I have not simply invented them ad hoc to provide an occupant of a logical space.

First, compare causal responsibility with moral responsibility in the full-blooded blame-licensing sense. A plausible assumption is that moral responsibility requires some form of causal responsibility, even though causal responsibility is not sufficient for moral responsibility. Choice and control of something are forms of causal responsibility for it.[8] We may assume, for example, that moral responsibility in the blame-licensing sense requires a specific form of causal responsibility such as choice or control, and that other causal relations are of the wrong kind and defeat blameworthiness.

If a choice does have causes, and if responsibility for it and for its causes is assumed to involve a causal relation such as choice or control, then regressive responsibility does begin to look impossible—and not just empirically impossible. To see this, notice that combining the substantive condition:

(1) A's responsibility for X requires A's choice or control of X

with the structural regression condition:

(2) A's responsibility for X requires A's responsibility for X's causes

---

8. This does not imply that agents cause their choices, but that choosing is a way in which states or properties of an agent are causally related to whatever is chosen. Control is also a way in which the controlling thing is causally related to the controlled thing.

entails:

(3) *A*'s responsibility for *X* requires *A* to choose or control the actual causes of *X* as well as *X*.

But the actual sequence of the causes of *X* goes back in time indefinitely, to times before *A* existed. So *A* could not possibly stand in the causal relations of choice or control to these causes. Because control and choice are causal relations, someone cannot choose or control what happened before he existed. This is not merely an empirical impossibility. If responsibility requires control or choice, regressive responsibility is incoherent. This point can motivate the claim that a regression requirement makes responsibility impossible (discussed in Chapter 3; see Strawson 1986; 1994).

Second, notice that sometimes a noncausal instead of a causal relation is required for responsibility: that is, a noncausal relation between agent and what he is regarded as responsible for. For example, hypothetical, counterfactual choice of *X* might be required instead of actual choice or control of *X*.[9] In Scanlon's example of the guilt-ridden believer, the agent did not choose and does not control the religious beliefs he was brought up with, and their associated burden of guilt. He would, however, have chosen them had he been able to, and would not choose to be without them. Thus, they are not plausibly regarded as matters of luck for him (see Scanlon 1986; Cohen 1989, 935 ff). The intuition is that he is responsible for them because of his hypothetical, counterfactual choices, despite the fact that he did not actually choose or control them.

Hypothetical, counterfactual choice of something is not a way of being causally responsible for it. You need not be in any actual causal relationship with something just because you would choose it if you could, or would not choose to avoid it if you could. If causal responsibility for *X* is not necessary for responsibility for *X*, then people can be responsible because of their hypothetical choices, in the absence of actual choice or control.

What is the effect of combining a substantive condition of hypothetical choice with a structural regression condition? For present purposes it does not matter exactly what formulation of a substantive condition best captures the intuitions that favor a hypothetical, counterfactual choice condition for responsibility, such as those appealed to in Scanlon's example. So we can let the phrase "hypothetical choice" stand for a suitable elaboration of such a condition. Then combining the structural regression condition (2) with the substantive condition:

---

9. As Cohen says, "counterfactual choice is not a kind of choice" (1989, p. 938).

(4) A's responsibility for X requires A's hypothetical choice of X

yields:

(5) A's responsibility for X requires A's hypothetical choice of the actual causes of X as well as of X.

But (5), unlike (3), does not lead to incoherence. There is no incoherence (as opposed to implausibility) in supposing that A hypothetically chooses the actual causes of X, however far back they go. If causal responsibility is not necessary for responsibility and A can be responsible in virtue of hypothetical choice, then regressive responsibility is not incoherent.

To sum up why a regression condition is incompatible with a requirement of choice or control but compatible with a hypothetical-choice condition for responsibility: a regression requirement is inconsistent with holding that A's responsibility for X requires A to be causally responsible for X in certain ways, such as by controlling X or by actually choosing X. It does not make sense to suppose that A could control or actually choose not just X but also X's causes, all the way back. Causes of X that occurred before A existed cannot possibly be the objects of A's actual choice or control.[10] So if responsibility does require causal responsibility in the form of actual choice or control, responsibility cannot consistently be supposed to be regressive.

By contrast, regressive hypothetical choice is not inconsistent. To stand in the relation of hypothetical choice to X need not be to have any kind of causal responsibility for X, even if X is an actual cause of something you do. For A hypothetically to choose the causes of X, all the way back, is not for A to stand in an actual relation of causal responsibility to them. It is merely for it to be true that A would have chosen them if he could have, or would not have chosen to avoid them. This is not incoherent.

In fact, we can go further. It is even possible in principle for A to choose hypothetically the stream of causes leading to his own character and dispositions to make certain hypothetical choices, including this very hypothetical choice. Though such self-referential higher-order hypothetical choice is not required by regression as stated, it might be regarded as a natural extension of a regression requirement. If hypothetical choice rather than actual choice or control is the substantive condition in question, then even such *extended regression* requires no actual choice of the agent's disposi-

---

10. Cf. Strawson 1986, p. 29: "True self-determination is logically impossible because it requires the actual completion of an infinite regress of choices or principles of choice."

tions to hypothetical choice. There is no inconsistency in a self-referential hypothetical choice of both (1) the primary act or choice, responsibility for which is at issue, with its whole stream of causes, and (2) the disposition to make just this hypothetical choice plus all the disposition's causes.

Thus, regression would require hypothetical choice of the causes of *X,* while extended regression would require self-referential higher-order hypothetical choice of the causes of dispositions to make hypothetical choices. When combined with a substantive condition of hypothetical choice, neither regression nor extended regression requires any actual choice or control of the agent's dispositions to hypothetical choice. Therefore, neither implies an impossible causal regress. If *A* can be responsible in virtue of hypothetical choice, then causal responsibility is not required for responsibility, and regressive responsibility is not incoherent.

5. The Tame Housewife and Other Objections to Hypothetical-Choice Accounts of Responsibility

The following objection may be made to hypothetical-choice accounts of responsibility, even when they include a regression or extended regression requirement. Whether someone is the sort of person who would have chosen to be that very sort of person if she could have, can itself be something for which she is not responsible. For example, it might be true that a "tame housewife" would choose to be the sort of person she is, if she could, and would endorse the causes of her choices and even the causes of her dispositions to hypothetical choice. But her dispositions to such hypothetical choices may have been formed under conditions of truncated opportunity or deprivation or manipulation (for relevant discussions see Sen 1987, Roemer 1996, Elster 1983). If the manipulation or oppression is extremely effective, she may even come to endorse *it* hypothetically. Even such extended and regressive hypothetical choice, however, does not make her responsible in the circumstances. We need to consider, the objection continues, not just why the agent does what she does but also why it is true of the agent—of Scanlon's believer, or of the tame housewife—that she would or would not choose certain things if she could.

While this objection is important, it is not an objection to my argument. The point for present purposes of distinguishing structural conditions for responsibility from substantive conditions is to show how regressive responsibility is even possible, in order to establish the double dissociability of regression and ability to do otherwise. It is not to defend a hypothetical-choice view of responsibility. The structural regression condition can be coherently combined with some substantive conditions for responsibility, but not others. If responsibility for X requires A's hypothetical choice rather than A's choice or control of X, then regressive responsibility is not impossible. Moreover, it is compatible with determinism. It can be true that an agent would have chosen what happened before he existed, if he could have. The whole sequence of causes of his choices and of his hypothetical choices could in principle be objects of his hypothetical choice. Even though he in fact cannot choose them, it is possible that if he could choose them, he would choose them. Hypothetical choice is causally costless and in principle indefinitely extendible.

Since the combination of a hypothetical-choice condition for responsibility with a regression requirement is coherent, it illustrates how regressive responsibility is possible. *But this provides no argument at all in favor of a hypothetical-choice conception of responsibility,* which faces various difficulties. The "tame housewife" objection given above argues that hypothetical choice is not sufficient for responsibility. There are further objections as well.

First, there are indeterminacy problems. The costless, indefinite extendibility of merely hypothetical choice, which makes it compatible with a regression requirement, also argues against its being sufficient for responsibility. There are too many things that people would choose, or would not choose to avoid, if they could. Surely people are not responsible for all these things. But then for which of them are they responsible? Mere hypothetical choice seems to leave it indeterminate. The relationship between the agent and what he is responsible for is not sufficiently constrained. Some further requirement is needed to take us from the too-large set of all those things that people would choose, or would not choose to avoid, if they could, to the smaller set of things that people are actually responsible for. The most plausible candidates to provide the needed constraint involve causal relations such as control or actual choice.[11] Perhaps some hybrid condition that requires actual choice or control as well as hypothetical choice could meet these concerns about indeterminacy (though that would again be incompatible with a regression requirement).

Second, under certain assumptions the counterfactual supposition that A can make the relevant choices ("if he could") may not make sense or

---

11. Though of course causal responsibility by itself is not sufficient for moral responsibility. See the discussion of animism in Chapter 3.

may be impossible. Then the truth of the hypothetical choice claims cannot be evaluated. This kind of worry makes hypothetical-choice requirements for responsibility less attractive than requirements of actual choice or control.

While there are various problems for hypothetical-choice approaches to responsibility, my point here is that it is possible to combine a hypothetical-choice requirement with a regression requirement. By thus explaining how regressive responsibility is possible, I have made good my claim that regression and ability to do otherwise are doubly dissociable, without appealing to causeless choice.

Since the regression requirement and the ability-to-do-otherwise requirement are doubly dissociable, we cannot argue for or against the former simply by reference to the latter. Someone could hold that alternate sequences are irrelevant to responsibility, yet still require responsibility to be regressive, or could adopt a requirement of ability to do otherwise while rejecting the regression requirement.

6. The Double Dissociability of Regression and Reason-Responsiveness

To be in a position to evaluate the regression requirement, we should distinguish the regression requirement from other actual-sequence conditions for responsibility. There is a rich variety of requirements that might be made of the actual sequence of causes leading up to an act. For example, we could require that a proximal cause of the act be a choice by the agent, and could further constrain this causal relation: the choice could be required to cause the act in certain ways and not others. Or, we could require that the act is controlled, in the sense that a complex set of dispositions constituting a control system characterize the actual sequence of its causes. We could also require that choices and reasons play certain roles in such a control system.

A chooser or controller is causally related to what she chooses or controls. A hypothetical chooser need not be causally related to what she hypothetically chooses: if I could, I would choose to sing like Maria Callas rather than like Emma Kirkby, though in fact I utterly lack the ability to do either. Nevertheless, a hypothetical choice requirement also imposes requirements on the actual sequence of causes of an act.

This may be confusing, so I'll pause to expand on this point. Hypothetical choice is not a kind of causal relation between the hypothetical chooser and what she is held responsible for in virtue of such hypothetical choice, namely, what she would choose if she could. In this respect, it contrasts with actual choice and control, as I have explained. Nevertheless, a hypothetical-choice condition for responsibility is an actual-sequence condition. What the agent would do under various counterfactual conditions is a dispositional property of the way the agent actually is and of the actual sequence of events. It is not an alternate possibility. The point is essentially the same as the point that conditional analyses of ability to do otherwise characterize the actual sequence rather than alternate sequence.

Thus, hypothetical choice, actual choice, and control conditions are all actual-sequence conditions. Within the class of actual-sequence conditions, some conditions are causal in that they require causal relations to hold between the agent and what she is responsible for, as in actual choice or control conditions. Other conditions are not causal in that they do not require such causal relations to hold. Either way, however, they are conditions on the actual sequence of events.

An important type of actual-sequence condition for responsibility is the requirement that an act be brought about in a way that is responsive to reasons (Fischer 1994; Fischer and Ravizza 1998). The latter does not require responsibility all the way back along the actual sequence as regression does. Rather, it imposes a dispositional condition locally on the causes of the act, namely, that the process that leads to the act is responsive to reasons. Notice now that regression and reason-responsiveness are also doubly dissociable.

On the one hand, a regression requirement could be satisfied while a reason-responsiveness requirement is not. Someone suffering from a mental illness might hypothetically endorse the whole chain of causes of an act that is a symptom of that illness, although the act is not brought about in a reason-responsive way. Indeed, the hypothetical endorsements might themselves be symptoms of the illness.

Conversely, a reason-responsiveness requirement can be satisfied while a regression requirement is not. The regression requirement projects a given substantive condition of responsibility backward onto the whole stream of causes of an act. But an act can be *locally reason-responsive*—that is, can result from a reason-responsive mechanism, where the causes of that mechanism are not themselves reason-responsive all the way back.[12]

---

12. See and cf. Fischer 1994, p. 209; Adams 1985. Fischer and Ravizza 1998 (chap. 6, esp. pp. 156, 161) concentrate on overdetermination cases as counterexamples to a

(Indeed, it is not clear that regressive reason-responsiveness even makes sense.) For example, suppose an agent is not responsible for the causes of her act, all the way back. Nevertheless, her act is brought about in a way that is responsive to evil subjective reasons, including a desire to cause pain to others. When her act is brought about in this way, she is disposed to act as she does just when doing so will hurt her victim, in order to hurt him.

Can an agent be responsible in virtue of such reason-responsiveness, even if the regression requirement is not satisfied? Klein, recall, holds that our intuitions about why people are not responsible in certain cases commit us to an actual-sequence regression requirement. She holds this while rejecting the alternate-sequence ability-to-do-otherwise requirement. However, she does not consider reason-responsiveness conditions as potential actual-sequence rivals to a regression requirement. We can agree with Klein that an actual-sequence condition of responsibility rather than an alternate-sequence condition is needed, without agreeing that the regression requirement provides the right one. And we can agree that regressive responsibility is not impossible, without agreeing that we are intuitively committed to a regression requirement. Could a nonregressive actual-sequence condition, such as a reason-responsiveness requirement, explain the intuitions that Klein believes can be explained only by the regression requirement? To address this question, we need to look more closely at the variety of reason-based views of responsibility.

7. Reason-Based Views of Responsibility: Wolf

Many philosophers, from Spinoza, Kant, and Hegel[13] through to the present, have conceived of freedom in terms of rational necessity, or have otherwise found close connections between rationality on the one hand and freedom and/or responsibility on the other. The reason-based views of responsibility of Susan Wolf and of John Martin Fischer, which I here com-

---

"transfer" principle that is closely related though not identical to a regression requirement. In a case of joint simultaneous assassination, I am responsible for the death even though I am not responsible for the other person's shooting, which is among the causes of the death. Such an example is thus technically a counterexample to a regression requirement. I regard such cases as relatively unimportant and peripheral rather than central to issues about regression. They leave untouched the reasons that people may be attracted to a regression requirement in cases not involving overdetermination. However, these are addressed by the later discussion of "taking responsibility" and manipulation.

13. And perhaps even further back, to Aristotle.

pare, can be seen as part of this broad tradition.[14] Wolf and Fischer both base their accounts of responsibility on the idea of responding to reasons, but they do so in different ways. Wolf (1990) gives an account of responsibility in terms of the ability to act in accordance with reason, which has both actual-sequence and alternate-sequence aspects. Wolf does not explicitly address Frankfurt Cases or clearly distinguish actual- and alternate-sequence conditions for responsibility, in the way that Fischer does.[15] Fischer (1994) gives a strictly actual-sequence account of responsibility, in terms of responsiveness to reasons. After explaining both their views, I summarize four main points of comparison, which can be used to characterize the space of reason-based views of responsibility.

On Wolf's Reason View, what matters for responsibility is the ability to act in accordance with reason, not the ability to act in some other way. This means that whether responsibility requires that the agent could have done otherwise depends on whether she actually acts in accordance with reason. Praise and blame are not symmetrical with respect to alternate possible sequences. If the agent does the right thing for the right reasons, then the requirement of ability to act in accordance with reason is satisfied, and she need not have been able to act otherwise—to act irrationally—in order to be responsible for what she does. Praise does not require an alternate possible sequence. As Wolf says, the ability to act in accordance with reason is compatible with the inability to do anything else (1990, p. 69). But if in fact the agent does not act in accordance with reason, it is then critical that she have been able to do so, to act otherwise. To be responsible for what she does when she does not act in accordance with reason, it must have been possible as things were for her to act in accordance with reason. Blame does require an alternate possible sequence. The objective normative commitments of the Reason View make it asymmetrical with respect to praise and blame.

The preceding paragraph gives Wolf's reason-based view of responsibility in a nutshell. I will now explain it in more detail, and in particular how it gives rise to an asymmetry between praise and blame. Wolf sets up a three-way contrast between the Autonomy View, the Real Self View, and the Reason View. She argues for the Reason View.[16]

The Autonomy View requires that to be responsible the agent must not

---

14. See Shatz 1986, sec. 7, for a discussion that locates contemporary reason-sensitivity accounts of responsibility in the broader context of contemporary approaches to responsibility.

15. Klein 1990 also draws this distinction.

16. I am grateful to Susan Wolf for discussions of her position.

only "control" her behavior via her will, but must have "ultimate control": "her will must be determined by her self, and her self must not, in turn, be determined by anything external to itself" (Wolf 1990, p. 10). The self that governs her will must be governed by her deeper self, and so on ad infinitum. On this view, if external forces such as those of heredity and environment determine her will, then her control is only intermediate and superficial. But it is no better if "the agent's control is controlled by nothing at all," or can be explained only in terms of random occurrences or brute inexplicable facts. The idea of an autonomous agent as a prime mover unmoved, whose self can endlessly account for itself and its behavior, can seem incoherent or impossible, even if necessary for responsibility (1990, pp. 13–14). "Ultimate control" appears to be, in effect, regressive control. So the Autonomy View appears to be committed to the regression requirement (though Wolf does not put it in these terms).

By contrast, the Real Self View denies that a responsible agent must be endlessly accountable to herself. In effect, it denies that responsibility must be regressive in the way the Autonomy View requires. Rather, it requires for responsibility that the agent's behavior be attributable to her real self: that she is able to govern her behavior on the basis of her will and able to govern her will on the basis of her valuational system. But it does not matter, on this view, where her real self comes from (Wolf 1990, pp. 33–35).

We can locate the contrast between the Autonomy View and the Real Self View within the space of actual-sequence conditions for responsibility. While the Autonomy View requires that control extend all the way back through the actual sequence of causes, the Real Self View is satisfied if the actual sequence leads back to the Real Self in the right way, even if the sequence does not stop there.

Wolf rejects the Real Self View. We can question the responsibility of a fully developed agent even when she acts in a way that is clearly attributable to her, because we can question whether she is responsible for her real self (1990, p. 37). Some forms of mental illness, for example, or cases of deprived or traumatic childhoods may raise this concern. (Recall that these are among the cases that lead Klein to think we are committed to a regressive conception of responsibility.) Wolf finds an unbridgable gulf between her own view and the view that in such cases people can be wholly responsible for their actions, even though they are not responsible for the real selves from which their actions result (1990, pp. 38–39). The claim that "To be a responsible agent is simply to be, as it were, a fully formed bad act-maker" seems to confuse the mere causal responsibility of the real self with its moral or deep responsibility (1990, pp. 40–43; see also Otsuka 1998).

Wolf's grounds for rejecting the Real Self View may seem to favor the Autonomy View, or to commit her to a regressive conception of responsibility. However, Wolf also criticizes the Autonomy View. On the basis of her criticisms of both the Real Self View and the Autonomy View, she develops a third view, the Reason View, which she favors. The Reason View does not respect the regression requirement.[17] It is a tricky matter to locate it in relation to the distinction between actual- and alternate-sequence conditions, as we shall see, since its alternate-sequence requirements are asymmetric as between praiseworthy and blameworthy acts.

The Autonomy View is committed not just to a regressive conception of responsibility, but also to the ability-to-do-otherwise requirement (Wolf 1990, p. 68). (This is not surprising; it is usual for the two principles to go hand in hand and unusual for them to be distinguished, as they are in Klein 1990.) Wolf's critique of the Autonomy View targets its commitment to an ability-to-do-otherwise requirement for praiseworthiness. An agent who cannot help choosing what she has most reason to choose is not autonomous. Autonomy requires radical freedom: that no basis for choice necessitates, that the agent have the ability to make choices on no basis even when a basis exists (1990, pp. 54–55). The autonomous agent who does the right thing could have done otherwise, even holding all the reasons there are for acting constant.

Wolf argues that this autonomous ability to be irrational is not desirable. Acting for a reason, in order, say, to save a drowning child, is no *more* praiseworthy if an agent could have declined to act in this way, all else constant. Acting nonautonomously but for such a reason deserves praise at least as much as acting the same way but autonomously (1990, pp. 60–61). Wolf considers the way in which skeptics about values and reasons for acting may think autonomy valuable, in the absence of any right answer to questions about what should be done, because the choices of an autonomous agent are more deeply hers, freer of bias and conditioning (1990, pp. 62–63). But, argues Wolf, unless we are such skeptics, what we should

---

17. Wolf's criticisms of the Real Self view may seem to commit her to a regression requirement. But since Wolf does not ultimately accept a regression requirement, her criticisms of the Real Self view should be either recast or reinterpreted so that they clearly do not depend on a regression requirement.

and do value is not radical freedom but the moderate freedom to act in accordance with reason. According to the Reason View advocated by Wolf, the valuable kind of flexibility is not the ability to act despite reason, but rather is built into the ability to act in accordance with reason. So someone who acts in accordance with reason can be responsible even if she could not have done otherwise (1990, pp. 63–66).

On the Reason View, what matters for responsibility is the ability to act in accordance with reason, not the ability to act in some other way. This means that whether responsibility requires that the agent could have done otherwise depends on whether she actually acts in accordance with reason. Praise and blame are not symmetrical with respect to alternate possible sequences. If the agent does the right thing for the right reasons, then the requirement of ability to act in accordance with reason is satisfied, and she need not have been able to act otherwise, to act irrationally, in order to be responsible for what she does. Praise does not require an alternate possible sequence. As Wolf says, the ability to act in accordance with reason is compatible with the inability to do anything else (1990, p. 69). But if in fact the agent does not act in accordance with reason, it is then critical that she have been able to do so, to act otherwise. To be responsible for what she does when she does not act in accordance with reason, it must have been possible as things were for her to act in accordance with reason. Blame does require an alternate possible sequence.[18]

Compare the conditions for praise and for blame on the Autonomy View, on the Real Self View, and on the Reason View. On the Autonomy View, both praise and blame require alternate possible sequences. On the Real Self View, so long as the real self is the actual source of the act, it does not matter whether there are alternate possible sequences. Since real selves can be the sources of bad acts as well as good acts, praise and blame are also on this view symmetrical with respect to alternate possible sequences. Behavior governed by a real self is behavior governed by certain disposi-

---

18. Wolf (1990) suggests in chap. 5 that these alternate possibilities could be identified at a psychological level of description, rather than a physical one, so that the agent could have done something else, holding his psychological history and all applicable psychological laws constant. Such alternate psychological possibilities are incompatible with psychological determinism. Whether such alternate psychological possibilities might nevertheless be compatible with physical determinism is a further and complex question, which I do not address here. Doing so might require that the actual/alternate sequence distinction, along with determinism, be relativized to levels of description. But at any given level of description, determinism will still be incompatible with the existence of an alternate sequence.

tions, to act in certain ways under certain conditions and in other different ways if conditions were otherwise, in accordance with the agent's character, values, and desires or subjective reasons. But such conditional dispositions are not the same thing as the outright ability to do otherwise, as things actually are.

It is more complex to characterize the alternate-sequence requirements of the Reason View. On that view, the regress of responsibility stops not with the agent's real self, her will and valuational system, or her merely subjective reasons for acting—the beliefs and desires she has that rationalize certain acts. Rather, it stops with what reasons there are, objectively. Someone can have beliefs and desires that rationalize a certain act, even though there are no objective reasons to do it. Her beliefs may be false or her desires out of line with objective reasons. But if objective reasons are the actual source of the act, if the agent does the right thing for the right reason, it does not matter if she is not responsible for those reasons or her responsiveness to them.[19] Nor does it matter whether there are alternate possible sequences. The agent who does the right thing for the right reason is praiseworthy. This is the nonregressive, actual-sequence component of Wolf's Reason View. The claim that alternate possible sequences are irrelevant to the praiseworthiness of right acts done for the right reasons can be regarded as expressing a restricted, asymmetrical form of the intuition that alternate sequences are irrelevant to responsibility. Like the Real Self View and unlike the Autonomy View, the Reason View is liberal with praise.

However, the objective normative commitments of the Reason View make it asymmetrical with respect to praise and blame. If reason cannot be the actual source of wrong acts or acts not done for the right reasons, then when the agent does not do the right thing for the right reasons, the conditions of responsibility on the Reason View are not necessarily met. Suppose that when we look at the actual sequence of causes of such acts, we do not find objective reasons.[20] Then the regress of responsibility

---

19. Why in general should we want to be responsible for the objective reasons to which we respond, anyway? Could they be objective if we were?

20. This assumption might be unwarranted if objective reasons for acting can come into ineliminable conflict with each other, so that a correct view of how to resolve the conflict does not eliminate the conflict or subsume the force of the overridden reason without remainder. (I argue that this is possible in Hurley 1989, chap. 7.) Where there is such a conflict, someone might be weak willed and do the wrong thing, all things considered, but nevertheless act for the conflicting objective reason.

cannot stop with objective reasons. When wrong acts are in question, the ability to act in accordance with reason requires the ability to act otherwise, as things are—to act in accordance with reason rather than against it. Blame requires alternate possible sequences (1990, p. 79; cf. Wallace 1996, pp. 203 ff). This is the alternate-sequence component of the Reason View. Like the Autonomy View and unlike the Real Self View, the Reason View is not liberal with blame.

The difference between the Real Self View and the Reason View turns on the difference between subjective and objective reasons. In Wolf's terms, according to the Real Self View someone is responsible if and only if she is able to form her actions on the basis of her values, whereas on the Reason View someone is responsible if and only if she is *also* able to form her values on the basis of the True and the Good (1990, p. 75). Deprivation and other unfortunate circumstances may disconnect real selves from objective reasons, and so explain, on the Reason View, why blame is inappropriate. The difference between responsibility and the lack of it is less a metaphysical difference than a normative difference, a difference in an agent's connectedness to objective reasons (1990, pp. 70–71, 76), which may result from the difference between a good upbringing and a deprived one.

While criticizing the Real Self View, Wolf appears to be sympathetic to a regression requirement. But in developing the Reason View, she makes it clear that praiseworthiness turns on the ability to act in accordance with reason, and is not undermined by failure to meet a regression requirement. So Wolf's position suggests a general line of response to the challenge to find some principle other than a regression requirement that explains intuitions about blame. Perhaps blameworthiness also turns on the ability to act in accordance with reason, not on a regression requirement. But if a reason-based account of blameworthiness imposes alternate-sequence requirements for responsibility, it will be in the target area of Frankfurt-style arguments against such requirements. Can a reason-based account avoid alternate-sequence requirements?

8. Reason-Based Views of Responsibility: Fischer

Wolf does not herself formulate her reason-based account explicitly in terms of the distinction between actual-sequence and alternate-sequence requirements (as I have). Nor does she address Frankfurt's arguments.[21]

---

21. Although, as indicated, her view in effect expresses an asymmetrical form of the

Fischer does both, and locates his own reason-based account of responsibility firmly in the actual sequence. His position thus helps to clarify how a reason-based view of responsibility could provide a strictly actual-sequence rival to the regression principle, one not vulnerable to Frankfurt-style objections to alternate-sequence requirements.

Fischer suggests that we view Frankfurt Cases as cases in which the actual mechanism on which the agent acts is at least weakly or loosely responsive to reasons, though the manipulative mechanism that would operate in the alternate, counterfactual-intervention sequence is not responsive to reasons. By the "mechanism" on which the agent acts, Fischer means the process that leads to the action, or the way the action comes about. In the case of Jones and Black, for example, when Jones acts for his own reasons, he acts on one kind of mechanism. When he does the same thing but because his brain has been manipulated by Black, he acts on a different kind of mechanism. If Jones acted because of a hypnotic suggestion implanted by Black, he would be acting on yet another different kind of mechanism. Fischer describes some mechanisms in terms of (reason-responsive) deliberation or practical reason, and others in terms of physical processes, such as (non-reason-responsive) central nervous system processes, which might, for example, realize the irresistible urge to take a drug on which an addict acts (1994, pp. 173–174; 1998, pp. 42, 46 ff). Reason-responsive mechanisms may be reflective, as in the case of practical reasoning, but need not be (Fischer and Ravizza 1998, p. 86). Fischer gives no general account of when the kinds of mechanism on which agents act are the same or different, but regards it as intuitive in many cases.

Reason-responsiveness in Fischer's sense requires that the mechanism that operates in the actual sequence have certain dispositional features: holding the mechanism constant, the agent would have responded differently in at least some circumstances in which the reasons were different. Fischer (1994) requires for blame only what I call "loose" reason-responsiveness.[22] That is, he requires only that the mechanism on which the agent acts would, in *some* (not all) possible worlds in which there is reason to do otherwise, lead her to act on that reason and hence to do otherwise. For example, someone who shoplifts, although there are sufficient pru-

irrelevant alternative intuition—an intuition I claim is also at work in Frankfurt Cases.

22. He calls it "weak" instead of "loose." In Fischer and Ravizza 1998, Fischer's 1994 view is revised in various ways. On the revised view, weak reason-responsiveness is too weak a condition for blameworthiness. See my discussion of moderate reason-responsiveness in Chapter 2, sec. 1.

dential reasons not to, might nevertheless not do so if she thought her daughter would find out. So Fischer does not require that the agent have an outright ability to act differently, holding all else constant, including whatever reasons there are.[23] Fischer's condition of loose reason-responsiveness does not support the asymmetry between praise and blame that Wolf defends; neither praise nor blame requires an alternate sequence.

On Fischer's view, so long as there is no responsibility-undermining factor in the actual sequence, the agent may be responsible. It doesn't matter if there is a responsibility-undermining factor in the alternate sequence, so long as it is not actually causally operative. Differences in responsibility depend or supervene on the actual history and causes of action, not merely on what nonactual sequences might have been like (1994, p. 158). What matters is the character of the actually operative mechanism of action, including its dispositional character, in particular, its responsiveness to reasons. Fischer makes a point similar to Wolf's point against the Real Self View: it is not enough for responsibility that there is a mesh between the agent's preferences and values, or first-order and higher-order preferences. We need to know more about how this mesh was actually produced, since it is possible for such a mesh to be produced by a bad mechanism, which is not even loosely responsive to reasons (1987; 1994, p. 208).

Fischer holds in his 1994 book that the only plausible threat to moral responsibility from determinism is the threat to the existence of alternate possible sequences. If Frankfurt Cases demonstrate that alternate sequences are not required for responsibility, then determinism is no longer a threat to responsibility.[24] Responsiveness to reasons and hence responsibility are compatible with determinism, even though the outright ability to do otherwise, all else constant, is not compatible with determinism. Fischer calls this combination of views "semicompatibilism" (1987, 1994).

However, to remove the threat of determinism we need to do more than register that the actual sequence is what matters. Some actual-sequence requirements may be compatible with determinism, but not others. As we have seen, cases of hypnotism, brain tumor, and so on lead Klein to endorse a regressive conception of responsibility that is arguably incom-

---

23. This and other varieties of reason-responsiveness are explained further in Chapter 2. See Fischer 1994, p. 244n; Fischer and Ravizza 1991, p. 277; 1998.

24. Fischer 1994, pp. 151, 205; though Fischer appears to have changed his mind about this in Fischer and Ravizza 1998.

patible with determinism.[25] Fischer accounts for some of these cases instead in terms of the failure of reason-responsiveness. In later work, he adds an additional actual-sequence requirement of "taking responsibility" to the requirement of reason-responsiveness.

9. A Four-Point Comparison of Wolf and Fischer

Fischer's 1994 version of a reason-based view of responsibility differs from Wolf's in at least four ways. First, Fischer requires that the mechanism on which the agent acts in the actual sequence have a certain dispositional character, namely, reason-responsiveness; he does not require alternate sequences. Wolf requires, by contrast, that the agent have the ability to act in accordance with reason. This requires there to be an alternate sequence when the agent does not act in accordance with reason, though not when the agent does do the right thing for the right reason. The idea of ability to act in accordance with reason cuts across the actual/alternate sequence distinction, while the idea of reason-responsiveness is located on the actual-sequence side of the distinction.

Second, Fischer requires only a loose link to reason for responsibility. On his 1994 view, someone who does not act in accordance with reason can be responsible in virtue of acting on a mechanism that is loosely disposed to respond to reasons—that responds to reasons in some counterfactual possible world. If Fischer were instead to require a tight link, then someone who did not act in accordance with reason would not be responsible. For Wolf, by contrast, when an agent does not act in accordance with reason, he may still be responsible, but only if there is an alternate sequence in which he does the right thing for the right reason, where other relevant factors are held constant and not allowed to vary counterfactually.

Third, Wolf's account clearly invokes objective reasons, the ability to form values on the basis of the True and the Good. The ability to act in accordance with reason that Wolf requires is the ability to act in accordance with the reasons there are, not just the reasons the agent takes herself to have. Fischer's position on objective versus subjective reason-responsiveness is not as clear as Wolf's.[26]

---

25. See Klein 1990, who argues this on the assumption that we are not responsible for the causes of our acts. The regression requirement can be regarded as a generalization of Klein's U-condition, though she does not use the term "regressive."

26. "Even an agent who acts against good reasons can be responsive to some reasons" (Fischer 1994, p. 167). Is this because the reasons in question need not be objective,

Fourth, praise and blame are asymmetric on Wolf's reason-based view, but are not on Fischer's 1994 loose reason-responsiveness account. We should, however, consider whether a reason-responsiveness account supports other sorts of asymmetry in responsibility. Fischer at one point defended an asymmetry between acts and omissions, which I reject (as he now does also). I argue, by contrast, that a reason-responsiveness account of responsibility can give rise to an asymmetry between certain talents and corresponding handicaps. In the rest of this section I explain these claims about asymmetry in more detail.

In 1991, Fischer and Ravizza endorsed an asymmetry between responsibility for acts and for omissions. On that view, responsibility for an act does not require the freedom to refrain from performing the act, while responsibility for failure to perform an act does require the freedom to perform (1991, p. 271; cf. Fischer 1994). However, their arguments for this view seem to rest on a misunderstanding of control and its relationships to reason-responsiveness and to alternative sequences. They later revised this element of their position (Fischer and Ravizza 1998, p. 147n)—though not thoroughly enough, in my view.

On their earlier position, since omissions do not involve "actual causal control" of movement, but responsibility does require reason-responsive control in some form, responsible omissions must instead involve "regulative control." The latter is an alternate-sequence requirement, demanding outright ability to perform. But the misunderstanding this involves can be corrected in Fischer's own terms.

Choosing how to act in response to reasons is closely related to the idea of control. Reason-responsiveness is a kind of control, which operates through choice. Not all control involves choice and reasons: consider a thermostat. But when someone chooses how to act in response to reasons,

---

or because the responsiveness in question needs only to be loose? Does pluralism about reasons allow that there are bad but objective reasons? In one example, Sam's reasons for killing are bad reasons, but "they are *his* reasons," and Sam is viewed as responsible and blameworthy (Fischer and Ravizza 1991, p. 258). If the counterfactual intervenor tracked objective reasons tightly, but these were not the agent's subjective reasons, would the alternate-sequence mechanism count as reason-responsive? For more recent discussion, see Fischer and Ravizza 1998. Also relevant here are the questions raised in note 20, this chapter: can objective reasons for action come into ineliminable conflict? Can it be the case that when someone acts in a weak-willed way against his correct better judgement, he nevertheless acts on and for an objective reason?

her choices and the reasons to which they respond form a control system. Her reasons provide a target, which may involve characteristics of her own behavior as well as external states of affairs. Her choices combined with exogenous events in the environment and acts by others produce joint results, in which the target is either achieved or missed to some degree. Her choices are adjusted in the light of information about the exogenous events and the joint results of them and her earlier choices in order to reduce error, or the gap between the target and the joint result.[27]

Thus, reason-responsive control involves dispositional properties of operative mechanisms in the actual sequence of events, rather than alternate sequences of events. It requires that a different response would be made under different conditions, which give rise to different relations between target and joint result: for example, if the reasons were different or if the circumstances were different and so differently related to the same reasons. If the error were such and such, her choices would be adjusted in a certain way; if the error were something else, her choices would be adjusted in another way; if there were no error, her choices would be yet something else. But reason-responsive control does not require that a different response could be made, holding all else constant. It does not require that an alternate sequence be possible outright (see Fischer and Ravizza 1998, pp. 53, 144n). Indeterministic control systems *can* be as good as imperfect deterministic control systems (though other things equal, indeterminism tends to degrade control, not to support it). But while indeterminism is compatible with control, it is certainly not necessary for it. An agent who acts in a reason-responsive way need not have been able outright to choose otherwise, holding reasons and circumstances constant.

These points apply to omissions as much as to acts. If the operative mechanisms when you omit to act are so disposed that you would have acted under different conditions and these dispositions characterize a reason-responsive control system, then your omission may nevertheless count as reason-responsive and as responsible. For example, you may be responsible for omitting something you should have done in virtue of reason-responsive dispositions characteristic of weak will or of dedication to evil.

In their 1998 position, Fischer and Ravizza no longer require for re-

---

27. See, e.g., Powers 1973; Marken 1986; cf. Ashby 1956. Fischer and Ravizza 1998, e.g. at 120, give an account closely related to basic control theory, though it uses very different language.

sponsible omissions a kind of control that involves alternate sequences. However, they still think that there is a kind of control, indeed the kind typically associated with moral responsibility, which they still call "regulative control," that does require alternate sequences (pp. 20, 24, 37, 338). I claim by contrast that *no* kind of control *requires* the outright possibility of an alternate sequence, all else constant.[28] Although control is compatible with indeterminism, "regulative control" is not a kind of control at all. Moreover, Fischer and Ravizza still in 1998 find it natural to think of the reason-responsiveness of an agent as requiring alternate sequences (p. 37), even if the reason-responsiveness of a mechanism does not. By contrast, I claim that agent reason-responsiveness no more requires alternate sequences than mechanism reason-responsiveness, for the same reasons given above.

Someone may still be tempted to ask the following question: When a different mechanism could have operated but didn't, did the agent control whether it operated or not? But this way of posing the question confuses an alternate-sequence condition with an actual-sequence control condition. It is a fundamental misunderstanding to suppose that control requires that someone could have done otherwise, all else constant. Again, control of X requires that X would have been otherwise under certain conditions, not that it could have been otherwise all else constant. Whether a different mechanism could have operated as things were is a question about an alternate sequence, about outright possibility, all else constant. But control, like reason-responsiveness, involves dispositional properties of the actual sequence.

As explained, control depends on dispositions to respond so as to maintain a target value under various counterfactual conditions. So, if the agent controls which mechanism operates, then the agent maintains the state of affairs with respect to mechanism operation at some target value in the face of exogenous disturbances, by adjusting her behavior accordingly to compensate for those disturbances. Moreover, if an agent is controlling something, he does otherwise in response to different circumstances: different exogenous disturbances demand different responses to maintain the target value of what he controls. If his variation in behavior is substantially independent of those conditions, he is not maintaining the target

---

28. See also Wallace 1996, pp. 86–87, 181, 189–190, 220–221, 262–263, who argues for powers of reflective self-control as a condition of accountability and that such powers are compatible with determinism.

value, hence not controlling whatever takes that value. Target maintenance against exogenous disturbance is essential to control. What are
needed for control are dispositions to act in certain ways under certain
counterfactual conditions. An ability to do otherwise, all else constant, is
not needed for control and if acted on could even undermine control.
(Hence what Fischer and Ravizza (1998) still call "regulative control" is
not a kind of control at all.)

The question arises whether the agent in turn controls the target value.
He may or may not. But if he does, that just pushes the conditional/
dispositional character of control back a step and begins a control hierar-
chy. Points similar to those I have made about control of a target value
apply also to control hierarchies. Meta-control no more requires alternate possible sequences than does simple control (cf. Fischer and Ravizza
1998, p. 31).[29]

Reason-responsiveness accounts of responsibility are structurally well
suited, as dispositional actual-sequence accounts, to capture the sense in
which responsibility requires control, whether by the agent or by a reason-
responsive mechanism. But by the same token they do not generate an
asymmetry between acts and omissions.

However, a reason-responsiveness conception of responsibility can support a different and more promising asymmetry, between certain talents
and corresponding handicaps. Omissions to act in worthwhile ways are
often explained not by the operation of mechanisms that are reason-
responsive in blame-supporting ways, but rather by sheer lack of reason-
responsiveness. Such a lack of reason-responsiveness can be regarded as a
kind of handicap. On a reason-responsiveness conception of responsibility,
people handicapped by lack of reason-responsiveness may make poor decisions, both to act and to omit, for which they are not responsible, even
though those with more talent at responding to reasons are responsible for
their acts. Of course there is no converse implication: people with various
independently identified handicaps need not lack reason-responsiveness.
Rather, the suggestion is the other way around: sheer lack of reason-
responsiveness can itself be regarded as a generic handicap, and reason-
responsiveness as a generic talent. If reason-responsiveness is held to be

---

29. These remarks about the dispositional character of control can easily be adjusted
to make explicit that control is compatible with indeterministic causation (see Clarke
1995). Control is logically neutral with respect to determinism. Cf. Otsuka 1998,
pt. 1.

necessary and sufficient for responsibility, this yields an asymmetry: people can be responsible in virtue of having such a talent, even though they are not responsible in virtue of having such a handicap. This asymmetry has interesting implications in relation to distributive justice (see Part II).

I have given a four-fold comparison of the reason-based views of Wolf and Fischer, elements of which are used in Chapter 2 to develop the intuition that the alternate sequence is irrelevant to responsibility. I now bring Klein's arguments for a regressive conception of responsibility back into the comparison.

10. Between Regression and Reason-Responsiveness

As we have seen, Klein holds that our intuitions about certain kinds of excuse or exemption from responsibility commit us to a regressive conception of responsibility. But she does not consider the possibility that reason-based views of responsibility might instead explain these intuitions. Could a causally local requirement of reason-responsiveness, without a regression requirement, explain our intuitions about such cases? Or is there some condition occupying a middle ground between regression and reason-responsiveness that can deal with these cases?

Consider acts that result from brainwashing or a brain tumor or mental illness or an arbitrary hypnotic suggestion or an extremely deprived upbringing. In some such cases, neither regression nor reason-responsiveness requirements are met. So we could explain why responsibility is lacking in terms of either.

However, in other cases—say, of deprived upbringing—we may have reason-responsiveness without regression. Even if someone is not responsible for the causes of his act all the way back to his deprived upbringing and beyond, he may nevertheless act on a loosely reason-responsive mechanism. It might dispose him, for example, to act in accordance with his deliberations in many situations where reasons conflict, even though not in this case.

Intuitions on reason-responsiveness without regression, like those about the converse issue, may depend on exactly how reason-responsiveness is specified: as tight or loose, as responsiveness to objective or merely subjective reasons. An act can issue from a mechanism that is tightly responsive to evil subjective reasons, or loosely responsive to objective reasons, or tightly responsive to objective reasons, where the presence of that mechanism can only be explained in terms of causes that are not themselves so responsive.[30] A process of upbringing that is itself less than reason-responsive could nevertheless result in a variety of reason-responsive characters: in evil, weak, or virtuous character. Does the failure of reason-responsiveness further back in the actual sequence matter? Can we blame or praise people for acts that result from such reason-responsive characters only if they are also responsible for their characters? Again, the answers may differ for different specifications of reason-responsiveness.

In some cases, a medical problem or manipulation of some kind may have the effect not of switching off reason-responsiveness altogether, but rather of replacing one kind of reason-responsiveness with another. If this is merely a transient change, followed by other transient changes that add up to no stable reason-responsive disposition, the net long-term effect may be to switch off any identifiable reason-responsive mechanism.

But the change could instead be stable. Scanlon suggests that a shift from a kind to a cruel disposition after a head bump, if it persists long enough and is not disowned by the agent, is likely to shift our sense of the agent. "Instead of disrupting the connection between the person and these [cruel] forms of behavior, the accident or the drugs come to make a change in what she is like. We may say, 'She used to be so wonderful, but after her accident she became a nasty person'" (Scanlon 1998, p. 279). In such a case, at least some specification of reason-responsiveness could be satisfied both before and after the bump on the head, even though a regression requirement is not satisfied. Suppose that Smith receives a bump on the head that substitutes a stable disposition to respond to subjective reasons for a prior disposition, which was the result of upbringing, to respond to objective reasons. Does the change in Smith brought on by the head bump exempt her from responsibility?

If responsiveness to objective, or to moral, reasons is required for responsibility, this requirement will not be met post-bump (given the way the case of Smith was described). A tight objective reason-based condition of responsibility will agree with a regression requirement in exempting from responsibility.

But a looser, subjective reason-based condition of responsibility could be satisfied both pre- and post-bump. Antiregressive intuitions may be ap-

---

30. Wallace 1996 argues for a version of a reason-based view, according to which what is needed for accountability are powers of reflective self-control, which involve the power to grasp and apply specifically *moral* reasons, and the power to regulate one's behavior by the light of such reasons; see pp. 86, 155, 157. For comparison with Fischer's views, see pp. 189–190.

pealed to as follows. Smith's pre-bump responsibility in virtue of reason-responsiveness is not intuitively undermined by the fact that she is not responsible for her upbringing. Therefore, her post-bump responsibility should not be undermined by the fact that she is not responsible for the bump on her head. Furthermore, it may be argued, Smith's post-bump dispositions may be qualitatively similar to White's dispositions, which have been the result not of a bump but of peer pressure and television. The fact that White is not responsible for the latter does not, intuitively, exempt White from responsibility. So why should the fact that Smith is not responsible for her head bump exempt her (see and cf. Wallace 1996, p. 197)? If Smith is not responsible after the bump, it must be for some more specific reason than that she is not responsible for the causes of her new reason-responsive dispositions and mechanisms.

In response, appeal may be made to the normal or ordinary character of the agents' reason-related dispositions. Does the bump disable Smith's ordinary or normal dispositions and substitute different, nonnormal ones, that are not really hers in some sense? If the new dispositions are stable for long enough, does that establish their normalcy, or does their source permanently compromise their normalcy? We may be more inclined to recognize a new set of "normal" or long-term dispositions as the agent's own when they are induced by an accidental head bump than when they are induced by chemical or surgical manipulation by a brain scientist. The intentional intervention and manipulation by another agent tends to preempt recognition of a new set of dispositions as normal or as the agent's own.

We saw earlier that dispositions to hypothetical choice could be manipulated, as in the case of the tame housewife. Similarly, dispositions to respond to reasons could themselves be manipulated. This possibility leads us to ask whether what is needed is an actual-sequence requirement weaker than regression but stronger than any reason-responsiveness requirement per se. Such a middle-ground requirement would aim to capture an intuition that what matters for responsibility is not just that certain reason-responsive dispositions be active, but also that they are in some sense the agent's own. It would add some actual-sequence normalcy or ownership or identification condition to a reason-responsiveness condition.

There are various forms that this additional actual-sequence requirement could take. It could take the form of adding various structural or content conditions to the agent's dispositions and attitudes at the time of acting, or it could take the form of imposing conditions further back on the process that leads to action (though not all the way back, as in the regression condition). Fischer and Ravizza develop one version of such a middle-ground requirement in their 1998 account of responsibility, which emphasizes the process by which the kind of mechanism on which an agent acts becomes his own. Fischer's 1994 account of responsibility is put solely in terms of reason-responsiveness. But in Fischer and Ravizza's 1998 view, action on a locally reason-responsive mechanism is not enough for responsibility; it is also required that the agent *take responsibility* for the kind of mechanism on which he acts (see especially their chap. 8). This means, roughly, that the agent must see himself as an agent and as an apt target for reactive attitudes in respect of actions that flow from the relevant kind of mechanism, such as practical reasoning. Moreover, these self-perceptions must be the results of a certain kind of *process*. They must be based in an appropriate way on the evidence the agent has, such as his experience of the effects of his choices and actions on the world, what his parents taught him, and his experience of various social and moral practices.[31] Taking responsibility on this view requires not just that a certain end-state of cognitive dispositions be reached, but that it actually be reached through a certain canonical kind of evidence-based process. However, the agent is not required to be responsible for this process. This middle-ground actual-sequence account requires more than mere local reason-responsiveness, but less than full-fledged regression.

This further process element of Fischer and Ravizza's account of taking responsibility is supposed to keep cases of manipulation from satisfying the requirements for responsibility. Consider how reason-responsiveness might itself be subject to manipulation. Suppose that unbeknownst to Jeremiah, a mad scientist implants in him a moderately reason-responsive mechanism on which he, Jeremiah, acts, with harmful effects (see and cf. 1998, pp. 232 ff). Intuitively, he is not responsible, even though he acts on a reason-responsive mechanism, because the mechanism has been implanted in such a way that it is not his own. The process element of the taking-responsibility condition confirms this intuition. Since Jeremiah does not know about the manipulation or the implanted mechanism, he does not see himself as an agent and an apt target for reactive attitudes with respect to actions that flow from this mechanism. Hence he cannot

---

31. "Taking responsibility" seems a misnomer, since it is "coming to have a certain cluster of beliefs (in a certain way)," rather than something one does voluntarily (see Fischer and Ravizza 1998, p. 217).

have taken responsibility for the kind of mechanism that has been implanted and on which he has in fact acted.[32]

Jeremiah might, however, come to know about the manipulation, and to see himself as an agent and an apt target for reactive attitudes with respect to actions that flow from the implanted mechanism, on the basis of appropriate evidence. The "manipulator" might be his therapist, who has given him a drug. In response to Jeremiah's questions, the therapist explains that the drug helps to control his mood swings and to think more calmly and positively, but that it very occasionally has undesirable side-effects, such as temper tantrums. This is true, and Jeremiah believes it. Thus Jeremiah takes the drug willingly, and enjoys the net improvement in his life and relationships that his new reason-responsive dispositions produce. Here, his view of himself in relation to actions on the new mechanism do seem to be formed on the basis of appropriate evidence. When he has a tantrum, he does not say: "It's not my fault; that is just the cost of controlling my moods." Rather, he says: "I'm sorry; please forgive me; I'll try to improve." Such "manipulation" is more like the stable change of disposition induced by the head bump, in that the change in which it results becomes the agent's own.

Could taking responsibility itself be manipulated? Again, the process element of Fischer and Ravizza's account of taking responsibility is supposed to prevent this. Perhaps Jeremiah's seeing himself as an agent and apt target of reactive attitudes in respect of the drug could themselves be implanted—not by appropriate evidence and experience with the drug, but rather by some other "softening up" drug or hypnotic manipulation

---

32. I said that there are various forms a middle-ground account could take. Fischer and Ravizza contrast their historical view of taking responsibility with Frankfurt's current-time-slice view in terms of the structure of the agent's attitudes and higher-order attitudes at the time of action (1998, pp. 199–200; Frankfurt 1987b). In their view, the essential process element of taking responsibility enables their middle-ground account to deal with cases of manipulation, in the way described in the text, and hence gives it an advantage over Frankfurt's structural account. Suppose certain endorsing higher-order attitudes and contemporaneous judgments are required for an agent to identify with his volitions, as in Frankfurt's account. Such identification could be required in addition to some condition of reason-responsiveness in a middle-ground account. But such attitudes and judgments could in principle be implanted, manipulatively induced in the wrong way (Fischer and Ravizza 1998, pp. 199–200, 233n). Similar points could be made about dispositions to hypothetical choice, if these were added to a requirement of reason-responsiveness in yet another version of a middle-ground account.

that induces deference to therapists. But then Jeremiah's views of himself are not formed in the appropriate sort of way (1998, pp. 235–236).[33]

Fischer and Ravizza, however, do not say much about how appropriate ways are distinguished from inappropriate ways. There is a danger that this distinction simply follows, rather than independently explains, our intuitions about manipulation and responsibility. It must be true that if responsibility requires that the very process by which agents come to "own" reason-responsive mechanisms have certain manipulation-incompatible features, then manipulation of that process cannot satisfy these requirements, even if it does lead to the same end result. But the challenge that remains is to give an independent account of the required manipulation-incompatible features of the process, one which could explain and not merely redescribe our intuitions about manipulation and responsibility in specific cases.

One way to respond to this challenge is to go objective. Suppose the process by which reason-responsive mechanisms and self-perceptions in relation to these mechanisms are acquired is one in which the agent is equipped with mechanisms that reliably and flexibly, across a wide range of possible situations, induce true beliefs and right actions. This does not count as manipulation but as the instilling of wisdom and virtue, regardless of what the hidden agenda of the instiller is. A process that connects the agent with objective reasons for belief and action is not a process of manipulation, even if it is intended to be.

But we now run into a problem. If we require the process to instill this degree of wisdom and virtue, to dispose the agent tightly to track objective reasons, then we rule out responsibility for weakness and evil. However, the incompatibility between manipulation and contact with objective reasons gives us a programmatic clue to what may be needed in a middle-ground actual-sequence requirement.

The something more than local reason-responsiveness but less than full-fledged regression that is needed may be a process of acquiring reason-

---

33. It may also be objected that the possibility of higher-order manipulation, of the process that leads to the process of taking responsibility, is not ruled out. A whole portion of someone's life and education could be staged, unbeknownst to him, so that the desired results are obtained through the "right kind" of process. However, the distinction between ordinary life and manipulation now begins to blur. Persuasion by others with their own agendas is one of the hazards of ordinary life. It is one of the background conditions against which we come to identify with what we are, not something that undermines our identifications.

responsive mechanisms or dispositions in which the agent is genuinely in contact with objective reasons—with the True and the Good, as Wolf might say—but which does not guarantee he will arrive at true beliefs and right actions. It may not be cost effective or even possible for evolution or culture to instill perfect wisdom and virtue, especially if objective reasons for action can ineliminably conflict. Instead, evolution and culture may equip us with mechanisms for arriving at beliefs and actions through a process of learning to respond to objective reasons in specific contexts. These mechanisms or heuristics may work most of the time and in many situations without being foolproof.

To summarize this section: when reason-responsiveness conditions of responsibility are pitted against a regression requirement in various cases, questions arise about whether the reason-responsive dispositions or mechanisms in question are the agent's own. In particular, cases of implanted mechanisms and similar manipulations cast doubt on the sufficiency of reason-responsiveness for responsibility, since it seems that reason-responsiveness itself could be implanted. However, it may be possible to do justice to intuitions about manipulation cases without going all the way to a regression requirement. A middle-ground account could require more than mere local reason-responsiveness but less than full-fledged regression. For example, in their 1998 theory, Fischer and Ravizza argue for the additional requirement that an agent "take responsibility" for the reason-responsive mechanisms on which he acts. They understand taking responsibility to involve a process that is incompatible with manipulative implantation.

The idea of a middle-ground requirement is promising, though it needs further development. More than reason-responsiveness may be needed for responsibility, but we do not yet have a full account of what. I argue in Chapter 3, however, that even if more than reason-responsiveness is required for responsibility, regression is not required.

11. Klein, Wolf, and Fischer: How the Debate Relocates to the Actual Sequence

I now want to stand back from the details of this philosophical landscape and draw together my various comparisons of Klein, Wolf, and Fischer.

We can see each of these illuminating philosophers as making good gaps in the others' discussions. Klein prompts us to distinguish between the actual-sequence regression requirement and the alternate-sequence requirement of ability to do otherwise. She addresses Frankfurt Cases and issues about regression. But she does not register the importance to responsibility of responsiveness to reasons, or its relationship to her distinction. Wolf (1990) explains the importance to responsibility of the ability to respond to reasons, and (unlike Fischer 1994) considers the challenge to reason-based views of responsibility from a regression requirement. But Wolf does not draw a distinction between actual-sequence and alternate-sequence requirements or consider the implications of Frankfurt Cases for reason-based views. Fischer does, and also considers how the actual-sequence/alternate-sequence distinction and reason-responsiveness are related. But he still faces Klein's challenge to explain the intuitions about responsibility that she thinks support a regression requirement. In their 1998 book, Fischer and Ravizza provide an alternative to a regression requirement by adding a requirement of taking responsibility to their reason-responsiveness account.

In this way the debate about whether determinism is compatible with responsibility relocates from the alternate sequence to the actual sequence. Klein and Fischer agree, following Frankfurt, that what matters for responsibility is what the actual sequence of events leading to an act is like, not whether the agent could have done otherwise. Fischer's actual-sequence reason-responsiveness condition leaves responsibility compatible with determinism. In his 1994 view, determinism could only threaten responsibility by threatening our ability to do otherwise, and this threat fails to materialize because responsibility does not require ability to do otherwise. But Klein thinks our intuitions commit us to an actual-sequence regression requirement, and that as a result responsibility is threatened by determinism.[34] So the question arises whether actual-sequence requirements other than regression can do justice to these intuitions, such as requirements of reason-responsiveness and taking responsibility (Fischer and Ravizza 1998).

These are the issues we are left with by an articulation of responsibility that follows and weaves together the leads of Klein, Wolf, and Fischer. They are still large issues, but they are differently drawn. The major threat to responsibility now looks to be a regression requirement rather than determinism per se, and the actual sequence is where the action is.

---

34. On the assumption that the causal chain leading to the agent's choice does not consist just in events of informed choosing by the agent.

2

Why Alternate Sequences
Are Irrelevant to Responsibility

In this chapter I develop further the argument that the alternate sequence is irrelevant to responsibility. I will be excavating what I take to be the fundamental intuition underlying Frankfurt Cases, but will generalize it in a certain way. As I develop it, the intuition can be evoked from a wider range of cases than classical Frankfurt Cases, and does not depend on science-fiction fail-safe devices to guarantee that the agent could not have done otherwise, as classical Frankfurt Cases do. The more general intuition is here called the *irrelevant-alternative intuition*.[1] According to this intuition, the outright possibility of doing otherwise, all else constant, is not what matters for responsibility. If the agent *wouldn't* have done otherwise whether or not she could have, then it is irrelevant whether or not she could have. I illustrate the irrelevant-alternative intuition by various cases involving weakness of will, evil motivations, and medical problems. This intuition operates not just against the ability-to-do-otherwise requirement, but also against the ability-to-avoid-blame requirement.

---

1. While my way of arguing that responsibility does not require alternate sequences can be seen as generalizing the intuition to which Frankfurt Cases appeal, that of Wallace (1996, esp. chaps. 5, 6) can be seen as complementing Frankfurt's approach. Wallace gives a brilliant account of the reasons for which we excuse or exempt people from responsibility in a variety of cases. He then argues powerfully and persuasively that the truth of determinism, hence the lack of alternative possibilities, would not constitute a generalization of these reasons. Wallace's arguments thus contribute to the strong overall case against alternate-sequence requirements for responsibility. However, Wallace does not focus explicitly on the separate threat to responsibility posed by actual-sequence requirements such as a regression requirement (but see pp. 197 ff).

1. The Space of Reason-Based Accounts of Responsibility

The comparison of Wolf and Fischer in Chapter 1 provides distinctions that are used here to characterize the space of reason-based accounts of responsibility. By reference to this characterization I then illustrate how the irrelevant-alternative intuition can be generalized beyond Frankfurt Cases. First, the link to reason required for responsibility can be tight or loose. Second, it can be a link to objective reasons, or merely to subjective reasons. Third, the link to reason can impose alternate-sequence requirements or can be characterized in terms of counterfactual conditionals expressing the dispositions of the mechanisms that operate in the actual sequence.

First, consider the distinction between tight and loose reason-responsiveness.[2] Both are counterfactual characterizations of the mechanism that operates in the actual sequence of causes leading to someone's act. If the causes of someone's act are tightly responsive to reason, then if there is good reason to act differently and the same mechanism were operating, she would act as reason requires. A *tightly reason-responsive* mechanism of action tracks reason. Someone who does not do the right act for the right reason is not acting on a mechanism that responds tightly to reason—that tracks reason closely—since reason requires doing otherwise than she does. But even so the causes of her act might be *loosely reason-responsive*. This requires only that there is *some* possible world, which need not be close to the actual world, in which there is good reason to do otherwise and the same mechanism operates and it leads her to act on such reason and hence to do otherwise. For example, what actually leads her to steal a book, wrongly and imprudently, despite sufficient reason not to, might be responsive to at least some incentives not to steal (cf. Fischer 1994, pp. 167; 1987). A loose reason-responsiveness requirement is, roughly, what lawyers are getting at when they ask whether a defendant would have broken the law if there had been a policeman at his elbow. But it may rule out very little other than cases in which reason gets no purchase at all on the operative mechanism, such as cases of reason-blindness, subrationality, or mental illness.

Weakness of will is compatible with loose reason-responsiveness but not

---

2. Fischer uses the terms "strong" versus "weak" reason-responsiveness (1994, pp. 164 ff).

tight reason-responsiveness. Suppose I go to the movies for a good reason. But, holding the deliberative mechanism on which I act constant, I would have gone even if I'd had a publication deadline that provided better reason not to go. That is, I would have been weak willed under those circumstances. The mechanism on which I act is not tightly reason-responsive. But, still holding the mechanism constant, I would not have gone to the movies if I would have lost my job by going, or if tickets had cost a thousand dollars. So the causes of my act are loosely reason-responsive. If such loose actual-sequence reason-responsiveness is sufficient for responsibility, then I would be responsible in the case of weak will. But if tight reason-responsiveness is required, someone who is weak willed is not responsible.[3]

Tight responsiveness to objective reasons provides a condition of responsibility that is maximal in two dimensions. Thus it can be weakened in two ways. It can be loosened, as we have just seen. Or, it can be subjectified: responsiveness could be required merely to subjective reasons, rather than to objective reasons. So there is logical space for at least three more kinds of reason-responsiveness: loose responsiveness to objective reasons, tight responsiveness to subjective reasons, and loose responsiveness to subjective reasons.

It might be thought that loose reason-responsiveness is too weak a condition for blameworthiness but that tight reason-responsiveness is too strong (Fischer and Ravizza move to this view in 1998). Is there attractive middle ground between responding to reason in all possible worlds and only in some possible worlds? Can some subset of possible worlds be specified that yields a condition intermediate between loose and tight reason-responsiveness? Further consideration of weakness of will suggests one way to do this.

Distinguish all-things-considered reasons to act ("It's the right thing to do") from specific reasons to act ("That would be the kindest thing to do, though not necessarily the fairest"). Assume that specific reasons for action may conflict, even if they are objective reasons (see Hurley 1989, chaps. 7, 8, on pro tanto reasons). A weak-willed agent does not act in accordance with the reasons she has, all things considered, but she does act for one of the conflicting specific reasons she has. Suppose distinct specific

---

3. See Fischer 1994, pp. 165–167. As explained in Chapter 1, Wolf's view is not a pure actual-sequence, reason-responsiveness view; her ability condition makes alternate-sequence demands. She thinks that someone can be able to act in accord with the True and the Good, but fail to do so nonetheless, thus that weakness of will is possible (1990, pp. 88–89).

reasons conflict over whether to do *x* or *y*. The agent deliberates and judges correctly that, all things considered, the right thing to do is *x*, and instead she does *y*. Moreover, she does *y* for the specific reason there is to do it, even though her all-things-considered, deliberative judgment to the contrary took account of this reason.

In this familiar type of situation, intermediate reason-responsiveness might require the mechanism on which the agent acts not only to respond to reasons in some other possible worlds, but to be responsive to deliberation in the face of conflicting reasons in some other possible worlds. More specifically, it could require the mechanism on which the agent acts to satisfy various combinations of the following conditions: (a) that it responds to specific reasons (of the types in play in the actual world) in some other worlds where reasons of those types obtain; (b) that it responds to all-things-considered, deliberative reasons in some other worlds where specific reasons conflict; (c) that it responds to all-things-considered, deliberative reasons in some other worlds when specific reasons of the types in play in the actual world obtain and also conflict. Each of these conditions could be strengthened to require "most other worlds" rather than "some other worlds."[4]

If we recognize intermediate kinds of reason-responsiveness between loose and tight responsiveness, we get another two categories of responsiveness: intermediate responsiveness could be required merely to subjective reasons, or to objective reasons. In fact, I am sympathetic to the claim that some form of intermediate reason-responsiveness may provide the most successful reason-based account of responsibility. Nothing in my argument here is incompatible with this claim. However, intermediate reason-responsiveness raises complications tangential to the present argument, which does not need to be formulated in these more complex terms. So this attractive conception of responsibility is not developed further here.[5] My argument will proceed by reference to the simpler, loose vs. tight, classification of reason-responsiveness conditions.

Second, then, consider the distinction between responsiveness to objective reasons and responsiveness to subjective reasons. Someone who had a

---

4. See and cf. Honore: "a person guilty of fault must have, besides a general capacity for decision and action, the ability to succeed most of the time in doing the sort of thing which would on this occasion have averted the harm" (1988, p. 531; see also 550–551).

5. See Fischer and Ravizza 1998, chap. 3, on what they call "moderate reason-responsiveness," which requires an appropriate *pattern* of responses (e.g., p. 66).

bad or deprived upbringing might fail to satisfy a requirement of objective reason-responsiveness but not a requirement of subjective reason-responsiveness. For example, a deprived upbringing might result in someone with evil motivations, who acts for evil reasons, in order to hurt others. These are subjective rather than objective reasons, but they might be tracked very tightly.

Agents can be more or less tightly disposed to respond to their own desires or to subjective reasons as well as to objective reasons. They can be weak willed in relation to their own self-interested desires, as well as in relation to objective reasons (see Hurley 1989, chap. 8). So the mechanism on which an agent acts should not be thought of simply as his desires. Rather, the mechanism on which an agent acts may be disposed to respond to various reasons, which may include desires, more or less tightly.

Notice that the distinction between subjective and objective reason-responsiveness cuts across the distinction between tight and loose reason-responsiveness, to yield four varieties of reason-responsiveness. If subjective reason-responsiveness is sufficient for responsibility, then someone who acts on dispositions that track evil reasons tightly can be responsible. But if objective reason-responsiveness is required, and assuming that there are no objective reasons to do evil and that there are objective reasons not to do evil, then someone who acts on a mechanism that is tightly responsive to evil cannot be responsible. However, someone who is less tightly responsive to objective reasons might act for an evil subjective reason: he might act on a disposition to injure someone a little, even though he would avoid acting to injure a lot. If only loose responsiveness to objective reasons is required for responsibility, then it is possible to do a bit of evil responsibly.[6]

Our choices between objective and subjective, and between tighter and looser, versions of reason-responsiveness will correspond to whether we allow that agents whose acts result from defective upbringing, weakness of will, or devotion to evil can be morally responsible for the resulting acts. For example, if we want to allow that someone can be responsible for a weak-willed act, we should require for responsibility something looser than tight reason-responsiveness. If we want to allow that it is possible to be dedicated to evil yet responsible for a resulting evil act, we should go

---

6. Although it could be regarded as odd to allow that someone can do a bit of evil responsibly, but would not be responsible if he were tightly responsive, or dedicated, to evil.

	Tight	Loose
Subjective	weakness of will: not responsible deprived upbringing: may be responsible dedication to evil: may be responsible occasional evildoing: may be responsible	weakness of will: may be responsible deprived upbringing: may be responsible dedication to evil: may be responsible occasional evildoing: may be responsible
Objective	weakness of will: not responsible deprived upbringing: not responsible dedication to evil: not responsible occasional evildoing: not responsible	weakness of will: may be responsible deprived upbringing: not responsible dedication to evil: not responsible occasional evildoing: may be responsible

Figure 1. Varieties of reason-responsivenesss that could be required for responsibility, and their implications.

for a form of subjective reason-responsiveness. But if instead we want only to allow the possibility of doing an occasional bit of evil responsibly, loose objective reason-responsiveness will do the trick (see Figure 1).

Third, notice that all these varieties of reason-responsiveness impose actual-sequence conditions for responsibility. What is required for responsibility is that the agent actually act on a mechanism that has certain dispositions to respond to reasons under counterfactual conditions, characterized in one of these ways. The actual causes of her acts must involve certain conditional dispositions to act on reasons. This is not in general, as Frankfurt Cases illustrate, the same thing as an outright possibility of acting otherwise, given the reasons there actually are. As Fischer might put the point, so long as in the actual sequence the agent acts on an appropriately reason-responsive mechanism, it does not matter what other mechanism might have operated instead.[7] So, in a Frankfurt Case, it does not matter if there is a counterfactual intervenor or fail-safe mechanism in an alternate sequence such that an ability-to-do-otherwise requirement is not satisfied. What matters is the dispositional character of the operative mechanism.

However, in the maximal case where tight objective reason-responsiveness is required for responsibility, it is hard to distinguish an actual-sequence requirement for blame from an alternate-sequence requirement. Praiseworthy acts can meet the requirement for responsibility that the actual causes of an act must respond tightly to objective reasons. But any failure to do the right thing for the right reasons indicates that the agent is not acting on a mechanism with this actual-sequence disposition. It is not relevant here to ask how the agent would have acted under different conditions; we are concerned with how she acts given the reasons there are. She cannot be acting on a mechanism of the required kind, since good objective reason is present and she does not act on it. It is not possible, on such a condition, to be blameworthy. The defect is in the actual sequence: in the disposition of the operative mechanism. But this is immediately tied to the failure to do otherwise given the reasons there are. Similarly, Wolf's Reason View can ignore Frankfurt Cases and the distinction between actual- and alternate-sequence conditions because it requires a tight link to objective reasons. Thus, maximal reason-responsiveness, like Wolf's ability to act in accordance with reason, generates an asymmetry between blame and praise. Blame does require an alternate sequence, even though praise does not.

An actual-sequence condition of tight objective reason-responsiveness makes responsible weakness of will or evildoing impossible. However, Fischer holds that weakness of will can in principle be responsible (1994, p. 168). This seems right, and surely the same is true of evildoing. A condition of responsibility that rules out these possibilities in principle cannot be correct. This argues for less-than-maximal reason-responsiveness as a condition of responsibility, which would allow these possibilities in principle. And weaker forms of reason-responsiveness do not support the asymmetry between praise and blame.[8] They permit us to distinguish the responsiveness to reasons of the mechanism on which the agent acts from

7. Fischer is sensitive to worries about how mechanisms are individuated, and to parallel worries in epistemology (1987; 1994; Fischer and Ravizza 1998).

8. See Fischer 1994, pp. 156 ff; Fischer and Ravizza 1991.

the agent's outright ability to act rightly. This distinction allows us to set up cases in which it is supposed that the agent *wouldn't* have done otherwise or have avoided blame, whether or not she *could* have. The irrelevant-alternative intuition then emerges. Responsibility turns on what the actual sequence of operative causes is like. If the actual sequence is such as to support or to defeat responsibility, adding or subtracting alternate sequences makes no difference.[9]

2. A Recipe for the Irrelevant-Alternative Intuition

Fischer and Ravizza argue that a mechanism-based approach to responsibility is more useful than an agent-based approach. Frankfurt Cases show that the operative mechanism can be reason-responsive even if the agent, and the mechanism that would operate in the alternate sequence, are not reason-responsive.

By "mechanism," they explain, they do not mean anything over and above the way the action comes about. Actions can come about in importantly different ways. It is crucial to distinguish between the way an action comes about in the actual sequence and the way it would come about in alternate sequences. But they confess they do not have any general formula for specifying when these are the same ways or different ways. Rather, they rely on relatively clear intuitions about sameness and difference of ways actions come about, or mechanisms on which agents act. Nor do they specify in a general way how to determine which mechanism is the relevant operative mechanism; again, they simply presuppose that there is an intuitively natural choice. If intuitions about mechanism individuation are unclear where intuitions about responsibility are also unclear, then the mechanism approach reflects pretheoretical fuzziness about responsibility (Fischer and Ravizza 1998, pp. 38–40, 40n, 46–47; see also Wallace 1996, p. 190n on mechanism worries).

In what follows I take over Fischer's intuitive idea of acting on a reason-responsive mechanism and use it to argue for a generalized irrelevant-alternative intuition. This strategy makes the generalized irrelevant-alternative intuition hostage either to the mechanism story or to there being some explanation that does the equivalent work. The essential work that needs to be done to support the irrelevant alternative intuition, as I ex-

---

9. There is a sense in which this is just the old intuition that indeterminism cannot make for responsibility in a new guise.

plain, is to underwrite the intuitive supposition that an agent would not have done otherwise in a given situation, whether or not she could have. I go on to suggest how this supposition could be explained.

Here is the general idea. Frankfurt Cases generate the irrelevant-alternative intuition by supposing that the actual-sequence condition for responsibility is met even though the alternate-sequence condition is not. However, we cannot generate the intuition in this way where the actual-sequence condition is tight objective reason-responsiveness, because of the way such maximal reason-responsiveness ties the actual and alternate sequences together. We can however pry the actual sequence and the alternate sequence apart the other way around. And this suggests a recipe for generating the irrelevant-alternative intuition even for weaker forms of reason-responsiveness and indeed where reason-responsiveness is absent. My general strategy will be to develop pairs of examples in which the relevant properties of the actual sequence are held constant. In one of each pair there is an alternate sequence, and in the other there is not. The irrelevant-alternative intuition is that adding or subtracting the alternate sequence makes no difference to responsibility. If the agent wouldn't have done otherwise in a given situation, whether or not she could have, then whether she could have done otherwise does not matter to her responsibility or lack thereof. This strategy generalizes the irrelevant-alternative intuition beyond the special scenario of Frankfurt Cases with their counterfactual intervenors.

Consider first a case in which the mechanism on which the agent acts is tightly disposed to respond to objective reasons. This is a property of the actual sequence, though one with implications for counterfactual situations. Suppose that Vivian is virtuous. If there had not been good objective reason to do the act and Vivian had acted on the same mechanism as she actually acts on, she would not have done it. But in fact there is good objective reason to do the act, and Vivian does it for that reason. A fortiori, she is able to do it. The ability to act in accordance with reason does not here require an alternate sequence. Here we have both the ability to act in accordance with reason and the operation of a reason-responsive mechanism. On both conditions, the act is responsible, and hence praiseworthy. Wolf's Reason View is formulated in terms of the ability, not the responsive mechanism. But which one is really doing the work in supporting the intuitions of responsibility in such a case?

To pry these conditions apart, we need to consider cases in which the agent does not do what reason demands. We have just seen that an implication runs from a responsive mechanism claim to an ability claim. From:

(6) Vivian acts on a mechanism that is tightly responsive to objective reasons

we get:

(7) Vivian responds to objective reasons by doing the right thing

and thus:

(8) Vivian is able to do the right thing.

So, contraposing, if Vivian is unable to do the right thing, she cannot be acting on a mechanism that is tightly responsive to objective reasons.

The implication does not run in the other direction, however. Salome may be able to do the right thing, even though the kind of mechanism on which she in fact acts is not tightly responsive to objective reasons. Perhaps it was possible outright for a different, more responsive mechanism to operate, so that it is true that Salome could have done the right thing in these circumstances for the reasons there were. But this is not the way things happened. Given the kind of mechanism on which she actually acted, she *would* not have done the right thing in this situation, whether or not she *could* have. The ability condition can be met even though the tight responsiveness condition is not met.

Compare this case with an otherwise similar case in which neither the ability condition nor the responsive mechanism condition is met. If we judge someone is not responsible in such a case, does our judgment turn on the lack of ability or the ill-disposed operative mechanism? To find out, we can consider a pair of cases. In the first case, neither condition is met. In the second, the responsiveness condition continues to fail in the same way as in the first case, but the ability condition is met; otherwise it is similar to the first. We thus compare a case in which someone could not have done the right thing with a case in which someone would not have done the right thing in the same situation, even though she could have. We hold the applicable reasons and operative dispositions constant, and vary the ability. We ask: Does the sheer ability, the outright possibility on its own, make a difference to responsibility?

How is this strategy related to the strategy of Frankfurt Cases? In a Frankfurt Case the agent is not able to do otherwise because in the alternate sequence a fail-safe mechanism kicks in. But the operative causes are such that this mechanism never actually intervenes. The intuition Frankfurt Cases appeal to is that this feature of the alternate sequence is irrelevant. An actual-sequence condition sufficient for blame can be met, even if the alternate-sequence ability-to-do-otherwise condition is not.

This precise strategy for eliciting such an irrelevant-alternative intuition cannot be pursued when the proposed actual-sequence condition for blame is that someone is acting on a disposition that is tightly responsive to objective reasons. That is because of the inference from this particular tight disposition to ability. As in the case of Vivian, if someone is unable to do the right thing, she cannot be acting on a disposition that is tightly responsive to objective reasons. When the actual-sequence condition is this tight, we cannot pry apart the actual and alternate sequences in the manner typical of Frankfurt Cases, by supposing the actual-sequence condition is met and the alternate-sequence condition is not.

However, Frankfurt Cases are a symptom of something more general: the irrelevant-alternative intuition. We can still elicit this intuition, *by prying apart the actual-sequence disposition and the alternate sequence the other way round*. This is the key to the generalization of the irrelevant-alternative intuition that emerges from considering reason-based views of responsibility.

Here is how the generalization emerges. Suppose that an agent did not do the right thing and so did not act on a tightly reason-responsive mechanism but nevertheless was able to act rightly. She would not have done the right thing, even though she could have. That is, the mechanism on which she acted was not disposed to respond tightly to reasons, even though there was an alternate possible sequence in which another mechanism operated, leading to the right action. The question then is: What more can be said about the mechanism on which the agent did in fact act? Is it reason-responsive in some weaker way, that is compatible with being able but failing to do the right thing? Could a plausible actual-sequence condition for blame be formulated in terms of such weaker reason-responsiveness? If so, we can then consider whether an agent is blameworthy because the actual-sequence condition of weak reason-responsiveness is met, or because the agent is able to do the right thing. Given that she would not do the right thing in this situation whether or not she could, does it make any difference if in fact she can?

The mechanism on which an agent acts when she acts wrongly cannot be tightly responsive to objective reasons, or she would not act wrongly. But it might be more weakly reason-responsive: either loosely responsive, or responsive merely to subjective reasons. For example, the agent might act wrongly because she is weak willed or because she is evil. If she is *weak willed,* her act may be caused in a way that is loosely but not tightly responsive to objective reasons: holding the mechanism on which she acts constant, she would respond to even stronger objective reasons to act in the right way, even though she does not respond to the objective reasons there actually are.[10] If she is *evil,* her act may be caused in a way that is tightly responsive to evil subjective reasons, such as a desire to hurt others. These examples fall short of maximal reason-responsiveness: tight responsiveness to objective reasons. But they still illustrate weaker forms of reason-responsiveness: loose, or subjective.[11] A third way in which the agent could act wrongly, however, is by acting on a mechanism that is not even weakly reason-responsive. This might be the case, for example, for *medical* reasons: if the ordinary reason-responsive mechanisms that would otherwise operate are actually preempted by a brain tumor, by mental illness, by hypnotists, or by brain scientists.

The preceding paragraph gives us three different dispositional characterizations of the kind of mechanism on which an agent can act when she fails to do the right thing: as loosely reason-responsive, responsive only to subjective reasons, or not reason-responsive at all. These are all characterizations of the actual sequence. Each falls short in one way or another of maximal reason-responsiveness. In each case we can intuitively say that the agent would not have acted rightly in a given situation, even if she could have.

We now need to bring into play alternate sequences and outright possibilities—what the agent could have done, all else constant, as opposed to what she would have done under various counterfactual conditions, given the conditional dispositions of the operative mechanisms of action. To this end, I compare two scenarios, for each of the three types of operative disposition.

In the first scenario, we stipulate that the agent, in each of these three types of case, *could* have acted rightly. In fact she acted on a mechanism such that she *would* not have acted rightly in this situation even if she could have. Nevertheless, there was indeed an alternate possible sequence, in which a different kind of mechanism operated. Since this kind of mech-

---

10. Perhaps she also satisfies a requirement of intermediate reason-responsiveness; she may be generally responsive to the results of rational deliberation about what should be done, all things considered, when objective reasons conflict.

11. Someone could be both evil and weak willed, but that doesn't raise any different issues. Reason-responsiveness that is both loose and subjective is not considered separately.

anism could have operated instead, the agent could have acted rightly. But as things actually were it played no causal role.

In the second scenario, holding the situation and the dispositions of the operative mechanism constant, we stipulate instead that, unbeknownst to her, she could not have acted rightly. There was no alternate sequence. In neither case does the agent believe that she cannot act rightly.

In both scenarios, the agent acts a mechanism with the same dispositions and for the same reasons, but in one scenario there is an alternate sequence and in the other there is not. We now compare these two scenarios, and ask: If the agent would not have acted rightly in this situation whether or not she could have, does it matter whether or not she in fact could have? If the actual causes of her act are not tightly responsive to objective reasons, so that she acts wrongly, and indeed they are such that she would not act rightly in this situation even if she could, why is it relevant whether it is possible for her to act rightly? This possibility plays no explanatory role in what she actually does.

3. The Recipe Applied: Weakness of Will, Evil, and Medical Problems

We can follow this recipe for each of our three actual-sequence characterizations: cases of weakness of will, cases of evil, and medical cases. These questions pry apart various actual-sequence conditions from alternate sequences, and in particular the two varieties of weak reason-responsiveness from the outright ability to act rightly.

Consider first weak-willed Wilma. The mechanism on which she acts is so disposed that even if she could do the right thing in this situation for the reasons there are, she would not—though she might do the right thing for stronger reasons, if there were any, or in different circumstances. Given this, does it make any difference to her responsibility if in fact she could? Compare two scenarios. In both, Wilma acts in a weak-willed way, and the mechanism on which she acts is such that she would not have done the right thing, in this situation and for these reasons, even if she could have. In one scenario, additionally, she could have done the right thing; there is an alternate sequence in which she does. In the other scenario, the dispositions of the mechanism on which she acts are the same but, unbeknownst to her, she couldn't have done the right thing; there is no alternate sequence. In neither scenario does she believe she could not have done the right thing. (This is the kind of comparison that I signal, elliptically, by asking if "someone would have done otherwise, whether or not she could have.") Is Wilma any more responsible in the second scenario? Is what matters for her responsibility the actual causes of her act and the dispositions they involve, or the outright possibility of an alternate sequence?

The descendant of Frankfurt's irrelevant-alternative intuition here is that what matters for responsibility is not the outright ability to act rightly instead of wrongly, all else constant, but rather the character of the operative disposition—namely, whether one would act rightly if one could. When someone is weak willed, her act is caused in such a way that she wouldn't have done the right thing for the reasons there were, even if she could have, yet she would have done the right thing if the reasons had been stronger. If this is enough for responsibility when there is an alternate sequence such that she could have done the right thing for the reasons there are, why not also when there is no alternate sequence, when she couldn't have done the right thing for the reasons there are? If she would have acted wrongly, on the same kind of mechanism and given the same reasons, whether or not there was an alternate sequence in which she did not act wrongly, then why should the alternate sequence matter to her responsibility? Why should the outright ability to act in accordance with reason be necessary for responsibility if she wouldn't have acted that way whether or not she were able to? These questions express the irrelevant-alternative intuition. The outright possibility of an alternate sequence seems to be extrinsic, irrelevant, makes no difference to her action or its explanation.

Notice that the irrelevant-alternative intuition is conditional and comparative. It is not an intuition that Wilma is responsible for acting wrongly in either scenario. Rather, it is the intuition that *if* she is responsible for acting wrongly when she could have done otherwise, she is no less responsible when she couldn't have, given that the mechanisms on which she acts in the two scenarios have the same dispositions, so that she wouldn't have done otherwise whether she could have or not. The irrelevant-alternative intuition ties the two scenarios together, but does not resolve whether we blame in both cases or neither. That turns on whether loose reason-responsiveness provides the right actual-sequence condition for blame, so that weak-willed acts are blameworthy in such cases. If we think that at least some weak-willed acts are blameworthy, we need to loosen up a condition of tight reason-responsiveness in some way.

Recall the other two actual-sequence characterizations: subjective reason-responsiveness and nonresponsiveness. I now explain how the irrelevant alternative intuition can be elicited for pairs of scenarios relevant to these disposition types.

Suppose that Ethel is evil. She desires to cause pain to others. We can suppose for the sake of argument that there are no objective reasons to do evil: no objective evil reasons. Nevertheless, suppose there can be subjective evil reasons, such as Ethel's desire to cause pain. That is, suppose that this desire, along with Ethel's belief that a certain act would be hurtful, do provide a subjective reason for her to do it. Now some people might act in ways that are tightly responsive to their subjective reasons, while others act in ways that are only loosely responsive to them. There is some interpretative play in the relations of subjective reasons to action; you can be weak willed when your subjective reasons conflict. But suppose that the mechanism on which Ethel acts when she acts in accordance with her subjective evil reasons is tightly responsive to these reasons. When she acts on this mechanism and does the wrong thing, in accordance with her evil reasons, it is true of her that she would not do as she does if she did not believe it to be hurtful. And when she does nothing, it is still true of her that if she believed she could do something hurtful, she would try to.

Ethel acts on a mechanism with these dispositions when she acts in accordance with her evil reasons, whether or not she could have done otherwise. Can it then make any difference to her responsibility for acting this way in a given situation whether there is an alternate sequence of causes such that she is able to do the right thing in this situation? Given that she would not do the right thing whether or not she could, why is it relevant whether she could? Either way, she actually does act on a mechanism that is tightly disposed to respond to evil subjective reasons. Even if she could act rightly, the alternate sequence would merely be standing by; it would do no work in explaining why she actually does what she does.

Again the irrelevant-alternative intuition is conditional and comparative. *If* Ethel is responsible when she acts in accordance with her evil desire and could have done rightly, then she is no less responsible when she acts in the same way and in accordance with the same evil reason, but could not have done rightly. If the mechanism on which she acts in both scenarios is so disposed that she *would* not have done rightly in this set of circumstances, it doesn't matter whether or not she could have. The character of the operative mechanism ties the two cases together. The mere presence of the irrelevant alternative, a possibility that plays no role in explaining what she actually does, cannot make a difference to her blameworthiness. It is a further question whether her disposition to evil makes her responsible in both scenarios or in neither.

Finally, consider Maude, who has a medical problem. She also acts in a hurtful way in a particular situation, but the mechanism on which she acts is not reason-responsive in general, either loosely or to subjective reasons. Her act is a symptom of her mental illness, and is caused by abnormal neurotransmitter fluctuations that bear no projectible relationship to reasons. On a reason-based view of responsibility, such a causal history would tend to defeat responsibility for an act. If the mechanism on which Maude acts is not responsive to reasons at all, and as a result she would not do the right thing in the given set of circumstances, whether or not she could, then an actual sequence reason-based view of responsibility will find her not responsible. Does it make any difference whether she indeed could have done the right thing? Suppose there is an alternate sequence of causes in which a different, reason-responsive mechanism operates, such that there is an outright possibility that she does the right thing. Does this make Maude any more responsible? After all, this alternate sequence plays no role in the actual causes of her act. The irrelevant-alternative intuition is again conditional and comparative: the outright ability to do the right thing makes Maude no *more* responsible, given that she in fact acts on a nonresponsive mechanism.

On the other hand, suppose that Alfred is an addict, and as a result couldn't do otherwise than he does in a given situation. (Compare Frankfurt 1971, pp. 19–20, on the willing addict.) Nevertheless, he does what he does for his own reasons; the addiction does not need to exert its power over him. Even if he were not addicted and could have done otherwise, he wouldn't have done otherwise. Indeed, he would choose to become addicted even if he weren't already, in order to guarantee that he does as he does. (Alfred would install his own counterfactual intervenor if the addiction didn't already constitute one.) The irrelevant-alternative intuition again says that it doesn't matter whether he could have done otherwise.

What if Alfred's act is the result of his addiction instead of being done for his own reasons? It is not then directly the result of a reason-responsive mechanism. If we only look this far, and if reason-responsiveness is required for responsibility, then Alfred is not responsible because his act did not result from a reason-responsive mechanism. The irrelevant-alternative intuition says that the addiction is relevant if it is the mechanism on which he acted and is not reason-responsive, but not because it makes it the case that he couldn't have done otherwise.

We could, however, extend the range of our search for reason-responsive mechanisms and ask whether the addiction itself is the result of a choice by Alfred to become addicted, for his own reasons, and whether it is still true of him that if he could choose to become addicted he would do so, for his own reasons. If we take this broader view, we may treat the act in question as effectively the result of a reason-responsive mechanism via the choice to become addicted. If we therefore regard Alfred as responsible, the irrelevant-alternative intuition says that it is irrelevant whether in fact Alfred could have done otherwise, or indeed could have chosen not to become addicted in the first place, since he wouldn't have done or chosen otherwise even if he could have.

4. How Could It Be That the Agent Wouldn't Have Done Otherwise, Whether or Not She Could Have?

The irrelevant-alternative intuition generalizes the point of Frankfurt Cases in a significant way. Frankfurt Cases involve a blameworthy actual sequence and a blame-avoiding alternate sequence, and so do my cases. In Frankfurt Cases, the agent couldn't have done otherwise because in the alternate sequence she does the same thing as she does in the actual sequence. The alternate sequence in those cases is associated with a counterfactual intervenor, a fail-safe mechanism that guarantees that in the alternate sequence the agent does not do otherwise. Comparing the presence and the absence of the counterfactual intervenor in the alternate sequence yields the intuition that what matters is the way the action is brought about in the actual sequence, not whether the agent could have done otherwise. By contrast, in my cases no fail-safe device guarantees that in the alternate sequence the agent does not do otherwise. But this counterfactual-intervenor strategy of argument turns out not to be critical; the intuition still emerges that what matters for responsibility is the way the action is actually brought about, not the properties of alternate sequences—or even their existence. What the generalized intuition does depend on is making sense of the supposition that the agent would not have done otherwise, whether or not she could have done otherwise, without the prop of a counterfactual intervenor in the alternate sequence.[12]

I want to pause here to forestall a misunderstanding that has arisen in discussion of my position. My claim is in effect that whether someone is

---

12. For the role of this supposition in Frankfurt's work, see, e.g., 1991, p. 19; 1969, p. 837.

responsible for an act depends or supervenes on properties, including dispositional properties, of the actual sequence of causes leading to an act, and does not require an alternate sequence. This is the claim the irrelevant-alternative intuition supports, which I express using the elliptical phrase "he wouldn't have done otherwise, whether or not he could have," on the understanding that the relevant dispositions and circumstances are constant across the variation in ability. My claim is not that an agent is responsible for an act if he would not have done otherwise, even if he could have.[13] For consider a world in which an agent can do otherwise and does not do otherwise, but acts on a quite different disposition than that operative in the actual world. In the actual world, he may act on a given kind of reason-responsive disposition, while in this other world he acts on a quite different disposition that is not reason-responsive. Then of course my supervenience claim would not hold that he is equally responsible in these two worlds, since the supervenience base—the relevant dispositional properties of the actual sequence—has been allowed to vary between the worlds.

So far, the supposition that an agent would not have done otherwise, whether or not he could have, has been understood in terms of Fischer's mechanism-based account of responsibility, although he, as he admits, does not give a full account of how mechanisms are individuated. But can we now do more to explain this supposition?[14] It requires that the agent acts on mechanisms with the same operative dispositional properties in both the couldn't-have-done-otherwise and the could-have-done-otherwise scenarios. For my purposes, the focus is not on the identity of the mechanisms across the two scenarios, but rather on the sameness of type of the operative dispositional properties of the mechanisms across the two scenarios. And sameness of type of the dispositional properties of the mechanisms is determined, within a reason-responsiveness approach, by the types of reason-responsiveness we regard as relevant to responsibility.

Wilma does the weak-willed act *X*, thereby acting on a mechanism that is loosely responsive to objective reasons in a particular way that tends to yield weak-willed actions. This disposition to weakness of will, the "WW disposition," is held constant across the couldn't-have-done-otherwise

---

13. This misunderstanding in effect collapses the higher-order, conditional and comparative claim I am making into a first-order claim.

14. Note that I have inherited the component idea that an agent could have done otherwise, all else constant, from traditional incompatibilism, though I use it within the supposition that an agent wouldn't have done otherwise, whether or not he could have, to argue against alternate-sequence requirements for responsibility.

and could-have-done-otherwise scenarios. I suggest that "Wilma wouldn't have done otherwise, whether or not she could have" can be understood in terms of the variable realization of such a disposition across deterministic and indeterministic worlds.

Suppose that the actual world, in which Wilma does X, is deterministic, so that there is no alternate sequence. Suppose also that there is a set of possible indeterministic worlds different from the actual world only in that these possible worlds contain an alternate sequence: in each of these possible worlds, unlike the actual world, it is possible that Wilma does X and also possible that Wilma does otherwise. Call these indeterministic worlds the "alternate sequence worlds," or "AS worlds." In different subsets of the set of AS worlds, different possibilities are actualized. There is a subset of the AS worlds in which, as in the actual world, Wilma acts on the WW disposition. There is another subset in which Wilma does not act on this disposition. To claim that Wilma wouldn't have done otherwise whether or not she could have is to claim that the AS worlds in which Wilma acts on the WW disposition are closer to the actual deterministic world than are the AS worlds in which Wilma does not act on this disposition (see Figure 2).

What could make this claim true? The AS worlds in which Wilma acts on the WW disposition could be closer to the actual deterministic world because they are similar in respect of the WW disposition, of which there might be both deterministic and indeterministic realizations. Causation need not be deterministic; causal mechanisms and dispositions can make counterfactuals about what an agent would have done true both in deterministic and indeterministic worlds.[15] A comparison between weakness of will and control may help to make the point.

There could be deterministic or indeterministic realizations of a given control system with its identifying dispositions. A thermostat that includes an indeterministic process can be just as good at controlling the temperature as one realized differently that includes no indeterministic process (see Clarke 1995, p. 129). Neither realization may be perfect. Determinis-

---

15. My position here may require me to take on arguments against Molinism; but I must reserve this question for another occasion. On indeterministic causation, see Anscombe 1993; Clarke 1995; Lewis 1986, pp. 175–184; Salmon 1993. Clarke considers that "recent efforts to provide accounts of such causation indicate . . . that we can make about as good sense of probabilistic causation as we can of any other sort of causation" (p. 127). Lewis writes: "I certainly do not think that causation requires determinism . . . Events that happen by chance may nevertheless be caused. Indeed, it seems likely that most actual causation is of just this sort" (p. 175).

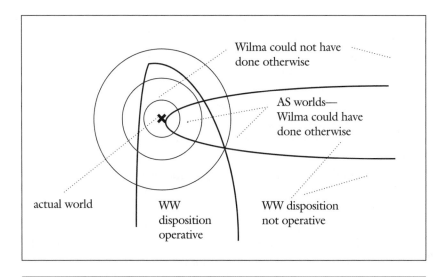

Figure 2. Wilma would not have done otherwise, whether or not she could have.

tic causation is no guarantee against minor malfunctions in a mechanism's operation; an indeterministic mechanism can in principle be just as reliable as many deterministic mechanisms. There may be trade-offs between the kinds of faults generated by deterministic and indeterministic hardware that leave the two realizations functionally equivalent at the macro level. Evolution, for example, might have used either equally well; natural selection might have operated on either in a similar way.

Similarly, a person who is realized in a way that includes indeterministic processes can be just as good a chooser, a controller, or a responder to reasons as a person who is deterministically realized. In particular, there could be deterministic or indeterministic realizations of the WW disposition, which are functionally equivalent. There is no reason in principle why the variable realization of macro-level features and dispositions cannot extend across the variation between determinism and indeterminism. As a result, it can be true that Wilma wouldn't have done otherwise, whether or not she could have. If causes can operate indeterministically, then a reason-responsiveness requirement could be satisfied by a disposition that has an indeterministic realization,[16] but need not be, since reason-responsiveness is not an alternate-sequence requirement.

---

16. In such a case, we could say that the way the dispositional properties of the actual sequence are realized can, but need not, involve alternate sequences.

Note that all the worlds inside the AS arc in Figure 2 are indeterministic. Thus, those AS worlds in which the WW disposition is operative are not guaranteed to be worlds in which Wilma does not do otherwise. In this sense, the disposition within the AS arc, so to speak, is spotty. However, this is not fatal to the supposition that the disposition is the same whether or not Wilma could have done otherwise. Even in a deterministic world, where an agent could not have done otherwise, a disposition can be imperfectly realized, as noted for control systems. Chaotic complexity and sensitive dependence on initial conditions in a deterministic world mean that the macro-level disposition of a deterministically realized mechanism could include unpredictable gaps and lapses of performance, just as does the macro-level disposition of an indeterministically realized mechanism. In the indeterministic world, the spots are at the metaphysical level. In the chaotic deterministic world, the spots are at the epistemic level. But this difference may not matter for purposes of holding constant either a disposition of weakness of will or the dispositions of a control system. The micro differences could cancel out at the macro level, so that the realizations are equivalent from a functional or evolutionary point of view.

Compare this account to Frankfurt's suggestion that the fact that an individual couldn't have done otherwise is relevant to responsibility only if he did what he did *only because he could not have done otherwise* (1969, pp. 837–839). What is it to do what you do only because you cannot do otherwise? Whatever it is, it must be the case that you cannot do otherwise and that this plays an essential role in why you do what you do.

Frankfurt says that if someone could not have done otherwise but did not do what he did because he could not have done otherwise, then he would have done the same thing even if he could have done otherwise. What makes it the case that he couldn't have done otherwise could be subtracted from the story without affecting what happened or why, and in particular without affecting his reasons. Whatever made someone do what he did would still have done so, even if he could have done otherwise (1969, p. 837). In Frankfurt Cases, the circumstances that make it the case that the agent couldn't do otherwise are in the alternate sequence: the counterfactual intervenor. These could be subtracted without affecting what happened or why because they are not what made the person do what he did: he acted for his own reasons. But what if the circumstances that make it the case that the agent couldn't do otherwise are in the actual sequence, in a deterministic world? This comparison shows yet again how the irrelevant alternative intuition generalizes the point of Frankfurt Cases. To spell this out:

If the world is indeterministic but you are in a Frankfurt Case, you could not have done otherwise. In such a case, this is because in the alternate world, the counterfactual intervenor would make you do the same thing as you actually do. You do what you do for your own reasons, and you could not have done otherwise because of the counterfactual intervenor. Do you do what you do only because you could not have done otherwise? No; since even if the counterfactual intervenor had not been there, you would have done what you did, for your own reasons.

If the world is deterministic, then you cannot do otherwise, because of the past and the laws. Indeed, you do what you do because of the past and the laws, which may operate through your reasons. But do you do what you do only because you cannot do otherwise? Not necessarily. You might have done the same even if you could have done otherwise, that is, even if the world were not deterministic, acting on the same reasons and the same reason-responsive disposition, differently realized.

My account of what it could mean to say that someone "wouldn't have done otherwise, even if she could have" can thus help to explain what Frankfurt's "only because she could not have done otherwise" formulation amounts to. For example, if you would have acted on the WW disposition even if you could have done otherwise, in the sense that the AS worlds in which the WW disposition is operative are closer than are other AS worlds to the actual deterministic world, then you didn't do what you did only because you couldn't have done otherwise. Closeness to the actual world might reflect, for example, the functional or evolutionary equivalence of deterministic and indeterministic realizations of a disposition.

My position thus agrees with Frankfurt's in tying assessments of moral responsibility to the explanation of why someone did what she did. But my argument generalizes Frankfurt's argument in a certain way: it does not depend on a counterfactual intervenor to make sense of the supposition that someone cannot do otherwise. It is directed against alternate-sequence requirements at large.[17] We can start with a situation, as in my

---

17. In a different dimension, Frankfurt's arguments are more general than mine, since they apply against conditionally analysed "could have done otherwise" requirements—a kind of actual-sequence requirement for responsibility—as well as against alternate-sequence "could have done otherwise" requirements. That is, Frankfurt's position is

weakness of will example, in which someone cannot do otherwise simply because she is in a deterministic world—not because she is in a Frankfurt Case. So my suggestion frees us from the special context of Frankfurt Cases, with their counterfactual intervenors and fail-safe mechanisms, and returns us to the more general deterministic context in which could-have-done-otherwise worries have traditionally arisen. It thus shows that the importance of the irrelevant-alternative intuition behind Frankfurt Cases cannot be resisted by objections to the peculiarity of Frankfurt Cases and their science-fiction apparatus.

In sum, the question whether you would have done otherwise whether or not you could have is closely related to the question whether you did what you did only because you couldn't have done otherwise, in the ways just indicated. My argument can be regarded as a way of developing and generalizing Frankfurt's claim that what matters is whether you did what you did only because you couldn't have done otherwise, and also of explaining the relationship of this claim to those few passages in Frankfurt in which the "wouldn't have done otherwise even if could have" formulation appears (see note 12, this chapter).

5. The Irrelevant-Alternative Intuition for Blame: Would the Agent Have Avoided Blame, Whether or Not She Could Have?

In order to appreciate the way in which my argument generalizes the irrelevant-alternative intuition, it is helpful to see it in operation against an alternate-sequence requirement other than the ability-to-do-otherwise requirement.

Michael Otsuka has recently argued that blameworthiness requires that the agent could have avoided blame, rather than that the agent could have done otherwise (1998; see also Wallace 1996, pp. 201 ff). He claims the ability-to-avoid-blame requirement is resistant to the Frankfurt-style counterexamples that embarrass an ability-to-do-otherwise requirement. His basic point turns on the fact that in a Frankfurt Case, even though the agent could not have done otherwise than perform an act of a given type, the agent could nevertheless have avoided blame for performing an act of

---

not just that the alternate sequence is irrelevant, but that it is irrelevant whether someone could have done otherwise even in a conditional, actual-sequence sense. I'm grateful to Harry Frankfurt and Gideon Rosen for discussion of this point.

that type. If Jones had wavered and induced Black's fail-safe mechanism to take over, then Jones would not have been blameworthy. Intuitively, Jones is not exempt from responsibility in such a case, even though he could not have done otherwise. Otsuka traces this intuition to Jones's satisfaction of a different alternate-sequence condition, namely, to the fact that he could have avoided blame, which Otsuka recommends. In this section I show that the irrelevant-alternative intuition operates against Otsuka's ability-to-avoid-blame requirement just as effectively as it does against the ability-to-do-otherwise requirement.

Again, compare two scenarios. The first, indeterministic scenario is a Frankfurt Case, where there are just two possible sequences. In the alternate "waver" sequence in which the counterfactual intervention occurs, the agent would avoid blame for her weak-willed act. If the mad scientist had predicted she would waver, he would have intervened to ensure that she acted in the same way. But he did not need to intervene. The counterfactual intervention is merely possible; it never actually occurs, and the fail-safe device never actually operates. In fact the agent acts on a mechanism with a loosely reason-responsive, WW disposition. She does the act for her own reasons, without intervention. Still, she could have avoided blame because the alternate waver sequence could have occurred instead. If it had, and the fail-safe device had operated, she would not have been blameworthy. Otsuka suggests that an agent is intuitively responsible in this kind of case because she could have avoided blame, even if though she could not have done otherwise.

The second, deterministic scenario is similar, except that there is only one possible sequence, no alternate waver sequence and no possible counterfactual intervention. So the agent could not have avoided blame. Nevertheless, in both scenarios she acts in the same way, on a mechanism with the same type of loosely reason-responsive, WW disposition and for the same reasons. In both scenarios, the dispositions involved in the processes by which the action is brought about are such that she would not have avoided blame, even *if* she could have. But in one scenario she could have, and in the other scenario she could not have; in one scenario but not the other the "if she could have" condition is counterfactual. The only difference between the two scenarios is that in the indeterministic scenario there is an alternate sequence, an outright possibility of waver and counterfactual intervention, and there is no such possibility in the other, deterministic scenario. That is, in the indeterministic scenario there is an outright causal possibility that the relevant action might have been brought about in a different way, by a functionally different kind of process, holding everything else constant. But in neither scenario was the action actually brought about in this different way, by this different kind of process. The difference is one in what might have happened, all else constant. It is not a difference in what did happen or in the relevant macro-dispositional reason-responsiveness properties of the process by which the action was actually brought about.

Is the agent any more blameworthy when in addition she could have avoided blame? Or is what matters the fact that she wouldn't have avoided blame, whether or not she could have? Does the existence of the alternate possibility matter, or the dispositional character of the actual causes of the act? The descendent of the Frankfurt intuition here is that what matters is the dispositional character of the way the action is actually brought about, not the outright possibility of avoiding blame. If she would not have avoided blame, whether or not she could have, then the alternate sequence is an irrelevant alternative, an extrinsic difference between the scenarios that does not affect her responsibility.

The outright possibility of an alternate sequence has traditionally been regarded as necessary for responsibility. By contrast, the irrelevant-alternative intuition casts it in an extraneous role, as not a feature of the agent that is operative or explanatory in the right way to be relevant to her responsibility. If the way in which the action is brought about is such that the agent would not avoid blame even if she were able to, but would act on her own bad reasons whether or not she could avoid blame, then the features of her and of her act that are relevant to blame are the same in the two scenarios. Why should it matter to her blameworthiness whether an alternate sequence exists? Her victims may think "It didn't have to happen!" and that may make their plight harder to bear. But she is just as bad and her act just as intrinsically blameworthy, just as much a proper object of resentment, either way. The intuition is that responsibility is independent of such irrelevant alternatives.[18]

---

18. This phrase suggests an analogy to intuitions that support independence or sure-thing axioms in rational choice theory. According to such intuitions, rational choice between two options cannot vary with the probabilistic context in which those options are embedded. So long as the options themselves do not vary between contexts, it is irrational for choice between them to depend on their probabilistic context, on what might have happened instead but did not. Some kinds of context-dependence are rational: my choice between red and white wine may depend on what's for dinner. After all, I consume them all together. But context-dependence across mutually exclusive

I have explained and defended the generalized irrelevant alternative intuition and shown how it can cut against other alternate-sequence requirements in addition to the ability-to-do-otherwise requirement, such as the ability-to-avoid-blame requirement. In what follows I shall take it that alternate sequences are not required for responsibility. So this cannot be a basis for holding that determinism makes responsibility impossible.

However, there may be other reasons for holding that responsibility is impossible. In the Chapter 3 I examine and rebut an argument that responsibility is impossible based on the actual-sequence regression requirement.

---

possibilities is arguably irrational: my choice between the options I face if tails comes up should not depend on which options I would have faced in the alternate sequence in which heads came up instead.

This argument is often responded to by reindividuating options: options in different "contexts" are actually different options—reviewing a paper versus watching a video are different options when I narrowly avoided a crash on my way home and when my trip home was uneventful. I am sympathetic to this move in certain cases (see the Introduction to Bacharach and Hurley 1991). Similarly, the irrelevant-alternative intuition in the text could be countered by insisting that operative dispositions cannot be relevantly the same across cases in which the agent could have done otherwise and cases in which he could not have done otherwise. But I am not sympathetic to this view, and argue against it in the text. Here the analogy runs out of steam.

3

Why Responsibility Is Not Essentially Impossible

This chapter argues against the claim that responsibility is essentially impossible. It focuses on the actual-sequence regression requirement. Recall from Chapter 1 that combining a regression requirement with a causal conception of responsibility—for example, in terms of choice or control—makes responsibility impossible. Galen Strawson has made related arguments for the claim that responsibility is indeed impossible. On my view, by contrast, responsibility is neither regressive nor impossible. Moral responsibility may possibly have a noncausal aspect, such as a requirement of hypothetical choice, and this component could be regressive. But moral responsibility must also have a causal aspect, such as a requirement of actual choice or control or reason-responsiveness. I have already argued, first, that purely noncausal conceptions of responsibility are inadequate and suffer from indeterminacy problems, and, second, that the causal components of responsibility are incompatible with a regression requirement. The right conclusion to draw from these points is not that responsibility is impossible, but that responsibility is not regressive overall.

1. Elimination versus Revision; Context versus Theory

In order to set up my argument about responsibility, I need first to draw some distinctions and to make some points about eliminativism in quite general terms. I do so very briefly in this section and the next.[1] In the remainder of the chapter I then apply these points to responsibility in particular.

Take any widely used concept *F*. We can distinguish between the con-

---

1. See Hurley 2000b for a fuller treatment of these general issues, which discusses aspects omitted here and considers more examples.

texts in which *F* is used and people's theoretical beliefs about *F*ness. If *F* is the concept of responsibility, we can distinguish between the contexts in which the concept of responsibility is applied and people's theoretical beliefs about responsibility.

Suppose contexts of application and theory are mismatched. Then the following issue arises: Does the mismatch show that the applications are wrong, because they don't satisfy the theory? If we go this route for all applications, we eliminate *F*ness. All applications of *F* are in error; nothing is really *F* after all. Or, does the mismatch show that the theory is wrong, because the theory doesn't apply to the canonical contexts of application of *F*? If we go this route, we revise our beliefs about *F*ness.

The issue here is quite general: When does a change of theory revise our beliefs about something, and when does it eliminate that thing? There are various familiar illustrations of this general question.[2] But there is no generally accepted answer. Back in the days when Steven Stich was an eliminativist about thought,[3] he claimed that nothing in the philosophy of science literature even comes close to giving a plausible general answer to this question (Ramsey, Stich, and Garon 1991, pp. 95–96). And old reference points are crumbling. We still think it was right to eliminate phlogiston; but these days some argue that there really were witches—we just had false beliefs about what they were like.[4]

This general issue about theory change and elimination is closely related to another issue: What determines the necessary or essential properties of something? Do the causal contexts in which a concept has been applied and its causal history determine the essential properties of what it applies to (see, for example, Putnam 1975)? Or does some theoretical role we assign to it do so (see, for example, Lewis 1970)? I call these *context-driven* versus *theory-driven* accounts of essence.[5]

The contrast should not be oversimplified. Subtle variations and grada-

---

2. Consider eliminativist views on thought (such as Ramsey, Stich, and Garon 1991; cf. Churchland 1993), Dennett on qualia (1988, pp. 44, 47), Parfit on persons (1984, pt. 3), Mackie on values (1977, chaps. 1, 2).

3. He later changed his mind about eliminativism (Stich 1991; 1996, esp. chap. 1).

4. See Stich's discussion of Luhrmann's (1989) claims in Stich 1996, pp. 68 ff.

5. I do not discuss here the currently less prevalent view that analysis of the sense of "*F*" reveals the essence of *F*ness. Cf. Moore 1952; Stich 1996, pp. 60 ff, 171 ff. Moore admitted that his account of analysis generated and did not resolve the "paradox of analysis": that some supposedly analytic truths are unobvious and open to disagreement (1952, pp. 665–666).

tions of position are possible. Some theories may give contexts of application an important part to play, but such that context is still responsible to theory. And the two approaches could be combined into a kind of reflective equilibrium approach to essences, which tells us to find a balance between context and theory. No one approach must be right for all concepts. Some concepts may be context-driven, others theory-driven.

What is the relation between the issue about elimination and the issue about essence? It is probably fair to say that context-driven accounts of the essence of *F*ness make it *harder* to sustain eliminativism about *F*s than theory-driven accounts do. If *something* in contexts of use of "*F*" stands in the right explanatory connections to uses of "*F*," it may not matter if our theories about *F*ness are seriously mistaken. Because such accounts make essence responsible to contexts of use rather than to the beliefs of users, they are very tolerant of error. Users can make wildly false claims about, say, stars, yet still be talking about stars. Suppose we hold the Mufasa theory: those sparkling things in the sky are the spirits of great kings of the past. We've got some serious revising of our beliefs about stars to do, but eliminativism about stars gets no support. Reference to an existent is more or less secured by context, and theory is up for grabs. This treatment has been given to witches (by Luhrmann 1989, discussed by Stich 1996): we were wrong about what witches are like—wrong, for example, to think witches must have magical powers instead of a certain social role. We should revise our beliefs about witches rather than eliminate them. By contrast, if our concept of *F*ness is wholly driven by a theoretical role, such as our concept of a social welfare function, and the theory turns out to be deeply wrong or incoherent (see Arrow 1963; Sen 1970), then there may not be anything that occupies the essential theoretical role, and *F*s are eliminated.

While it may be harder to eliminate when we are dealing with context-driven essences than with theory-driven essences, I claim that this is only a tendency. Again, we shouldn't oversimplify. In fact, the distinction between context-driven and theory-driven essences cuts across the distinction between elimination and revision. (In Figure 3, the shaded boxes represent the tendency, but the other boxes are also occupied.)

On the one hand, theory change can support elimination for context-driven concepts. Of course, on context-driven accounts, we can find out that some apparent *F*s are not really *F*s: planets are not stars. By contrast, the error postulated by eliminativism is global. Even this can be accommodated by context-driven concepts, however. We may find out that there is nothing in contexts of use that stands in appropriate explanatory relations

	Theory-driven essence	Context-driven essence
Eliminate	conventional view on witches Parfit on persons Dennett on qualia Mackie on values earlier Stich on thought Arrow on social welfare functions	phlogiston wizards arbitrary hodge-podge, gruesome concatenation
Revise	Owens on triangles	revision of the Mufasa theory of stars Luhrmann on witches later Stich on thought

Figure 3. Theory change: elimination versus revision.

to uses of F; users have accidentally latched onto an arbitrary hodge-podge with no natural or functional explanatory unity (see and cf. Cussins 1993). Then even on a context-driven account of Fness, Fness may be eliminated by deconstruction. For example, the contexts of uses of "wizard" may have no natural or functional unity at all, be just a gruesome concatenation. It's not that we were wrong to think wizards must have magical powers, when really they just play a certain social role. Rather, wizard-kind is no kind at all, either natural or functional.[6] Nothing in the contexts of use of "wizard" has explanatory depth.

---

6. Cf. Putnam's denial that the members of the extension of a natural kind term necessarily have a common hidden structure. "It could have turned out that the bits of liquid we call 'water' had no important common physical characteristics except the superficial ones. In that case the necessary and sufficient condition for being 'water' would have been possession of sufficiently many of the superficial characteristics." But

On the other hand, theory change can support revision for theory-driven concepts. Our theory of *F*ness may be partly wrong, while the essential theoretical role of *F*ness, or enough of it, is preserved. Then even on a theory-driven account of *F*ness, there are still *F*s, but we have to revise our view about them. For example, triangle is plausibly regarded as a theory-driven concept. Our theory about triangles used to have two elements: triangles are bounded by three straight lines, and have interior angles that add to 180 degrees. We then figured out that things that have the first property do not necessarily have the second property (see Owens 1992, pp. 64–65). Triangles haven't been eliminated; rather we've revised our view of them. The theoretical role that is essential to triangles can accommodate this shifting of weight. We can hold on to part of the theoretical role while rejecting another part, and so revise rather than eliminate.

Nevertheless, if eliminativism is harder on context-driven accounts, whether we take a context-driven or theory-driven view of *F*ness can affect whether we eliminate or revise in response to theory change.[7] This raises further questions. Which issue is properly the cart here and which the horse? Our position on whether a concept is context- or theory-driven

---

this does not mean that water might not have had a hidden structure, but rather that various bits of liquid with no common hidden structure, with only superficial characteristics in common, might have looked and tasted like water, filled lakes, etc. (1975, pp. 240–241). This suggests that we cannot infer from lack of any common hidden structure to elimination. Enough commonality to support reference to a kind may be found at a different, perhaps more superficial level.

If elimination is not to be impossible on context-driven accounts, however, there should be a distinction between cases where the explanation of the kind is relocated (say from hidden essences to superficial characteristics, or from a physical to a functional essence) and cases where there is no explanation and the unity of the kind is illusory. This distinction requires there to be some constraint on arbitrary or accidental concatenations of properties counting as the referents of kind terms. The text appeals to explanatory depth to make this distinction. In the hodge-podge scenario, nothing has explanatory depth, even relatively shallow explanatory depth, in relation to the relevant contexts, so deconstruction/elimination rather than revision is appropriate.

7. See and compare Stich 1996, chap. 1, on the defects of the top-down "semantic ascent" strategy, lack of clarity about what a theory of reference is supposed to do, and why the bottom-up "normative naturalism" strategy doesn't resolve issues about eliminativism either; Papineau 1996 on how the theoretical role approach bears on eliminativism. See also Jackson and Pettit 1983, p. 302; Salmon 1982, chap. 6.

may already reflect our intuitions about elimination versus revision in particular cases. Is this acceptable, or should we derive our views about elimination versus revision from prior views about whether a concept is context- or theory-driven?

These large questions are, to put it diplomatically, still unresolved. Do not imagine that the little tail of responsibility is going to wag this monster. Rather, in this chapter I locate issues about responsibility in the broader debate, and try to engender some skepticism about any position that takes responsibility to be essentially impossible while ignoring this cluster of issues.

Notice that both context-driven and theory-driven views of essence give essences explanatory depth. Essential properties have to do explanatory work. This will be important in the argument that follows.

On a context-driven view, for example, having the composition H_2O is essential to water because this property explains the behavior of the relevant stuff in the contexts in which "water" is applied. Theory does have a role in discovering essences on this view, but what needs explanation, thus what theory is responsible to, is determined by worldly contexts of use. Our beliefs may be wrong because the theories they are embedded in fail to explain our uses in relation to worldly contexts of use. For example, on a context-driven view, star-essence has to do explanatory work in relation to those twinkling things themselves, not just in relation to our beliefs about those twinkling things, namely, that they are the spirits of the great kings of the past. That might be done by a religious or social theory. However, context-driven views do not have to understand explanatory depth in a strictly scientific, causal-explanatory way. For example, a normative account could be given of the contexts in which a normative term is used.

On theory-driven views, essences also have explanatory depth, but here it is theory-internal, of a coherentist or justificatory or normative character. Some subset of properties the theoretical role assigns to kind F may do better than any other subset at preserving the internal coherence and point of the theory. For example, a theory-driven account of justice may see equality as essential to justice. Yet equality of resources may be argued to have greater theory-internal explanatory depth than equality of welfare, and therefore to provide reasons to revise certain beliefs about justice (see Dworkin 1981a; 1981b). Or, a theory-driven account of qualia could preserve some of the theoretical role traditionally assigned to qualia while revising one aspect of it, so, for example, regarding qualia as relational rather than intrinsic properties of mental states.

To sum up the two main points of this section: first, context-driven accounts tend to support revision rather than elimination, and eliminativism tends to sit more easily with a theory-driven account. If contexts of application anchor reference, there is greater freedom of movement with respect to theory; if theoretical role anchors reference, there is greater freedom of movement with respect to applications. But these tendencies should not be overstated. In principle the distinction between context-driven and theory-driven accounts of reference and essence cuts across the distinction between revision and elimination as a response to theory change. Second, on both context-driven and theory-driven accounts, essences are essential in virtue of explanatory depth of one sort or another.

2. Why Impossible Essences Are Weird

Before returning to responsibility, I want to make one more general point. I claim that a certain kind of eliminativism, *impossible-essence eliminativism,* is fundamentally problematic.

It's one thing to hold that nothing *in fact* has the essential property of F-kind. It's another thing to hold that nothing *could possibly* have the essential property of F-kind. Impossible-essence eliminativism claims that there are no Fs because F-kind has an impossible essence. For example, Galen Strawson claims that "true self-determination is both necessary for freedom and logically impossible" (Strawson 1986, p. 56). I argue that there is something weird about the very idea of an impossible essence.

We have seen that on a context-driven view, essences do explanatory work. The essence of the kind explains its behavior in contexts in which the kind term is used. In virtue of this, an essence can show up local errors in a term's application as well as globally mistaken theories. And in the arbitrary hodge-podge, gruesome concatenation scenario, where there is no unified explanation of the relevant contexts at any level, a kind may be eliminated. But this isn't because the purported kind does have an impossible essence. It simply has *no* essence.

Could impossible properties be essential to a kind on a context-driven account? No, because *properties in virtue of which things are impossible cannot do the relevant explanatory work.* We could not come to realize that an impossible property explains what is going on in worldly contexts in which *"F"* is used. Perhaps one property explains the behavior of certain stuff in the context of *these* uses and another property explains the behavior of other stuff in the context of *those* uses, and it is impossible for anything to have both properties. This could be a case of local error in application: one set of uses is mistaken—these are really planets, not stars. Or, it could be a case like that of jade, in which the level of explanation is relocated: this is the jadeite kind of jade, and that is the nephrite kind of jade, and they have superficial characteristics and functions in common (see and cf. Putnam 1975, p. 241). Or it could be a case of arbitrary hodge-podge or misconceived composite: perhaps one property is relational and functional, and the other is intrinsic and microstructural, and it's just a confusion to suppose the different sorts of context have anything with even fairly shallow explanatory depth in common. But none of these are cases of impossible essence.

Essences discovered from worldly contexts of application are not going to be much use to the eliminativist. Nor are properties that could have applied but in fact turn out not to apply to anything: they can hardly explain anything that happens in the relevant contexts. If wizards turn out not to have magical powers, then those powers cannot be essential to wizard-kind in virtue of explaining what wizards get up to in the contexts in which "wizard" is applied. Elimination on a context-driven approach turns on lack of essence—the arbitrary hodge-podge scenario.

Still, there is something further wrong with the idea of an impossible essence, if essences are supposed to have explanatory depth. When Fs do not have P, then P is not the essence of F-kind. If wizards do not in fact have magical powers, then magical powers are not the essence of wizard-kind. But if is not impossible for wizards to have had magical powers, then we can imagine a different world in which magical powers might have been explanatory. It would have to be different in lots of ways, a world of different kinds and different essences. Perhaps there are no wizards, only sorcerers. But having magical powers might have been essential to sorcerer-kind, in virtue of the explanatoriness of such powers in another possible world. If things *were* different in lots of ways, including that stuff superficially similar to F—call it G—had P, then G *could* behave in various ways in various contexts that would be explained by its having P. In virtue of the intelligibility of this counterfactual, P is a possible essence.

But if P is an impossible property, no similar counterfactual is clearly intelligible. If things *were* different so that some stuff has an impossible property, *could* that impossible property have explained that stuff's behavior? There is a general difficulty about knowing what would be the case if something impossible were true. It is, if anything, even more difficult to understand how there could be possible worlds in which impossible properties are explanatory. It seems not just false that impossible properties have explanatory depth, not just false that they are essences. They *couldn't* be. If it is essential to essences to have explanatory depth, we can eliminate impossible essences. When *P* is impossible, it is not even a possible essence.

This point does not turn on whether we know that some property is impossible. We may be wrong about whether a property is impossible, just as we may be wrong about whether it is instantiated. Hence we may be wrong about whether a property can do explanatory work. Whether or not we know that a property is impossible, if it is, it cannot possibly do the explanatory work required of context-driven essences.

So, a context-driven approach does not bode well for impossible-essence eliminativism. How do impossible essences fare if we shift from a context-driven perspective to a theory-driven perspective?

On this approach, a subset of the properties the theoretical role assigns to the kind *F* may do better than any other subset at preserving the internal coherence and point of the theory. Such a subset has normative status within the theory. But if the specified subset of properties turns out to be impossible to satisfy, it faces the difficulties impossible properties have in playing explanatory roles, even coherentist, theory-internal explanatory roles. Impossible properties can't do explanatory work of a normative or justificatory kind either. Impossibility internal to a theoretical role *can* play a part in eliminativism, not via the claim that the impossible property is essential to the theoretical role but rather via the unsalvageable shambles it makes of the theoretical role. But here the eliminativism is based on lack of any explanatory role hence of any essence, not on an impossible essence.

Whether explanatory depth is theory-internal or not, it is hard to understand how an impossible property or set of properties could be explanatory. So, impossible-essence eliminativism is weird on any view that gives essences explanatory depth. This point applies whether the explanatory depth required is internal to a theoretical role or rather relates to worldly contexts of a term's use, as in a context-driven approach.

I suppose someone might suggest that certain impossible properties are essential to *F*-kind in virtue of what anyone who knows what "*F*" means must understand. Stich 1996 goes over some of the many problems with this idea, but for present purposes I pass over it (see note 5, this chapter). I think it is extremely implausible that when people disagree about whether responsibility is essentially impossible, they are talking past one another. Rather, they are having a deep normative disagreement (more on this below).

But there is a further, more general worry about the idea that meaning-driven essential properties are impossible, at least on certain views about meaning. In the face of intuitive disagreement about whether a certain property is essential to Fs or not, to resolve that disagreement in favor of the impossible essence is uncharitable. If intuitions diverge about what is necessary in virtue of meaning, it seems perverse to interpret what we mean to involve incoherence. Within the broadly Davidsonian "charity is not optional" methodology, we can trade off oddness of meaning or desire against truth of belief. Perhaps in some cases an interpretation that assigns an odd meaning but a true belief is more charitable overall than one that assigns a familiar meaning but a false belief. But the impossible-essence eliminativist is not in this position. He wants to pull off a kind of interpretative double-whammy: to claim it is both nonempirically impossible and necessary for Fs to be P. The methodology of nonoptional charity sees these claims as at least in tension with one another. That methodology is itself controversial and hardly counts as neutral ground here, but it nevertheless provides a further source of worry about meaning-based impossible essences.

I haven't given a knockdown argument against impossible-essence eliminativism, but I hope at least to have engendered some skepticism about it. It should not simply be taken for granted, assumed without argument, that an impossible property can be essential, on either context-driven or theory-driven accounts. With this background, I now apply some of these general points to responsibility in particular.

3. Is Responsibility Essentially Impossible?

Consider eliminativism about responsibility, based on the argument that no one is ever responsible for anything because responsibility essentially requires regressive choice or control yet regressive choice or control is impossible.[8] While regressive hypothetical choice is possible, I have argued that a purely noncausal conception of responsibility, such as a pure hypothetical-choice conception, is inadequate. I thus accept that responsibility must have a causal component, such as a requirement of choice or control.

---

8. See and cf. Strawson (1986) on how true self-determination is "both necessary for freedom and logically impossible" (p. 36). It is, he claims, "logically impossible because it requires the actual completion of an infinite regress of choices or principles of choice" (p. 29).

But such causal components are not compatible with a regression requirement. Combined with a requirement of choice or control, regression requires that you choose or control not just what you are responsible for,
but its causes, and their causes, and so on, all the way back. This is impossible, as I argued in Chapter 1. If responsibility has such a causal component, it cannot be regressive overall (even if any noncausal component
considered separately can be). Consider then the view that responsibility
must have a causal component such as choice or control but also must be
regressive, and that this is impossible. Can such eliminativism about responsibility be defended?[9] I argue that it cannot.

Given that intuitions conflict about whether responsibility is regressive,
why doesn't the impossibility of regressive responsibility count in favor of
a nonregressive view of responsibility rather than in favor of eliminating
responsibility (pace Nagel 1979, pp. 26–27)? This question has no *obvious* answer. Neither position should simply be taken for granted. The belief that responsibility is essentially regressive requires defense; it is not
something we are simply stuck with, like it or not. On the other hand, we
need to know what could make it the case that someone who denies that
responsibility is regressive is talking *about responsibility* rather than just
changing the subject. What could give us enough of a grip on responsibility to enable us to deny that *it* is regressive, or to insist that anything that
would count as responsibility must be regressive and hence impossible?

In the rest of this chapter I consider how context-driven and theory-
driven accounts of responsibility bear on these issues. First, I describe
the contexts of use and the theoretical role of responsibility. Second, I
plug the relevant features of responsibility into a context-driven account,
to consider whether impossible-essence eliminativism about responsibility

---

9. It may be asked if it is appropriate to treat issues about whether responsibility is
impossible under the heading of eliminativism. Does this wrongly imply that responsibility is, if it exists, an entity? No. We can take the same breezy tack that Stich takes
about eliminativism for beliefs and desires: "if it rankles to talk about beliefs and desires as entities, we can construe eliminativism as claiming that there are no such
things as *believers,* or *desirers* because predicates of the form '___ believes that p' and
'___ desires that q' are never true of anyone. Viewed this way, what the eliminativist
is claiming is that the extensions of these predicates are empty" (Stich 1991, p. 235;
cf. Hannan 1993, p. 176n11). Similarly, what is at issue here is whether "___ is responsible for x" is ever true of anyone, whether the extension of this predicate is
empty.

can be supported. Finally, I do the same for a theory-driven account of responsibility. I conclude that responsibility is not essentially impossible.

4. Responsibility: Context and Theory

This section gives a rough sketch of some features of the term "responsible," covering both its contexts of use and the theoretical beliefs people have held about responsibility. Both of these change over time. People differ in their intuitive applications and their theoretical beliefs about responsibility at present, as well as comparing past to present. At least some such current differences are not merely semantic, but reflect ethical disagreement. Some theoretical beliefs people have held about responsibility are inconsistent with others.

Contexts of use. For a long time now, people have been making applications of "responsible" and accordingly holding one another accountable for their actions, deserving of praise or blame, reward or punishment, gratitude or resentment. Nowadays people are not generally regarded as responsible for what they do when it results from brain damage, brainwashing, hypnotism, or mental illness. There is disagreement over whether people are responsible for what they do when it results in part from serious deprivation. People generally are regarded as responsible for what they do when it results from personality traits or tendencies within a normal range and with normal causes, without attention to whether these traits are genetically influenced or otherwise unchosen or outside the person's control.

Theory. Many people believe that responsibility satisfies various general conditions or descriptions, some of which are more controversial than others. A set of such conditions could be regarded as collectively defining a theoretical role. For example, it is widely held that responsibility for something requires choice or control of it. It is also widely held, though more controversial, that responsibility is regressive: that to be responsible for something you must be responsible for its causes. Together, these conditions define the role of regressive choice or control.

In Chapters 1 and 2, I discussed various theoretical beliefs about responsibility. I'll review the taxonomy briefly. In the class of alternate-sequence requirements, which require indeterminism, I considered the views that responsibility requires the agent could have done otherwise, and that it requires the agent could have avoided blame. I argued against such requirements, and also that such alternate-sequence requirements are independent of other, actual-sequence requirements.

In the class of actual-sequence conditions of responsibility, I distinguished noncausal and causal conditions. Take noncausal conditions first, which could be held to be either necessary or sufficient for responsibility. For example, an agent may be disposed to make hypothetical choices about the causes of his action. Such hypothetical choices are not ways in which the agent is actually causally responsible for the objects of his hypothetical choices, even though they express dispositional properties of the agent. Recall that in Scanlon's example of the guilt-ridden believer, the agent did not choose and does not control the religious beliefs he was brought up with, and their associated burden of guilt. Yet they are not plausibly regarded as matters of luck for him, because he would have chosen them if he had been able to and would not have chosen to be without them. If people can be responsible because of their hypothetical choices, in the absence of causal relations such as relations of actual choice or control, then causal responsibility may not be necessary for responsibility. Satisfaction of a noncausal condition may suffice.

However, even if hypothetical endorsement is necessary for responsibility, it is implausible to regard it as sufficient for responsibility. Recall that I argued in Chapter 1 as follows. First, the adaptive preferences of the indoctrinated believer or the tame housewife aren't enough to make them responsible, even if they are (extendedly) regressive; we need to know why they have them, their genesis. These preferences may be a self-protective response to oppressive and inescapable conditions, or the result of manipulation. Second, hypothetical choice is too easy, too causally costless; it leaves it too indeterminate which, among all the things people would hypothetically choose if they could, they are responsible for.

The insufficiency of purely noncausal conceptions of responsibility argues for a view that includes a requirement of causal responsibility. But of course it does not follow that mere causal responsibility is sufficient for full-blooded moral responsibility.[10] The implausible view that causal responsibility is sufficient for responsibility could be called *animism*. It may be part of what has at times motivated people to punish the bearers of bad

---

10. Recall that when I use "responsibility" without the qualification "causal," it is intended in the sense of full-blooded, blame-licensing, accountability-implying moral responsibility.

news, or part of what motivates children to fear and personify inanimate objects that hurt them.

Actual choice or control of an act or an outcome are particular ways in which a person can be causally responsible for it, so can be ways of meeting a requirement of causal responsibility. However, even if choice or control is necessary for moral responsibility, neither seems sufficient for responsibility. A thermostat, or an infant with well-trained parents, might control effectively, but is not responsible for what it/she controls. An animal or a child or someone suffering from a mental illness might choose without being responsible for what he chooses. Attributions of responsibility should be restricted to persons who are mature and rationally competent in ways the theory of responsibility tries to spell out.

Additional specific causal requirements may further narrow down the scope of moral responsibility, such as requirements of reason-responsiveness and/or taking responsibility. The question still arises whether the resulting combined requirement is sufficient for responsibility. Some noncausal condition, such as hypothetical choice, may still be required in addition.

Finally, I considered the structural regression requirement. This needs to be combined with a substantive requirement for responsibility. The regression requirement demands that any substantive requirement it is combined with be satisfied all the way back through the actual sequence of causes leading to the act in question. As we have seen, this requirement is impossible to satisfy if combined with a causal requirement such as choice or control, but can be satisfied if combined with a noncausal requirement such as hypothetical choice (see Figure 4).

Impossibility internal to theory. Certain conditions of responsibility are incompatible. Consider the pairwise consistency of animism, a regression requirement, and a choice or control condition.

Animism is inconsistent with a regression requirement. If an object or animal is causally responsible for a significant effect, someone with animist tendencies will be inclined to treat that object or animal as morally responsible, as deserving of reward or punishment, praise or blame, gratitude or resentment. But an animist does not suppose such objects or animals are responsible for the causes of what he takes them to be responsible for: to be either responsible for themselves or for the stream of further causes leading from the significant effect beyond them back into the past.

While animism is inconsistent with a regression requirement, we can

	Necessary?	Sufficient?
Causal: choice, control, reason-responsive mechanism, taking responsibility	Yes: required to avoid indeterminacy	Animism: mere causal responsibility sufficient for responsibility Causal conditions are not sufficient if a noncausal condition is also required
Noncausal: hypothetical choice	Could be held to be necessary in addition to a causal requirement	No: tame housewife, indeterminacy, impossible antecedents
Structural: regression	No: not compatible with causal requirements	No: must be combined with substantive condition

Figure 4. Actual-sequence conditions for responsibility.

reject the regression requirement without supporting animism. This is important, because there may be a subliminal tendency to view the denial of the regression condition as a kind of remnant of animism: as something we moderns can no longer be comfortable with for the same reasons, but must put behind us, into our collective childhood. But we have found in the variety of actual-sequence requirements for responsibility plenty of scope for improving on animism, for restricting responsibility to persons and in other ways, without accepting a regression requirement.

Causation itself is not regressive: to cause something does not require causing its causes in turn. For X to cause Z may involve X's causing Y, where Y is among Z's causes, but it cannot require X to cause Z's causes all the way back to D, C, B, and so on, which are among X's own causes.[11] So, if causal responsibility is sufficient for responsibility, as the animist holds, then responsibility is not regressive either. Of course, since animism is false

---

11. So causation can be transitive even if it is not regressive.

and causal responsibility is not sufficient for responsibility, this implication does little to resolve conflict about the regression condition.

More importantly, but for related reasons, neither choice nor control is intrinsically regressive either. Choice of something does not require choice of its causes. Control, whether in nature or in human affairs, involves maintenance of a variable at a target value in the face of exogenous disturbance, where the variable is caused to take values jointly by factors endogenous and factors exogenous to a control system. To control something not only does not require control of its causes as well, but in fact presupposes causes exogenous to the control system.

I explained in Chapter 1 why it is impossible to satisfy a regression requirement for responsibility and also a requirement of choice or control (and see Strawson 1991, p. 29; 1994; cf. Nagel 1979, pp. 26–27). Recall that it does not make sense to suppose that A actually controls or chooses not just X but also X's causes, all the way back. It is not possible for causes of X that occurred before A existed to be the objects of A's actual choice or control.

I also argued that, by contrast, regressive hypothetical choice is not incoherent. Recall that for A hypothetically to choose the causes of X, all the way back, is not for A to stand in a relation of actual causal responsibility to them. It is merely for it to be true that A would have chosen them if he could have, or would not have chosen to avoid them. This per se is not problematic, so long as in some (nonactual) world A can choose the relevant causes (that is, the antecedents of the relevant counterfactuals are not impossible). Nor is extendedly regressive hypothetical choice incoherent. A could choose hypothetically the stream of causes leading to his own dispositions to make certain hypothetical choices, including this very hypothetical choice. If A can be responsible in virtue of such hypothetical choices, then causal responsibility is not required for responsibility and regressive responsibility is not impossible.

Given the incompatibility of requirements of regression and of causal responsibility (such as actual choice or control), if we want to avoid eliminativism about responsibility we should reject one or the other of these requirements. If we are determined to hold on to regression, we may consider a purely noncausal conception of responsibility. But we have found good reasons not to go this route. Some kind of causal responsibility seems necessary, if not sufficient, for responsibility, and that means that responsibility cannot be regressive overall, even if some noncausal component of it is regressive.

For example, consider a hybrid account that requires for responsibility both regressive hypothetical choice and nonregressive choice or control, perhaps in the form of reason-responsiveness. Such a combination would at least avoid some of the indeterminacy worries about pure hypothetical-choice accounts. And it would not make responsibility impossible. By not requiring regressive choice or control, only regressive hypothetical choice, such a hybrid view would provide one way to avoid any pressure to eliminativism set up by the incompatibility of regression and causal responsibility.

Changes in contexts of use and theory. Over time, both tendencies to apply "responsibility," and beliefs about the general conditions of responsibility, have changed. Older applications of "responsible" in, say, feudal contexts were probably less restrictive than contemporary applications, and corresponding beliefs about responsibility were less prone to recognize a regression requirement.

It also seems plausible that adults made more animistic attributions of responsibility in the past than now. Even so, despite the implausibility of animism to most modern people, animistic attributions of responsibility to inanimate objects and animals that are not persons are still made, accompanied by blame and resentment. This may be a natural or primitive tendency: perhaps the result of the distinctively human trick of interpreting other minds being applied indiscriminately. It is very common in young children, though some adults seem also to be intuitive animists. But the tendency to animism is still natural enough that it needs to be guarded against. Children are encouraged to grow out of it, and it is regarded as a regrettably childish trait in adults.

Intuitive conflict and disagreement. Even now, intuitions conflict and people disagree about whether certain general conditions hold. Among contemporary adults there is widespread (though not universal) agreement on some version of a choice or control condition as a requirement for responsibility, and also on the rejection of animism. But the regression condition is highly controversial between people; intuitions continuous with an older tendency may not recognize this requirement at all. Individuals may also have internally conflicting intuitions about whether responsibility must be regressive.

According to one natural set of intuitions, a person need not be responsible for being what he is in order to be responsible for choices that are determined by what he is. If we understand "foundations" in causal terms, then Robert Nozick seems to reject a regression requirement for desert when he says that the foundations underlying desert don't themselves need to be deserved, all the way down (Nozick 1974, p. 225). And Galen Strawson describes common intuitions about responsibility that are not committed to a regression requirement when he writes:

> Many people accept that they are, ultimately, entirely determined in all aspects of their character by their heredity and environment. But it follows from this that, whether the heredity-and-environment process that has shaped them is deterministic or not, they cannot themselves be truly or ultimately self-determining in any way. And yet they do not feel that their freedom is put in question by this—even though they naturally conceive of themselves as free in the ordinary, strong, true-responsibility-involving sense. . . . This is a very common position. (Strawson 1986, p. 106)

But there are conflicting intuitions. For example, despite his recognition of the "very common position" just described, Strawson also views us as deeply committed to a regressive choice conception of responsibility, even though it makes responsibility impossible.[12] On this view, a person's responsibility requires that she be self-determining, in a sense that makes her responsible for how and what she is. But this is impossible, because it requires the actual completion of an infinite regress of choices of principles of choice (Strawson 1986, pp. 8, 26–30, 49–50).

> It may be objected that the kind of freedom this argument shows to be impossible is so obviously impossible that it is not even worth considering. To this the reply is simple: the kind of freedom that it is an argument against is just the kind of freedom that most people ordi-

---

12. Deep commitment to a regressive conception of responsibility could be such that when we press the question what such responsibility could be, or what it would require, we are led into the regressive-choice story, even though we never ordinarily think of such regresses. This is what Strawson has in mind (personal communication). Deep conceptual commitments may not be superficially accessible, may require such reflective questioning to reveal. Suppose this is what our commitment to a regressive-choice conception is like. Such a commitment still constitutes us as having conflicting intuitions if at the same time we do not feel that our freedom is put in question by the fact that we cannot be truly or ultimately self-determining. Thanks to Galen Strawson for prompting clarification here.

narily and unreflectively suppose themselves to possess. The idea that we possess such freedom is central to our lives.[13]

Strawson also regards us as "stuck with" a natural sense of self that is "irremediably incompatible" with any deep acceptance of the idea that all we are and do is determined (1986, p. 101). "[W]hat one naturally takes oneself to be . . . is a truly self-determining agent of the impossible kind."[14]

Ethical character of disagreement. Disagreement about conditions of responsibility is ethical disagreement. For example, people disagree ethically when they disagree about whether responsibility has to be regressive, and hence about whether people can genuinely deserve reward or punishment, praise or blame, gratitude or resentment, if they are not regressively responsible for the causes of what they do. This is a deeply normative, substantive disagreement, not simply a semantic disagreement. If Adam claims that people deserve the fruits of their talents even though they don't deserve their talents, and Karl denies this, Karl has not simply changed the subject. If this doesn't count as a substantive ethical and political disagreement, what does? Even if Karl is wrong, he is disagreeing with Adam, not talking past him. We use "responsibility" in a way that

---

13. Strawson 1986, p. 30. Strawson later revises this claim as follows: "But the freedom that is shown to be impossible by this sort of argument against self-determination is just the kind of freedom that most people ordinarily and unreflectively suppose themselves to possess, even though the idea that some sort of ultimate self-determination is presupposed by their notion of freedom has never occurred to them. It is therefore worth examining the argument in detail. For the idea that we possess such freedom is central to our lives" (1991, p. 30).

Two points in response to this revision: first, my points are not ad hominem but directed to a position, so Strawson's earlier statement can still serve to put the position in play. Second, the revision does not in fact affect the points to be made. For present purposes, it doesn't matter whether what people presuppose has occurred to them or not. Suppose people do not feel that their freedom is put into question by the influence of heredity and environment, which means that they cannot be truly or ultimately self-determining. Suppose also they presuppose that their freedom has a feature that is incompatible with such influence. Then they are conflicted. This is true whether or not the presupposition they make has occurred to them, and whether or not they realize that they are conflicted. Thanks again to Galen Strawson for prompting clarification.

14. 1986, p. 96; see also p. 88. Nagel also suggests ("Moral Luck," in Nagel 1979) that we are conflicted, tending sometimes to more restrictive, sometimes to less restrictive views of responsibility. See Chapter 4.

permits such substantive disagreements. If regressivity is essential to responsibility, this is a deep explanatory truth that it is possible to get wrong, not a truth that must be understood by anyone who knows the meaning of "responsible." We cannot settle the issue about regression or preempt such ethical disagreement by appealing to what anyone who understands the meaning of "responsibility" must know. Neither side can dismiss the other as simply using "responsibility" in a different sense. In particular, the impossible-essence eliminativist who believes that responsibility is impossible cannot immunize his position against ethical disagreement by dismissing opponents in this way.

In this section I have collected various observations about responsibility concerning: contexts in which attributions of responsibility are made or withheld; theoretical beliefs about responsibility, some of which are compatible and some incompatible; the ways in which both contexts of use and theory change over time; the ways in which intuitions about responsibility conflict; and the ethical character of many disagreements about responsibility. Context-driven and theory-driven views of responsibility will differ in the way they handle these features of responsibility. I now want to consider whether either way of handling them provides a basis for impossible-essence eliminativism about responsibility.

5. Responsibility as Context-Driven

Impossible-essence eliminativism about responsibility says that responsibility is essentially impossible because it requires regressive choice or control. I argue that such a position cannot be defended on a context-driven account of responsibility. A context-driven account of responsibility may or may not be plausible, but it won't help the eliminativist in any case.

Some aspects of context-driven approaches may tempt the eliminativist. Since essential properties can be controversial, the eliminativist may be tempted to claim that responsibility essentially requires regressive choice or control, even though there is substantive disagreement over regressivity.

But brief reflection should dispel this temptation. On a context-driven account, the essential properties of a kind have explanatory depth in relation to worldly contexts of the kind term's use. How could conditions of regressive choice or regressive control describe properties with explanatory depth in relation to contexts of the use of "responsible"? The very impossibility of satisfying these conditions cuts against their title to context-driven essentiality. We couldn't come to realize, despite previous disagreement, that they do the relevant explanatory work. Impossible properties are not instantiated in any contexts of use and cannot do explanatory work, so cannot have the required explanatory depth. It is not just that regressive control or choice *turn out* not to be involved in the relevant contexts and hence not essential; they're not even *possible* essences. So the context-driven approach to reference does not give the eliminativist a way to defend the claim that regressivity is essential to responsibility despite substantive disagreement about it.

A context-driven approach does allow that some of our applications may be in error: planets are not stars; pyrite is not gold; falling stones, ravening wolves, and some people with brain damage are not responsible. But this is not enough for the eliminativist, who claims that all our positive applications of "responsibility" are in error.

What might do the work of elimination would be an argument not that something impossible is essential to responsibility, but rather that the contexts in which "responsibility" is applied are an accidental, arbitrary hodge-podge, a gruesome concatenation. Such a deconstruction of responsibility would reveal that nothing has the right explanatory relationship to the various contexts in which the term is applied, not even at the cost of revealing some of those applications to be in error, or of relocating the level of explanation. Uses of the kind term have no unifying point, cotton on to no kind at all. Certain applications in certain limited contexts may have a point or an explanation, but it is quite unrelated to, or at a different level from, or utterly at odds with the point or explanation of other applications. This would be an argument for what we can call *deconstructive eliminativism*, not for impossible-essence eliminativism. But deconstructive eliminativism carries a heavy burden: that of showing, without trading on implicit assumptions of impossible essence, that no satisfactory account of responsibility can be given.

Eliminativists about responsibility sometimes suggest the following argument. Only a regressive control or choice requirement can explain why people are not responsible in cases of brain damage, hypnotism, and so on. But this requirement cannot be reconciled with recognizing responsibility in more ordinary cases, since it is impossible to satisfy. So no one is ever responsible (see and cf. Klein 1990, chap. 4).

From a context-driven perspective, there are several related things wrong with such an argument. First, it gives explanatory priority to contexts in which the term in question does not apply, and tries to use those "negative contexts" to correct all our positive applications. But this gets things backward. We don't start with an explanation of things not being stars, and use that to correct all our applications of "star." Rather, we first explain what stars are, and then use that explanation to explain further why some things are not stars. A context-driven account gives explanatory priority to contexts of positive use, though it can admit that some of these are mistaken.

Second, there is the problem with attributing explanatory depth to impossible properties. It may be possible to explain why some things are not *F* by reference to their failure to meet a requirement on *F*s, namely, that *F*s have property *P*. Pyrite is not gold, and behaves differently from gold, because it turns out not to have the essential properties of gold. But such negative explanation, of non-*F*-hood by non-*P*-hood, is parasitic on the explanation of *F*-hood by *P*-hood in other cases. The essential properties of gold do have explanatory depth in relation to instances of gold. Where *P* is impossible, *F*-hood cannot ever be explained by *P*-hood. So parasitic negative explanation is not available. On a context-driven approach, it is an illusion to suppose that a condition that is impossible to satisfy can explain why people are not responsible.

Third, even if we don't assume that contexts of positive use have priority, the eliminativist seems to be assuming the opposite. Why should we correct our ordinary positive applications to bring them into line with our exemptions of people from responsibility, rather than the other way round? The regression condition provides no independent leverage here, since it is at least as controversial as our normal positive applications of "responsible."

Fourth, it is not at all clear that no explanation can be given of both our ordinary positive applications of "responsibility" and our exemptions of the brain damaged, the hypnotized, and so on, from responsibility (cf. Klein 1990, chap. 4; Wallace 1996).

Context-driven theories of reference are more obviously attractive to the anti-eliminativist, who denies that responsibility is essentially regressive and hence impossible. She may be tempted to secure her claim to be talking about responsibility rather than something else (when she disagrees about its regressivity) in terms of the immunity of context-driven reference to bad theory. The theory of regressive choice or control is a bad theory of responsibility, just as animism was a bad theory. Neither theory has explanatory depth, neither has an explanatory relationship to contexts of use that reveals what is essential to responsible acts. Just as animism fails to capture the point of responsibility by licensing its attribution too widely, the regressive choice or control theory fails to capture the point of responsibility by restricting its attribution to the vanishing point.

A better theory would strike a middle ground. It would explain the point of our positive attributions of responsibility in a variety of contexts, and would do so in a way consistent with our exempting from responsibility not just the inanimate realm, but also people suffering from brain damage, acting under hypnotic suggestion, and so on (see, for example, Wallace 1996). Perhaps some combination of the various necessary and sufficient conditions we have considered would do this work, perhaps a hybrid theory with both nonregressive causal and regressive noncausal components. The successful theory may not be easy to find, but then we have only fairly recently learned not to confuse actual-sequence and alternate-sequence conditions, such as regression and ability-to-do-otherwise requirements. That's progress, but it also suggests we may still have a long way to go. On a context-driven view, the successful theory may be quite different from existing theories. And it doesn't have to validate all our applications of the term in question; we may be mistaken in a variety of cases, just as original users were mistaken if they made animistic applications. But on a context-driven account, not all of our positive applications of "responsibility" can miss their mark: some such applications must anchor our talk about responsibility.

So, on a context-driven approach, the dispute between the eliminativist and his opponent could take the following shape. The opponent tries to find a theory, however novel, that accounts for the contexts in which "responsible" is applied, even if not all of them. The eliminativist tries to deconstruct responsibility by arguing that there is no such account, that responsibility is an arbitrary hodge-podge. But this would not be eliminativism that relies on the claim that responsibility essentially requires regressive choice or control and hence is impossible. On a context-driven approach, the prospects are dim for impossible-essence eliminativism, since impossible essences cannot do the explanatory work required of essences.

6. Responsibility as Theory-Driven

Let's shift now from a context-driven to a theory-driven approach. This makes things a bit easier for the eliminativist. Contexts of use of a term exist, even if our existing theories are very misguided. But the essential theoretical role assigned to something can be such that no existing thing has it. On both views, however, essential properties have explanatory depth. On context-driven accounts, they explain something about actual worldly contexts of a kind term's application, while on theory-driven accounts, the reveal the deep structure and coherence of the theoretical role assigned by users.

Of the various conditions of responsibility we have canvassed, some may be less controversial than others: conditions of choice or control seem to be more widely assumed than a regression requirement. Alternate-sequence requirements are incompatible with determinism. Animism, and requirements of choice, control, or reason-responsiveness are compatible with both deterministic and indeterministic causation. A regression requirement could also in principle be applied to indeterministic as well as deterministic causes. Some combinations of requirements are coherent while others are incoherent. Regression is incompatible with choice or control requirements and with animism, but compatible with hypothetical choice requirements. Regression and ability-to-do-otherwise requirements are compatible; indeed, they have often not been distinguished, though neither entails the other.

As a result of these features and relationships, some conditions or combinations of conditions may have greater theory-internal explanatory depth than others. To support a claim about the deep structure of the theory of responsibility, we should look for a subset of essential conditions that are mutually coherent, a subset that, other things equal, excludes more controversial conditions rather than less controversial ones.

Various trade-offs to achieve coherence are possible. For example, we could hold onto choice or control and reject regression, or vice versa. Or we could combine requirements of nonregressive choice or control and regressive hypothetical choice in a hybrid view. Once we settle on the most coherent account of the deep theoretical structure of responsibility, we may find out that nothing in the world satisfies this account. We might thus end up as eliminativists about responsibility. But again, that would not be because responsibility has an impossible essence. A combination of properties that is impossible to satisfy could not have even theory-internal, coherentist explanatory depth.

Another possibility is that it turns out there is no good account of the deep theoretical structure of responsibility that preserves its coherence and point; it is simply an unsalvageable shambles and we should abandon it. That would also eliminate responsibility rather than merely revise our view of it. But eliminativism would not be based on an impossible essence in this case either. A theoretical role that is an incoherent shambles with no deep structure does not have an impossible essence, something we could mourn or regret the impossibility of. It is not poignant, just confused.

It may be indeterminate whether a theoretical role is just confused, or has a coherent deep structure, if only we could figure it out. In that case it may be indeterminate whether or not the theoretical role has an occupant and whether or not eliminativism is warranted. Perhaps responsibility provides an example of such indeterminacy. But that would not show that responsibility is essentially impossible either.

7. Context and Theory in Reflective Equilibrium

I close this chapter with two morals. First, we are not stuck believing responsibility is impossible. If the contexts in which we apply "responsible" are an arbitrary hodge-podge or if the theoretical role of responsibility is unsalvageably confused, then it may be that no one is ever responsible for anything, and eliminativism about responsibility is correct. But this would not be because responsibility is essentially impossible. And these are big "ifs," far from settled.

Second, rather than rely on either a context-driven or a theory-driven approach to adjudicate these matters, we might do better to combine them into a reflective-equilibrium approach. The essence of F-hood would, on such a view, have explanatory depth in relation both to the contexts of application of "F" and to theoretical beliefs about Fs. Rather than either context or theory having priority in determining essence, perhaps they work together. This idea applied to justice is familiar from Rawls's work; it is natural to extend the idea to responsibility (and it also appears to have wider application, outside ethics). This view would not presuppose that either the contexts of our uses of "responsible" or our theoretical beliefs about responsibility have priority as explananda. Rather, it would require us to bring applications into systematic contact with theoretical role, revising and correcting each in the light of the other, and to seek a coherent deep structure or essence that sheds normative light on both contexts of use and theoretical role. This balancing approach would make it unlikely either that a wholly new theory of responsibility is needed or that all our positive applications of responsibility are mistaken.

In light of the arguments of this and previous chapters, a plausible working hypothesis is that an account of responsibility that can achieve such reflective equilibrium will have certain features. First, it will not require alternate sequences. Second, it will include causal actual-sequence requirements: not just choice or control, but some form of reason-responsiveness, and perhaps a further requirement such as a "taking responsibility" requirement. Third, it will not require responsibility to be regressive in its overall structure, though it may include regressive noncausal subcomponents, such as requirements of regressive hypothetical choice. These features still leave a large space of possible accounts to be explored. But there are some attractive approaches on the market today, to be found in this space. The prospects are encouraging. Eliminativists about responsibility should think again.

4

Responsibility, Luck, and the "Natural Lottery"

Part I of this book is about responsibility. Part II is about the relationships between responsibility, luck, and justice. A focus of Part II is the luck-neutralizing approach to distributive justice, which makes responsibility central to justice. This chapter argues for a certain conception of the relationship between responsibility and luck, thus acting as a bridge between the book's two parts.

I distinguish a thin concept of luck from various thick conceptions. On the thin concept, luck is simply the inverse correlate of responsibility, so that what is a matter of luck for someone is what he is not responsible for. On alternative thick readings, luck has more specific implications; for example, it may be associated with luck in lotteries, or lack of control, or lack of choice. I argue that we should adopt the thin usage of "luck" for purposes of moral and political philosophy.

In particular, I apply the distinction to constitutive luck, and use it to criticize the thick conception of constitutive luck expressed by the idea of a "natural lottery." This metaphor does no work in helping to understand constitutive luck. The concept of a lottery does have independent implications, first about the identity of the agent who enters the lottery, and second about the role of chance in lotteries. But both of these implications are misleading and confusing when applied to constitutive luck. The identity-dependence of lotteries gives rise to a bare self problem, and the relationship of chance to responsibility is not what the lottery metaphor suggests, whether chance is understood metaphysically or epistemically. The natural lottery metaphor is positively unhelpful in understanding constitutive luck, and is best avoided.

1. Terminological Tidiness: Thin Luck versus Thick Luck

In a well-known pair of essays both titled "Moral Luck," Thomas Nagel and Bernard Williams comment on the Kantian idea that morality must be independent of luck in some sense (Nagel 1979; Williams 1981). They both think it is basic to our intuitive ideas of morality that what people are morally responsible for cannot depend on mere luck, though Williams is skeptical about this aspiration and thinks it is bound to be disappointed. As Daniel Dennett notes, both Nagel and Williams take the concept of luck more or less for granted in these essays (Dennett 1984, pp. 81, 92 ff). By contrast, Dennett (rightly, in my view) regards luck as a curious and treacherous concept.

I argue in this chapter that we should distinguish between *thin luck* and *thick luck*. This distinction has not been drawn in discussions of moral luck. Conflation of thin luck and thick luck has, I believe, contributed to unclarity and ambiguity surrounding uses of the notion of luck in moral and political philosophy. I briefly introduce the distinction in the context of the discussions of moral luck by Williams and by Nagel, and explain how thick luck ramifies into a variety of thick conceptions of luck. I go on to argue that the thin concept of luck is more useful and appropriate in moral and political philosophy, and apply the distinction between thin and thick luck to issues about constitutive luck and the "natural lottery." I follow my own advice in Part II of this book, where the concept of luck looms large, and use the thin concept of luck except where I indicate otherwise.

Thin luck is simply the inverse correlate of responsibility, in the full-blooded sense that licenses and is implied by praise, blame, moral assessment, moral accountability, and resentment and other reactive attitudes. What is a matter of thin luck for an agent is what he is not responsible for, and what he is responsible for is not a matter of thin luck for him.[1] Thin luck is just the absence or negation of whatever it is that makes for responsibility. The thin concept of luck is transparent. It simply follows, inversely, the bottom line about responsibility, and contributes no independent theory or content to our understanding of responsibility and what defeats it.

---

1. It is a further issue whether something is a matter of luck for you, or you are responsible for it, only under certain descriptions of it. My argument here is not, as far as I can see, hostage to this issue.

Thin luck provides a handy conceptual correlate of any independently arrived at conclusions about responsibility.[2]

Thick luck, by contrast, is not simply the inverse correlate of responsibility. Rather, it ramifies into a variety of thick conceptions of luck, such as lottery luck, lack of control, lack of choice, and so on. They all have some implications or content more specific than the negation of our bottom-line judgments about responsibility, though this content can differ considerably between different thick conceptions of luck. Thick luck can therefore purport to make some independent substantive contribution to our understanding of responsibility. It does not simply follow that understanding, but can in principle cut across it. When something is a matter of thick luck for an agent, it is an open substantive question whether he is responsible for it. Thick luck may or may not be inversely correlated with responsibility.

For example, one thick conception of luck is that of luck in the ordinary sense in which winning a gamble or lottery is a matter of luck: *lottery luck*. This thick conception of luck is often combined with the idea of constitutive luck in the metaphor of a natural lottery of constitutions, which is taken to express our lack of responsibility for our constitutions. I argue below that the thick conception of lottery luck has implications about the identity of the agent who enters the lottery and about the role of chance in lotteries. These implications diverge from those of thin constitutive luck and raise substantive questions about responsibility; we cannot simply assume that lottery luck is inversely correlated with responsibility. I argue

---

2. A minor qualification is this: we normally only speak of something being a matter of luck—good or bad—for someone if it is relevant to their interests in some way. I am not responsible for how long it takes Pluto to orbit the sun, but that is not a matter of luck for me one way or the other if it in no way bears on my interests or concerns. So the concept of luck implies not just lack of responsibility but lack of responsibility in relation to something that affects the interests or concerns of the person in question. I will take this qualification as read in what follows.

Note also that in my usage here, thin luck is thin *in relation to* responsibility. In an alternative usage, however, it might be thin in relation to something else, such as desert. But luck cannot be the inverse correlate of both responsibility and desert, since they are not the same thing and can dissociate. This is relevant to the equivocation between responsibility and deservingness discussed in Chapter 7, especially sections 6 and 8. Within the luck-neutralizing account of distributive justice, luck is primarily opposed to responsibility and responsibility-related notions such as choice and control, but there is a tendency to slip into opposing it to desert as well, which can lead to equivocation.

that lottery luck cuts across responsibility: we can be responsible for what is a matter of lottery luck, and not responsible for what is not a matter of lottery luck. As a result, the idea of a natural lottery is confusing and misleading as a metaphor for our lack of responsibility for our constitutions, or thin constitutive luck.[3]

2. Williams and Nagel on Moral Luck

Williams does not say exactly what he means by "luck." He claims, as he puts it, to "use the notion of 'luck' generously, undefinedly, but, I think, comprehensibly" (Williams 1981, p. 22). Williams agrees with Nagel that it is basic to our ideas of morality and justice that the subjection of morality to luck is incoherent. But Williams is skeptical: he holds that the Kantian aim to immunize morality against luck is bound to be disappointed. Moreover, he holds that such "[s]cepticism about the freedom of morality from luck cannot leave morality where it was," but calls our intuitive moral conceptions into question (1981, pp. 22, 36n, 39). Our judgments of moral responsibility are subject to luck in ways that conflict with the Kantian aspiration.

Williams's usage of "luck" is ambiguous in relation to the thick–thin distinction, but is probably best interpreted in terms of an undifferentiated thick concept of luck. As just explained, he uses it not just to report that intuitive morality regards the subjection of morality to luck as incoherent, but also to express skepticism about the aspiration of intuitive morality to immunize morality against luck. So on his dual use of "luck," it must make sense to ask whether the aim to immunize morality against luck could conceivably be disappointed, whether someone could properly be regarded as morally assessable and hence morally responsible for something that is a matter of luck.[4] In the thin sense of luck, these questions do not make

---

3. A person can gamble without involving other people, while lotteries involve more than one person, with an implication of interdependence between persons: your winning is not independent of my losing. However, as far as I can see these features of lotteries do nothing to protect the idea of a natural lottery from my criticisms. Thanks here to Geoffrey Brennan.

4. On an alternative interpretation of Williams, he aims to show that people can be morally assessed in respects for which they are not morally responsible. It is not clear which is the correct interpretation. I find this alternative interpretation hard to understand: if someone is *morally* assessed for an action he is thereby being regarded and treated as morally responsible for it, whether or not he has met various specific condi-

sense. Thus, though Williams does not positively explain the specific sense of "luck" he has in mind or its relationship to responsibility, he appears to be using an undifferentiated thick concept of luck.

Nagel uses a specific thick conception of luck, which expresses lack of control:

> Where a significant aspect of what someone does depends on factors beyond his control, yet we continue to treat him in that respect as an object of moral judgment, it can be called moral luck. (Nagel 1979, p. 26)

In his usage, to require control for responsibility is to reject moral luck. Since significant aspects of what we do are almost always in part beyond our control, a control requirement for responsibility would threaten to erode most moral assessments. But such a requirement seems correct to Nagel even so.

Luck as lack of control can be compared with luck in the ordinary sense in which the outcome of a lottery or gamble is a matter of luck for someone. Lack of control is necessary but not sufficient for lottery luck. If the outcome of a lottery is a matter of luck for someone, he does not control that outcome. If he does control it, there is cheating going on; the outcome is not a matter of luck. So lottery luck implies lack of control. But not everything that someone lacks control over is the outcome of a lottery. So, we can in this way distinguish two related thick conceptions of luck: lack of control, and lottery luck.

Nagel explains that the erosion of moral judgment by the requirement of control is a natural consequence of ordinary intuitive ideas of moral assessment and of responsible agency. These ideas he regards as incompatible with the understanding of actions as events in the world and of agents as things in or parts of the world:

> Once people are seen as parts of the world, determined or not, there seems no way to assign responsibility to them for what they do. Ev-

---

tions for responsibility. Of course, people can be held accountable for an act in various other ways, such as legally or institutionally, even when they are not morally responsible for it. There may be good institutional or pragmatic reasons for doing so, even good moral reasons. But this is not the same thing as morally assessing the action in question. I do not see a gap between morally assessing an action and regarding someone as *morally* responsible for it, even though he may not have had control, been able to do otherwise, and so on.

erything about them, including finally their actions themselves, seems to blend in with the surroundings over which they have no control. (Nagel 1986, pp. 120 ff; see also 1979, p. 36)

In Nagel's view, when we see people as parts of the world, we cannot make sense of the idea that what people do depends ultimately on them. What we do is gradually eroded by the subtraction of what happens, until the responsible self disappears, and we can only celebrate or deplore, not praise or blame. Alternatives are just alternative courses the world might take. That the world somehow includes or makes up the agent does not make the alternatives alternatives *for him*. The world is not an agent, and cannot be held responsible. The intuitive idea of responsible agency, in demanding that I be able to act in light of everything about myself, from outside myself and indeed from outside the world, becomes unintelligible (paraphrasing Nagel 1986, pp. 120 ff).

Notice that more than just control is at issue here. Control itself is part of the natural world, as in genetic control. Nor is there any difficulty in understanding artificial control systems, such as thermostats, as part of the natural world. We do not argue that genes and thermostats could not really control anything because they are part of the natural world. Neither does a person's being part of the natural world show that she does not really control anything. This suggests that Nagel implicitly requires more than just control for responsibility.

What he seems to be requiring is *regressive control,* which is control of a special kind. Regressive control of X requires control of X's causes as well as of X itself. As explained in Chapter 3, control of X does not in itself require control of X's causes. For example, a thermostat controls the temperature of a room: it maintains room temperature at a target level by compensating for exogenous causes, such as sunlight coming through a window, or clouding over, or nightfall. But the thermostat does not control these exogenous causes, or others further back in the causal chain, and is not required to in order to control room temperature. Indeed, it could not control causes which ex hypothesi are exogenous. So a thermostat controls but does not regressively control room temperature. Lack of control of causes is luck in causes, in Nagel's thick sense of "luck." If responsibility requires regressive control, then lack of control of causes is incompatible with responsibility.

Nagel distinguishes luck in the consequences or effects of action, luck in the circumstances of action, and *constitutive luck:* luck in the kind of person you are, your inclinations, capacities, and temperament. Nagel understands constitutive luck thickly, as a specific sort of *luck in causes*, namely, lack of control of the causes of who and what you are—such as luck in having ancestors with genes for certain talents and without genes for serious diseases, in having a mother who did not smoke when she was pregnant with you, and so on—and thus in the causes of your actions. The idea of constitutive luck has played important roles in political philosophy (though not always under that name). For example, it often motivates familiar arguments about distributive justice, to the effect that since our native abilities, talents, and so forth are mere matters of luck, we are not responsible for differential earnings or other social consequences that flow from them,[5] and hence such earnings are properly subject to redistributive taxation.

We can apply the distinction between luck in causes and luck in effects to various thick conceptions of luck. For example, compare lack of control of consequences with lack of control of causes. We can try to immunize acts against lack of control of consequences by paring our acts down to an inner act of pure will, a choice or intention or trying, with contents determined independently of their consequences, and by restricting responsibility accordingly.[6] But this paring-down tactic does not work against lack of control of causes, which Nagel also regards as incompatible with responsibility. We cannot control the causes of what we try to do any more than the consequences.

---

5. But compare the views of Ginger the Cat, in Beatrix Potter's *Tale of Ginger and Pickles* (1909):

> When it came to Jan. 1st there was still no money, and Pickles was unable to buy a dog licence.
> "It is very unpleasant, I am afraid of the police," said Pickles.
> "It is your own fault for being a terrier [said Ginger]; I do not require a license, and neither does Kep, the Collie dog."

6. This is rather like trying to immunize against epistemological skepticism by paring the objects of perception down to sense data, with contents determined independently of their causes. The result is the familiar inward retreat of the disappearing self: the effect of luck in contracting the scope of responsibility parallels the effect of the skeptic's hypotheses in contracting the scope of knowledge. I have no more sympathy for this internalist tradition in relation to responsibility than in relation to epistemology (for more on the parallels, see Hurley 1998, chap. 6). On the paring down to tryings, compare Hornsby 1980.

If one cannot be responsible for consequences of one's acts due to factors beyond one's control, or for antecedents of one's acts that are properties of temperament not subject to one's will, or for the circumstances that pose one's moral choices, then how can one be responsible even for the stripped-down acts of the will itself, if *they* are the product of antecedent circumstances outside of the will's control?

The area of genuine agency, and therefore of legitimate moral judgement, seems to shrink under this scrutiny to an extensionless point. Everything seems to result from the combined influence of factors, antecedent and posterior to action, that are not within the agent's control. *Since he cannot be responsible for them, he cannot be responsible for their results.* (Nagel 1979, p. 35, emphasis added)

The final italicized sentence just quoted gives expression to the regression requirement for responsibility: in order to be responsible for something, one must also be responsible for its causes. As we have seen in earlier chapters, this principle applied recursively generates a regress: responsibility entails responsibility for causes, all the way back. Lack of responsibility, or luck, anywhere back among the causes is transmitted forward to effects. That is, anything that is among the effects of luck in causes is itself a matter of luck. Responsibility is not causally local.

It is worth pausing here to emphasize the difference between, on the one hand, luck in the effects of X, and, on the other hand, the effects of luck on X. These have very different logical relationships to luck in the causes of X. For X to be among the effects of luck is for X to have luck among its causes. To neutralize the effects of luck on X is thus to neutralize luck in X's causes (rather than luck in X's effects). You can in principle aim to neutralize *luck in X's effects* but not luck in X's causes, or vice versa: these are logically independent. But aiming to neutralize *the effects of luck on X* just is aiming to neutralize the effects *of luck in X's causes*. The aim to neutralize the effects on X of luck that occurs anywhere back among X's causes is a way of giving effect to the regression requirement.

The regression requirement is often assumed in discussions of constitutive luck, when it is supposed that someone is not responsible for his choices because he is not responsible for the constitution from which they result. However, the idea of constitutive luck does not entail the regression requirement. We could agree that someone did not control and was not responsible for his constitution, but still think he was responsible for certain choices that flow from his constitution. We could hold that lack of control of causes, or Nagelian thick constitutive luck, is compatible with responsibility for the resulting choices. This would be to reject the regression requirement.[7]

The regressive-control conception of responsibility results from combining two requirements. First, control is required for responsibility. Nagel understands constitutive luck as involving lack of control of causes, which negates our responsibility for our constitutive properties. Second, responsibility is required to be regressive. Combined with the control requirement, this means that responsibility requires control all the way back along the chain of causes.[8] The combination implies that lack of control over one's constitutive properties, or Nagelian constitutive luck, negates responsibility for choices that result from those properties. It is this combined requirement, rather than the condition of control alone, that seems incompatible with naturalistic understanding. Indeed, it makes responsibility impossible, as discussed in Chapters 1 and 3.

Note also that the components of this Nagelian conception of responsibility as regressive control are doubly dissociable. Since control is not in itself regressive, it could be held that responsibility for X requires control of X, but not regressive control. On the other hand, responsibility might be thought to require regressive choice rather than regressive control. To choose something is not necessarily to control it, or vice versa. Thermostats control but do not choose, and many choices do not exercise control.

3. How Thick Luck Generates an Empty Ramification of Issues, and a Proposal

So far we have compared one thick conception of luck as lack of control with a second thick conception of lottery luck. Since a control requirement is distinct from a regression requirement for responsibility, a distinct third thick conception of luck is lack of regressive control, according to which lack of control of any of X's causes suffices for X itself to be a matter of luck. A fourth thick conception of luck is suggested by the fact that con-

---

7. Cf. Nozick (1974, p. 225), who suggests that you do not have to deserve to be everything you are in order to deserve the results of what you do. This is to reject a regression requirement for desert.

8. John Roemer's conception of responsibility is also a control conception, and sometimes appears to be a regressive-control conception. See, e.g., Roemer 1996.

trol and choice can come apart, and by the way Cohen (1989) opposes luck to choice: something is a matter of luck for someone in this sense just if it is not chosen by him. Note that lack of choice does not always correlate with lottery luck: people may choose to enter lotteries in ways that give rise to so-called option luck. On a choice theory of responsibility, people can be responsible for their option luck, or the outcomes of chosen lotteries. A fifth thick conception of luck could bring hypothetical choice into play as well. These various different thick conceptions of luck have different implications and inferential commitments.

In this way, thick luck ramifies into various distinct thick conceptions of luck, which cut across one another in various ways. But now notice something. The articulation of different thick conceptions of luck runs in parallel to that of conceptions of responsibility. The same distinctions emerge, along with parallel sets of issues. Is luck more closely linked to lack of control or to lack of choice? Is responsibility more closely linked to control or to choice? Is luck lack of control or lack of regressive control? Does responsibility require control or regressive control?

I claim that this is a redundant and empty ramification of issues, which leads to unclarity and confusion. These distinctions between different thick conceptions of luck are derivative. It is very important not to run together distinct conditions of responsibility; the articulation and differentiation of various conditions of responsibility (by Frankfurt, Klein, Wolf, Fischer, and others, as described in Chapter 1) has advanced our understanding of responsibility greatly. But it is not helpful for purposes of moral and political philosophy to conceive luck to admit of a parallel variety of distinct conceptions. Luck is not an independently contested concept, for these purposes. There is no *separate* body of evidence or intuitions to which questions about whether luck is really lack of control, or lack of choice, or lack of regressive control, and so forth are responsible. These are not fruitfully different substantive questions from questions about whether responsibility requires control or choice or is regressive.

If we were to suppose that there is One Big Threat to responsibility, it may seem natural to ponder, using a thick conception of luck tied to that One Big Threat, whether luck really does threaten responsibility. But if in fact there are different candidate conditions of responsibility, which cut across one another in various ways, then it becomes unclear which thick conception of luck we are pondering with. If we claim, with Williams, that responsibility is subject to luck after all, then luck cannot just be whatever defeats responsibility, as in the thin usage. Rather, it must be one of the specific things commonly, though wrongly, taken to defeat responsibility. But which? Failure to keep track of which thick conception of luck is in play lends itself to equivocation and confusion.

For example, suppose I hold that responsibility for X does not require control of the causes of X. It would be misleading to express this view by saying that responsibility is subject to luck after all. That would suggest either that "luck" *really* refers to one specific condition among the variety of potentially responsibility-defeating conditions, or that it is not important to distinguish them, that they can harmlessly be run together. But both suggestions are wrong. There is no basis for associating luck with one or another of these conditions, independent of their relations to responsibility. And recent literature (including that canvassed in Chapter 1) has shown how important and fruitful it is to distinguish conditions of responsibility that have often in the past been run together.

Therefore, on grounds of conceptual hygiene, tidiness, and clarity, I recommend suppressing the thick usage of "luck" in moral and political philosophy. We do better to adopt a thin concept of luck, which is simply the inverse correlate of responsibility, with no independent commitments. This is a frank piece of conceptual legislation. The thin concept of luck cannot be used to wonder whether the aim to immunize responsibility against luck is bound to be disappointed (cf. Williams 1981). This may sound like a reasonable, even philosophically profound, thing to wonder; but the hygienic legislation proposed deflates this wonder. However, the proposal leaves open all the relevant substantive questions about responsibility: Does it require control, choice, alternate sequences; is it regressive; and so on. It treats the parallel questions about luck as derivative and as answering to arguments about responsibility rather than to independent arguments about luck. This proposal thus recognizes needed distinctions while avoiding the empty ramification of issues.

In the remainder of this chapter I apply the distinction between thin and thick luck to issues about constitutive luck and the "natural lottery." I show how the metaphor of the natural lottery expresses a thick conception of constitutive luck that cuts across issues about responsibility for our constitutions and hence across a thin conception of constitutive luck. The thick natural lottery conception of constitutive luck has different implications and inferential commitments from the thin concept of constitutive luck. The metaphor is misleading, and we do better in particular to adopt a thin concept of constitutive luck.

4. Constitutive Luck and the "Natural Lottery"

Recall that constitutive luck involves luck not in the effects of our actions, but rather in their causes, and in particular luck in who and what we are. We can distinguish different thick conceptions of constitutive luck from thin constitutive luck.

A thick conception of constitutive luck would reflect some specific conception of luck, such as lack of control, or lottery luck. Nagel's thick conception of constitutive luck involves lack of control of causes. A different thick conception of constitutive luck, however, is suggested by the widely used metaphor of the natural lottery, which supposedly deals us good or bad luck in the form of morally arbitrary natural or social advantages or disadvantages: innate talents or handicaps, advantageous or disadvantageous family situations. To the extent that what we get in the natural lottery constitutes us as persons, determines who or what we are, what we get is a matter of constitutive luck.

By contrast, a thin concept of constitutive luck simply expresses the judgment that someone is not responsible for his constitution, without indicating the particular basis for that judgment.

In the following sections I examine the relationship between thin constitutive luck and the thick conception of constitutive lottery luck expressed by the idea of a natural lottery. I consider the implications of the idea of a natural lottery for someone's responsibility for his constitution. Does the idea of a natural lottery help to understand our responsibility for what we are and our natural assets, or provide a distinctively luck-related reason for judgments on these matters?

I argue that it does not. The idea of a lottery of constitutions is a misleading guide to thin constitutive luck. Lottery luck is a kind of luck in consequences, and it has implications that do not project smoothly to luck in causes in general or to constitutive luck in particular. Specifically, there are two ways in which lottery luck has misleading implications in the context of concerns about responsibility for our constitutions. These concern the identity-dependence of lottery luck and the role of chance in lotteries. I conclude that the metaphor of a natural lottery should be handled more critically than it usually is. It is not helpful in understanding our responsibility for our constitutions. We do better to stick to the thin usage of constitutive luck, and avoid the natural lottery metaphor. This specific claim aligns with my more general proposal to adopt the thin concept of luck.

5. Lottery Luck as Identity-Dependent

The first way the idea of a lottery of constitutions is a misleading guide to thin constitutive luck concerns the identity-dependence of the luck involved in lotteries. Lottery luck requires that there is an agent whose luck is in question and whose identity is constant across the different possible results of the lottery.

Identity-dependent harm is an idea familiar from discussions of the impact of environmental policies on future generations. In such discussions, the point is made that if different environmental policies have cumulative effects on everyday life, then different sperm and egg cells will unite and so different people will be conceived as a result of different environmental policies. Hence policies of depleting resources may not be worse for anyone: this can be referred to as the *nonidentity problem*. The people who would exist given such policies would not have existed at all under different policies. No one is harmed by depletion if harm is identity-dependent, because the identities of people are not constant between the depletion scenario and alternative scenarios. The idea of harm involves a comparison of two states of affairs, one of which is worse than the other for the person harmed. If harm is identity-dependent, then the person's identity must be constant across the states of affairs compared. Identity-dependent harm or benefit is harm or benefit *to someone*.[9]

A qualification may be needed. If the lives of people who live given environmental depletion are so bad as to be not worth living, depletion of resources might be said to make them worse off. If so, we do not compare their situation with an alternative in which they are better off, but with an alternative in which they do not exist. Because depletion is *so* bad for them, it might be said to be worse than nonexistence *for them*. This is a kind of limiting case of identity-dependent harm. But if it makes sense, it does so only if a life is so bad as to be not worth living. And while existence may count as a harm to someone in such a limiting case, it does not follow that nonexistence counts as a benefit to him. This asymmetry is characteristic of such a limiting case.[10] The idea of harm to a person is extended as it were by courtesy to such a case.

There is a similar sense in which good or bad luck in gambles or lotteries

---

9. See Parfit 1984, pt. 4, on the nonidentity problem.

10. We might also say, in this limiting sense, that if someone's life is well worth living, then there is a manner of speaking in which existence might be said to benefit her; but it does not follow that nonexistence would harm her.

is also identity-dependent: it must be luck *for someone*. And there must be someone whose identity is constant between various possibilities that would count as good or bad luck, in order for them to count as good or bad luck *for that someone* (as opposed to just impersonally good or bad, or good or bad for mankind as a whole).

The idea of a gamble or a lottery expresses an identity-dependent conception of luck. A hand reaches into the barrel and pulls out a prize ticket or a penalty ticket. Since the hand might have pulled out either, what it does pull out is a matter of good or bad luck for its possessor. The same agent's hand might have pulled a different ticket out of the barrel, with different consequences. If that is not so, then the idea that the result is good or bad luck for the hand's owner loses application. So does the idea of a gamble or lottery. These ideas are identity-dependent. Without an identity that is constant across alternatives, we do not have a gamble or lottery but merely different possibilities—some good, some bad—in which different entities exist and different things happen. Not all such arrays of possibilities count as lotteries. The idea of a lottery, like that of a gamble, is tied to the idea of a constant identity, external to these possibilities, that could in some sense survey them and for which the outcome of the lottery counts as good or bad luck.[11] That is, the idea of a lottery is tied to the idea of good or bad luck *for someone*. The someone in question need not actually be a person: it could be an animal, or an honorary person, a nation or a corporation, but it must be an entity treated as having a unified perspective or constant identity for purposes of the gamble.

Lottery luck is normally a kind of luck in consequences: it is the consequence of an act of gambling that counts as a matter of good or bad luck. The identity-dependence of lotteries is normally unproblematic for luck in consequences. A person does an act, the consequences of which may be one thing or another. One result may be good luck for that agent, another bad. The agent of the act whose consequences are in question is the same, whatever the consequences turn out to be.

But when we turn to luck in causes, as in a natural lottery of constitutions, identity-dependence is not so straightforward. It may be good or bad luck *tout court* that this happened rather than that, but if it is not good or bad luck *for someone,* then it is not the result of a lottery or a gamble. It might be a matter of good luck that the sperm and the egg from which Mozart developed came together, rather than some others. But this does

---

11. Must agency be an attribute of the identity in question? Must a lottery be chosen, or can it be thrust upon one? Either way, luck is identity-dependent.

not mean Mozart might have been someone else, and that he was lucky to have been Mozart; only that he might not have existed at all, and that it is lucky for the rest of us that he did.

Is a qualification needed here too? Suppose we have a limiting case of identity-dependent harm. In one possibility, someone's life is not worth living. Existence counts as a harm to him. In no other possibilities does he exist at all. Does it follow that his situation is bad luck for him in the sense of lottery luck? Does it follow from a limiting case of identity-dependent harm that there is a limiting case of identity-dependent bad luck? If it makes sense to say that his very existence counts as a harm to him, does it also make sense to say that his very existence counts as bad luck for him?

Two points can be made in reply to these questions. First, even if such a limiting case of bad lottery luck for someone does make sense, it does so only when someone's life is so bad as to be worse for him than nonexistence. That condition will certainly not be met by many people who suffer from various handicaps. Second, it is not clear that it does make sense. The identity-dependence of lottery luck is intuitively more stringent than the identity-dependence of harm. The difference between saying that something for which someone is not responsible counts as a harm to him and that it counts as bad luck for him precisely reflects the stronger identity-dependence of lottery luck. Even if we can make sense of harm by comparison with nonexistence, it is not clear that we can make sense of bad luck in the outcome of a lottery by comparison with nonexistence. Such bad luck intuitively requires identity to be constant across possibilities; it does not admit the limiting case qualification.[12]

The thick conception of lottery luck thus has certain specific content and implications, apparently independent of our bottom-line judgements about responsibility. It is a conception of luck as identity-dependent: the outcome of a lottery or a gamble must be good or bad luck *for someone*. Return now to the idea of a lottery of constitutions. Can the outcome of such a lottery be good or bad luck for someone? Is the thick conception of constitutive luck informed by the idea of lottery luck even coherent?

6. The Bare Self Problem

It depends on what we mean by "constitution." In at least one sense of that term, your constitution is that without which you would not be

---

12. Is death bad luck? Perhaps this is a limiting case. But dying is either something someone does or something that happens to her. Not existing is neither.

you, your essential properties. Constitutive luck challenges the Kantian requirement that, as Williams puts it, "what I most fundamentally am" should be beyond luck (Williams 1981, p. 38). In this strong sense, your constitution fixes your identity, *who* you are. In a weaker sense of "constitution," your constitution is *what* you are in various respects, but these need not be essential to your identity. What you are could be different even though who you are is the same.

In discussions of the nonidentity problem for future generations, it is often assumed that an essential property of you is the combination of particular sperm and egg cells from which you develop. There may be a sense in which it is a matter of chance that these two came together. But this does not mean it is a matter of chance that you developed from those cells, as opposed to some others, only that it is a matter of chance that you existed at all. There may be other essential properties of persons. Let us put aside for the moment the question of how a person is constituted in the strong, identity-fixing sense.

We are now in a position to pinpoint the first problem with the concept of a lottery of constitutions. This is the result of combining the identity-dependence of lottery luck with the strong identity-fixing sense of constitution. The thick conception of constitutive luck that expresses this combination is indeed incoherent. This is what we sense when we puzzle: "But who or what is it that could have had different constitutions or essential properties?" For there to be a lottery, there must be identity constant across possibilities. But if the possibilities are different identities, this is impossible. Identity cannot be constant across different possible identities. There can be no pre-entity whose good or bad luck it is to have one or another identity or set of essential properties or constitution in the strong sense. There can be no proto-self or possible self or bare self who might-have-existed-as-you or who might-have-existed-as-someone-else (however mathematically convenient it might be to suppose the contrary!). But the metaphor of a lottery of essential properties may encourage us to think in these incoherent terms. We can call this the *bare self problem* for the idea of a natural lottery.[13]

The bare self problem for the natural lottery can be avoided. It depends on a purely logical point, the force of which turns on what we take to be the identity-fixing essential properties of persons. The problem extends

---

13. Cf. Honoré 1988, p. 549; Rawls 1982. The fact that I can imagine being someone else through imaginative role-playing does not show that I can conceive as a logical possibility that I might have been someone else; see Williams 1973, p. 45.

only to a lottery of constitutions in the strong sense of "constitution." Concerning aspects of what people are that are not essential to their identities, there is no threat along these lines to the coherence of the idea of a lottery of constitutions. So far, then, the idea of a lottery of constitutions is misleading for the strong sense of "constitutive" but not for the weak sense. It could be said that we are not responsible for our constitutions because the outcome of the lottery of constitutions is arbitrary. But the coherence of this usage is restricted to the weak sense of "constitution." So its coherence depends on whether the property whose constitutive luckiness is in question for someone counts as essential or not. And this may be unclear or controversial.

The bare self problem can also be avoided if the natural lottery is taken to operate over different epistemic possibilities about what my essential properties are, since the identity-dependence requirement can be satisfied across such different epistemic possibilities (thanks here to comments from Mike Ridge). For example, I may only find out at age forty-five whether I have a certain genetic defect, and I may consider that if I do turn out to have the defect that will be bad constitutive luck for me. But the idea of the natural lottery so construed still has a more restricted range of coherent application than does the thin concept of constitutive luck. We can speak of constitutive luck when there are no relevant different epistemic possibilities, when it is plain what someone's constitutive properties are, and there is no ignorance or controversy about it.

Notice that the bare self problem does not arise for luck in consequences. Luck in the consequences of an action does not in the same way threaten to undermine the identity of the agent. There is no logical difficulty about an agent with a given identity entering a lottery in which the different possible outcomes are the different possible consequences of some action or choice of his. The bare self problem arises when we try to project the identity-dependent conception of lottery luck from luck in consequences to luck in causes, and to constitutive causes in particular.

The first way the idea of a lottery of constitutions can be misleading has been traced to the incoherence of combining the identity-dependence of lottery luck with an identity-fixing sense of "constitutive." This gives rise to the bare self illusion. But the idea of a lottery can still be applied to aspects of what people are that are not essential to them. The coherence of the lottery of constitutions idea is thus restricted to the weak sense of "constitution," in the way I have described. We can avoid the incoherence if we register this restriction. But in practice, the idea of a lottery of constitutions may still lead to confusion, since it may be unclear whether people are implicitly disagreeing about which properties are essential.

By contrast, the thin concept of constitutive luck is not so restricted. We can coherently judge that people are not responsible for their essential properties or their inessential properties, and even when it is clear what their essential properties are. So even if we avoid the danger of incoherence, the lottery of constitutions idea cannot explain such unrestricted judgments about constitutive luck.

7. Lottery Luck and Chance

I now want to move on to the second way the thick conception of constitutive luck in terms of a lottery of constitutions has misleading implications in relation to thin constitutive luck. This concerns not the role of identity in lotteries, but the role of chance. In order to distinguish this from the first problem, I assume for present purposes that the constitutive properties in question are nonessential, so that problems about identity-dependence do not arise.

Ordinary gambles and lotteries are closely associated with alternative possibilities and chance. For example, you have good lottery luck if various different outcomes of the lottery were possible, in one or another sense of "possible," and by chance you got the most desirable one; or, when everyone in a lottery had the same chance of winning a prize, and you win it. Chance and possibility here might be understood in different ways. Chance might be understood to require different physical possibilities and hence indeterminism. Alternatively, it might be understood to require merely different epistemic possibilities and mere unpredictability rather than indeterminism. After all, roulette wheels are deterministic, yet there is a sense in which the outcome of a spin is a matter of chance: for all we know, it could have been anything. Determinism does not entail predictability, even in principle.[14]

A lottery entails different possibilities and chance. If this point is applied to the idea of lottery of (nonessential) constitutive properties, there are two alternative implications, depending on whether chance is understood metaphysically or epistemically. On the metaphysical understanding of chance, the outcome of the lottery is indeterministic: my (nonessential) properties could have been different because they result from an indeter-

---

14. As the study of nonlinear dynamic systems has shown.

ministic, chance process. On the epistemic understanding of chance, the outcome of the lottery is unpredictable: for all we know, my (nonessential) properties could have been different.

The idea of a lottery of constitutions thus has implications about chance, understood either in terms of indeterminism or unpredictability. But I now argue that thin constitutive luck, or lack of responsibility for one's own properties, does not have such implications. First, lack of responsibility does not entail indeterminism, whether we are considering responsibility for causes or for effects. Second, lack of responsibility for causes does not entail their unpredictability. And though there are links between responsibility for effects and predictability, we still do not get a clean parallel to the implications of lottery luck. So again the idea of a lottery of constitutions is a misleading guide to thin constitutive luck. My conclusion is that the thick conception of constitutive luck in terms of a lottery of constitutions is multiply misleading and we do better to stick to a thin usage of constitutive luck that simply reflects our judgments about responsibility for constitutions.

8. Chance, Indeterminism, and Responsibility

Let us begin with the indeterminism reading of chance. Does thin luck, or lack of responsibility, entail indeterminism? No. If it did, then something's being causally determined would entail that it was not a matter of luck. But that cannot be right!

Some philosophers deny that responsibility is compatible with causal determinism. That is, they take responsibility to entail indeterminism. From the fact that X was fully causally determined and could not have been otherwise, they conclude that the agent is not responsible for X.

But if lack of responsibility entailed indeterminism, then determinism would entail responsibility: precisely the opposite of what these philosophers take it to entail! They would have to be not just wrong, but perversely wrong. Now in fact I think these philosophers are wrong, and that determinism does not entail lack of responsibility (as argued in Chapter 2). But they are not perversely wrong. We have to work hard to specify the conditions under which determinism is compatible with responsibility. The mere fact of determinism does not suffice for responsibility. Thus, lack of responsibility, or thin luck, does not entail indeterminism.

It might be thought that lottery luck would be a better guide to responsibility for consequences than to responsibility for causes and constitutions. So let us focus on luck in consequences specifically. Does lack of responsibility for consequences entail indeterminism? If so, then determinism would entail responsibility for consequences. But that does not seem right either.

Suppose someone does an act that causally determines certain effects. That by itself does not tell us whether the agent is responsible for those effects or not. We need to know more. In some such cases, cases of so-called *option luck,* a person is responsible for these effects, even if they are unintended.[15] For example, if someone deliberately opts to do an act with uncertain effects and decides not to take out insurance in order to spend the cost of insurance on his favorite hobby instead, he is responsible for whatever the effects turn out to be (within limits, perhaps). But in other cases a person may not be responsible for the uncertain effects of his act, even if they are causally determined by his act. The situation of his choice may be such that we regard the consequences of his act as a matter of so-called *brute luck,* for which he is not responsible. Perhaps what happens to the agent is not the result of his action at all. Perhaps the agent did not know something critical about the circumstances of his act, so did not even realize he was taking a gamble. Perhaps the effects of his act were not merely unpredictable, but so unlikely that they would not be foreseeable even as possibilities to a reasonable person. Perhaps other agents intervened in the causal chain. Tort law aims, among other things, to sort cases of option luck from cases of brute luck in a principled way.

For present purposes, the relevant point is that determinism does not suffice for responsibility for consequences; this turns on further issues. Thus lack of responsibility for consequences does not entail indeterminism.

Nor, by the way, does the entailment run in the other direction: deter-

---

15. See Dworkin 1981a, p. 293. Note that "option luck" is not luck in the thin sense at all, but a kind of lottery luck, which turns on a "deliberate and calculated gamble," hence implies responsibility. Brute luck involves no such gamble. Indeed, it need not involve risk at all, but could be the result of deterministic processes, whether predictable or not, such as developing a disease that results from a gene carried by both one's parents. Brute luck, I suggest, is thin luck: something is a matter of brute luck for someone if he is not responsible for it (and it impacts on his interests or concerns). Using the term "luck" for both of these is at odds with my proposal to adopt a thin usage of luck. In order to avoid confusion and ambiguity, it would be better to avoid talk of "option luck" and to find another label. I think the clarity gained by adopting the thin usage more than compensates for this awkwardness. I doubt that there is an alternative proposal that similarly clarifies and disambiguates "luck" while saving all existing uses.

minism does not entail lack of responsibility for consequences, as the example of responsibility for option luck shows. In such a case, indeterminism does not protect from responsibility for effects.

In this section I have given half of the argument that the implications of lottery luck regarding chance do not hold for thin luck. Lottery luck entails chance, which can be understood metaphysically, to involve indeterminism. But lack of responsibility does not entail chance in this sense, whether we are concerned with responsibility for causes or responsibility for consequences. The causal determination of your constitution does not entail that you are responsible for it. And the causal determination of the consequences of your act does not entail that you are responsible for them either; they may still be a matter of brute luck.

9. Chance, Unpredictability, and Responsibility

Next, the other half of the argument: the implications of lottery luck regarding chance can be understood epistemically instead of metaphysically. But these implications do not hold for thin luck either. So again, lottery luck is not a good guide to thin luck or lack of responsibility.

If a lottery can operate by means of a deterministic mechanism, then the outcome is a matter of chance only in the epistemic sense: it is unpredictable. For all we can know, it might be anything, whether or not it is causally determined. Does this reading of the idea of a lottery of constitutions help to understand our responsibility for our constitutions, or thin constitutive luck? Does thin constitutive luck, or lack of responsibility for my constitution, entail its unpredictability? No.

Suppose a woman is exposed to a certain chemical when she is pregnant. It may be predictable that she would be exposed to this chemical when pregnant, and it may be predictable that if she was, the chemical would induce a certain condition in the resulting child, which only begins to have harmful effects after the child reaches adulthood. The adult in question can thus predict these harmful effects, as could his mother and others who knew them. They are nevertheless bad constitutive luck for that person: he is not responsible for this aspect of his constitution. This judgment is in no way undermined by the predictability of the condition and its harmful effects.

Turning next to responsibility for effects, we can consider whether lack of responsibility for the effects of an act entails their unpredictability by the agent. Here, we still do not get a clean parallel between the implications of lottery luck and of thin luck. Admittedly, the predictability of the effects of an act by the agent does seem at least to be relevant to the agent's responsibility for such effects. Whether someone is responsible for the results of a gamble he chose to take depends on, among other things, whether the various possible outcomes of the gamble were predictable: whether they should have been foreseen, or would have been foreseen by a reasonable person. However, tort law raises issues about whether mere predictability is sufficient for responsibility for effects, in the absence of actual foresight or other conditions. While the predictability of the effects of an act by the agent at least cuts in favor of the agent's responsibility for such effects, the implication seems more secure in the other direction: the unpredictability of effects argues against the agent's responsibility for them more strongly than the agent's lack of responsibility argues for their unpredictability. Predictability may be necessary though not sufficient for responsibility for consequences.

Even to the extent lottery luck does have implications about predictability that hold also for thin luck in effects, its implications about predictability still do not hold for thin luck in causes, or constitutive luck, as already argued. The implications of lottery luck concerning predictability do not generalize from luck in effects to luck in causes, or constitutive luck.

10. Concluding Remarks and Transition to Part II

I conclude that the thick conception of constitutive luck expressed by the idea of a lottery of constitutions is unhelpful, and even positively misleading, in relation to our responsibility for our constitutions. The implications of lottery luck concerning the identity-dependence of luck do not combine coherently with the strong sense of "constitution." Moreover, lottery luck and thin constitutive luck come apart in their implications concerning chance, whether understood in terms of indeterminism or unpredictability. We do best to avoid the confusing metaphor of a lottery of constitutions and adopt instead the thin usage of constitutive luck. On this proposal, to say that someone's constitution is a matter of luck is just to say that she is not responsible for it. The grounds for such a claim are whatever the grounds are for judging that people are not responsible for something.

This recommendation can leave it seeming rather puzzling that it is so natural to use the same word, "luck," in such different ways. If lottery luck is not the clean inverse correlate of responsibility, why is it so common to use "luck" both for lottery luck and for lack of responsibility?

To venture a diagnosis: perhaps we uncritically and mistakenly generalize from the limited link between unpredictability and responsibility for effects to a link between lottery luck and responsibility in general, including responsibility for causes. Moreover, both control and choice loom large as conditions of responsibility, and lottery luck is not under control and not chosen. So lottery luck and responsibility do have some inverse commitments, at least in relation to predictability, control and choice. Perhaps our pretheoretical understanding of luck simply does not register the distinction between luck in effects and luck in causes, or that control and choice (along with other pairs of conditions for responsibility) are doubly dissociable.

I will end Part I by briefly reviewing the points about responsibility made thus far that are carried forward and used in Part II, in connection with distributive justice.

In Part II, I use "luck" in the thin sense argued for in this chapter, unless otherwise indicated. The philosophical landscape drawn in Part I is used to navigate throughout Part II. My arguments in Part II invoke the actual sequence / alternate sequence distinction, and the distinctions between various different actual-sequence conceptions of responsibility. For example, I apply the distinction between alternate- and actual-sequence conditions of responsibility in the context of arguments about incentive inequality and the choices of the talented about how hard to work. I also show how different actual-sequence conceptions of responsibility, in terms of regressive choice or control, or regressive hypothetical choice, or nonregressive reason-responsiveness, have different implications for issues about incentive-seeking by the talented.

Part I argues that, under plausible assumptions, regressive responsibility is impossible, and argues against a regressive conception of responsibility. In Part II, I consider the implications of these positions for issues about distributive justice. For example, I consider how a regressive conception of responsibility is related to a view of egalitarianism as aiming to neutralize the effects of luck, as well as to the assumption that luck and responsible choice are separable. And I consider the relationship of a regressive conception of responsibility to assumptions about bare selves.

The worries expressed in Part I about the insufficiency of a pure hypothetical-choice view of responsibility are developed further in Part II, where I describe a closely related indeterminacy problem. I explain why this problem means that responsibility cannot tell us *how* to redistribute goods, even if it can tell us *what* goods to redistribute. I also explain, in light of this problem, the importance of distinguishing responsibility from deservingness in theories of distributive justice.

In Part II I want not only to show how different views of responsibility have different implications for distributive justice, but also to display some of the implications of the most promising view. Part I leaves reason-responsiveness conceptions of responsibility in play after alternate-sequence, hypothetical choice, and regressive choice or control conceptions have been criticized. I accordingly rely on the plausibility of reason-responsiveness conceptions in responding to issues about incentive inequality. I also explain how the asymmetry between certain talents and handicaps generated by a reason-responsiveness view of responsibility bears on the interpretation of maximin principles of distributive justice.

II

JUSTICE

5

Philosophical Landscape: The Luck-Neutralizing Approach to Distributive Justice

What is the relationship between responsibility and luck, on the one hand, and distributive justice, on the other? Egalitarians believe that distributive justice favors equality across persons. But equality of what? The answers to that question that have developed over the past three decades have given concepts of luck and responsibility an increasingly explicit role. A prevalent view now is that there is little reason to be concerned with inequalities for which agents are suitably responsible, while inequalities that are a matter of luck demand redistribution. This is the luck-neutralizing approach to distributive justice.

This chapter sketches a second philosophical landscape, a background against which the rest of Part II is argued. It briefly and selectively lays out the development of the luck-neutralizing approach, providing reference points from Rawls through Sen and Dworkin to Cohen and Roemer. (This chapter can be skimmed over by those already familiar with this body of work.) In this literature the concepts of responsibility and luck operate for most purposes as black boxes, without explicit commitment to substantive accounts of responsibility. My hypothesis is that the roles responsibility can properly play within theories of justice are constrained by the nature of responsibility. Subsequent chapters distinguish, probe, and assess various possible roles responsibility might play in theories of justice, in light of the new articulation of responsibility canvassed in Part I.

1. Rawls as a Luck Neutralizer

John Rawls cast his 1971 liberal egalitarian *Theory of Justice* in terms of primary goods. Primary goods are understood as goods that everyone needs: whatever specific conception of the good you have, whatever you value in life, you need primary goods to pursue your own particular ends. They are

133

universal means to whatever your ends happen to be. They include basic resources like income, which provide food, shelter, clothing, and so on.[1] People who differ widely in their conceptions of the good and their tastes and preferences can be presumed to want such primary resources. Rawls departed from utilitarianism by focusing not on welfare but on such primary resources, and by requiring not the maximization of a total or an average across people but rather that departures from equality across people maximize the primary goods position of the worst off people. His egalitarianism was significantly motivated by the thought that many differences between people, such as differences in natural endowments and family status and consequent earning abilities, are morally arbitrary, a matter of luck.

Rawls's attitude to responsibility is complex. He wants to avoid making justice depend on preinstitutional concepts of responsibility or desert. But he wants also to conceive of people as responsible for their own ends and conceptions of the good. Whether these aims are in tension has been discussed in the literature, if not resolved (see and cf. Nozick 1974, p. 214; Cohen 1989, pp. 914–915; Scheffler 1992, p. 321; Scanlon 1988; Ripstein 1994; Woodard 1998).

Less discussed is a different but more fundamental tension in Rawls's attitude to responsibility.[2] Suppose it is true that concepts of responsibility and desert play no significant role in a theory of justice at the level of fundamental principle. How then could it be fundamental to our conception of justice that no one is responsible for or deserves his distribution of natural assets, or that it is unjust to allow distributive shares to be influenced by such morally arbitrary factors? (See and cf. Rawls 1971, secs. 12, 48; Scheffler 1992; Roemer 1996; Arneson forthcoming; Woodard 1998.) The motivating thought that natural assets are a matter of luck is not independent of the thought that people are not responsible for them. If the former is fundamental to justice, then so is the concept of responsibility.

Now part of the answer may lie in the way Rawls's thought has developed, from the more Kantian, luck-neutralizing emphasis of *A Theory of Justice* to his later focus on pluralism, political neutrality, and the avoid-

---

1. This description of primary goods does not resolve the question whether the list or the universal means formulation is more basic, if these come apart. It also does not address the place of liberty.

2. But it surfaces in the contrast between the incompatible readings of Rawls found in Roemer 1996 and in Scheffler 1992.

ance of controversy over metaphysics and ideals (1985; 1993; 2001.).[3] Perhaps the charge that the noted tension is present in Rawls's work can be defended against by differentiating his earlier and later views. I doubt, however, that this is the whole story; the tension is to some extent internal to *A Theory of Justice* (compare secs. 12 and 48).

But let's put this exegetical issue aside. It is worth spelling out and emphasizing the substantive point. If you judge that no one is responsible for his natural assets, you make a negative judgement, true. But it is still a judgment about responsibility, which essentially employs the concept of responsibility. A negative application of a concept is no less an application of it than a positive application. If significant consequences for distributive justice flow from such negative applications, then this concept does indeed play a fundamental role in the theory of justice. To judge that rewards are not required because people are not responsible for their natural abilities makes responsibility just as central to distributive justice as it would be if

---

3. He is especially concerned by claims to metaphysical and moral truth. Rawls writes that his conception of justice as fairness "presents itself not as a conception of justice that is true, but one that can serve as a basis of informed and willing political agreement between citizens viewed as free and equal persons." Given the existence of "conflicting and incommensurable conceptions of the good," a fundamental feature of modern societies that social theory must recognize, we secure this agreement by trying, "so far as we can, to avoid disputed philosophical, as well as disputed moral and religious, questions. We do this not because these questions are unimportant or regarded with indifference, but because we think them too important and recognize that there is no way to resolve them politically . . . Philosophy as the search for truth about an independent metaphysical and moral order cannot, I believe, provide a workable and shared basis for a political conception of justice in a democratic society." "[A] conception of the person in a political view . . . need not involve . . . questions of philosophical psychology or a metaphysical doctrine of the nature of the self. No political view that depends on these deep and unresolved matters can serve as a public conception of justice in a constitutional democratic state." In such a state, under modern conditions, conflicting and incommensurable conceptions of the good are bound to exist; this fundamental social fact must be recognized by any viable political conception of justice that avoids reliance on authoritarian use of state power. The absence of commitment to moral ideals, even liberal ideals such as autonomy, he regards as essential to liberalism as a political doctrine; there is no practicable answer for political purposes to the question of the true good, since public agreement cannot be obtained. Rawls 1985, pp. 230–231, 245, 249. See also Rawls 1993 on why the idea of moral truth is not a suitable basis of public justification, e.g. at p. 129, and the chapter titled "The Idea of Public Reason."

instead one judged that rewards are required because people are responsible, if not for their natural abilities, then nevertheless for the actions they enable.[4]

That is a short argument for a luck-neutralizing view of the deep structure of Rawls's egalitarianism in *A Theory of Justice*—almost certainly too short. But the literature on the currency of egalitarian justice that took Rawls's theory as a point of departure can be given a more elaborate interpretation to the same effect. Sen and Dworkin considered the question "equality of what?" and put forward various cases that any plausible answer had to handle correctly. Cohen, Arneson, and Roemer went on to diagnose the constraints these cases imposed as reflecting the luck-neutralizing deep structure of egalitarianism. According to some versions of the luck-neutralizing account (see, e.g., Roemer 1996), the fundamental role of responsibility was already implicit in Rawls's theory of distributive justice. What follows provides an overview of the "equality of what?" debate, so interpreted.

2. Welfare and Resources, Handicaps and Expensive Tastes

In his "Equality of What?" (1980), Amartya Sen contrasted resource egalitarianism not just with utilitarianism, but also with welfare egalitarianism. He distinguished the aim to equalize people's welfare levels (levels of utility or of preference satisfaction) from the aim to equalize their resource levels (levels of income or of Rawlsian primary goods). He criticized both aims, and proposed instead the aim to equalize people's basic capabilities. Sen's influential discussion was followed shortly afterward by a pair of articles by Ronald Dworkin (1981a; 1981b), in which Dworkin argued that distributive justice should be conceived not in terms of equality of welfare but rather in terms of equality of resources. But Dworkin's conception of resources was refined in order to deal with Sen's criticisms of using income

---

4. These remarks in effect side against Scheffler's reading of Rawls as avoiding fundamental dependence on concepts of responsibility and with Roemer's reading of Rawls as containing the embryo of the later explicit egalitarian concern with responsibility. See Roemer 1996; 1987, p. 216; see also Arneson forthcoming, who attributes the fundamental concern with compensating for misfortune or bad luck to Rawls. My view similarly reads Rawls as holding that people are not responsible for their natural assets, hence as employing the concept of responsibility, rather than holding that the concept of responsibility is incoherent.

or primary goods as the currency of justice, and to incorporate some of Sen's concerns with capabilities.

The "equality-of-what?" discussion revolves around several salient reference points (paraphrased here from Sen and Dworkin). Consider first the principle of equalizing income or primary goods (similar remarks apply to a maximin resource principle, such as Rawls's Difference Principle, which allows departures from equality of resources that benefit the worst off). Such a principle does not give any more resources to a disabled person than to others, in virtue of his disability. As a result, he may be worse off than others with respect to basic capabilities and to welfare. A given income level may support various basic capabilities, including normal mobility, for people without handicaps. But it will not support the same capabilities, for example, for a blind person who needs to spend a significant part of this income just to feed his guide dog. Moreover, other things equal, it arguably takes more income to get a disabled person to the same welfare level as someone without a handicap; handicaps tend to make for the inefficient generation of welfare. The aim to equalize resources ignores these differences. The motivating intuition here is that resource egalitarianism so understood does not treat handicaps correctly.

Consider next the principle of equalizing welfare levels. This principle gives more income or resources to the disabled in order to get them to the same level of welfare as those without handicaps. However, it also gives more income to people with expensive tastes. Why? If we simply plot welfare against income, we find that expensive tastes look like handicaps: they make for inefficient generation of welfare. Both make people less well-off than others are, other things (including income) equal.

But surely there is a distinction relevant to justice between a handicapped person and someone with champagne tastes. We don't want to be forced to subsidize expensive tastes just because we do want to subsidize the handicapped. But the principle of equalizing welfare does not distinguish between these cases. It just sees what they have in common: the inefficient generation of welfare. From the point of view of justice we want to know more: we want to know *why* welfare is generated the way it is, how things came to be that way. The operative intuition here is that welfare egalitarianism does not correctly distinguish between handicaps and expensive tastes.

Nor does it consider, when someone has cheap tastes, whether a truncated conception of success in life has been the only viable survival strategy for that person, as in the case of the "tame housewife." Welfare egalitarianism would take her preferences, which cost relatively little to satisfy, at face value without enquiring into their genesis, and so would give her fewer resources. This and other cases of endogenous preference formation raise further complex issues (see Roemer 1996; Elster 1983; Barry forthcoming).

Focusing on levels of primary goods instead of welfare treats whether people have cheap or expensive tastes as their own business. It does avoid subsidizing expensive tastes. But, as we have seen, it also treats whether people have handicaps as their own business, and fails to compensate for them. So this version of resource egalitarianism does not correctly distinguish handicaps from expensive tastes either.

So far we have two constraints as reference points: the need to compensate for handicaps, and the need to distinguish between handicaps and expensive tastes. A third is provided by the case of someone who, despite being disabled, has an unusually cheerful, well-adapted personality: Tiny Tim. Suppose he is so cheerful that he reaches higher welfare levels, other things equal, than people without handicaps. Neither the principle of equalizing resources nor the principle of equalizing welfare will give Tiny Tim extra resources to compensate for his disability per se. The principle of equalizing welfare may even take resources away from him, since he is so content. The constraining intuition here is that this is unfair. Tiny Tim should receive compensation for his disability. If he manages to be well-adapted and happy despite that, the more power to him. A just distribution would not divert resources from him relative to others because of his cheerful disposition.

3. Capabilities, Internalized Resources, and Dworkin's Distinctions

Sen and Dworkin make different but related proposals to handle these three cases, among others. Both resource and welfare egalitarianism suffer, in Sen's view (1980), from their failure to focus on what given resource levels allow different people to do. He develops this insight into the proposal that distributive justice requires equal basic capabilities, which he distinguishes from both resource and welfare egalitarianism. The disabled should be compensated so as to give them the same basic abilities to function as others, not in order to raise them to certain welfare levels. So Tiny Tim's cheerfulness is not held against him: he should have the same basic capabilities as others, however content he is. Nor are expensive tastes a ground for compensation, unless it can be argued that they disable basic functionings.

We can relate the idea of basic capabilities to the idea of primary goods. For purposes of distributive justice, primary goods are often assimilated to income and other external resources. But in retrospect, the conception of primary goods as universal means to whatever your ends happen to be can in principle accommodate basic capabilities themselves as among primary goods, even if this is not the way the conception was originally applied. Normal capabilities to get around, to see, and so on, are just as much universal means to whatever your ends happen to be as income, food, and other external goods. If such capabilities count as resources, then handicaps should count as negative resources, and equalizing resources will compensate for handicaps and will at least have a tendency to equalize basic capabilities.

Dworkin makes a proposal along these lines that he offers not as an alternative to equalizing resources but as a better understanding of what it is to equalize resources. He argues that handicaps are indeed negative resources, and equality of resources demands that disabled persons receive extra resources in compensation. More generally, he holds that resource egalitarianism should be understood to have the general aim of equalizing people with respect to their differential endowments, but not their differential ambitions. The refined conception of resources should reflect the distinction between people and the circumstances they find themselves in. People's preferences reflect differences in people themselves, while endowments—including some talents and handicaps—are merely circumstantial. Differences attributable to people themselves, such as expensive tastes, will be left undisturbed by Dworkin's resource egalitarianism, but differences attributable to different circumstances will be corrected. If Tiny Tim's sunny disposition is attributable to him rather than to his circumstances, it will not offset compensation for his handicap. Dworkin develops this distinction between people and their circumstances, and a measure of resources that reflects it, by means of the idea of a hypothetical insurance market, in which people could buy insurance against turning out to be handicapped. The insurance premiums model the tax payments people make under a progressive tax system.

Suppose two people have the same talents and other initial endowments. One chooses hard work and gets rich; the other chooses a more leisurely life and does not get rich. Dworkin's resource egalitarianism will respect their different preferences between wealth and leisure. Since the two have equal earning abilities, their difference in wealth does not flow from a negative resource endowment that demands compensation, as a handicap would. The two have the same resource endowment, valued ex ante. This is not altered by whether they prefer to transform it into wealth or leisure, or their resulting levels of welfare. So Dworkinian equality of resources will not equalize the income levels that result from their different choices.

What about different preferences about risk? If people choose to gamble when they could have insured, but they lose, justice does not require they be compensated, on Dworkin's view. The gamble is valued ex ante, not after the result is known. Like their choices between work and leisure, people's choices to accept or avoid risk are respected, even if these choices result in unequal income or welfare levels.[5] Good or bad "option luck" is attributed to people, since they choose to run the relevant risks instead of avoiding them by, say, insuring. By contrast, good or bad "brute luck" is attributed to circumstances. People who are born with handicaps do not choose to run the risk of being disabled, and cannot actually take out insurance against being born disabled. Such handicaps count as bad brute luck, so demand compensation.

We may wonder why people are to be identified with their preferences but not their endowments. If you ask people which aspects of themselves they identify with and which they regard as merely the circumstances they find themselves in, you would no doubt find that many people identify more strongly with certain inborn characteristics, such as their race or their gender, than with anything else (see and cf. Moon 1988). Should people be identified in terms of their preferences if they identify themselves most strongly with their endowments? Of course, people are far more likely to identify with their talents than with their handicaps, as Dworkin recognizes (1981b, p. 316). This raises issues about whether talents and handicaps should be treated symmetrically—as good and bad luck, respectively.[6]

4. Differences for Which People Are Not Responsible

People versus circumstances; preferences versus endowments: the two distinctions don't quite line up. Against this background came Gerald Co-

---

5. When identical choices to gamble yield different outcomes, this may be hard to accept; see Roemer 1986, chap. 7.

6. I take a pass at related questions in Chapter 10.

hen's claim that the fundamental distinction motivating egalitarian intuitions about how to handle the critical cases correctly is not exactly either
of these, but rather the distinction between responsibility and brute luck.
"For anyone who thinks that initial advantage and inherent capacity are
unjust distributors thinks so because he believes that they make a person's
fate depend too much on sheer luck" (Cohen 1989, p. 932). People are
responsible for aspects of their situation attributable to choice, but not for
aspects of their situation attributable to brute luck. Egalitarianism should
aim to neutralize differences due to luck, for which people are not responsible, whether these are differences in welfare or resource levels. But it
should not aim to neutralize differences due to choice, for which people
are responsible, again whether these are welfare or resource differences.
Cohen sums this up by claiming that what should be equalized is *access to
advantage*.[7]

Dworkin's distinctions may often be relevant to the issue of responsibility, but they do not settle it. We may assume that people are not responsible for their handicaps, but normally are responsible for their preferences,
including expensive tastes. That would explain why we normally think
handicaps but not expensive tastes require compensation. But if someone is actually not responsible for her expensive tastes, equal access to advantage requires that they should be treated like handicaps and provide
grounds for compensation. As Cohen explains, advantage has both resource and welfare dimensions. Tiny Tim would be compensated despite
his high welfare levels on the assumption that his movement disability but
not his happy disposition is properly regarded as a matter of luck. On the
other hand, if someone can move but after moving suffers pain, his welfare
deficit may be a matter of bad luck that requires compensation so that he
can buy expensive medicine to prevent the pain.

Cohen articulates the deep structure of the "equality of what?" debate by relocating Dworkin's cut. Responsibility versus luck is the dis-
positive issue, not preference versus endowment and not welfare versus resources. Cohen claims that his distinction between responsibility and luck
is truer to the motivation of Dworkin's resource-egalitarian theory than
Dworkin's own distinctions. The distinction between responsibility and
luck cuts across the distinction between welfare and resources. Rather
than refine our conception of resources and endowments, as Dworkin

---

7. Arneson (1989; 1990) develops a closely related view that focuses on opportunity
for welfare as equalisandum. See also the discussion in Roemer 1996, chap. 8.

does, to try to capture the responsibility / luck distinction, we should admit that the two are independent and that the responsibility / luck distinction is fundamental. Either resource or welfare differences require redistribution if they are morally arbitrary or due to luck, but not if they are due to responsible choice.

Cohen's most fundamental contrast is between responsibility and the lack of it. Luck is understood negatively, as whatever negates responsibility. He opposes luck variously to choice, to control, and to hypothetical choice (see, e.g., 1989, pp. 916, 924, 938). These are not equivalent, but they all arguably bear on responsibility.

In response to an example of Scanlon's, Cohen concedes that the contrast between choice and luck does not do quite all the work needed to delineate the equalisandum of distributive justice. Scanlon's religious believer has a particularly onerous, guilt-inducing creed. Differences in religious beliefs can produce differences in welfare levels. Such beliefs are often not chosen, but come with upbringing. But even so it can seem distinctly odd to regard someone's unchosen but burdensome religion as a matter of bad luck and a basis for compensation. That would be incompatible with regarding it as a matter of commitment and conviction, valued and adhered to as correct even if not chosen.

Cohen admits that it is neither because of his choice nor because of bad luck that Scanlon's believer suffers. Not just actual choice, but also hypothetical choice, can be opposed to luck. The disadvantages that do not count as bad luck are not just those traceable to the subject's actual choice but also those costs so intrinsically connected with his unchosen commitments that he would not choose to be without them even if he could. Because the religious believer identifies with his unchosen commitments and would not choose to be free of them if he could so choose, they do not count as bad luck. Unfortunately, as Roemer (1996, chap. 8) points out, this amendment also tells us not to compensate the tame housewife if she identifies with her lowly preferences and would not choose to be without them.

Roemer (1996, chap. 7) credits Dworkin with moving issues of responsibility, which appeared only embryonically in the work of Rawls and Sen, to center stage, but he questions Dworkin's criterion of responsibility. He sees Dworkin's cut between ambitions and endowments as motivated by the view that people are responsible for their preferences, so long as they identify with them and are glad they have them, regardless of whether they were voluntarily or involuntarily cultivated (see also Scanlon 1986; 1988).

But Roemer doubts that people should necessarily be held responsible on this basis for their preferences, tastes, and ambitions.[8]

If someone is not responsible for her circumstances, Roemer asks, why should she be responsible for the preferences she has adopted because of them? Is it enough to answer: Because she identifies with them and would not choose not to have them? Compare two reference points: the tame housewife and the person brought up in an ascetic religion. Both have cheap tastes, and both identify with them and would not choose not to have them. But Roemer doubts the two cases for that reason raise similar demands of distributive justice. Intuitively, there is a stronger case for giving extra resources to the housewife than to the ascetic. The identification and hypothetical-choice criteria of responsibility for preferences do not capture the difference between the ascetic and the tame housewife: these criteria count neither as a case of bad luck. Unfortunately, the difference is not captured by the criterion of voluntariness or by the criterion of responsibility for circumstances, either: neither the tame housewife nor the ascetic voluntarily acquired the relevant beliefs and preferences, and neither is responsible for the circumstances that produced these preferences, so on these criteria both would count as cases of bad luck. Roemer suggests that the critical point is that the tame housewife's truncated preferences were adopted as a survival strategy, because opportunities were objectively lacking. But the relationship of this survival-strategy criterion to responsibility is unclear. These remain hard cases for everyone.

Roemer reads resource egalitarianism not as unconcerned with welfare, but rather as concerned only with the morally arbitrary part of welfare. He proposes that resource bundles should be measured by the degree of mor-

---

8. Roemer (1996) sees Dworkin as adopting an identification-based conception of responsibility and so taking a questionable view of responsibility as extending to preferences, but nevertheless as intending a responsibility / luck cut. By contrast, Roemer sees Cohen as adopting a different, control-based conception of responsibility such that, because of this semantic difference between Dworkin and Cohen, Cohen does not see Dworkin's cut as a responsibility / luck cut but rather as in need of relocation to align it with a responsibility / luck cut. Roemer does not regard this semantic difference as deep, and sees Cohen's view, and Arneson's closely related view, as the intellectual descendant of Dworkin's placing of responsibility in a central role.

However, in view of Cohen's invocation of hypothetical choice to deal with Scanlon's case, the contrast between his view and Dworkin's is more subtle than this; see Cohen 1989, pp. 937–938.

ally arbitrary welfare they produce. To the extent different abilities to generate welfare are a matter of luck, they count as different resources. Suppose people's different constitutions lead to different endorphin levels and hence to different preferences and different abilities to generate welfare. If people are not responsible for their constitutions and hence their endorphin levels, then the measure of these internal resources is the degree of welfare they produce. On Roemer's view, what initially appears as a difference between people for which they are responsible, the result of their own preferences, turns out, when we reflect on the further causes, to be a difference traceable to endowments or internal resources, for which people are not responsible. The thought that people cannot be responsible for their preferences if they are not responsible for their causes ultimately threatens the distinction between welfare egalitarianism and resource egalitarianism. If people are not responsible for their preferences, then equalizing resources understood in this way requires equalizing welfare (Roemer 1986; cf. Roemer 1996, chap. 7; Scanlon 1986).[9]

5. Luck-Neutralizing: Interpretation versus Aspiration

The luck-neutralizing account of egalitarianism explains the deep structure of recent debates about distributive justice. As a diagnosis or interpretation of contemporary egalitarianism, it is illuminating and convincing. However, recognition that this is what we have been up to in theorizing about distributive justice can prompt a renewed critical distance. With this deepened understanding, we can step back to consider whether luck-neutralization is indeed the best way to develop or to defend egalitarianism. Is this conception best as aspiration as well as best as interpretation?

In asking this, we do not risk changing the subject. Justice is a deep concept; there is no definitional stop, no sharp line between understanding and revising our concept of justice. Even if certain links between justice and responsibility have been assumed, they may not hold up under critical probing. Placing responsibility in certain demanding roles at the heart of

---

9. To avoid complications, this brief noncomprehensive survey omits the influential contributions of Arneson to the development of luck-neutralizing egalitarianism. While these are important, they do not raise different issues for my purposes here than do the contributions of Cohen and Roemer. In particular, I do not believe they provide a way around my arguments about the limitations of luck-neutralizing egalitarianism (for insightful discussion of Arneson's position, see Roemer 1996, chap. 8.1).

distributive justice may make justice hostage to questions about the conditions and extent of responsibility, in the way that Rawls's later work especially tries to avoid. It may mean that what justice demands will depend on exactly what, if anything, we are responsible for (cf. Roemer 1987, p. 216; 1993; 1995). It may call for judgments about responsibility for which there is simply no clear basis.

Perhaps, as Cohen suggests, it is just tough luck that justice is up to its neck in difficult problems about responsibility and free will: something we have to live with (1989, p. 934). But we can look again at the possible roles of responsibility in justice. Some of them may cohere better than others with what we have learned about responsibility. The luck-neutralizing account of justice backs into the role of responsibility from a focus on intuitions about distributive justice. A complementary approach, which is taken in this book, is to articulate various conditions of responsibility and their relations to control, choice, hypothetical choice, and so on, and then to work forward to consider the possible roles of these concepts in an account of justice. Perhaps we can avoid placing responsibility in highly problematic roles within a theory of distributive justice, while still giving it its due.

6

Why the Aim to Neutralize Luck
Cannot Provide a Basis
for Egalitarianism

1. Introduction

Gerald Cohen has claimed that a large part of the fundamental egalitarian aim is to neutralize the influence on distribution of luck, that is, of factors for which people are not responsible (Cohen 1989, p. 908).[1] In his view, recall, "anyone who thinks that initial advantage and inherent capacity are unjust distributors thinks so because he believes that they make a person's fate depend too much on sheer luck" (1989, p. 932). His version of egalitarianism is guided by the thought that "the fundamental distinction for an egalitarian is between choice and luck in the shaping of people's fates" (1989, pp. 907–908).

Cohen argues that his cut between choice and luck is truer to the motivation of Ronald Dworkin's resource-egalitarian theory of justice than Dworkin's own suggested cut between preferences and resources. While luck can fall on either side of the preference / resource divide, genuine choice contrasts with luck (1989, p. 931). Cohen in this way incorporates

---

1. Dworkin (1981a) and Cohen (1989) distinguish "brute luck" from "option luck." On this usage, people can be responsible for the results of option luck, for example, by choosing to run risks. But people are not responsible for what is a matter of brute luck. In Cohen's view, egalitarians aim to neutralize brute luck, or influences on distribution for which people are not responsible. However, there has also been a tendency simply to use "luck" rather than "brute luck" to refer to factors for which people are not responsible; Cohen himself slips into this thin usage of "luck" later in his 1989 article. On this usage, Cohen's view is that egalitarians aim to neutralize luck. I adopt this thin usage, defended in Chapter 4. If people are responsible for their "option luck," then, in the thin sense, it is not really a matter of luck for them. Option luck, rather, is luck in the thick sense of lottery luck; see Chapter 4.

within his version of egalitarianism what he regards as the most powerful ideas in the arsenal of the anti-egalitarian right: the ideas of choice and responsibility.

I agree that it has been implicit in much egalitarian theorizing that the fundamental motivating aim of egalitarianism is to neutralize luck. Cohen, along with John Roemer and Richard Arneson, have made this assumption explicit and articulated it with admirable clarity. They have advanced the discussion of justice to a new stage by doing so.

Nevertheless, I argue that the aim to neutralize luck cannot provide a basis for egalitarianism. The term "basis" is ambiguous, but I choose it deliberately to cover two possibilities. The luck-neutralizing aim might be held to provide a basis for egalitarianism in at least two different senses; I deny that it can do so in either sense.

First, the aim to neutralize luck could explicate egalitarianism. It could contribute to identifying and specifying what egalitarianism is and what it demands, though without providing any independent justification or reason for egalitarianism. I refer to this as the *specification* sense of "basis."

Second, the aim to neutralize luck could provide some independent, non-question-begging reason or justification for egalitarianism. I refer to this as the *justification* sense of "basis." The literature on luck-neutralizing egalitarianism does not always make it clear which of these two claims is in play.

In order to argue that the aim to neutralize luck cannot provide a basis for egalitarianism in either of these senses, I will assume that there is some minimal independent constraint on what could count as egalitarianism. Otherwise, anything that the luck-neutralizing aim leads to could be stipulated to be egalitarianism, and the issue would degenerate. The minimal constraint I adopt is this. To count as egalitarian, a doctrine must, for some X, favor relatively more equal patterns of distribution of X over relatively less equal patterns of X, other things equal. It must, that is, count relative equality in the pattern of distribution in some dimension as pro tanto a good thing, even if it can be outweighed by other values. This assumption provides a *patterning* constraint: a constraint on *how* egalitarianism distributes whatever it distributes, rather than on *what* it distributes. It is a weak constraint because it does not require that genuine egalitarianism favor absolute equality, only that it favor relatively more equal patterns of distribution over relatively less equal patterns. Moreover, it does not require that this preference for more equal patterns override other values, only that it holds other things equal.

For example, an egalitarian view could hold that equalities in some dimension do not need to be justified, while departures from equality do. Or, it could show how relatively equal patterns of distribution in some dimension tend to be justified, while relatively unequal distributions tend to be more difficult to justify. But a view that requires all possible patterns of distribution to be justified on the same terms, and has no differential tendency to favor equal patterns of distribution, would not count as genuinely egalitarian, given this minimal patterning constraint.

If we combine this patterning constraint on what counts as egalitarianism with my claim that the aim to neutralize luck cannot provide a basis for egalitarianism, we get the following. First, the aim to neutralize luck does not specify a demand for relatively more equal patterns of distribution, other things equal, nor does it specify that equality should be treated as a default position, departures from which need justification. The aim to neutralize luck per se has no inherent tendency to hit the target of relatively more equal patterns of distribution. Second, the aim to neutralize luck cannot provide any independent reason or justification for favoring relatively equal patterns of distribution, other things equal.[2]

It may be tempting to think that even if the luck-neutralizing aim cannot provide any independent reason for egalitarianism, it can nevertheless at least contribute to specifying egalitarian patterns of distribution. It may seem possible to avoid my arguments, that is, by adopting the less ambitious specification strategy and forgoing any claim to luck-neutralizing justification. But I hope to show that this move does not succeed.

In this chapter, I first distinguish two roles responsibility might have in theories of distributive justice: a currency role, in determining *what* we redistribute, namely, the currency of distributive justice, and a patterning role, in determining *how* we redistribute whatever the currency is. If the aim to neutralize luck is to provide a basis for egalitarianism, then responsibility would need to play a patterning role, not just a currency role. Given the minimal constraint on egalitarianism I described above, responsibility would have not just to tell us what to distribute, but also to say something about how to distribute, and in particular to specify or justify relatively equal distributions, other things equal.

I next argue that responsibility cannot play a patterning role—cannot

---

2. In Chapter 10, I argue that egalitarianism does not need the luck-neutralizing aim, and indeed may be stronger without it.

tell us how to distribute. We cannot derive an answer to the "how?" question from a luck-neutralizing answer to the "what?" question. In particular, the aim to neutralize luck neither specifies nor provides any independent reason for favoring patterns of distribution that are more rather than less equal. There is no inherent connection between aiming to redistribute goods that are a matter of luck, and aiming to redistribute them equally. I explain how the assumption that luck-neutralization can play a patterning role in egalitarianism runs a danger of committing the *egalitarian fallacy* and is open to the *luck-neutralizer's dilemma*.

Finally, I focus on a special case of the claim that responsibility cannot play a patterning role. It may be especially tempting to suppose that, *at least if no one is responsible for anything*, then the luck-neutralizing aim requires an equal pattern of distribution. But I argue that this is not the case. I explain how the aim to neutralize the *effects* of luck is closely linked to the regression principle, which holds that responsibility for something requires responsibility for its *causes*. As we have seen in Part I, on certain plausible assumptions the regression principle makes responsibility impossible. But the universal defeat of responsibility does not provide a basis for egalitarianism either. The aim to neutralize luck cannot play a patterning role, whether responsibility is possible or impossible.

These are not arguments against egalitarianism. They are rather arguments that clarify why egalitarianism cannot be based on the aim to neutralize luck, where luck is opposed to responsibility. Perhaps egalitarianism can be based on something else, such as appeals to fairness or to desert. But these should be more carefully distinguished from appeals to responsibility than they have been in the luck-neutralizing literature. Luck-neutralizing egalitarianism is reasonably interpreted as having given responsibility, rather than something else, star billing. It is worth taking it at its word and making explicit why responsibility cannot do the needed work (even if something else can).

2. What to Distribute versus How to Distribute

Luck-neutralizing egalitarianism gives responsibility a role in defining what it is that distributive justice distributes: in defining the *currency* of egalitarian justice, as Cohen (1989) puts it. In effect, responsibility acts as a filter, which yields the equalisandum or currency of egalitarian justice. We only aim to redistribute goods that are a matter of luck for people, not goods people are responsible for. For example, we do not redistribute goods people are responsible for via their choices, including the outcomes of chosen gambles.[3] But we do redistribute manna from heaven.

However, responsibility in its currency role cannot do all the work of specifying norms of distributive justice. For present purposes, there are at least two respects in which this is true.

First, there is an obvious preliminary point, which is nevertheless helpful to keep in mind as background to my arguments. Responsibility in its currency role contributes to telling us *what* to redistribute, by in effect acting as a filter on some independently specified good or goods, but it does not determine that independent specification. For example, we could aim to equalize resources for which people are not responsible, or welfare for which people are not responsible, or both. As Cohen (1989) argues, the luck / responsibility distinction cuts across the resource / welfare distinction; both resources and welfare are covered by Cohen's conception of "advantage." The obvious point is that some such independent specification of the good is needed; it is not provided by responsibility. We don't aim to equalize just anything and everything of any kind for which someone is not responsible; that would be absurd. For a given conception of the good, responsibility filters out goods within the original specification, only letting goods pass through into the currency of distributive justice to the extent people are not responsible for them, to the extent they are a matter of luck. For example, on a choice-based understanding of the responsibility / luck distinction, goods that are (at least partially) the result of suitable choices are (at least partially) exempted from redistribution.

Second, we should distinguish the question of *what* we aim to redistribute from the question of *how* we aim to redistribute: the currency of distributive justice from the pattern of distribution demanded by justice. A rule or function specifying a pattern of distribution cannot be applied until what we are distributing is defined. In that sense currency issues are prior to patterning issues. Nevertheless, knowing *what* to redistribute does not tell us *how* to redistribute it. Applied to luck-neutralizing views, the point is that the currency role of responsibility does not specify any particular pattern of distribution of the currency. The fact that we aim only to redistribute goods that are a matter of luck, for which people are not responsible, does not tell us how to distribute these goods or to favor more equal

---

3. Again, if people are responsible for their "option luck," then it is not part of what luck-neutralizing egalitarian aims to neutralize.

distributions in particular. This second point is central to my arguments in this chapter.

For example, consider the distinction Parfit (1995) draws between equality and priority. This is a distinction in the space of patterns, not currencies: in "how" space, not in "what" space. Equality proper is an interpersonal relation, between the actual states of different people. By contrast, views that give priority to the worse off, such as a maximin view, are concerned with the relations between individuals' actual states and other possible states they might have been in, with whether people are worse off than they might have been, and with absolute levels of well-being. According to priority views, benefits to the worse off matter more, not because of the relationship of the worse off to other people, but because of the absolute level the worse off are at. Maximin can be regarded as an extreme form of a priority view, according to which benefits to the worst off matter most. On a priority view, equality between people can, under certain assumptions, be a means to making the worse off better off (see Cohen 1992), but the relation of equality between people per se is not an essential concern. Equality between people is of merely instrumental value on the priority view.[4]

Suppose we aim to redistribute goods that are a matter of luck—manna from heaven. Does this determine whether we should aim to equalize goods that are a matter or luck or instead aim to maximin goods that are a matter of luck? No.

This aim may seem to favor equality over maximin for the following reason. If maximin requires an unequal distribution of goods that are a matter of luck, because of incentive and trickle-down effects, then there will be differences between people with respect to goods that are a matter of luck. It may thus seem that maximin does not neutralize luck, whereas equality would.

However, this is an illusion. If we equalize instead of maximin goods that are a matter of luck, then there will be equalities between people with respect to goods that are a matter of luck. But people are no more responsible for an equal distribution of goods that are a matter of luck than they are for an unequal distribution. Equalities can be just as much a matter of

4. This may be an advantage to the priority view. While the priority view has egalitarian consequences, it will not be subject to some of the objections that a view favoring equality per se is subject to, such as objections to leveling everyone down to the worst-off position for the sake of equality.

luck as inequalities. The fact that people are *not* responsible for *difference* does not entail that they *are* responsible for *nondifference*. There is no more a priori reason to assume that equalities are not a matter of luck than there is to assume that differences are not a matter of luck: people may not be responsible for either. If so, then equalizing no more neutralizes luck than maximining does. Aiming to redistribute only goods that are a matter of luck does not require us to eliminate only one kind of relation that is a matter of luck and not another: to eliminate only differences and not equalities that are a matter of luck. Since this aim neither specifies nor justifies favoring equality as a default position, it does not favor equality over maximin. In particular, it does not require us to equalize rather than to maximin manna from heaven. People are not responsible for equal amounts of manna, or any other particular amounts; they are not responsible for it at all.

The point can be put more formally as follows. It is a fallacy to infer from:

(9) It is a matter of luck that *a* and *b* are unequal

to:

(10) It would not be a matter of luck if *a* and *b* were equal.

This is just as fallacious as the move from:

(11) It is a matter of luck that *a* and *b* are equal

to:

(12) It would not be a matter of luck if *a* and *b* were unequal.

The move from (9) to (10) can be called the *egalitarian fallacy,* since it could be used in an attempt to specify or justify an egalitarian pattern of distribution. While the move from (9) to (10) might be subliminally tempting to egalitarians, the move from (11) to (12) will not be. But both moves are fallacious. One reason for this is that both fail to respect the scope distinction between internal and external negation (that is, between negation outside the scope of the operator "It is / would be a matter of luck that . . . ," and negation inside its scope). In the arguments that follow I expose points at which the egalitarian fallacy might be tacitly relied on. However, I am not accusing any particular egalitarian of committing this fallacy. Since the move is obviously fallacious when made explicit, it would be present only implicitly and would raise exegetical issues that are not my concern here.[5]

I have argued that there is no inherent connection between equality and what people are responsible for. Giving people what they are responsible for is what would neutralize luck, not giving them something else they are not responsible for. Therefore, there is no inherent connection between equality and neutralizing luck.

Here is an objection. It might be agreed that responsibility neither specifies nor justifies taking equality as a default position. Nevertheless, it might be held that equality should be taken as a default position anyway, perhaps on some other basis. Then responsibility can be used to justify departures from equality. Call this the *equality-default view*. Within such an egalitarian view, responsibility does seem to play a role in determining how to redistribute, since inequalities are either permitted or not by reference to responsibility. This view does not *argue* for the claim that it would not be a matter of luck if *a* and *b* were equal, so there is no danger of its being

---

5. For example, see and compare Steiner 1994, p. 216: "[I]f . . . no criterion for relevantly differentiating cases can be eligible to serve as a standard of distributive justice, the inference must be that no cases can be regarded as relevantly different: that is, all cases are relevantly alike. In this context that means that the freedom distribution mandated by justice is an equal one, that everyone is justly entitled to equal freedom."

Does this passage express the egalitarian fallacy? It depends on whether there is a valid scope distinction between "it is not the case that there is a relevant difference between *a* and *b*" and "*a* is not-relevantly-different from *b;* that is, *a* is relevantly similar to *b*." And that may vary with the specific standards of relevance in play. In the latter, internal sense of lack of relevant difference, lack of relevant difference would be conceptually equivalent to relevant similarity. The very same considerations that would be needed to establish relevant similarity would be needed to establish lack of relevant difference. But in the former, external sense of lack of relevant difference, there would simply be an absence of evidence for relevant difference. This is compatible with an equal lack of evidence for relevant similarity.

Suppose that what makes for a relevant similarity between *a* and *b* is their responsibility for similar positions and that what makes for a relevant difference is responsibility for different positions. Then it could be true that *a* and *b* were neither relevantly similar nor relevantly different, since it could be true that *a* and *b* are neither responsible for similar positions nor for different positions. Under this interpretation (which may be somewhat strained and which I do not claim is the correct way to interpret Steiner), Steiner's remark would be an expression of the egalitarian fallacy.

propped up by the egalitarian fallacy. Rather, it is simply not concerned with whether equalities are a matter of luck or not.

The equality-default view is at issue when the formulation "neutralize differences that are a matter of luck," or similar formulations in terms of "advantages" or "disadvantages," are used to express the luck-neutralizing aim. If we aim only to neutralize *differences* that are a matter of luck, then we are not concerned with whether equalities are a matter of luck or not. This view in effect helps itself to equality as the default position. If you equate the aim to neutralize luck with the aim to neutralize only differences, as opposed to other relations, that are a matter of luck, then you are equating the aim to neutralize luck with the equality-default view. It is critical for my purposes to distinguish the aim to neutralize only differences that are a matter of luck from the more general aim to neutralize luck. Only by distinguishing them can we register that the general aim to neutralize luck neither specifies nor justifies aiming to neutralize only differences that are a matter of luck.

Suppose we concede for the sake of argument that responsibility can contribute to determining what counts as an egalitarian pattern, within the equality-default view. Inequalities are either allowed or disallowed by reference to responsibility. But this is still not a case in which responsibility provides a basis for egalitarianism, since responsibility ex hypothesi provides no basis for the specifically egalitarian aspect of this view: that is, for its assumption of equality in particular as the default position, departures from which require justification.

To see this, consider a different view, the *inequality-default view*. This view instead takes an unequal distribution as the default position: aristocrats should have more than peasants, whether this is a matter of luck or not. Departures from this inequality, including equality, need to be justified by responsibility. Only equalities for which people are responsible are permitted, not equalities that are a matter of luck.

Responsibility plays a patterning role in the inequality-default view to just the same extent it does in the equality-default view. The specifically egalitarian character of the equality-default view owes nothing to the aim to neutralize luck. The choice of default position is a feature that can vary quite independently of the patterning role of responsibility. There is no inherent connection between luck and responsibility, on the one hand, and the choice of equality as default, on the other. Thus, the aim to neutralize luck does not specify the egalitarianism of the equality-default view, even if it does play a patterning role once the default has been independently specified.

In response, someone may grant the importance of distinguishing the currency and patterning roles—the "what" and "how" questions about distribution—and concede that knowing what does not tell us how. But he may go on to suggest that responsibility be used only to answer the currency question, to act as a filter that yields the equalisandum of distributive justice. It need not be used to answer the question about pattern, about how to distribute. Something else, such as fairness, can be used to answer the question about pattern.

My reply is that this suggestion concedes that the luck-neutralizing aim does not provide a basis for egalitarianism. For it to do that, it must be possible to derive some egalitarian patterning implications from the luck-neutralizing aim. Here I am appealing to the minimal patterning constraint on what can count as egalitarianism. For example, there is no reason to regard a doctrine that tells us to redistribute what people are not responsible for as a form of egalitarianism, if it tells us to redistribute very unequally, in a way that exaggerates rather than mitigates any prior inequalities. If responsibility merely tells us what to redistribute, but something else, such as an appeal to fairness or to deservingness, tells us to favor relatively equal distributions, then in the relevant sense responsibility does not specify an egalitarian pattern of redistribution in particular, even if it plays some role in specifying egalitarian demands overall. Responsibility and luck are not doing the essentially egalitarian pattern-specifying work. I emphasize that I am not claiming that nothing else could do that work, only that responsibility and luck cannot.

3. The Luck Neutralizer's Dilemma

So far I have argued that the aim to neutralize luck does not favor equality over priority views, and that the equality-default view does not provide a counterexample to my claim that this aim can neither specify nor justify egalitarianism. In this section I give a more general argument for this claim by means of a dilemma. In the following section I argue that there are deeper underlying problems with the very idea that responsibility can specify any particular pattern as the goal of redistribution, whether egalitarian or otherwise.

What is meant by "bad luck"? The phrase is ambiguous, between interpersonal and counterfactual readings. In the *interpersonal* reading, I compare my situation with other people's situations. I have bad luck when what I and others have is a matter of luck, and I am worse off than others. In the *counterfactual* reading, I compare my actual situation with other possible situations I might have been in. I have bad luck when what I have is a matter of luck and I am worse off than I might have been. The badness of my luck can be assessed by comparison either to how well off others are, or by comparison to how well off I might have been.

For example, suppose each of us has the same amount of goods, which is a matter of luck for each of us. This is not interpersonal bad luck for any of us, and it may or may not be counterfactual bad luck for each of us, depending on how well off each person might have been instead. Suppose we then all become worse off by the same amount, and none of us is responsible for the respective results. In the interpersonal sense, the result is still not bad luck for anyone. In the counterfactual sense, the results are bad luck for each of us, on the assumption that each of us might have been better off (as we were originally). If only one of us had become worse off, and was not responsible for the result, the result would be both interpersonal and counterfactual bad luck for that one.[6]

In neither sense of "bad luck," I shall argue, does the aim to neutralize bad luck either nontrivially specify or justify equality as a principle of redistribution. Here's the *luck neutralizer's dilemma:*

First horn of dilemma: On the one hand, consider interpersonal bad luck, which involves my situation's being worse than that of others with respect to goods that are a matter of luck. Inequality is used to identify the badness of my luck. So an equal pattern of distribution of whatever is a matter of luck would neutralize the badness of my luck. But this specification of equality by the aim to neutralize interpersonal bad luck is trivial. By definition, I would not have interpersonal bad luck if I were no worse off than others in respect of goods that are a matter of luck. Using inequality to identify the badness of luck in this way provides no luck-related reason to favor equality as a pattern of distribution of whatever is a matter of luck. Even if equality in matters of luck does not count as interpersonal *bad*

---

6. The interpersonal and counterfactual readings of bad luck should strictly be expressed as matters of degree: how bad my luck is is a matter of how much worse off I am, relative either to others or to myself in other possible situations. The range of comparisons that calibrates the degree of good or bad luck is given either interpersonally or counterfactually. But for the sake of simplicity I shall omit this refinement; it does not affect the argument.

luck, nevertheless, equality can be just as much a matter of luck as inequality. The aim to neutralize interpersonal bad luck begs the question of justification and just helps itself to the goal of equality (see and cf. Parfit 1995, p. 27).

The point about the way the aim to neutralize interpersonal bad luck begs the question of justification is closely related to points already made about the equality-default view. On the interpersonal understanding of neutralizing bad luck, the aim is to eliminate just *in*equalities for which people are not responsible. Equalities for which people are not responsible are ignored. So of course the result of the exercise will be to equalize people in respects for which they are not responsible! But there is no inherently luck-related basis for favoring or defaulting to equality. (Notice that this point applies to the distribution of what is a matter of luck. Inequalities for which people *are* responsible are not here relevant.)

Second horn of dilemma: On the other hand, consider bad luck in the counterfactual sense. How well off I might have been is now used to identify the badness of my luck. So eliminating all better worlds possible for me, or putting me in the best world possible for me, would neutralize the badness of my counterfactual luck. Ditto for you. But doing this for each of us would have no inherent tendency to leave you and me equally well off. Eliminating all better worlds possible for each of us would leave us in unequal positions if we started in unequal positions. And the best world possible for me, if it is even determinate what that is, may be very different from the best world possible for you. As a result, my position could be better or worse than yours.

It might seem that a more attractive way to neutralize counterfactual bad luck would be to neutralize the *luck*, as opposed to the *badness* of the luck. What pattern are we left with when counterfactual bad luck is neutralized in this way? Again, there is no reason to think it would tend to be an equal distribution, or more equal than the starting distribution. Suppose you and I each have counterfactual bad luck. Suppose my situation is a matter of luck, and that if the factors for which I am not responsible were eliminated, then my situation would be better than it is, and I would be responsible for it. Parallel remarks apply to you. If you and I were put into these respective counterfactual positions, our bad luck in the counterfactual sense would have been neutralized. But, again, there's no reason to think the result would be equality between you and me, or would even tend toward more equal patterns of distribution. The situation I would be responsible for, if my counterfactual bad luck were neutralized in this way, may be very different from the situation you would be responsible for if your counterfactual bad luck were neutralized. Suppose it is determinate in the first place what you and I would be responsible for under these counterfactual suppositions—about which I shortly argue there is room for doubt. Even so, neutralizing counterfactual bad luck is no more inherently likely to lead from inequality to equality than to lead from one inequality to another inequality. Indeed, you and I might start out equal, as a matter of bad luck for each of us; we could both have been better off, though differently well off. In that case, neutralizing our counterfactual bad luck might lead us from equality to inequality. (Of course, someone who aims to neutralize luck does not aim to eliminate inequalities that are *not* a matter of luck, for which people *are* responsible. The point here is that rather there is no reason to think that eliminating inequalities that reflect counterfactual luck will tend to lead to equality rather than to different inequalities.)

Thus, there is no inherent connection between neutralizing counterfactual luck and equality. The idea of neutralizing bad counterfactual luck does not specify or justify an egalitarian pattern of redistribution either.

You might think you can get around the luck neutralizer's dilemma if you believe that no one is responsible for anything, or if you first use responsibility to filter the currency so that the only goods you are interested in redistributing are goods for which people are not responsible—manna from heaven. But considerations of responsibility and luck neither specify nor justify equalizing even pure manna from heaven. If people are not responsible for anything, or for any of the manna, it does not follow that they are all responsible for the same thing, or for the same amount of manna. If everything is a matter of luck, equality is no less a matter of luck than any other distribution. If no one is responsible for anything, then responsibility cannot specify or favor an equal pattern of distribution, or indeed any other. I enlarge on this specific point in section 6 below.

So the luck neutralizer's dilemma is this: the idea of bad luck is ambiguous. On the interpersonal reading neutralizing bad luck specifies equality but only trivially, by building inequality into bad luck, and does nothing to justify equality. On the counterfactual reading, neutralizing bad luck neither specifies nor justifies redistribution toward equality rather than toward various other possible patterns of redistribution. The aim to neutralize bad luck can seem to lead to equality nontrivially if one equivocates between these two readings. But on neither the interpersonal nor the counterfactual reading does the aim to neutralize bad luck provide a basis for egalitarianism. Parallel points hold for good luck. The idea that considerations of responsibility and luck justify equality as a pattern of distribution may be an illusion born of this ambiguity.

4. Problems of Interpersonal and Counterfactual Responsibility

Someone might be persuaded by the luck neutralizer's dilemma that the aim to neutralize luck cannot provide a justification for egalitarianism, but still believe that it can provide at least a specification of egalitarianism. I now want to focus on why luck neutralization cannot even do this. There are underlying problems with the very idea that responsibility could specify any particular pattern as the goal of redistribution, whether egalitarian or otherwise. These are reasons for thinking that responsibility is by its nature unsuited to a pattern-specifying role in theories of distributive justice.[7]

First, *responsibility judgments are not primarily about interpersonal relations, relations between the goods positions of different people.* I may or may not be responsible for my income level. But this is a very different question from whether I am responsible for the relation between my income level and your income level. For reasons that will emerge, I call this the *boring problem.*

Second, *responsibility judgments may not extend in any determinate way to counterfactual situations.*[8] When people are not responsible for what they have, there may not be anything determinate, either to be found or constructed, that they would be responsible for instead, under counterfactual conditions in which factors for which they are not responsible are

---

7. One qualification: as already indicated, an exception to the claim that responsibility cannot play any patterning role at all is the case in which responsibility is used merely to permit departures from an independently specified default pattern. But as I have argued above, this exception provides no counterexample to my general claim that responsibility cannot provide a basis for egalitarianism. Responsibility does not specify that only differences that are a matter of luck should be of concern, hence, that equality is the default. So I set this case aside and consider in this section the difficulties for responsibility in any more substantial patterning role, whether egalitarian or not.

8. Note that parallel problems do not arise for retributive justice: the latter does not aim to give people what they are responsible for, or would be under counterfactual conditions, but rather what they deserve on the basis of acts for which they actually are responsible. Thanks to Gerald Cohen for discussion of this point.

eliminated. For example, if Sam had not had the deprived childhood that makes his current low income bad luck for him, what would he have been responsible for instead? He might have chosen to be a workaholic or a surfer, or anything in between. I call this the *indeterminacy problem*. It makes responsibility unsuitable for any patterning role, egalitarian or otherwise.

I'll elaborate these points, beginning with the boring problem. Even when people are responsible for their own positions, it obviously does not follow that they are responsible for the *relations* between their own positions and the positions of others. Judgments of responsibility seem prima facie not to have the right form to specify a pattern of distribution across persons. Consider the judgments that I am not responsible for my musical gifts but am responsible for the wages I earn for my hard work as a psychiatric nurse. Such responsibility judgments are primarily about *relations between people and goods:* between individuals and the goods to which they are causally or constitutively related, whether by choice or by factors that are a matter of luck. These judgments are needed for responsibility to play a currency role: certain goods are up for redistribution to the extent they are a matter of luck for their possessors.

But notice what would be needed in order for responsibility to play an interpersonal patterning role. What would be directly at issue is not whether *someone's level of goods* is a matter of luck *for her.* Rather, it would be whether *relations between the levels of different people* are matters of luck *for them.* An interpersonal patterning role for responsibility would require a shift of focus from responsibility relations between an individual and the goods she enjoys to the relations between the goods positions of different people, such as relations of equality and inequality. If responsibility were to play such a role, it would require us to consider in the first instance whether people are responsible for the *relation* of their own position to that of other people—for example, whether *differences* are a matter of luck. However, this may depend on whether people are responsible for the goods they have.

How is my responsibility for my relation to others related to my responsibility for my own level of goods? Consider first the following questions about *interpersonal* luck and responsibility. Let X and Y be levels of goods enjoyed by individuals. If Ernest is responsible for X and Bertie is responsible for $X + Y$, is either responsible for the difference between their goods positions? If Eleanor is responsible for X and Kate is also responsible for X, is either responsible for the sameness of their goods positions?

In both cases, despite each person's responsibility for his or her own position, the relations between persons are at least partly a matter of luck for each of them, for a simple, uninteresting reason.

Consider responsibility for difference first. If Ernest is not responsible for Bertie's position, then he is not wholly responsible for the difference between his goods position and Bertie's.[9] While Ernest's own goods position is not a matter of luck for him, the relation between his position and Bertie's is partly a matter of luck for Ernest. Reciprocal remarks apply to Bertie. There may well be no one person who is responsible for the *relation* between Ernest and Bertie's positions, even if Ernest and Bertie are collectively responsible for it or each is partly responsible for it.

Parallel remarks apply to Eleanor and Kate and responsibility for sameness. If neither is responsible for the other's goods position, then neither is wholly responsible for the sameness of their positions. The sameness of their position may be partly a matter of luck for each of them, even though they are both responsible for their own positions.

So, if individuals are not generally responsible for other people's positions, then individuals are in general no more responsible for interpersonal sameness than for interpersonal difference of position, for this same boring, obvious reason. Even when individuals are responsible for their own positions, relations between them are at least partly matters of luck.[10]

Next consider the following questions about *counterfactual* luck and responsibility. We have just seen that even when Ernest and Bertie, Eleanor and Kate are each responsible for their own positions, it does not follow that they are responsible for the relations between their positions. But if such relations are at least partly a matter of luck for them, are there other, counterfactual relations between them that would not be a matter of luck? No, for the uninteresting reason already given: if one person is not respon-

---

9. A qualification is needed: it is conceivable that Ernest has so arranged things that whatever Bertie's currency level is, Ernest has Y less than Bertie. Then Ernest might be responsible for the difference between their currency positions even though he is not responsible for Bertie's position. A similar qualification applies to Eleanor and Kate. But these stipulations make for special and quirky cases, and do not alter the main argument of the text.

10. Roemer's framework, discussed in Chapter 7, can be regarded as clarifying what it means to talk about whether actual interpersonal differences are a matter of luck or not, and so as providing a way around the boring problem. But even if this is admitted, I argue in that chapter that Roemer's framework still does not provide a solution to the indeterminacy problem.

sible for what another is responsible for, then the relations between their positions are at least partly a matter of luck for him. This boring point applies in other possible worlds as much as in the actual world. One person is no more responsible for counterfactual relations between his position and another's position than for actual relations. We have not yet got a use for the idea that counterfactual relations between people—whether of difference or sameness—might neutralize luck, even in the straightforward case where all individuals concerned are responsible for their own actual positions.

A luck neutralizer may reply that so long as each person is responsible for her actual position, he is not concerned with whether relations between them are nevertheless partly a matter of luck. Fair enough. Let's therefore now consider a situation in which Ernest and Bertie, Eleanor and Kate are *not* responsible for their own actual positions. This is the kind of situation that we would be addressing if we had already used responsibility in its currency role to filter out goods for which people are responsible. Can we now go on to give responsibility a patterning role? No, because the prospects of finding a clear sense in which counterfactual relations between people might not be a matter of luck are now even worse. We now face not just the boring problem that one person isn't responsible for the relation, whether actual or counterfactual, between his position and other person's; we also face an additional problem—the indeterminacy problem.

It is hard enough to say whether people are responsible for what they actually have. But to neutralize luck understood counterfactually, we need to know more than this, to answer a further question. We would have to be able to say, when people are not responsible for what they actually have, what they *would* be responsible for instead, if factors for which they are not responsible were eliminated. Otherwise we would merely be moving from one distribution that is a matter of luck to another, which might be equally a matter of luck. The point here is not just that there is no reason to assume we'd all be responsible for the same thing. More fundamentally, it is highly doubtful that we have any general, nonarbitrary basis for answering this further question. In many cases the answer is simply indeterminate.

Hard as it is to arrive at judgments about whether someone is responsible for the position she actually has, we can often reasonably decide that someone is not. Suppose, for example, we adhere to a reason-responsiveness view of responsibility. Then we might judge that someone is not responsible because the actual sequence of causes leading to the actions that result in her position do not meet a reason-responsiveness requirement. But it is another thing entirely to say what she would have been responsible for instead if the responsibility-defeating factors did not obtain. In some cases it will be possible, but it many cases it will be simply indeterminate. For example, how can we say what someone would have chosen or done or been responsible for if she had, counterfactually, satisfied a reason-responsiveness condition?[11] Different reasonable people can make different reason-responsive choices. Indeed, if we are not determinists, we might think that any given reasonable person can make different reason-responsive choices.

---

11. The following objection may be made (here I am indebted to Larry Temkin): suppose I am right that it is generally indeterminate what would not be a matter of luck for someone, when their actual situation is a matter of luck. If so, then why isn't it also indeterminate whether someone wouldn't have done otherwise, whether or not she could have? Yet I depend on suppositions of this form in Chapter 2. Putting the objection the other way around: if I can make determinate sense of suppositions to the effect that someone wouldn't have done otherwise, whether or not she could have, as I claim to do in Chapter 2, why not also of suppositions about what someone would choose under counterfactual conditions, hence of suppositions about what someone would be responsible for under counterfactual suppositions?

In Chapter 2 I gave a variable realization explanation of what could make it the case that someone wouldn't have done otherwise, whether or not she could have, hence whether or not determinism is true. This appealed to the way in which there could be different—deterministic and indeterministic—realizations of a macro-level disposition that are functionally equivalent at the macro level. By contrast, when significant features of someone's actual circumstances or character, such as his upbringing or his degree of reason-responsiveness, are a matter of luck, judgments of counterfactual responsibility require us to abstract from those features. What would the person have done if those features had not been present? For example, would someone have chosen to be a workaholic or a surfer if he had not had a privileged upbringing or a deprived upbringing, or if he had satisfied a reason-responsiveness condition instead of failing to do so? The relevant counterfactuals here vary macro-structural features that are not in general separable from choice dispositions. We cannot assume that choice dispositions are in general independent of such features. The idea that a given choice disposition could have both deterministic and indeterministic realizations does not support this assumption. When such features are varied counterfactually, it will generally be indeterminate what people would choose. The idea of variable realization thus does not undercut my skepticism about counterfactual responsibility.

Let me spell out why judgments about whether individuals are responsible for their actual goods positions leave an indeterminacy problem. Suppose we have made such judgments. Doris is a surfer and part-time janitor. She is responsible for her relatively low goods position, X, so it is exempt from luck-neutralizing redistribution. We leave her position as it is. Sam is not responsible for his relatively low goods position, X; his low income is bad luck for him. What goods position should he be in instead? Joe is only partly responsible for his goods position, $X + Y$; his high income is partly good luck for him. What goods position should he be in instead?

Sam's goods and part of Joe's goods are matters of luck for them, so are within the currency of redistribution given the currency role of responsibility. But if responsibility is to play a patterning role as well as a currency role, it must tell us not just *what* to redistribute, but *how*. Judgments about whether people's actual goods positions are matters of luck for them cannot by themselves show us what pattern of redistribution we should try to achieve instead. If responsibility is to play this patterning role as well as a currency role, further counterfactual judgments of responsibility are needed—for example, if Sam had five times his actual income, that would not be a matter of luck for him; if Joe had a third of his actual income, that would not be a matter of luck for him. If responsibility is to play a patterning role, it must tell us what luck-neutral baseline we should aim to put a person at through redistribution, when her actual goods position is a matter of luck. It must tell us what someone would be responsible for instead, when she is not responsible for what she actually has.

Such judgments, however, are in general highly problematic. They would go beyond our ordinary practices of judging whether people are responsible for what they actually have. What could be the basis for them? Can our practices of using the concept of responsibility in some way be extended to answer these questions? When people are not responsible for what they actually have, what is it for them to be responsible for something else instead, for something else not to be a matter of luck? And how can we know what that something else is?

Perhaps in some cases we can say. If Joe had not received a lucky legacy from a distant uncle, he would have one-third of his actual income, and that would not have been a matter of luck for him because it would be due to his own choices and efforts and hard work. But such clear-cut cases are the exception rather than the rule. If Sam had not had the deprived childhood that makes his current low income bad luck for him, what would he

	Choice: workaholic	Choice: surfer
Good luck	D	B
Bad luck (Sam's actual position)	C	A

Figure 5. Nonseparability of luck and choice.

have been responsible for instead? He might have chosen to be a worka-holic or a surfer, or anything in between.

The indeterminacy problem can be regarded as the result of a kind of nonseparability of luck and responsible choice. To simplify, suppose that there are two possible luck levels and two types of responsible choice for Sam. Suppose that as things are, Sam has had bad luck and surfs (he wouldn't have earned very much by working hard anyway). But that does not mean that if Sam had had good luck instead he would have surfed; he might well have worked hard instead (finding hard work more worth-while). From A we cannot infer B (see Figure 5). Alternatively, suppose that as things are, Sam has had bad luck and works hard. Again, that does not mean that if Sam had had good luck instead he would have worked hard; he might well have surfed instead. From C we cannot infer D. Dif-ferent luck levels may feed into the formation of Sam's character and dis-positions and hence affect the content of his responsible choices. Sam isn't responsible for his good or bad luck, but he can still be responsible for choices he makes, given that luck. This leads to the difficulty of under-standing how we should redistribute in order to neutralize luck.

It may be replied that if the choices for which Sam is supposedly respon-sible are not separable from his luck levels, then he is not really responsible for them.[12] But this claim is far too strong. Responsibility is not regressive, as I argued in Part I. That means that to be responsible for something you need not be responsible for all its causes. For example, factors that are matters of good or bad luck, for which Sam is not responsible, may be

---

12. I am indebted to Thomas Pogge for discussion of these issues.

among the causes of his having one or another reason-responsive disposition, in virtue of which he is responsible for resulting choices. Sam doesn't have to be responsible for all the causes of his having such a disposition in order to be responsible, in virtue of having such a disposition, for his choices.[13]

If choices were regressively responsible, would luck and responsible choice be separable? It is difficult to answer this question, since regressive choice is impossible. Perhaps an implicit assumption that responsibility must be regressive motivates people who are tempted by the assumption that luck and responsible choice are separable. But we have seen in Part I that on plausible assumptions the regression requirement would make responsibility impossible, so that no one would ever really be responsible for anything. In the following sections of this chapter I consider whether the elimination of responsibility could provide a basis for equality.

It is tempting to avoid the indeterminacy problem by assuming that when people are not responsible for what they have, we should redistribute in a way that leaves them all equally well off. This is what you are doing if you respond to the indeterminacy problem by reverting to the equality-default view and the aim to neutralize only differences that are a matter of luck.

Now, perhaps we should make this assumption. My point here is not to deny this, but rather to deny that considerations of responsibility and luck specify that equality should be the default pattern and that only differences that are a matter of luck need to be neutralized. Some other basis for this choice of default is needed. There is no reason to assume that the baseline of what people would be responsible for, when they are not responsible for what they have, is the same for different people. People might not be responsible for what they actually have, even when each has the same as the others; equal goods positions can be no less matters of luck than unequal ones. Simply to assume equality as the default position may indeed be the right thing to do. But we should not suppose we are neutralizing luck when we do so. Considerations of luck and responsibility do not resolve the indeterminacy problem.

Responsibility does not justify taking equal option sets as a default posi-

---

13. I use reason-responsiveness to illustrate the general point most simply. Here I am abstracting from the further issues, considered in Chapter 1, about whether something more than reason-responsiveness but less than regression is required for responsibility.

tion either (see and cf. Arneson 1989; 1990). Someone may or may not be responsible for the set of options he faces, but whether he is does not depend on whether he faces the same options as others. And if someone can acquire responsibility for goods by certain choices he makes within his set of options, he does not cease to be responsible because of the relation of his option set to that of others. Someone's responsibility given the choices he makes within his set of options does not depend on his having the same set of options as someone else. Responsibility does not depend on equality, or build equality in.

Is the indeterminacy problem just an epistemological problem, a problem of how we can *know* the answers? Or is it rather a problem about *what it is in virtue of which certain counterfactual claims are true,* namely, claims about what in particular someone would be responsible for under counterfactual conditions, given that she is not responsible for what she actually has? The indeterminacy problem may have both aspects, in different cases. But either way, I strongly doubt that these are problems we can or should or need try to solve. We have a use for confirming someone's responsibility for what he does and for what he has. We also have a use for excusing people from responsibility. But when we excuse, we do not generally reinstate responsibility for some counterfactual state of affairs. Our judgments of responsibility often simply do not extend determinately this far. Efforts to wring more determinacy out of our concept of responsibility than it is designed for invite arbitrariness.

Note that the indeterminacy problem does *not* turn on a claim that redistribution to achieve inegalitarian patterns neutralizes luck just as effectively as redistribution to achieve an egalitarian pattern, so that there are competing luck-extinguishing patterns. That is not my claim. Rather, it is that both egalitarian and inegalitarian patterns of redistribution may *fail* to neutralize luck: the new pattern in both cases may be just as much a matter of luck as the one we started with. There is no luck-neutralizing point in substituting one distribution that is a matter of luck for another. But nothing in the idea of responsibility singles out the egalitarian redistribution as any less a matter of luck than other possible redistributions.[14] Perhaps it is fairer to redistribute equally than unequally. But fairness is not the same thing as responsibility.

The problems with counterfactual responsibility just sketched are closely related to problems for the idea of hypothetical choice as a suf-

---

14. I am grateful to Gerald Cohen for discussion of this point.

ficient condition for responsibility. As I explained in Part I, hypothetical choice, unlike actual choice and control, need involve no actual causal relationship between the person and what he would counterfactually choose. Its very causal costlessness makes for indeterminacy: I would choose to be a brilliant mathematician if I had the talent, or a brilliant artist, musician, novelist, or scientist. So what? There are too many things that people would choose, or would not choose to avoid, under various counterfactual conditions. Further constraint is needed to narrow the focus down to those things people are actually responsible for. The most plausible candidates to provide such constraint, such as actual choice or control, involve causal relations between people and what they are responsible for. (However, a hypothetical-choice requirement may be a plausible component of a hybrid account of responsibility that also requires some such causal relation.)

5. Neutralizing the Effects of Luck and the Regression Requirement

In the rest of this chapter, I focus further on whether the luck-neutralizing aim can do any more to provide a basis for egalitarianism if we assume that no one is responsible for anything. I first argue, in this section, that the aim to neutralize the *effects* of luck is closely linked to the regression requirement, according to which responsibility for something requires responsibility for its *causes*. As we have seen in Part I, on certain plausible assumptions the regression requirement makes responsibility impossible. I go on to argue that the universal defeat of responsibility would not provide a basis for egalitarianism either. For the purposes of the rest of this chapter, it is crucial to distinguish the aim to neutralize the effects of luck from the aim to neutralize luck. The latter does not entail the former, and it is the former that is linked to the regression requirement.

Cohen concedes that finding a contrast between choice and luck at the heart of views about distributive justice may land the latter in the morass of thorny problems about freedom and responsibility. But that may just be the way things are. Moreover, while Cohen admits that "there is no aspect of a person's situation that is wholly due to genuine choice," he also suggests that theories of distributive justice don't need an absolute criterion of genuine choice, but may make do with criteria of differences in degree of genuineness and aim to redress disadvantage *to the extent* it does not reflect genuine choice (Cohen 1989, p. 934).

What, however, if no aspect of a person's situation is even partly due to genuine choice? What if everything is a matter of luck, because responsibility is an illusion or is impossible? It may be natural to assume that the complete elimination of responsibility would provide a basis for equality as a pattern of distribution. But egalitarians should not rely on this assumption.[15] Just as responsibility cannot play a patterning role in distributive justice, neither can the complete absence of responsibility. I elaborate this argument in the following section. First, however, we need to examine more closely the relationship between the luck-neutralizing aim and the view that responsibility is impossible, which is the task of this section.

A certain familiar train of thought can suggest that more or less everything is a matter of luck, that no one is really responsible for anything. Three examples of it follow.

The first is expressed by Parfit (1995, pp. 10–12). Begin with windfall luck: people could be just the same in their efforts and skills except that manna falls from heaven on some but not others. It is a small step from that to the notion of productive luck: people do the same work with the same skill but some are more productive because they happen to be surrounded by richer natural resources. The next step is a slightly larger one, to the notion of genetic luck: people make the same efforts with the same resources, but some are better off because they "happen" to have richer inner resources or talents. Parfit suggests that the most important question in the whole debate about distributive justice may be whether the infusion of effort by the talented cancels out the arbitrariness of genetic luck. But he goes still further, to consider the case in which people are equally talented and have the same natural resources, but make differential efforts: if genetic luck with respect to one's talents is arbitrary, why not luck in one's ability to make an effort also? This leaves only differences resulting from the choice to try; but why aren't the choices people make also a kind of luck—"choice luck?" If we object to natural inequalities because they are a matter of luck, why shouldn't the objection extend to inequalities due to choice? Why should differences be acceptable merely because

---

15. Cohen concedes the power of Nozick's response to egalitarian determinism, namely, that "denigrating a person's autonomy and prime responsibility for his actions is a risky line to take for a theory that otherwise wishes to buttress the dignity and self-respect of autonomous beings . . . One doubts that the unexalted picture of human beings Rawls' theory presupposes and rests upon can be made to fit together with the view of human dignity it is designed to lead to and embody" (Nozick 1974, p. 214; cited by Cohen 1989, p. 915).

people happened to make good or bad choices? After all, choices are also among the effects of luck. How can even choice hold out against the responsibility-corroding effects of luck?

The second version is expressed by Roemer, when he discusses where to draw the line on the slippery slope between what is and what is not a matter of luck for someone. He writes:

> Dworkin, for example, maintains that the distribution of income should be ambition-sensitive but not endowment-sensitive. By this he means that ambition is an attribute of the person from which he deserves to benefit . . . But if you are more ambitious than I, is it not because you have more endorphins than I, or a different pattern of synaptic connections, or some other biological endowment? Or if not, perhaps it is because we had exposures to different external resources, such as family wealth or family attitudes. But should not these experiences that differentiate us count as resource differences? Can we not always reduce the differences between people to "resources", things over which they have no control or choice, things whose distribution is morally arbitrary? (Roemer 1986, p. 781; see also his 1985 article)

Suppose that internal talents, abilities or disabilities, are features for which we are not responsible, hence are resources within the jurisdiction of resource egalitarianism. Roemer argues that this supposition leads ultimately to the conclusion that all differences between people are a matter of luck, and thus undermines the distinction between equality of resources and equality of welfare. Suppose people have different preferences over some list of goods; there must be a cause. Perhaps that cause takes the form of another "good" or resource with respect to which we differ, such as different levels of endorphins, or different patterns of synaptic connections, or exposures to different families. "If we list a sufficient number of such 'resources', some of which are internal to the person and some external, then you and I can be represented as having the same preferences—we differ 'only' in our consumption of different vectors of resources." In this way Roemer reduces apparent differences in the preferences of agents, from which responsibility does flow, to differences in their resource endowments, from which it does not. Resource egalitarianism requires compensation for resources whose distribution is morally arbitrary, a matter of luck, even if they are not transferable. If no line can be defended between different preferences, from which responsibility does flow, and different resource endowments, from which responsibility does not flow, then all differences between people are a matter of luck. Roemer thus argues that one cannot consistently distinguish between equality of resources and equality of welfare while also advocating the view that talents are internal resources within the jurisdiction of resource egalitarianism. (Roemer 1985, pp. 178–179).

I now want to express the line of thought that seems to make everything a matter of luck in yet a third way. This turns explicitly on a particular formulation of the aim to neutralize luck, which I think is at least implicit in Parfit's and Roemer's thinking. This aim is often formulated as the "aim to neutralize *the effects of* luck." This turn of phrase may seem innocent, but it is not. The aim to neutralize the effects of luck is operationally equivalent to adopting the regression principle, discussed in earlier chapters.

To see why, recall from Part I the way in which responsibility appears to be impossible if you think both that it requires choice or control and that it must satisfy the regression principle. The regression principle says that responsibility for something requires responsibility for its causes. Suppose you choose or control something. Regression requires that you choose or control the causes of that thing, and the causes of those causes, and so on, all the way back. But the causal chain goes back to times before you existed. It is impossible for you actually to choose or control what happened before you existed. No one can actually choose or control the causes of an action or choice, all the way back.[16]

With this impossibility in mind, we can now see the significance of aiming to neutralize not just luck but the *effects* of luck. Recall from Chapter 4 that for X to be among the effects of luck is for it to have luck among its causes. To neutralize the effects of luck on X is to neutralize luck in X's

---

16. Recall from Part I that this point is distinct from the claim that determinism is incompatible with responsibility because the latter requires an unconditional ability to do otherwise. The ability-to-do-otherwise requirement, which is incompatible with determinism, is an alternate-sequence requirement. By contrast, the regression requirement, that responsibility for anything requires responsibility for its causes, is an actual-sequence requirement. The argument that regressive responsibility is impossible does not turn on determinism; rejecting determinism does not avoid the point. Given the regression requirement, so long as your acts have causes for which you are not responsible, then you are not responsible for those acts either, even if the links between cause and effect are not deterministic (see and cf. Strawson 1986, pp. 26–30, 494–450, 56; Scanlon 1988, pp. 152–153; 1998, p. 250).

causes (rather than luck in X's effects). Thus, if we aim to neutralize the *effects* of luck anywhere back in the causal chain, we are effectively refusing to hold people responsible for something unless they are also responsible for its *causes* (cf. Roemer 1987, p. 216). We are in practice imposing a principle that the regression requirement makes explicit: that lack of responsibility anywhere back in the causal chain that leads up to some event propagates forward to that event. On this view, responsibility cannot genuinely emerge; it must have been there all along. But since on plausible assumptions no one can be responsible for causes all the way back, we are thus effectively refusing to hold anyone responsible at all. The aim to neutralize the effects of luck is operationally equivalent to use of the regression principle to argue that everything is a matter of luck.

Note that it is important here to distinguish the aim to neutralize the *effects* of luck from the nonequivalent aim to neutralize only *differences* that are a matter of luck. The latter was discussed earlier in this chapter under the heading of the equality-default view. Neutralizing the effects of luck and neutralizing only differences due to luck are not only not equivalent: they are incompatible. To neutralize only differences due to luck is to fail to neutralize all the effects of luck, since equalities can also be among the effects of luck.

To illustrate the connection between the aim to neutralize the effects of luck and the regression requirement, consider something that is a matter of luck for me and that I'm therefore not responsible for—say, some gene of one of my great grandparents for extraordinary musical talent. Suppose that this has effects on my constitution and hence on my choices and actions and hence on my share of goods. For example, my extraordinary musical gifts make it possible for me, and attractive to me, to become a world-famous opera star. As a result, I command a very large income. Then the aim to neutralize the effects of luck is an aim to neutralize these effects on my goods position. It operates so as to treat me as not responsible for those *effects* just because I am not responsible for their *cause*, namely, the gene that was a matter of luck. The luck-neutralizing aim appeals to effects, and the regression principle to causes; but the practical upshot is the same. Just as, on plausible assumptions, the regression principle makes responsibility impossible, so the aim to neutralize the effects of luck treats everything as a matter of luck.

It may be objected that choice can be opposed to luck in a way that preempts the reasoning I have just given. Now this objector should concede that factors for which we are not responsible have effects on our choices, via, for example, constitutive luck. This is true whether causes operate deterministically or indeterministically. While I may choose to develop my musical talents, my choices themselves may be among the effects of my constitutive luck. However, the objection might nevertheless be made that we can hold the effects of choices to be exempt (or partially exempt) from the project of neutralizing the effects of luck, even when choices themselves are among the effects of luck since they have causal antecedents that are a matter of luck.

Perhaps this choice exemption can be justified by an account of how choice makes for responsibility. But even so, this move would be a move away from the aim to neutralize *all the effects* of luck, which include choices, and thus an implicit rejection of the regression principle. Our choices, and their effects in turn, are among the effects of factors for which we are not responsible. If the intervention of choice cancels the aim to neutralize the effects of luck, then the operative aim is not simply an aim to neutralize the effects of luck. Something else is doing essential work. The operative aim should be formulated differently.

A luck-neutralizing view does not need to be formulated in terms of the effects of luck, or to be implicitly committed to a regressive conception of responsibility. Its aim can be expressed simply as the aim to neutralize *luck*, rather than the *effects of luck*. This would allow us to evaluate directly, using a nonregressive account of responsibility if we so like, whether someone's goods position is a matter of luck. We could take the genesis of someone's goods position via his choices into account in whatever way our account of responsibility might require. Perhaps I am only partly responsible for my high income, since it results only partly from my choices. Then, by the currency role of responsibility, only part of my high income would be included in the currency of distributive justice. It is a further question what pattern of distribution of that currency is required.

If we believe that responsibility is possible and reject the regression requirement, we should avoid formulations of egalitarianism that aim to neutralize the effects of luck, which is what associates the luck-neutralizing aim, at least operationally, with the regression principle. The luck neutralizer might aim to neutralize the effects of luck only selectively, if these effects fail to meet some further condition for responsibility (such as not resulting in the right way from choice). But then the aim to neutralize the effects of luck is not doing all the work.

I have just explained how the aim to neutralize the effects of luck operationalizes the view that everything is a matter of luck. I now turn to the promised argument that rampant luck and the elimination of responsibility provide no basis for egalitarianism.

6. Rampant Luck Provides No Basis for Equality

Arguments were given in earlier sections of this chapter that the aim to neutralize luck cannot provide a basis for egalitarianism. These arguments do not turn on whether the "effects of luck" formulation is used, with its implicit regressive character. They hold even for regressive conceptions of responsibility that make responsibility impossible. However, it may be especially tempting to regard the aim to neutralize luck as providing a basis for egalitarianism if responsibility is assumed to be impossible. It may seem that, even if it is conceded that considerations of responsibility cannot provide a basis for egalitarianism in general, at least on the assumption that responsibility is impossible, that very impossibility does provide a basis for egalitarianism. I argue in this section and the next that this is an illusion. Egalitarians should not suppose that egalitarianism somehow would gain support if responsibility were to be impossible.

Why might the view that everything is a matter of luck seem to provide a basis for egalitarianism? First, it may seem to do so if a version of the egalitarian fallacy is committed. Second, it may seem to do so if something like autonomous bare selves are assumed to be common to all people. I explain the first suggestion in this section, and the second in the next.

To see how the egalitarian fallacy might arise here, notice a way in which my version of the train of thought about rampant luck differs from Parfit's and Roemer's versions (in the previous section). Parfit and Roemer try to show how all *differences* between people may seem to be a matter of luck. But I tried to show how *everything* could seem to be a matter of luck, not just differences between people.

I have been pressing the question: Why should only *differences* be regarded as a matter of luck, and not *nondifferences*? If responsibility is impossible, people are no more responsible for nondifference than for difference; equalities are among the effects of luck as well as differences. The aim to neutralize the effects of luck makes sameness of position just as much a matter of luck as difference of position—to the extent it makes sense to regard relations between people as a matter of luck at all!

Why then might someone only be concerned with differences that are a matter of luck? One possibility is that they assume that if no one is responsible for anything, then equality should be assumed as a default position or normative baseline, as in the equality-default view. What would justify this assumption? There may indeed be some way of justifying it. But I have claimed that considerations of responsibility and luck cannot do so.

I now emphasize that this claim holds even if no one is responsible for anything. In particular, the aim to neutralize luck *when combined with the view that no one is responsible for anything* still provides no basis for taking equality to be the default position. The most basic point here turns on exposing a version of the egalitarian fallacy. That some difference between *a* and *b* is a matter of luck does not entail that it would not be a matter of luck if *a* and *b* were equal in this respect. This point holds even when all differences between people are a matter of luck. If people are not responsible for anything, it does not follow that they are all responsible for the same thing. If everything is a matter of luck, equality is no less a matter of luck than any other distribution. The aim to neutralize luck does not favor egalitarian luck over inegalitarian luck.

This basic point should make us wary of a non sequitur. If we aim to neutralize the effects of luck, but ultimately everything turns out to be among those effects, then at best it is *indeterminate* what would neutralize the effects of luck. We cannot infer that equality will do so.

There is also a further danger, however, of incoherence. If we hold that responsibility is essentially impossible, then by the same token it is *impossible* to neutralize the effects of luck (not merely indeterminate what would do so): no possible state of affairs could do so. But this impossibility in itself provides no basis for taking equality as default position. Going for equality as the default position cannot be a way of doing the impossible—that is, of neutralizing luck—even if it has some other justification. It is incoherent to hold both that responsibility is impossible and that equality would neutralize luck. If responsibility is impossible, then everything must be a matter of luck and it is impossible to neutralize luck.

Note again that I have not argued against the possibility that other considerations, independent of luck neutralization, justify taking equality as a default position. Nor have I argued against the view that we should not even try to derive equality from other considerations but should simply assume equality as a normative baseline. My target is the view that luck neutralization provides a basis for egalitarianism, not that something else does, or that we should assume equality as our default position directly without any independent basis.

7. The Lurking Bare Self

It may be objected that we have still not really got to the bottom of the assumption that eliminating responsibility somehow supports equality. Even when we recognize and avoid the egalitarian fallacy, the temptation to make this assumption is not completely disarmed. It may have another source as well, in an implicit view that each of us harbors something like an autonomous bare self.

On this view, even if everything seems to be a matter of luck, our bare selves, stripped of all the contingent differences that are matters of luck, are ultimately autonomous. Moreover, they are qualitatively identical, so any pattern their residual autonomy indicates must be one of equality. For example, in Roemer's argument described in section 5, once the causes of our differences, mere matters of luck, are stripped away, you and I have identical underlying preferences from which responsibility flows.[17] Our equal claims are based on the underlying autonomy of our bare selves. This line of thought moves from a picture of identical bare selves with the same residual autonomy to equality as the default position or normative

---

17. However, in later work Roemer claims, in the course of discussing Arneson's position, that the formation of preferences can never be autonomous, at least in the sense Arneson requires. See Roemer 1996, p. 271.

Compare the ways in which bare selves lurk in Roemer's earlier (1985; 1986) versions of luck-neutralizing egalitarianism and in Harsanyi's version of utilitarianism (1976 and elsewhere). In Harsanyi's version, the stripping down is accomplished by putting all causes of preferences that are not universal into the objects of preference. "Extended preferences" operate over all-embracing objects that include the causes of all the differences between lower-order preferences between persons. As a result, there is supposedly one universally shared extended preference ordering from which normative consequences can be derived. The ordering is universal because any causes of differences in preference have been put into the content of the universal extended preference ordering. It has normative status because it is the object of a universal preference from which all contingent, differentiating influences have been purged.

But these suppositions are no more justified than the supposition that eliminating the influence of luck must leave a common autonomous preference ordering. The objection now is somewhat different. The causes of differences in preference are not neutralized merely by incorporating them into the all-embracing objects of extended preference. Causes may still operate even when they are made objects of preference by reflective people. So even the extended preferences of different persons may differ. See and cf. Broome 1993; Hurley 1989.

baseline for purposes of neutralizing luck. Thus, only differences need to be neutralized. Sameness is not a matter of luck, but can somehow be regarded as reflecting the equal autonomy of identical bare selves. I don't find this reasoning completely clear. But let's grant the reasoning for the sake of argument, and ask where it gets us.

Notice first that to believe in a bare self that is the bearer of such residual autonomy is to believe in something that is ultimately not a matter of luck. It is thus to retreat from the view that luck is rampant and responsibility impossible. So this is not strictly speaking an account of how the complete elimination of responsibility might support equality. The line of thought I have just sketched, leading from bare selves to equality, in effect takes back the view that everything is a matter of luck and adopts a quite different view according to which bare selves are autonomous. Arguments that everything is a matter of luck not only give no support to this different view but are inconsistent with it. If everything is a matter of luck, so are the identical preferences of my "bare" self and your "bare" self, and these selves are not autonomous after all.

The premises of the argument from bare selves to equality are the following:

(13) We each harbor a bare self, which is what is left when all factors that are a matter of luck are stripped away;

(14) These are autonomous selves;

and:

(15) These are qualitatively identical, since all qualitative differences are matters of luck and hence are part of what is stripped away.

Even if we allow for the sake of argument that from these premises we can argue for equality, what reason do we have to believe them? Our ordinary, everyday practices of attributing responsibility do not support these claims. Kant postulated noumenal selves with something like this residual equal autonomy. I will not attempt to provide an argument against noumenal selves here, but it seems safe to say that today few people believe they exist. Kantian noumenal selves aside, there are powerful reasons to reject these premises.

Against (13): We may be persuaded that everything is indeed a matter of luck and that responsibility is impossible. Where would this leave bare selves? If they are understood as whatever is left when everything that is a matter of luck is stripped away, but everything is a matter of luck, then there are no such things as bare selves.

Against (14): Even if we are not persuaded that everything is in fact a matter of luck, we may share Nozick's doubts about whether any coherent conception of a self is left when all contingent, particular traits are stripped away (Nozick 1974, p. 228; see also Sandel 1982; Watson 1987, pp. 278–279). Even if as things are, not everything is a matter of luck, nevertheless, when everything thing that is a matter of luck is stripped away, there may be no selves at all left. And if there are no selves left, they cannot be autonomous or identical. Stipulating that the bare self is whatever is left when luck is stripped away does not support the substantive claim that any intelligible self survives. Luck may take the self and responsibility with it.[18] Responsibility and autonomy may be properties of selves that, to be selves at all, *must also* have some features that are a matter of luck. The myth of the autonomous bare self, on this view, badly misunderstands the nature of the self and of autonomy and responsibility.

Against (15): Suppose we grant that when luck is stripped away, we are indeed left with bare selves, and moreover that they are autonomous—since if they weren't, luck would not yet have been completely stripped away. It still does not follow that distinct bare selves would be qualitatively identical. Rather, it is simply being assumed that no differences, only samenesses, survive the stripping process. But why assume that all differences are matters of luck? If bare selves are autonomous, why can't they be qualitatively different? If they could be, then no argument for equality would be in the offing from these premises. So we need some reason for assuming that they cannot be, which does not simply amount to a question-begging assumption of equality. Even if we grant the previous assumptions about autonomous bare selves, if considerations of responsibility are to provide a basis for egalitarianism, we need a responsibility-related basis for holding that autonomous bare selves cannot be different. But it is very unclear what that basis might be.

Does the aim to neutralize luck in combination with bare selves provide a basis for egalitarianism? The prospects are not good here either.

---

18. Compare: we could not argue that the mind is what is left when everything that is not conscious is stripped away; when everything that is not conscious is stripped away, the mind may go with it.

8. Summary

I have claimed that the aim to neutralize luck cannot provide a basis for egalitarianism. It can neither (nontrivially) specify nor justify an egalitarian pattern of distribution. Luck and responsibility can play a role in determining *what* justice requires to be redistributed, but from this we cannot derive *how* to distribute: we cannot derive a pattern of distribution from the currency of distributive justice. Nor does responsibility provide a basis for aiming to neutralize only *differences* that are a matter of luck, in effect taking equality as a default position, departures from which must be justified. My argument for these claims was developed in terms of a dilemma, according to whether luck is understood in interpersonal or counterfactual terms. On the one hand, the aim to neutralize interpersonal bad luck does specify an egalitarian pattern of distribution, but only trivially, since interpersonal inequality is used to define bad luck, and it does nothing to justify an egalitarian pattern. On the other hand, the aim to neutralize counterfactual bad luck does not specify or justify an egalitarian pattern of distribution.

It may be tempting to think that, even if responsibility does not provide a basis for egalitarianism in general, at least if it is held that everything is a matter of luck, then egalitarianism would be supported. I have explained how the aim to neutralize the effects of luck ends up treating everything as among the effects of luck and operationalizes a regressive conception of responsibility that, under plausible assumptions, makes responsibility impossible (see Chapters 1 and 3). If everything turns out to be among the effects of luck, this gives us no reason to think that equality would neutralize the effects of luck. And if responsibility is impossible, then it is also impossible to neutralize the effects of luck.

It might be thought that we can argue to equality from the supposition of identical autonomous bare selves common to all people, which are supposedly what is left when everything that is a matter of luck is stripped away from the self. However, there are powerful objections to this line of argument. If everything is a matter of luck, then there are no such things as autonomous bare selves. Moreover, responsibility and autonomy may be properties of selves that, to be selves at all, must also have some features that are matters of luck. And even if stripping away factors that are matters of luck were to leave autonomous bare selves behind, there is no evident reason to assume that there would be no relevant differences between such autonomous bare selves.

Note that my arguments in this chapter have depended critically on distinguishing formulations of the luck-neutralizing aim that are often run together. The aim to neutralize luck is not the same thing as the aim to neutralize specifically differences due to luck or the aim to neutralize the effects of luck. The latter two formulations have implications that the first in itself does not.

Finally, I emphasize again that I have not argued against egalitarianism, or against the view that equality should be taken as a default position when people are not responsible for what they have. Rather, I have argued that considerations of responsibility and luck do not provide a basis for these views. But there may well be some other basis for them. We need to think further about what that could be.

7

Roemer on Responsibility and Equality

1. My Target versus Roemer's Intentions

John Roemer gives an illuminating and ingenious account of what it would be to neutralize luck, which he offers as a "pragmatic theory" for the egalitarian planner. Roemer's account of luck-neutralization is clearer, more fully developed, and more operational in character than any other I know of in the literature on distributive justice, and has the potential directly to influence political and legal policies.

Recall from Chapter 6 that Gerald Cohen has claimed that the aim to neutralize luck provides the fundamental motivation of egalitarianism (1989, pp. 908, 932). Roemer (1996, chap. 8) conceives his position to follow on from Cohen's. In this chapter I consider whether Roemer's account can be used to defend Cohen's claim. Thus, my target is not exactly either Roemer or Cohen, but Roemer's-account-in-service-of-Cohen's-claim. I take this concatenated position as my target because I believe Cohen has most clearly articulated an important claim about the aim to neutralize luck that is implicit in much contemporary discussion of distributive justice, and because, despite my criticisms of Roemer's view, I believe that he has gone farther than anyone else in trying to work out what it would be to neutralize luck.

I argue that, despite its merits, Roemer's account does not show how the aim to neutralize luck could provide a basis for egalitarianism. This claim is not itself a criticism of Roemer, since it is not clear that Roemer intends his account to provide a basis for egalitarianism. Rather, his account makes operational the conception of equality he favors, which he calls "equality of opportunity" (see, for example, 1998, p. 4). Roemer himself may see the role of responsibility in his proposal as telling us what to distribute rather than how to distribute (see, for example, 1998, p. 7).

I argue that what Roemer's scheme does is show how to reward people equally who make equal efforts to behave in ways we regard as meritorious or deserving. If Roemer's scheme is properly limited to specific, democratically adopted policies that favor and encourage particular kinds of behavior, it may well be a valuable and effective tool of policy implementation. Nevertheless, giving people what they deserve on account of their efforts is not the same as giving them what they are responsible for. Nor is equalizing what people are not responsible for the same as giving them what they are responsible for. Moreover, depending on what behavior we regard as deserving, a Roemerian system of rewards may or may not favor egalitarian patterns of distribution. Treating like cases alike in the way Roemer spells out is not enough to guarantee that relatively equal patterns of distribution are favored over relatively unequal ones, other things equal.

The argument in this chapter thus expands the argument for the main claim of the previous chapter. The aim to neutralize luck may tell us *what* to distribute, namely, goods that people are not responsible for, which are a matter of luck for them. But it cannot tell us *how* to distribute such goods, or in particular to favor more equal over less equal distributions, other things equal. The aim to neutralize luck, understood as goods people are not responsible for, neither specifies nor justifies a distinctively egalitarian *pattern* of distribution, even if it does contribute to specifying a *currency* of distribution. Something else must do that work.

2. What It Would Be to Neutralize Luck: Roemer's Framework for Addressing the Problem

In a schematic version of Roemer's framework, we consider four persons who have four different goods positions. A is better off than B, who is better off than C, who is better off than D. Consider all the factors that contribute to how well off these characters are. Some of the contributing factors undermine their responsibility for their positions to some degree, such as congenital disabilities, poor quality of education, deprivation or abuse during childhood, and so on. Other factors support their responsibility for their positions, such as their reasoned choices as to how to behave. Suppose that society has in some way arrived at various judgments about just which factors undermine responsibility. Though he often speaks of responsibility in terms of choice or control, Roemer claims that his theory is not committed to any particular view about what factors undermine responsibility, but leaves this question open for each society to decide for itself.[1] His theory is rather about what we do once we have these judgments, how we can use them to discover how to redistribute justly. I assume a choice-based view of responsibility for purposes of setting out his framework.

Roemer suggests that we take all the responsibility-undermining factors and circumstances, and use them to define a *type* of person. One type collects persons who are similar in respect of the factors we have judged to undermine responsibility. For example, in type *T* (for *talented*) are people who are born without congenital disabilities, who received relatively good educations, and had happy, healthy childhoods. In type *U* (for *untalented*) are people who have inherited some mental or physical weakness, had relatively poor educations, and had childhoods involving privation or abuse of some kind.

We could make our specification of types finer-grained, but this will do to convey Roemer's scheme. The persons in one type need not be exactly similar, but they are similar to whatever degree of accuracy we wish to stipulate. The bottom line is that they are similar enough for us to be willing to say that any differences between people within one type are not a matter of luck.[2]

Suppose next that A and B belong to type *T*. Recall that A is better off than B. Suppose this is because A is a workaholic and B is a surfer.[3] There is no relevant difference between A and B in respect of responsibility-un-

---

1. This disclaimer notwithstanding, he appears to be sympathetic to the regression requirement, that responsibility for something requires responsibility for its causes. He does not distinguish the regression requirement from the ability to do otherwise requirement. "One could construct a tree of causes . . . leading backward from any action the person takes, rooted finally in an initial set of genetic and circumstantial variables beyond the reach of her powers. Freedom requires that an alternative action be possible, which this tree of causes does not leave room for" (1995, p. 4, col. 1).

I have explained how the regression requirement, on plausible assumptions, makes responsibility impossible. And if responsibility is impossible, then there would be no scope for Roemer's notion of variation within a type that is not a matter of luck.

2. If the types are so finely specified that each type can contain only one person behaving in one way, then all differences are a matter of luck. This is a limiting case of Roemer's general scheme. The case we are interested in at present, however, is not this limiting case, but the case in which some differences are matters of luck while others are not, so that there is more than one person in each type.

3. This is my illustration; Roemer uses different illustrations, considered below.

dermining factors, since they belong to the same type. Recall that all factors judged to make someone less responsible than another have been used to define the type. So however responsible A and B are for their respective positions, they are *equally* responsible for their respective positions. A may be more prudent than B, but B is just as responsible for his own position as A is for his. The difference between A and B is due, say, to their different choices of work versus leisure, and is therefore not a matter of luck. Thus the difference between A and B is not one that a luck neutralizer should wish to eliminate.

Similarly, C and D belong to type *U,* and there is no relevant difference between C and D in respect of responsibility-undermining factors. However responsible C and D are for their respective positions, they are equally responsible for them. Yet C is better off than D; again, suppose that C is a workaholic while D is a surfer. And again, C may be more prudent than D, but C and D are equally responsible for their own positions. This difference is also down to the different choices of C and D, and therefore is not a matter of luck. So the difference between C and D is not one that a luck neutralizer should wish to eliminate either. (See Figure 6.)

However, the kinds of circumstance in which A and B have made their choices are very different from the kinds of circumstance in which C and D have made theirs. The type to which A and B belong is, in ways for which no one is responsible, more conducive to advantage than the type to which C and D belong. It is so much more conducive to advantage that even though B has chosen to be a surfer, he is still better off than C, who has chosen to be a workaholic. The difference between being a member of type *T* and being a member of type *U* is a matter of luck, by hypothesis. It seems then that any of the intertype differences might be, at least in

	Choice: workaholic	Choice: surfer
Luck: talented type	A: best off	B: second best off
Luck: untalented type	C: third best off	D: worst off

Figure 6. Illustration of Roemer's framework.

part, matters of luck and require some redistribution: the differences between A and C, between A and D, between B and C, and between B and D. Roemer aims to preserve differences within types, for which people are responsible, while equalizing between types what people are not responsible for.

So far I have followed Roemer's lucid way of setting out the problem, though using a different example.[4] Roemer's framework explains how actual differences between people could be judged to be a matter of luck or not. Given these judgments about luck and nonluck, how should we redistribute? Which positions, if any, should be made equal?

3. Why Solving the Problem Requires Judgments of Counterfactual Responsibility

At this point I begin to diverge from Roemer, since I do not agree with the solution he proposes to the problem he sets out so clearly. I argue that the judgments of responsibility that would be needed to solve the problem as set out are not in general available. As I showed in Chapter 6, to equalize what people are *not* responsible for is not to give them what they *are* responsible for: equality may be as much a matter of luck as inequality. Moreover, Roemer's own proposed solution seems to involve an equivocation between desert and responsibility. To give people what they *deserve* because they make more effort is not to give them what they are *responsible* for, either.

Notice first that we cannot eliminate all of the intertype differences, while leaving alone the differences between A and B (in type *T*) and between C and D (in type *U*), which are not matters of luck.

For example, should we eliminate the difference between A and C or the difference between B and C? We cannot do both while respecting the

---

4. It is interesting to compare Roemer's technique with that of attribution theory, as described and criticized in Schoeman 1987 in connection with the Milgram experiments. In particular, Schoeman questions the assumption that the more atypical an act type is in given circumstances, the more the individual performing the act is accountable for it. People can be responsible for doing something, Schoeman suggests, even if nearly everyone in their situation does the same. Cf. Roemer 1996, p. 277: "To take an extreme case, if all sixty-year-old steelworkers smoked for thirty years, we would say that the choice of 'not smoking' is not accessible to steelworkers: as a steelworker, one would have had no effective opportunity but to smoke for thirty years."

difference between A and B, who by hypothesis are equally (though not wholly) responsible for their different respective levels of goods. What we need to know is what counterfactual position for C would make it the case that the relations between A and C and between B and C are not matters of luck either, given that the actual relations between A and C and between B and C are at least partly matters of luck. Would it not be a matter of luck if C were to have the same level of goods as A? As B? Or some other, different level? Is C responsible for the same position as A or for the same position as B or for some other position? All the same questions arise for the relations of A and B to D also. Answers must respect the differences between C and D as well as between A and B, which are not matters of luck.

This is the general form of the problem of finding a pattern of distribution that would neutralize differences that are matters of luck. If judgments of luck and responsibility can be used to solve this problem, then they can play a patterning role. An example of the kind of judgment that would be needed to solve this problem is this:

> A and C are responsible for the same goods position and B and D are responsible for the same goods position, where the first position is better than the second. That is, it would not be a matter of luck for A and C to be equally well off and for B and D to be equally well off, such that A and C are better off than B and D.

This particular judgment, of course, is only an example of the kind of judgement needed to solve the problem. Different particular correlations could be established, by different judgments of luck and responsibility.

However, let's continue to focus on this particular judgment as an example, and consider its implications. If we do implement this particular judgement, we will redistribute to equalize the positions of A and C, and of B and D. Notice that this will reverse the positions of B and C. Before redistribution, B was better off than C; after redistribution, C is better off than B. If responsibility underwrites this pattern, we are not only judging that the actual difference (such that B is better off than C) is a matter of luck. Nor are we merely adding to this that a counterfactual state of equality (between A and C and between B and D, respectively) would not be a matter of luck. We are also implicitly judging that some particular counterfactual *difference* (such that C would be better off than B) would not be a matter of luck. If this tacit judgment of counterfactual responsibility is not confirmed, then redistribution would merely move us from one difference that is a matter of luck to another. And that would not neutralize luck.

This feature of the particular example generalizes, even if different correlations are established. If luck-neutralization is to solve the patterning problem, some such tacit judgments that counterfactual differences would not be a matter of luck are unavoidable. That is, judgments are needed not just about whether or to what degree people are responsible for their actual positions, or that certain actual interpersonal differences are or are not a matter of luck. We can concede that such judgments are legitimate in Roemer's framework. But further judgments are also needed, which are more problematic, about what counterfactual situations people should be judged to be responsible for instead, and what counterfactual relations between people would not be a matter of luck. And some of these must take the form of judgments that particular counterfactual *differences* would not be a matter of luck.

4. Skepticism about Counterfactual Responsibility

What general basis we could have for such judgments? Indeed, what could the truth of such judgments amount to, even apart from our knowledge of their truth? The skepticism about counterfactual responsibility I argued for in Chapter 6 applies again here. It is hard enough to determine whether B's actually being better off than C *is* a matter of luck. But if we judge that it is, this does not mean that we can go further and identify some particular counterfactual relation between B and C that would *not* be a matter of luck. Our normal practices of judging whether people are responsible do not in general extend to specifying other possible states of affairs for which they would be responsible, when they are not responsible for the actual state of affairs. When actual differences between people are due to luck, there is no reason to assume we can in general identify what counterfactual relation between them would not be a matter of luck.

There may be intuitive answers to this question in some particular cases involving limited departures from actual circumstances. But any general principle claiming to answer this question in relation to all actual circumstances due to luck seems bound to be arbitrary. If most of a person's basic life circumstances, or some very influential aspects of them, are a matter of luck, what particular choices would he have made in the absence of luck? What choices would someone make if his life had been a very different life? We are not justified in assuming that luck and responsible choice are separable, so that someone would have made "similar" responsible choices in very different circumstances. More generally, I doubt such questions have answers at all in many cases. The idea of what people are responsible for is underconstrained and indeterminate when it is disconnected from people's actual situations and the actual consequences of their actual choices, in actual or close-to-actual circumstances. This seems to be a case in which our language makes grammatical space for a type of judgment but we should nevertheless be wary of occupying that space. We may have a form of words, but we do not have the substantive resources to underwrite such judgments of counterfactual responsibility. The judgments of counterfactual responsibility needed for responsibility to tell us how to distribute outrun the determinate content of the concept.

Perhaps C would have chosen to be a surfer rather than a workaholic if she had been more talented (she might have perceived more clearly the futility of the rat race). Perhaps that means that being a workaholic is to some degree a matter of luck for her.[5] But nevertheless, there is no causal relationship between C and the counterfactual state of affairs in which she is a surfer. While actual choice and control are causal relations between a person and what is chosen or controlled, hypothetical choice is not a causal relation between a person and what is hypothetically chosen. On pure hypothetical-choice accounts of responsibility, causal responsibility is not necessary for responsibility. As I argued in Part I, this is a problem for such accounts.[6] There are too many things that people would have chosen, if they could have. It is too easy, causally costless, to meet this condition. Surely responsibility requires a more specific, restricted relationship. To

---

5. It does not follow that she is not responsible for her resulting choices, unless the regression requirement is assumed.

6. Roemer himself makes a different criticism of such accounts. He is concerned that someone's self-identifications and hypothetical preferences or choices are often influenced or determined by circumstances for which one is not responsible, as in the case of the tame housewife who is glad she has her overly modest ambitions (1996, p. 249; see also 1998, p. 19). But this criticism in effect switches from a hypothetical choice account of responsibility to some other account, such as a control account. Why, otherwise, assume the tame housewife is not responsible for the relevant circumstances? Her self-identification may be such that she would choose all these circumstances if she could, even though she evidently does not control them. As I have pointed out in earlier chapters, hypothetical-choice accounts of responsibility are compatible with the requirement of regressive responsibility for causes, if hypothetical choice itself can take the chain of causes leading up to actual and hypothetical choices as its object.

hold that responsibility requires causal responsibility, say in the form of actual choice or control, is one way of meeting this point. Of course, causal responsibility is not sufficient for responsibility, even if it is necessary.[7]

What we have now seen is that for responsibility to tell us how to distribute in Roemer's scheme, it must be detached from causal responsibility. His scheme requires us to judge that certain counterfactual differences between people in different types would not be a matter of luck. The needed judgments of counterfactual responsibility, about what people would be responsible for when they are not responsible for their actual situations, break any causal link such as actual choice or control between a person and what she is judged responsible for. As a result, these judgments are open to the same kind of objection that was made against hypothetical-choice accounts of responsibility. Basically, the truth of these judgments of responsibility is underdetermined. There are too many possible counterfactual states of affairs: Which of them is the one someone should be judged to be responsible for, when she is not responsible for the actual one? Why assume this question must in general have a determinate answer? We cannot appeal here to causal relations such as actual choice or control to narrow down the range of possible answers this question. Appealing instead to hypothetical choice merely pushes the problem back a step: there are also too many things people would choose if they could, under various counterfactual conditions. They cannot be responsible for all of them.

The point can be made more concrete by returning to our example. We have two talented characters in type T: workaholic A and surfer B. We also have two untalented characters in type U: workaholic C and surfer D. A is better off than B, who is better off than C, who is better off than D. What judgment about responsibility could warrant the view that redistribution should instead make C better off than B? Perhaps the judgment that if C had been talented, C would still have chosen to be a workaholic rather than a surfer. But that merely postpones the problem. What could make it the case that if C had been more talented, she would not have chosen to be a surfer instead (say, because she perceived the futility of the rat race), or various other things? Her hypothetical choices may well not be separable from her talents (see again Figure 5 in Chapter 6). And the problem isn't just one of how we *know* which of such claims is true. It is one of what it could *be* for a particular one or the other of such claims to be true.

---

7. See Chapter 3.

Let me take stock. The idea that neutralizing luck could provide a pattern for redistribution is tempting. But when we work out exactly how it could do so, we find that we would need judgments about exactly what counterfactual differences between people would *not* be matters of luck, given that actual differences *are* matters of luck. That is, we would have to say not only that some people are not responsible for what they actually have, but go further and specify some other possible state of affairs they should be judged to be responsible for instead. But there are reasons to doubt that our concept of responsibility provides a determinate basis for such judgements of counterfactual responsibility.

5. An Objection, and Why the Equality-Default View Needs to Defend Counterfactual Differences

It may be objected here that we should take equality as the default position. It may just be basic to egalitarianism and to Roemer's view in particular that *only differences that are a matter of luck* need to be eliminated. Egalitarians simply aren't worried about whether equal positions are a matter of luck. Judgments of responsibility are only needed, on this view, to justify differences, not to justify equality. For example, the objection might continue, why not simply take the monetary value of actual differences that are a matter of luck and redistribute it equally among all persons? That way, someone who makes more effort would end up with more of the relevant good than someone who makes less effort, and those who make equal efforts would end up with equal amounts, regardless of their types.

This proposal does not give people what they are responsible for, but what they deserve on the basis of effort, which is quite different (this point is developed further in section 6 below). It does not neutralize luck, since we have no reason to assume that if luck were eliminated people would be responsible for equal amounts of the relevant good rather than unequal amounts. However, this proposal may appear to avoid the need for problematic judgments of counterfactual responsibility by assuming equality as a default position without requiring any justification for doing so in terms of luck and responsibility.

One reply to this proposal has in effect already been made in Chapter 6. The equality-default view adopts equality as default, without trying to show that luck and responsibility either specify or justify this particular default setting. So this view in effect concedes that responsibility does not do the work of specifying or justifying the choice of equality as the default position.

A further reply can now also be made. The equality-default view says that equalities need not be defended, only differences. But if differences do have to be defended in luck-neutralizing terms, then such a defense will still rely on problematic judgments of counterfactual responsibility, as can be shown by reference to Roemer's scheme.

In our example, this proposal would have us estimate the monetary value of the differences between types T and U, take that amount away proportionately from those in type T, and then redistribute it equally among A, B, C, and D. Would this avoid the need to rely on problematic judgments of counterfactual responsibility? No. As before, the effect would be to make C better off than B. This is a difference, not an equality, so it needs defense. If differences need to be defended in terms of responsibility, then we must ask: Is this counterfactual difference a matter of luck? If not, it is acceptable. If so, we would need to eliminate it also. There is no point in replacing differences that are a matter of luck with different differences that would also be a matter of luck.

But how, when the actual differences between people are a matter of luck, can we identify different differences between them that would not be a matter of luck? I have claimed that in many cases there is no determinate answer to this question. If we uncritically assume that we can answer this question, the answers we come up with are likely either to be arbitrary or to reflect some unscrutinized assumptions or implicit value judgments that are really doing the work. We do better to admit that luck and responsibility cannot play this patterning role, and to scrutinize explicitly whatever is doing this work.

In fact, the work of defending counterfactual differences in this proposal is really being done by judgments of deservingness, not by judgments of responsibility at all.

6. Equivocation between Responsibility and Deservingness

I suggest that in many cases with the structure of our example, what prompts us to make C better off than B is indeed a tacit value judgment, such as the judgment that C's choice to work harder than B chooses to work is the better choice, and deserves reward. We may want people to work hard; we may approve when they do, and want to reward them more the harder they try to work. Moreover, we may prefer people to choose what we regard as productive work or work we think is good for them, so that "working hard" at surfing doesn't really count as working hard. In a different sense of "responsible" than that in play up to now we may regard hard workers as more responsible than slackers: they are more prudentially responsible and hence more deserving. (I assume here that deservingness is understood prudentially, but my arguments are unaffected if it is understood socially or ethically instead.) According to this value judgment, other things equal, workaholics are more prudentially responsible, hence deserving, than surfers: so A is more prudentially responsible than B, and C is more prudentially responsible than D.

However, this value judgment is controversial. For example, someone who advocates the right to a basic income might reject this value judgment, and regard it as socially and/or prudentially counterproductive and unjustifiably paternalistic and perfectionist (see and cf. Van Parijs 1995). Moreover, the real world is not as simple as my toy world of surfers and workaholics. People may choose to work very hard at one job, which they regard as more worthwhile, even though they would be more talented or productive in another job. I may choose to neglect my extraordinary musical talent in order to work hard as a relatively low-paid psychiatric nurse. A controversial value judgment is needed to say which choice is more prudentially responsible (or indeed more socially responsible) and hence deserves greater reward (for discussion, see Vandenbroucke 1999, chap. 1).

Moreover, this *must* be a different sense of "responsible" than the one we have been using up to now. Someone can be responsible for making prudentially (or socially) irresponsible choices; indeed, someone can be responsible for doing evil. We assumed in setting up our example that A and B are equally responsible for their positions, as are C and D. A and B are responsible for different choices and hence for different levels of goods, and we regard A's choices as more prudentially responsible than B's. Nevertheless, A and B are equally responsible for their choices, since all responsibility undermining factors have been used to define the type to which they both belong. Equivocation on these two senses of responsibility leads to implicit incoherence. A cannot both be more responsible than B and in the same sense equally as responsible as B. A clear distinction is needed between what people are responsible for and what people deserve or how prudent they are. Rather than speaking of how prudentially "responsible" someone is, it would serve clarity and avoid equivocation to speak instead of how prudent, or how deserving, someone is.

Roemer makes his own suggestion about how to resolve the issues I have been discussing. Unfortunately, his proposal fails to register the distinction just drawn between claims about whether people are responsible for their positions and claims about how prudentially responsible, or deserving, people are. Let us now switch to Roemer's own example, involving the choice to smoke.

Again, we collect all the factors society judges to undermine someone's responsibility for some type of behavior. The basis for these judgments about responsibility is left open. These factors are used to collect people into types. People with one type are in the same position as one another with respect to factors that are matters of luck. Therefore, differences between people within one type are not matters of luck. Suppose that there is a range of behavior within type 1. For example, among all those smokers with a given age, gender, ethnicity, economic class, level of education, and smoking parents, some will have smoked for two years and some for twenty years. Now consider a different type, type 2, identified by the same age but different gender, ethnicity, class, education, and so on. Again, there will be a range of behavior within type 2. Roemer suggests types of sixty-year-old white female college professors and sixty-year-old black male steelworkers.

Roemer proposes that we focus on the median behavior within each type of population.[8]

> [S]ociety has already accounted for, in the definition of type, all the circumstances affecting smoking behavior which it takes to be beyond a person's control. Now let us compare two people of different types, both of whom are at the median of their respective type-distributions of years of smoking. Although it might not make sense to say they have exercised the *same* degree of responsibility, we can say that each has exercised a comparable degree of responsibility, taking into account what others in his type have done. (Roemer 1993, pp. 150–151; see also 1996, pp. 276–279; 1998, pp. 8–12)

Suppose the type 1 median white female college professor has smoked for eight years, while the type 2 median black steelworker has smoked for thirty years. Roemer regards these two behaviors as equally accessible, because exactly half of the type 1 people smoked for less than eight years and

---

8. He makes a different, more complex suggestion in later work (1998, p. 27), but the earlier proposal will do to illustrate the problem, which arises for both proposals.

exactly half of the type 2 people smoked for less than thirty years. The median types, he claims, have exercised similar degrees of will power or effort, or have taken comparable degrees of "responsibility". In this way Roemer argues for an egalitarian ethic that requires these two people, at the medians of their respective types, to be equally indemnified by society against the ills that result from smoking. If society pays all the medical costs of the type 1 median character, it should do the same for the type 2 median character.

Roemer does not in general require that those who make more effort within a type should get more goods than those who make less. All individuals in a type face the same policy, which might allocate goods in a variety of ways to individuals, according to their effort. Equalizing opportunity in Roemer's sense means choosing the policy that equalizes outcomes across types, at each level of effort.[9]

In effect, Roemer is proposing to normalize a measure of deservingness by using the range of behavior within each type to measure effort. Within type 1, someone who has smoked for two years is presumed to make more of an effort and thus be more prudentially responsible than someone who has smoked for twenty years. As a result, it may be felt that within type 1, someone who has smoked for only two years deserves more medical help than someone who has smoked for twenty years. The critical point is that equal efforts across types get equal reward: for example, that someone in type 2 who has made the same effort not to smoke as the person in type 1 who has smoked for two years gets the same level of medical help. This is to tailor social assistance to how prudentially responsible, or deserving, someone's behavior is. It is to rely on our value judgments about how prudentially responsible certain behavior is, in order to arrive at a pattern of distribution of medical resources.

But it is *not* to neutralize differences that are a matter of luck or to give considerations of luck a patterning role. To do that, we would need to know not *how deserving* people are, but *what they are responsible for: what is not or would not be a matter of luck for them*. It is exactly this difference that Roemer's proposal fails to register. Judgments about how prudentially responsible, or deserving, someone's behavior is should be distinguished from judgments about how responsible each person is for his or her situation. Within type 1, someone who has smoked for two years is just as responsible for her choice to smoke for two years as someone who has

---

9. My thanks to John Roemer for this clarification of his position.

smoked for twenty years is for her choice to smoke for twenty years, even though the choice to smoke twenty years is less prudentially (and socially) responsible and the twenty-year smoker has exerted less effort not to smoke. By hypothesis, the difference between two years and twenty years within a type is not a matter of luck. The type is defined so as to ensure that differences within types are differences for which people are responsible; all differences for which people are not responsible are used to distinguish the types.

Roemer's proposal conflates issues about *how* prudentially responsible, hence deserving, people are with issues about *what* they are responsible *for*. Are different people equally responsible for the results of their choices? Even if they are, they can make different choices, some more prudentially (or socially) responsible than others, with different results. This distinction is blurred by Roemer's talk of "comparable responsibility." Within a given type, by hypothesis, people are equally responsible for their choices to smoke different amounts. Smoking less is in this sense no less accessible than smoking more. Perhaps it takes more will power or effort to smoke less. But someone who smokes more is just as responsible for doing so as someone else within the same type who smokes less.

7. The Paternalism of Roemer's Proposal

We may judge it better—whether prudentially, socially, or ethically—to smoke less and regard those who do so, other things equal, as to that extent more deserving. We may wish to redistribute in accordance with this value judgment. As a result, we may wish to reward people equally who try equally hard not to smoke. But that does not show that someone's position after redistribution would not be a matter of luck for her. Indeed, it may be a matter of luck for her that we make this value judgment at all; she may regard it as an utterly daft value judgment that happens to produce a windfall for her.

It is not enough to say that people who expend equal effort should end up equally well off. We have also to ask: *Effort at doing what?* And we must justify our answers. Some people may try very hard to do just the opposite of what others try to do. Someone can try very hard to do things of which we do not approve. Jack may try hard to smoke more in order to fit in with his peer group and not care much about his long-term health, but be unable to smoke more because of his asthma (cf. Roemer 1998, pp. 43–44). People make different trade-offs between various goods worth striving for, not just between one good and effort. People's own differing valuations of what they try to do are not captured by Roemer's scheme; rather, our valuation is imposed.[10] Although Roemer claims that "reward is due to persons according to their propensity to expend effort" (1998, p. 15; see also p. 104n), it is not someone's degree of effort per se that interests Roemer, but degree of effort made toward doing *what we value* (1998, pp. 33–34, 52, 115). Our valuations are imposed by the choice of dimension of advantage along which effort is assessed.

This prompts the question: Why should we aim to reward people for how hard they try to do what we judge they should do, when no explicit basis for that valuation or its democratic relationship to their own values has been given? I am sympathetic to liberal perfectionism (see Chapter 10), but it requires explicit defense in relation to liberal democratic values, and care should be taken that it is not disguised by incorporation within formal structures that protect it from scrutiny. Roemer is clear that the definition of types on his proposal is the outcome of a contentious process, since people may disagree in their judgments about what factors people are not responsible for, and these are deep ethical disagreements (1998, pp. 8, 28 ff; 1996, p. 277). But his proposal requires not just that society somehow resolve these deep issues about responsibility in order to define types, but also that society somehow determine that reward is deserved for efforts to do some things, but not others, whether or not the expenders of effort agree. As Roemer admits, his planner is paternalistic (1998, p. 52; see also pp. 114–115).

In Roemer's scheme, such admittedly paternalistic value judgments about "advantage" and *which* efforts deserve reward are in effect occupying the vacuum left by the indeterminacy of the concepts of responsibility

---

10. Roemer writes: "Underneath their circumstances, then, persons are not presupposed to be identical—they differ in their propensity to expend effort." He regards this as a sufficient basis for saying that individuals retain "some kind of deep individuality" (1998, p. 15). By contrast, I suggest that this is only the tip of the iceberg of individuality and of the deep differences in all-things-considered value judgments that express individuality. This difference is closely related to my worries about the paternalism of Roemer's view, discussed in the text. Roemer's conception of individuality takes us not very far at all away from the bare selves with their universal preferences who lurk in Roemer 1995 and 1996, discussed in Chapter 6. The deeply paternalistic character of Roemer's proposal comes closer to the surface in more recent formulations, such as 1998, pp. 22–24, 33–34, 52, 114–115; see also Vandenbroucke 1999, chap. 1.

and luck as applied counterfactually. Since there is no way to answer the question of what counterfactual differences between types would not be a matter of luck, in the sense opposed to responsibility, we answer a different question instead, namely, what counterfactual differences between types would reward people in accordance with our valuation of their efforts and how deserving they are. People who are equally deserving because they have made equal effort *in the direction we favor* should be rewarded equally. Such tacit value judgments are really doing the work, and accordingly need explicit scrutiny by democratic processes. They may be controversial either on specific grounds or on general antipaternalist or antiperfectionist grounds.

Our answers to this different question can indeed play a patterning role. But there need be nothing especially egalitarian about our valuations of merit and the pattern they support. For example, we might value efforts to earn more money rather than less within each type, and wish to reward high earners within each type by redistributing in their favor. We would then, following Roemer's proposal, regard the median person within each type as equally meritorious and reward them equally, but we would redistribute the value of the intertype differences in favor of higher earners rather than lower earners within each type, *increasing* the disparity between them. We would still be rewarding equally across types those who make equal efforts to earn money. But this would hardly be egalitarian in a more substantive sense; nor would it satisfy the minimal egalitarian constraint (see Chapter 6) that requires that relatively more equal patterns of distribution be favored, other things equal. We have to start with egalitarian value judgments to ensure that an egalitarian pattern of distribution will be supported by them.

8. A Diagnosis of the Equivocation between Responsibility and Deservingness: Monotonic Valuation

Shifting from one to the other of the two senses of "responsibility" I have distinguished amounts to changing the subject. We started out to find whether judgments about responsibility in one sense could justify an egalitarian pattern of distribution. The relevant sense is the one we use when we ask whether someone is responsible for something, as a result, say, of choice, or whether instead it is a matter of luck for him. This is the sense that, on the face of it, is invoked by the luck-neutralizing approach to distributive justice. I denied that the aim to neutralize factors for which people are not responsible supports equality, or any other pattern of distribution. But Roemer's scheme is not actually in the business of showing how the aim to neutralize factors for which people are not responsible supports any particular pattern of distribution.

It may seem to be, however, because of equivocation between the two senses of "responsibility." Roemer uses responsibility in the first sense to divide people into types: people in a given type are similar with respect to all factors for which people are not responsible, such as their parent's education levels, their race and sex, and so on. But Roemer then uses responsibility in the second sense, that of *deservingness*, to allocate resources to people within types according to the merit of their choices along some dimension. In doing so, he is appealing to our value judgments about how deserving someone's choices have been in some particular respect.[11] Roemer shows how the aim to reward effort according to deservingness can play a patterning role. He shows how under certain assumptions we can equate the degrees to which effort is made across types, so that we can reward equally behavior that is equally deserving.

But, as I have emphasized, rewarding effort according to deservingness is not the same thing as neutralizing factors for which people are not responsible. What someone deserves is not equivalent to what he is responsible for. Some can deserve his situation even though he is not responsible for it: as a matter of serendipity an unsung hero may receive a windfall that he richly deserves, or a blackguard may get his comeuppance. Conversely, someone can be responsible for his situation even though he does not deserve it: a saint may reasonably and deliberately take a calculated risk, and lose; a sinner may do the same, and win.

Why might these two different aims be conflated? One possible explanation is that the idea of luck can be opposed to deservingness instead of to responsibility. Is the situation of the unsung hero with the windfall a matter of luck or not? Yes, in the sense opposed to responsibility, since he is not responsible for it. But not in a sense opposed to desert, since he deserves it. However, it would be fallacious to argue from the claim that the windfall is not a matter of luck in the sense that it is deserved to the claim

---

11. Peter Vallentyne (personal communication) has raised the question whether Roemer is concerned with how morally or socially deserving someone's choices are or rather with how prudentially deserving someone's choices are. Roemer is not explicit about which he intends. I have interpreted him in terms of prudential deservingness in the text. But the points I make about monotonicity and paternalism would apply either way.

that it is not a matter of luck in the sense that he is responsible for it. I have no objection to "luck" being used as the inverse correlate of desert instead of responsibility, so long as the two uses are clearly distinguished and equivocation is avoided. My complaint is that they have not been.

We have been concerned with luck in the sense that is relevant to responsibility-driven accounts of distributive justice. But the question now arises whether we should conceive of distributive justice in desert-driven rather than responsibility-driven terms. Notice, however, that we cannot make do with desert as the fundamental concept in Roemer's account. Suppose A is more deserving than B because A makes more effort, but A and B are equally responsible for what they do because they are in the same type. A and B must be equally responsible in some sense of "responsible" that does not simply amount to deservingness. Roemer's scheme needs two different concepts: one to partition people into types, another to assess people's different choices within types. Neither desert nor responsibility can play both roles.

A further diagnosis of the conflation of responsibility and deservingness within Roemer's framework is this. Notice how, if the range of behavior within a type is one-dimensional in a certain sense, then this conflation becomes very natural. Suppose we make the value judgments that smoking ought to be resisted, that effort not to smoke is prudentially responsible, and that it is better to smoke less, within any type. Merit therefore increases monotonically as amount of smoking reduces. We wish to redistribute across types in a way that rewards people in accordance with these value judgments. Roemer's proposal is that the median position within each type involves the same degree of merit. In this example it is merit in making an effort to resist smoking. But in another of his examples, concerning years of education undertaken, the one-dimensionality or monotonicity feature is also present. The assumption there is that it is better to undertake more education rather than less. Merit increases monotonically with years of education; it is merit in making an effort to get an education.

This monotonicity feature of Roemer's examples obscures the points I have been making, and lends itself to talk of "comparable responsibility" that blurs the distinction between whether someone is responsible for something and how deserving he is. The effects of smoking are bad: bad health. The effects of education are good: greater income. So we can assume that people are more prudentially responsible the more effort they make to avoid smoking and to acquire education. If we aim to reward such prudentially responsible behavior, then someone who smokes less or ac-

quires more education, other things equal, deserves more reward, according to these value judgments. But within one type, the person who smokes
less is no more responsible than the person who smokes more; he just
makes a different, though better, choice.

In sum: when such monotonic valuation is assumed, degree of reward
can be correlated with degree of merit normalized within each type. And
we can express this by saying that the median person within each type deserves the same reward. But this sense of desert directly reflects our value
judgments and desire to reward meritorious efforts, rather than what people are responsible for.

It is not clear how Roemer's proposal would apply unless this monotonicity assumption is made (see and cf. Roemer 1996, p. 279 ff; Vandenbroucke 1999, chap. 1). And this assumption may be justified in some
cases, such as his smoking and education examples: perhaps it simply is
better, other things equal, to smoke less and to get more education. But
monotonicity is not in general justified. We cannot in general presume
that behavior at one end of a range within a type ought to be encouraged
or resisted.

In my example, we had workaholics and surfers. It is controversial
whether these are points on a spectrum along which merit increases monotonically. We might reasonably judge that both extremes are undesirable
and wish to discourage them, and instead regard midspectrum behavior as
deserving of reward. Or, more fundamentally, we may regard it, within
broad limits, as none of society's business and objectionably paternalist or
perfectionist to make assumptions about where on this spectrum people
should fall, or even whether equal effort made in one direction or the
other deserves equal reward. Ditto for assumptions about whether people should work at the jobs at which they happen to be most talented or
efficient or rather at those they regard as most worthwhile or satisfying. Which of such choices is more prudentially responsible or deserving
is a controversial normative issue normally reserved to private decision-
making. If a public policy is needed on such an issue, the issue should get
explicit exposure and democratic deliberation. We cannot simply assume
that efforts to be efficient are more deserving than efforts to do something
one finds satisfying. Nor can we assume that people who make the same
degree of effort to be efficient rather than to do something satisfying deserve the same reward. Different people may rightly make different trade-
offs between different aims and values, and accordingly make different ef-

forts. For many dimensions of effort, it is not for society to decide which efforts are more, less, or equally deserving.

To take another example, consider the number of children people have within two different types. Suppose the median for type 1 is one child, while the median for type 2 is three children. In this example, monotonicity fails. In the absence of some particular population policy, we cannot assume that having more children is either to be encouraged or resisted. It is a matter of free private choice within natural constraints, and within each type people are equally responsible for the results of their different choices. They may be equally deserving as well, both prudentially and socially. More merit does not attach to having either more or less children. Some people make tremendous efforts to have more children, others to avoid having any. In the absence of monotonic valuation, the median position lacks the significance Roemer wants to give it. There is no reason to reward type 1 persons with one child to the same degree as type 2 persons with three children. Occupying the median within a type is mere happenstance.

I have been emphasizing that luck-neutralizing approaches to distributive justice should respect the distinction between responsibility and deservingness, and should not trade on equivocation between them by opposing luck to both of them simultaneously. Perhaps appeal to something other than responsibility, such as desert or fairness, can provide a basis for egalitarianism. But this should be clearly distinguished from an appeal to what people are responsible for.

Return now to the suggestion that we conceive distributive justice in desert-driven terms. Someone might object: Well, what is wrong after all with taking the basis for distribution to be deservingness rather than responsibility? We can grant that the two shouldn't be confused and that both concepts have roles to play, but that responsibility cannot tell us how to distribute. And we can grant that the dimensions along which we reward deservingness should be limited to those for which a degree of paternalism or perfectionism is appropriate, in light of the results of democratic processes. But once we've distinguished responsibility from deservingness, and limited our concern with deservingness appropriately, perhaps it is indeed deservingness that should tell us how to distribute. Perhaps our general aim should be to distribute in accordance with deservingness, to give people not what they are responsible for after all, but rather what they deserve, whether they are responsible for it or not.

This objection raises a very deep issue. I find the idea that we should re-distribute in accordance with deservingness deeply unattractive as a general basis for distributive justice (and of course others have argued against this kind of view, such as Rawls 1971). Basing distributive justice on deservingness is worrying in relation to liberal democratic values in a way that basing distributive justice on responsibility is not. Moreover, I doubt that the concept of deservingness would prove less damagingly indeterminate in general than does a conception of responsibility detached from causal responsibility, such as a pure counterfactual choice conception. What people deserve extends counterfactually well beyond what they are responsible for, and would in many cases be highly controversial. How in general would a theory of distributive justice resolve controversial issues about what people deserve to have, when they do not deserve what they do have? Should distributive justice in a pluralistic liberal democracy be based on such judgments about deservingness?

Perhaps these concerns would be disarmed by appropriate limitations to specific democratically adopted policies. But then would we really have a general theory of distributive justice, as opposed to a theory of how to implement specific policies? Policies that reward desert along specific dimensions can indeed result from properly democratic processes. A democracy might adopt, for example, a policy of rewarding people for choosing more education rather than less, or for choosing healthier lifestyles. Under certain circumstances, it might adopt a policy encouraging or discouraging certain numbers of children. Roemer's scheme may well have valuable practical applications and offer effective guidance in carrying out public policy, so long as it is limited to rewarding efforts along specific dimensions that have been explicitly targeted in policies adopted through democratic processes. This is quite different, however, from providing a general basis for egalitarian distributive justice.[12]

I have not tried here to give a decisive argument against the aim to redistribute in accordance with deservingness. What I have done is to argue, more modestly, that this aim should not be confused with the aim to neutralize factors for which people are not responsible, and to suggest some reasons for doubting that the former aim can provide a general basis for

---

12. Perhaps Roemer's scheme should be conceived as part of a theory of complex equality and used to carry out specific policies within particular "spheres" of justice (see Walzer 1983).

distributive justice, as opposed to a way of implementing specific policies with a liberal democracy.

9. Summary

Let's now review the basic points that have been made about Roemer's framework. People can be equally responsible for very different outcomes. Within each of Roemer's types, people are by hypothesis equally responsible for what happens to them. The types are defined so as to ensure that people are responsible for the differences within the type; all differences for which they are not responsible result from the factors used to distinguish one type from another. Within a type, a person at the median, who, for example, has smoked for eight years, is just as responsible as a person at the eightieth percentile, who has smoked for fifteen years. They simply make different choices. To the extent different results flow from those choices, they are responsible for different results.

But across types, differences are partly due to luck. How, then, can we correct for differences across types that are a matter of luck while preserving differences within types for which people are responsible? We cannot eliminate all differences across types while respecting differences within types as due to choice. If the aim to neutralize differences that are a matter of luck can answer this question, then it can play a patterning role and tell us how to distribute.

For it to do so, however, we would need to know, when actual differences between types are a matter of luck, what counterfactual differences between types would not be a matter of luck. And this is generally indeterminate. In many cases our judgments of responsibility simply don't reach this far. Roemer's proposal doesn't in fact even try to use the aim to neutralize differences that are a matter of luck to answer this question. It doesn't try to tell us what counterfactual differences would not be a matter of luck. Rather, it tells us what counterfactual differences would reward people across types in accordance with our value judgments about their efforts to behave in certain ways, so as to reward equal, and equally deserving, efforts equally. This aim, not the aim to neutralize differences that are a matter of luck, is what plays a patterning role in Roemer's scheme. So his scheme is not a counterexample to my claim that considerations of luck and responsibility cannot play a patterning role. And it is constrained in its scope of application by the need for the valuations that are doing the work to avoid antipaternalist and antiperfectionist scruples and satisfy democratic constraints.

10. Concluding Thoughts

People are, to some degree, responsible for doing certain things, and as a result for certain goods. They are not responsible for other goods. When responsibility plays a currency role in distributive justice, it tells us what goods to redistribute. It tells us that goods are exempt from redistribution to the extent to which people are responsible for them and that distributive justice is only concerned with redistributing goods that are a matter of luck for people. This provides another view about the currency of distributive justice: along with welfare-egalitarianism and resource-egalitarianism, we have "luck-egalitarianism."

If responsibility could play a patterning role, it would have to tell us not *what*, but *how* to redistribute. I have argued that it cannot play this role, and that responsibility provides no basis for equality in particular as a pattern of distribution.

Why have the *what* and *how* roles not consistently been clearly distinguished? A diagnostic answer is that talk about "differences that are a matter of luck" and "differences for which people are not responsible" and people being "worse off through no fault of their own" has been engaged in uncritically, without adequately examining what it could mean. Responsibility is in the first instance a relation between people and what they do or what results from what they do, including goods. Talking instead about responsibility for relations between people, such as differences or sameness of their goods positions, makes it natural to run together the *what* and the *how* issues about distribution. If what people are responsible for, or not responsible for, is a difference or a sameness in interpersonal relations, then it seems that knowing what people are responsible for immediately tells us something about interpersonal patterns of distribution. That is, it seems as if what people are responsible for immediately tells us how we should redistribute.

But this immediacy is illusory. When we scrutinize talk about whether people are responsible for differences, we find that we need to substitute for differences that are supposedly a matter of luck other, counterfactual differences, but with no general basis for holding that they would not be just as much a matter of luck. The imagined patterning role of responsibility falls apart in our hands.

Even though I claim that the aim to neutralize luck cannot, on reflection, provide a basis for egalitarianism, I agree with Roemer that the articulation of responsibility-based accounts of distributive justice has been the signal achievement in this field in the last fifteen or so years (Roemer 1996). It has brought deep assumptions to the surface where they can be probed and assessed. While my arguments in this chapter and Chapter 6 have taken issue with Cohen and Roemer, my own perspective on these matters is heavily indebted to their seminal work.[13]

---

13. Cf. Anderson 1999 for a critique of luck-egalitarianism very different from that offered here.

8

The Currency of Distributive Justice and Incentive Inequality

1. Introduction:
Four Possible Roles of Responsibility in Justice

Luck-neutralizing egalitarianism gives responsibility a role in defining what distributive justice distributes—in defining the currency of egalitarian justice, as Gerald Cohen puts it. In previous chapters I have contrasted questions about how to distribute with questions about what to distribute. If responsibility tells us how to distribute, it plays a patterning role. I have argued in the previous two chapters that responsibility cannot play a patterning role. If, on the other hand responsibility tells us what to distribute, it plays a currency role. My arguments that responsibility cannot play a patterning role leave open whether it can, or should, play a currency role.

As I explained in Chapter 6, we can think of the currency role of responsibility in luck-neutralizing accounts of distributive justice as follows. Responsibility acts as a filter on goods (such as welfare, resources, or both, that is, advantage), and what passes through the filter is *what* distributive justice is concerned to distribute, the currency of distributive justice. We only aim to redistribute goods that are a matter of brute luck for people, but not goods people are responsible for, for example, via their choices.[1] This chapter focuses on the currency role of responsibility, and especially its relationship to issues about incentive inequality. I also examine the way the implications of the currency role concerning incentive inequality depend on the conception of responsibility in play.

Chapter 9 goes on to consider the relationship of the goods-filtering,

---

1. Recall again that goods for which people are responsible can include the outcomes of chosen gambles, which count as matters of "option luck" rather than brute luck.

currency-defining role of responsibility in luck-neutralizing egalitarianism to two further and distinct roles that responsibility can play in distributive justice. In one role, conceptions of responsibility and beliefs about responsibility act as parameters on which the range of possible incentive-seeking behavior depends. This is referred to for short as the *incentive-parameter role* of responsibility. It is an aspect of a more general role that beliefs about responsibility can play in motivating productive activity. In another role, both truths and beliefs about responsibility can constitute part of people's well-being. This is referred to for short as the *well-being role* of responsibility.

By the end of the next chapter, then, I will have distinguished and examined four possible roles that responsibility might play in distributive justice: it might tell us how to distribute, what to distribute, set the parameters of possible incentive-seeking behavior, or constitute part of well-being. The patterning or "how" role has been rejected. The currency or "what" role will turn out to be problematic. However, the incentive-parameter and well-being roles will emerge as important. The relationship of these two roles to the currency role will be considered. How do these three distinct roles interact: do they conflict, or constrain one another, or create unstable interdependencies, or admit of stable equilibria? Finally, I will consider how these various roles appear from an alternative, cognitive perspective, one concerned to neutralize bias rather than luck.

2. Incentive Inequality: How Well Off Could the Worst Off Be?

Should luck-neutralizing egalitarianism countenance incentive inequalities? My general strategy in this chapter is to ask: How can Cohen's luck-neutralizing view of the currency of distributive justice be combined with his separate arguments against incentive inequality? The currency role of responsibility within luck-neutralizing egalitarianism is already familiar. The next task is to provide a brief exposition of Cohen's arguments about incentive inequality, which raise revealing and important questions. Then I ask how the currency view and the view on incentive inequality can be brought together.

Why should some be badly off, when others are well off? In "Incentives, Inequality, and Community" (1992), Cohen pursues this fundamental egalitarian issue. In general, he sees unnecessary hardship as wrong, and equality as a means to making the badly off better off. In particular, he criticizes an incentive-based argument for inequality apparently countenanced by Rawls: *the maximin argument for incentive inequality.* This attempts to justify inequalities that derive from incentives to the talented on the grounds that they are needed to improve the position of the worst off. The argument has a maximin principle as normative premise, namely, that the worst off should be made as well off as possible, a version of which is incorporated into Rawls's difference principle. The argument also has a supposedly descriptive premise, namely, that the position of the worst off will be maximally improved by giving the talented incentives to work harder than they would otherwise choose to work, incentives that will generate departures from equality. This is because the benefits of this extra work will, if there is enough of it by enough of the talented, trickle down to improve the position of the worst off as well. Moreover, the talented will in general do the extra work just if they are given such incentives.

Cohen distinguishes inequalities that are absolutely necessary in order to make the worst off better off from inequalities that are only necessary relative to certain intentions or choices, taken as given. He points out that incentive inequality benefits the badly off only within the constraint fixed by the attitudes of the talented. In particular, the incentive-seeking attitudes of the talented are critical, and their corresponding dispositions to withdraw or withhold labor in the absence of incentives. These attitudes and dispositions underwrite the supposedly descriptive premise of the incentive argument—that the position of the worst off can be maximally improved by giving the talented extra incentives. However, these very attitudes in many cases run counter to the normative maximin premise of the argument.

Cohen does not reject the difference principle, but he denies that it justifies special incentives to the talented. He conjectures that if inegalitarian incentive-seeking attitudes and choices are not taken as given, then incentive inequality harms the worst off relative to another, more egalitarian possible state of affairs in which the extra work of the talented is performed without extra incentives and so with greater benefit to the worst off. More simply, if the talented did not withhold labor in the absence of incentives, the worst off could be better off still.

Cohen holds that the talented choose to make the supposedly descriptive premise of the incentive argument true. Given this, he argues, there is a kind of incoherence between their utterance of the "descriptive" premise and their endorsement of the normative maximin premise, to which their own choices run counter. The attitudes that make the "descriptive" premise true, which the utterances of the talented express, conflict with the normative premise. The more disposed the talented are to affirm the normative premise of the incentive argument, the less disposed they should be to make its factual premise true. The talented cannot justify the truth of the premise that their own choices make true, namely, that incentives to themselves are needed in order to benefit the worst off, consistently with the normative premise that the worst off should be made as well off as possible. Cohen focuses attention on the character of utterances of the incentive argument in the mouths of the talented when directed to the badly off, and argues that the incentive argument can justify inequality only where there is a lack of community.

This claim of incoherence assumes that it is indeed possible for the talented to work just as hard to benefit the worst off without the extra incentives. For example, it is possible for them to work just as hard at, say, 60 percent top tax rate as at 40 percent. There is a factual question here, but Cohen finds the answer to it clear and downplays the issue. Luxuries, he asserts, are not strictly needed for performance. Perhaps extra effort requires some compensation so that it does not leave the talented badly off themselves, to avoid the "slavery of the talented." But Cohen suspects that the income gap standardly required to meet the costs of extra effort is "surely only a fraction of the one that obtains even at 60% top tax" (1992, p. 228). *Special burden cases,* in which the relevant extra effort without extra compensation leaves the talented as the worst off themselves, he regards as statistically uncommon (cf. Roemer 1985). In *standard cases,* working harder at the higher top tax rate would leave most of the talented still much better off than most others are, with both higher incomes and more fulfilling jobs. "In my opinion," he writes, "there is not much truth in th[e] contention" that the talented just cannot get themselves to work as hard without the incentives, just cannot resist knocking off at five instead of six o'clock, taking longer holidays, and so on. The kind of morose reluctance that operates as a drag on performance, he suggests, may itself be a function of habituation and normative expectations, which should not be taken as given and can be changed. Cohen admits, however, that he has not shown that there are no deeper restrictions on motivation. Incentives may elicit motivation that cannot be summoned at will. *And what one is able to do may depend on one's reasons for doing it.*[2]

Cohen thus assumes a positive answer to the factual question about

---

2. This important point is developed in Chapter 9's discussion of the incentive-parameter role of responsibility.

whether it is possible for the talented to work harder without extra incentives. In this context, he finds an ambiguity in the difference principle:

> [I]n its strict reading, it counts inequalities as necessary only when they are, strictly, necessary, necessary, that is, apart from people's chosen intentions. In its lax reading, it countenances intention-relative necessities as well. (Cohen 1992, p. 311)[3]

The strict difference principle cannot be implemented by government alone. But the lax difference principle could allow quite large inequalities, if the talented seek large incentives where no special burdens are involved. The degree of inequality permitted by the lax difference principle may be incongruent with the idea that talented are lucky to be talented. Those talented who seek large incentives where no special burdens are involved are not living by an egalitarian conception of justice that aims to maximin advantages that are a matter of luck. This aim conflicts with the lax reading of the difference principle[4] and supports the strict reading.

In this way Cohen draws critical attention to the way maximin principles of justice can be constrained by assumptions and attitudes about incentive seeking that are not themselves normatively neutral. Given the large impact such attitudes can have on the upshot of maximin principles, it is surprising that they are often treated purely as empirical matters, or as exogenous to norms of justice. But while Cohen is surely right to bring these attitudes under normative scrutiny, there is more than one way of looking at the issues he raises.

In his view, the answer to the factual question whether it is possible for the talented to work harder for less is clearly "yes." Therefore, an ambiguity arises in the difference principle as between the lax and strict readings. But a different view is that the difference principle is not ambiguous; the "strict" difference principle just is the difference principle. Its correct application, however, depends on the factual issue about what is possible.[5]

---

3. Does this way of drawing the distinction assume that people's intentions cannot themselves be necessitated?

4. More generally, the luck neutralizing aim conflicts with the Pareto argument for inequality; see and cf. Cohen 1995.

5. There is some reason to attribute this alternative view to Rawls. Rawls (2001, p. 63) explains the relationship between "OP" curves and the difference principle as follows. "Other things being equal, the difference principle directs society to aim at the highest point on the OP curve of the most effectively designed scheme of coopera-

Cohen finds an ambiguity in the difference principle by downplaying any serious issue about what is possible. The alternative view denies there is an ambiguity but holds that how the difference principle applies turns on the issue about possibility. What on Cohen's view amounts to a lax reading of the difference principle, on the alternative view amounts to a different view about what is in fact possible. If it is not possible for the talented to do extra work without incentives, then the difference principle supports incentive inequality as a means to making the worst off as well off as possible. But if it is possible for the talented to do extra work without incentives, then their doing so may be the most effective means of maximining. While the difference principle permits incentive inequality in principle, we need to know what is possible before we can apply the difference principle or determine whether it permits incentive inequality in fact. Once the factual issue is resolved, there is no ambiguity in the difference principle.

Is the answer to the factual issue really as clear-cut as Cohen assumes? Many egalitarians believe that people "need" (in a way that is not directly subject to their choice or control) some kind of personal incentive, such as social esteem, yet want to resist the idea that people need money incentives. But if people may genuinely need the former, why not the latter?[6] More argument is needed here. It seems that Cohen ignores this alternative view because he does not envisage serious disagreement with his claim that it is possible for the talented to work harder for less and that only their choice makes the "descriptive" premise of the incentive argument true. Nevertheless, he makes some concessions on this point that, as we shall see, can fruitfully be pursued.

This chapter and the next consider issues raised by Cohen's illuminating discussion of incentive inequality. The focus of this chapter is the supposed choice of the talented about whether to work harder for less, in the context of a luck-neutralizing approach to justice. Though points of departure are found in Cohen's position, the arguments are not intended to be ad hominem. My primary aim is not to interpret or criticize Cohen's position, but rather to pursue in their own right questions suggested by his discussion. The emphasis in this chapter and Chapter 9 is on the suppos-

---

tion." Moreover, "[o]ne scheme is more effective than another if its OP curve always give a greater return to the less advantaged for any given return to the more advantaged." Thus, we have to decide on the most effective scheme in order to apply the difference principle.

6. Thanks to Frank Vandenbroucke for this formulation.

edly descriptive premise of the maximin argument for incentive inequality. In Chapter 10 I turn to the normative maximin premise.

3. The Choice-Exemption Argument and the Talented Choice Dilemma

We are now in a position to consider how Cohen's luck-neutralizing position on the currency issue combines with his separate arguments against incentive inequality. Cohen opposes choice to luck in specifying the currency role of responsibility in justice. How does the choice of the talented about whether to work harder for less, which Cohen also emphasizes, relate to the currency role of responsibility? That depends on how responsibility is understood, and the resulting implications about choices by the talented. If responsibility is understood in terms of choice (as indeed Cohen appears to understand it), so that choice is used to filter goods out of the currency of redistribution, what should happen to extra goods resulting from the choice of the talented to work harder for less?

On luck-neutralizing assumptions about the currency of distributive justice, there seems to be something self-defeating about claiming that the talented could and should choose to work just as hard at 60 percent top tax rate as they do at 40 percent, for the benefit of the worst off. Suppose the talented could choose either to work harder or less hard, under the higher tax rate, and they choose to work harder. Then why wouldn't they be responsible, at least in part, for their harder work, in virtue of their choice to do it? Why aren't they thus entitled, on a luck-neutralizing view of the currency of distributive justice, to additional benefit from their harder work, that is, to a lower tax rate? The apparent danger of self-defeatingness here turns on the idea that goods for which people are responsible are to be filtered out of the currency of distributive justice, to be exempt from redistribution. If the exemption from luck and hence from redistribution is based on choice, then why isn't the result of the choice to work harder for less exempt? More precisely, why aren't goods that are in part the result of the choice to work harder for less at least partly exempt?

We can spell out this *choice-exemption argument* using Cohen's example. Suppose that the marginal tax rate is held constant at 60 percent. What work levels are possible for the talented to choose at this marginal rate? Suppose a higher level and a lower level of work are both possible. Levels of work can be understood in terms of type of work as well as period of work: working harder can involve working at a more productive job as well as working longer hours. Suppose it is possible for them to choose to work just as hard with marginal tax rates at 60 percent as they would personally like to work if rates were instead at 40 percent. Or, they could choose to work less hard than this, which is what they would personally prefer with rates at 60 percent. It is up to them. If they do not work harder with rates at 60 percent, it is because they have chosen not to. It is not because it was not possible for them to choose to work harder without extra reward, in the form of lower marginal rates. Recall that in Cohen's example these are standard cases, not special-burden cases: both the higher and the lower levels of work at the higher tax rates would still leave the talented better off than many others. Compensation is not due them on special burden grounds if they choose to work harder.

Suppose, still holding rates constant at 60 percent, that the talented decide to work harder. This choice generates more product than there would have been if they had chosen the lower level. In virtue of their choice to produce, they are responsible at least in part for this extra product. Not all of it counts as a matter of luck for them. So some of it should not be up for redistribution, and should be returned to them. What is at stake is the difference between the lower amount they would personally prefer to produce at 60 percent and the higher amount they nevertheless choose to produce at 60 percent. If some of this difference is exempt from luck-neutralizing redistribution, then the 60 percent marginal rates should be lower after all.

Notice that the choice-exemption argument does not assume that the results of choice are wholly exempt from redistribution, but only partially, reflecting the way choice contributes to those results.

The choice-exemption argument provides the first horn of a dilemma argument that I call the *talented choice dilemma:* On the one hand, if the talented could choose to work harder without additional incentives, that is, holding high marginal tax rates constant, then their extra product should they so choose would be attributable at least in part to their choice. So it is not wholly within the scope of luck-neutralizing redistribution. That suggests they should get some of that extra product back in the form of lower marginal tax rates. On the other hand, if the talented could not choose to work harder without additional incentives, the original maximin argument for incentive inequality stands: incentives are needed to maximize the position of the worst off.

Cohen finds an incoherence between endorsing a maximin normative principle and choosing not to work harder for less, when the choice to work harder for less is open and would most benefit the worst off.[7] By contrast, the choice-exemption argument appeals not simply to a maximin normative principle, but to one explicitly limited along luck-neutralizing lines by a choice-based filter on the currency of redistribution. We can see the choice-exemption argument as the result of attempting to combine a luck-neutralizing view of the currency of distributive justice with Cohen's argument against incentive inequality. The choice-exemption argument suggests that there is at least a tension between arguing, on the one hand, that the talented could choose to work harder for less and, on the other hand, that they should do so on normative grounds provided by a maximin principle subject to the choice-based exemption.[8] This apparent tension turns critically on the currency role of responsibility.

Here the following point can be made. The choice-exemption argument, and the first horn of the talented choice dilemma, may show that it is justified to reward the talented who choose to work harder by returning some of their extra product to them. This may require a tax cut. But even if so, such rewards would not be justified on *incentive* grounds, but on grounds of their responsibility in virtue of their choices. Rewards are backward looking; incentives are forward looking.

This point could be conceded for present purposes. A choice exemption will still provide the first horn of the talented choice dilemma, even if it is justified in terms of responsibility rather than incentives. The second horn of the dilemma is the incentive inequality argument proper. In practice,

---

7. At this point, issues arise about the site of distributive justice (see Cohen 1997). I am pursuing related issues, but in a rather different way.

8. Frank Vandenbroucke (personal communication) has provided an example of a simple world in which the choice exemption and the rejection of incentive inequality are consistent. In his example, there is one type of job and perfect information about individual productivity and how many hours each person chooses to work. Issues of incentive compatibility that arise from lack of information are thus not relevant. People choose how many hours to work, but their level of productivity per hour worked is a matter of luck. Tax is 100 percent, and citizens are paid a wage per hour that equals average productivity per hour.

In response, I would point out that the consistency in this case appears to be an artefact of the simplistic assumption that there is only one type of job. This means that all work is equally productive, and eliminates the relevant difference between the talented and the untalented. The interesting cases arise when talented people, who are capable of doing more productive jobs, can choose not just how many hours to work, but whether to work at more or less productive jobs.

however, a choice exemption, which allows people to reap rewards from the results of their choices to work harder, can operate to provide incentives even if it is not justified in terms of incentives.

It can also be replied, however, that as a matter of principle the distinction between rewards as backward looking and incentives as forward looking is artificial and depends on taking a static rather than a more realistically dynamic view of the motivations of temporally extended agents.[9] Incentives and rewards operate through time in a way that makes them continuous with one another. From the dynamic perspectives of both agents who provide them and agents who receive them, incentives and rewards are two sides of the same coin, seen from different temporal perspectives but with awareness of the continuity between these perspectives. Incentives may work, have good consequences, and hence be justified in part because they reward certain choices and are not seen as a matter of luck. And rewards flowing from certain choices, again not seen as a matter of luck, may best provide incentives, and indeed have a formative influence on the very motivations to which incentives appeal. These do not appear to be merely arbitrary, contingent facts, but reflections of something deep about the motivation of temporally continuous, responsible agents in social environments and hence about the nature of incentives and rewards. This reply leads into the point developed in Chapter 9 about the way facts and beliefs about responsibility can act as parameters of incentive-seeking behavior. General facts about whether people are responsible for their choices and whether as a result rewards are appropriate feed into the operation of incentives and affect the need for them and hence their justification.

The choice-exemption argument distinguishes people's positions all things considered from their positions with respect to the currency of distributive justice. The argument can concede that the position of the worst off would be best all things considered if the talented chose to work at the higher rather than the lower of the possible work levels, holding marginal rates constant at 60 percent. This would maximally benefit the worst off all things considered in so far as the highest percentage of the greatest total product would flow to the worst off. But the argument goes on to insist that the maximin norm does not apply to all-things-considered positions,

---

9. I would defend a related criticism of the standard distinction between backward-looking and forward-looking justifications of punishment. See and cf. Hurley 2000a, on punishment and deep deterrence; see also Andenaes 1974.

but only to goods that are within the currency of distributive justice and not filtered out by the choice exemption. Hence the maximin norm does not capture all of the differential product of such a choice by the talented. The currency role of responsibility limits redistribution to goods that are a matter of brute luck, for which people are not responsible. On a choice-based reading of responsibility, it thus exempts from redistribution the consequences of qualifying choices, whether they are good or bad. If there is some reason why the choices in question by the talented don't qualify as exempting, we haven't yet seen what it is.

The rest of this chapter examines this argument further and considers various responses to it. I draw on work done in Part I in considering how the talented choice dilemma and choice exemption argument are affected by different views of responsibility.

4. Responses to the Choice-Exemption Argument: Lack of Responsibility for Talents, and Regression

The most immediately tempting response may be as follows: "The talented may choose how hard to work, but at least in many cases they do not choose to be talented. Their talents enable them to be extra productive if they so choose, but in many cases their talents are a matter of luck; they are not responsible for their talents."

Perhaps in some cases talents are the result of choice, and not a matter of luck. But we can set these aside for the sake of argument. There will surely be many other cases in which this is not so, in which talents are at least partly a matter of luck. Even so, there are problems with this tempting response.

Suppose that the talented could choose to work harder, and so produce more, holding higher marginal tax rates constant. If choice is properly opposed to luck, then the extra goods produced by such a choice would not be wholly attributable to luck, even if the choice was the result of talents that were unchosen and were themselves a matter of luck. Otherwise, choice does not exempt from luck, since any choice will have among its causes some factors that are unchosen matters of luck, whether talents or something else. This will be true whether causation operates deterministically or indeterministically. And, as indicated Chapter 6, we do not aim to redistribute everything that is a matter of luck for anyone. Rather, we slice human affairs according to some independent specification of the goods in question, such as welfare or resources. On a luck-neutralizing view of the currency of distributive justice, such goods are then in effect filtered by responsibility, so that goods for which people are responsible are exempt from redistribution.

Luck and choice can intermingle to produce effects. Perhaps both the choices of the talented and their good luck in being talented combine to yield the extra product in question in such a way that some of it should be exempt from redistribution, though not all of it. But that is all the choice-exemption argument requires. If the talented are responsible for their choice about whether to work harder or less hard at the higher marginal rate, and choose to work harder, then luck neutralization has not yet reached a stable equilibrium at those rates. Unless the choice-based exemption is nullified, not all of the extra product of choice can be up for redistribution on the grounds that talents are a matter of luck. It may be true that their good luck in being talented, not their choices alone, enables the talented to be this productive. But it may also be true that without their choices, the talents would not produce the extra goods.

Now the natural thing for a luck neutralizer to say at this point may be that it is fine for the talented hard worker to be better off than the equally talented slacker, but that the talented hard worker should be no better off than the person who makes as good an effort but lacks the talent.[10] This, however, is essentially Roemer's proposal. Differences in talents that are a matter of luck put people into different Roemerian types. Within types, differences in effort justify inequalities. Between types, equal effort should be treated equally. I have assessed this proposal in Chapter 7. The critical point for present purposes was the use of deservingness (rather than responsibility) to tell us how to distribute, even if responsibility tells us what to distribute. Roemer's proposal may provide an appropriate way to implement specific policies (such as antismoking or pro-education or population policies), which have been adopted through democratic processes and so are not subject to antipaternalist or antiperfectionist objections to the specific judgments of deservingness in question. But I suggested that the role of specific judgments of deservingness in this proposal makes it inappropriate as the basis for a general theory of distributive justice. If this is correct, then this proposal does not provide a model of how responsibility can have a currency role (even if not a patterning role) within a general theory

---

10. A point made to me by both Gerald Cohen and Joshua Cohen.

of distributive justice, which is my present concern. So it cannot tell us how the currency role of responsibility is related to the choices of the talented within such a theory.

These replies to the first response invite a more radical response, which invokes a regression requirement for responsibility. At this point let me briefly remind readers of various points from earlier chapters. A regression requirement, recall, holds that responsibility for something requires responsibility for its causes. The requirement applies regressively: responsibility for causes in turn requires responsibility for the causes of these causes, and so on, all the way back. Recall also that to aim to neutralize all the effects on relevant goods of any cause that is a matter of luck is operationally equivalent to accepting a regression requirement for responsibility. To treat as a matter of luck anything that is an effect of luck anywhere back in the causal chain is equivalent to treating responsibility for something to require responsibility for its causes. While luck-neutralizing accounts are sometimes described in terms of the aim to neutralize the *effects* of luck, they do not have to be. Responsibility can be given a currency-defining role even if the regression requirement is rejected.

To illustrate, consider Fiammetta. Suppose her grandfather's genetic constitution and native musical ability, which she inherited, were a matter of luck in causes or constitutive luck for her. Many of her choices, as well as her musical talent, operatic performances, and prima donna's income are among the effects of such luck. Suppose we regard all these as matters of luck for her on the grounds that they are among the effects of luck, even if some of those effects are brought about in part by her choices. Then we are effectively imposing a regression requirement.

The more radical response to the choice-exemption argument, then, is the following *regression argument:* "Talents are among the causes of the productivity of a talented person such as Fiammetta. We are allowing for the sake of argument that these talents are at least in part a matter of luck. So the talented person is not fully responsible for them. But if we look at the causes of the talents of any given talented person, and the causes of those causes, and so on, we soon reach factors and events for which that talented person could not possibly be responsible, because she did not yet exist. So, since she is not responsible for the causes of her higher work level and extra product, all the way back, she is not responsible for her work or product either. The intervening or commingling of choice does not alter this. The same points could be made about the causes of her choices. Since she is not responsible for the causes of her choices all the way back, she is not responsible for her choices or their consequences either. Choices are also among the effects of luck. So choice does not exempt from luck-neutralizing redistribution after all."

5. Talents and Regressive Responsibility: Actual Choice or Control versus Hypothetical Choice

To address the issues raised by the regression argument, we need to consider more closely the structure of various conditions of responsibility. As I explained in Part I, there is more than one way to characterize a regressive conception of responsibility. In this section I consider how particular specifications of responsibility as regressive affect the present issues about talents and choices of how hard to work. I first consider how the talented choice dilemma and choice-exemption argument are affected by assuming a regressive choice or control conception of responsibility, and then how they are affected by assuming a regressive hypothetical choice conception of responsibility. Recall that regression is incompatible with choice and control requirements for responsibility but compatible with hypothetical-choice requirements. Recall also that regression is an actual-sequence requirement, which is doubly dissociable from the alternate-sequence ability-to-do-otherwise requirement. I will remind readers briefly of the relevant arguments from Part I as I proceed.

Alternate-sequence conditions do not concern the actual stream of causes leading to whatever it is responsibility for which is in question. Rather, they concern what might have been instead, other possible sequences of events. The salient example of an alternate-sequence condition for responsibility is the requirement that someone could have done otherwise—not just conditionally, if something else had also been different, but absolutely, holding all else constant.

Return to our talented opera star. When marginal rates go from 40 percent to 60 percent, suppose Fiammetta chooses to work less. She cuts back on the number of performances she gives and spends less time practicing. This reduction in operatic product affects others: all the supporting workers, the media, the public, and so on. But suppose that it was possible for her to choose to work just as hard at 60 percent as she had at 40 percent. She could have chosen otherwise, absolutely, not just conditionally on something else being different, such as incentives. Moreover, if she had indeed chosen to work just as hard after rates went up, it would still be true that she could have chosen otherwise: she could have chosen to work less hard. Holding other things constant, including marginal rates at the higher level, both choices were possible. Then whichever she chose, there was an alternate-possible sequence. She could have chosen otherwise.

By contrast, *actual-sequence conditions* of responsibility concern the character of the stream of actual causes and operative mechanisms, not the possibility of different sequences of events. The regression requirement— that responsibility for something requires responsibility for its causes—is an example of an actual-sequence condition of responsibility. For example, suppose Fiammetta works just as hard when marginal tax rates go up, and produces just as much. What are the actual causes of this work and production? Suppose they include both her choices and her endowment of talents. What are the causes of these causes? Suppose they include her upbringing, which was both musical and socialist, her resulting dispositions, and her native musical ability. The causes of these factors include, in turn, her parents' upbringing, before she was born, their genetic constitution, that of her grandparents, and so on.

Before we have gone very far back, the stream of actual causes extends to factors that Fiammetta has not actually chosen or controlled. A regression condition requires responsibility for causes all the way back. If responsibility is also held to require actual choice or control, as was implied in the regression argument above, then responsibility is impossible (as has been argued in earlier chapters). This would hold whether causation operates deterministically or indeterministically. Since no one can actually choose or control what happens before she exists, a regressive choice or control condition of responsibility means not only that Fiammetta is not responsible for her work and product, but that no one is responsible for anything.

How does such a regressive choice or control conception of responsibility affect the choice-exemption argument? By eliminating responsibility, a requirement of regressive choice or control nullifies the choice exemption from redistribution, regardless of whether there was an absolute possibility of doing or choosing otherwise. Choice filters out none of the goods subject to redistribution, because it does not negate luck after all. We can still aim to redistribute goods of the specified kind that are a matter of luck, but the qualification adds nothing: if responsibility is eliminated, all goods of the specified kind will be a matter of luck.

How does a regressive choice requirement for responsibility affect the talented choice dilemma? It may seem to provide a way out of the dilemma. For reasons just given, a regressive choice requirement blocks the first horn of the dilemma, the choice-exemption argument. Choice does not exempt from redistribution, even given the ability to do otherwise. But a regressive choice requirement does not force us onto the second horn of the dilemma, which is the claim that if the talented could not choose to work harder without incentives, then the original maximin argument for incentive inequality is in force. Nonregressive choice can still be choice, even if choice does not make for responsibility.

Here it is helpful to keep in mind the difference between an actual-sequence requirement such as the regression requirement and an alternate-sequence requirement such as the ability-to-do-otherwise requirement. Suppose choice does not make for responsibility because it does not satisfy the regression requirement, with the result that choice does not exempt from redistribution. It might still be possible for the talented to choose to work harder, holding high marginal rates constant. An alternate sequence might be possible, even though this would not satisfy regression either.

So, technically, the regression argument may provide a way to avoid the talented choice dilemma. But this still leaves us in an unsatisfactory position, for two reasons. First, the luck-neutralizing egalitarian is now supposedly free to combine two claims. Not only *could* the talented choose to work harder, holding higher rates constant. But if they do, this would maximally benefit the worst off: since the talented themselves would not be responsible in virtue of their choice for any of their extra product, all of it would be within the scope of redistribution.

But where does the egalitarian argument go from there? Can it claim that the talented therefore *should* make the choice to work harder for less, if they endorse a maximin normative principle? There is something odd or unstable about combining a claim that people could make a certain choice and should do so on normative grounds with a claim that if they do so they are not responsible in virtue of that choice for what they choose to do or its consequences.

It's as if two different criteria of responsibility are being used: one to deny that choice exempts from redistribution because choice is not regressive, another to urge that people could and therefore should make a certain choice. (This is an example of the way in which an actual-sequence regression requirement can come apart from an alternate-sequence ability to do otherwise requirement.) If people are not responsible in virtue of choice because choice does not satisfy a regression requirement, how can it be the case that they should do one thing or another because they could choose to? Arguments based on normative commitments and the ability to choose to honor those commitments presuppose responsibility. This presupposition fights with the denial that people are responsible in virtue of choice and hence that choice exempts from redistribution.

The second problem is that a conception of responsibility that makes responsibility impossible, as the regressive choice conception does, is a high price to pay to avoid the dilemma argument. As I argued in Chapter 3, it is doubtful that such a conception can be independently justified. So it's worth considering how other accounts of responsibility would bear on the present issues about incentive inequality.

Someone wedded to a regressive conception of responsibility may be tempted to substitute a condition of hypothetical choice for a requirement of actual choice or control. As I argued in Part I, regressive hypothetical choice is possible. How does assuming this view of responsibility affect present issues about talent and choices to work harder?

A hypothetical-choice conception of responsibility does not concern what alternate sequences of events are possible absolutely, or whether Fiammetta had the ability to do otherwise, holding all else constant. Rather, it concerns counterfactually conditioned dispositional properties of the actual sequence of causes and its operative mechanisms. Within the class of actual-sequence conditions, we can distinguish those that concern dispositions someone actually has to make choices under various counterfactual conditions from those that concern choices someone actually makes. In virtue of the causal mechanisms on which someone actually acts, she could actually have a disposition such that she would choose something under counterfactual conditions, even if in fact those conditions do not obtain and she does not actually choose that thing. A hypothetical-choice conception of responsibility is concerned with whether Fiammetta would choose something if she could, or would choose to avoid it if she could, under various counterfactual conditions, rather than whether she actually chose or controlled it.

For example, we can ask what dispositions Fiammetta actually has with respect to all the actual causes of her extra work and product, when she chooses to work more rather than less at high marginal rates. Would Fiammetta choose to avoid any of these causes if circumstances were such that she could? It can be true that Fiammetta would not choose to avoid them if she could, even though she didn't actually choose any of them and indeed could not have chosen those that preexisted her. So a regressive hypothetical-choice condition of responsibility could be satisfied, even though a regressive actual-choice requirement makes responsibility impossible.

Suppose that in fact Fiammetta would not choose to avoid any of the actual causes of her work and product, all the way back. She endorses and identifies with her socialist upbringing and her native musical ability, her parents' upbringing and genetic constitution, and so on. She even endorses, self-referentially, her own dispositions to endorse her own hypothetical choices and their causes. If regressive hypothetical choice is held to be sufficient for responsibility, then she would be responsible for her work and product.

This conception makes responsibility for the results of talents too easy to come by. Few talented people would, if they could, choose to avoid the causes of their talents. Mere hypothetical choice is not a proactive or causally substantial enough relation to underwrite responsibility, even if regressive. As I argued in Part I, people would choose a wide variety of things, if circumstances were such that they could, to which they stand in no more direct causal relation. Surely the truth of such unconstrained counterfactuals does not make people responsible for things they would choose if they could, even if such hypothetical choices are regressive and reflect dispositional properties of operative mechanisms in the actual sequence of causes leading to action. Perhaps the correct account of responsibility does involve dispositional actual-sequence conditions (as, for example, a reason-responsiveness account does). Nevertheless, mere hypothetical choice of the object responsibility for which is in question is not enough, even if regressive. A pure hypothetical-choice account does not provide sufficient constraint on such dispositional features, does not pinpoint the right dispositional features of the actual sequence.

These points apply with special force to responsibility for the results of talents, because people will be differentially disposed to (regressive) hypothetical choices of things that lead to good results for them.[11] A pure hypothetical-choice conception of responsibility is thus likely to yield an indiscriminate exemption for the results of talented choice. But people are surely not responsible for such results just because of such dispositions to hypothetical choice! Some such good results may be a matter of luck despite these dispositions.

Let's take stock of how the actual-sequence conditions for responsibility

---

11. More generally, people are more likely to identify themselves with their talents than with their handicaps.

we have considered interact with the choice exemption and issues about talented choice. On the one hand, a requirement of regressive actual choice or control makes responsibility impossible. It nullifies the choice exemption, but at the same time implies that the talented are not responsible for failing to work harder for less in order to help the disadvantaged. On the other hand, a hypothetical-choice condition suffers from the opposite problem, even if it is applied regressively. It makes it too easy to exempt the results of talented choice from redistribution.

When their implications are drawn out, neither of these options on how to specify the currency role of responsibility may be very attractive to egalitarians after all. Perhaps something in between these two extremes may be more attractive.

6. Talents and Responsibility as Reason-Responsiveness

Consider next actual-sequence conditions of responsibility that drop the regression requirement, but retain a requirement of choice or control. Conditions of reason-responsiveness are found in this category. A luck-neutralizing account of the currency of distributive justice could adopt a reason-responsiveness conception of responsibility and use this to filter the currency of distributive justice. In this section I consider how assuming a reason-responsiveness conception of responsibility affects our present concerns with talent and choices about how hard to work.

At this point let me remind readers briefly of salient points about reason-responsiveness from Part I. Like a hypothetical-choice condition, a reason-responsiveness condition for responsibility is a dispositional actual-sequence condition with counterfactual implications. These conditions, however, are unlike in specifying different dispositions. A hypothetical-choice condition is concerned with what the agent would choose, or would choose to avoid, if she could. By contrast, a reason-responsiveness condition is concerned with whether, in making the choices she actually does make, the agent acts on a mechanism that would respond in certain ways if certain reasons were present (Fischer 1994; Fischer and Ravizza 1998). There is variation within the class of reason-responsiveness conditions: for example, responsiveness to objective or to subjective reasons can be required, and responsiveness can be required to be tight or only loose. These options yield different judgments about the responsibility of the weak-willed and the evil. Someone who responds to reasons makes choices to act that are guided by reasons and so would not do the same thing in some cases in which the reasons were different or in which the circumstances were different and so differently related to the same reasons. Reason-responsiveness is a kind of control, which operates through choice. When someone chooses how to act in response to reasons, the reasons determine her ends or targets and her choices are adjusted in the face of exogenous events so as to reduce the gap between the target and the joint result of these events and her choices. This process essentially involves dispositional properties of the actual sequence of causes and operative mechanisms rather than alternate sequences. Indeterminism is compatible with control, but not necessary for it. A reason-responsive agent need not have been able to choose otherwise, all else constant. Moreover, control is not regressive, and responsiveness to reasons does not require control of those reasons.

The idea of reason-responsiveness defines a class of nonregressive actual-sequence conditions of responsibility and provides an attractive way of incorporating requirements of choice and control into an account of responsibility. Within this class we find alternatives to the two unsatisfactory extremes considered in the previous section. Instead of adopting conditions that make responsibility either impossible or too easy and insubstantial, perhaps a luck neutralizer should adopt a reason-responsiveness conception of responsibility as the filter that yields the currency of distributive justice. How would such a view bear on the choice-exemption argument and issues about incentive inequality?

The issue raised by the choice-exemption argument was: Why doesn't the very choice of the talented to work more rather than less, holding high marginal tax rates constant, show that they are partly responsible for the resulting additional product? Given the currency role of responsibility within luck-neutralizing accounts of distributive justice, this would provide a reason to reduce marginal tax rates. One response, that had unattractive implications, was that despite their choice to work more, they are not responsible for the talents that enable them to be especially productive. The unattractive implication was the regression requirement, that to be responsible for something you must also be responsible for its causes. A reason-responsiveness account of responsibility avoids this unattractive implication. But now we want to know: What is the relationship of reason-responsiveness to talent and to the extra product of the talented?

The answer will evidently depend on the details of the account of reason-responsiveness. Is reason-responsiveness sufficient for responsibility, or necessary, or both? How tightly are choices required to respond to reasons? Are they required to respond to objective or to subjective reasons? Some talents, for example, mathematical or scientific talent, may be abilities to respond to objective reasons. Sheer intelligence or rationality, as a kind of generic talent, may involve abilities to respond to both objective and subjective reasons. Other talents may not involve reason-responsiveness at all. The market may not always value reason-responsiveness, and may value abilities that are not forms of reason-responsiveness. But if the market rewards some trait or ability, then cultivating or exploiting can be a way of responding to at least subjective reasons, even if the ability itself is not a form of reason-responsiveness.

Return to our socialist opera star. We can consider the relationship of Fiammetta's talent and productivity to reason-responsiveness both in general and with respect to her choice of how much to work. Her native musical ability and her musical training have given her a talent that could be described as an ability to respond to musical reasons. Her singing is nuanced in ways that reflect her understanding of and thought about the music, its structure and harmonies and modulations. Her practice sessions are carefully and thoughtfully designed to bring out the best in her voice and in the music. The market values her musical abilities. Moreover, her socialist upbringing has given her an ability to respond to ethical and political reasons (abstracting for the moment from whether her political views are correct). So, in choosing how much to work, that is, to practice just as hard and to do just as many performances at 60 percent as she had been doing at 40 percent, even though she would personally prefer to do less work, she responds to ethical and political reasons. And in actually performing, she acts on mechanisms that are responsive to musical reasons. So far, she seems a good candidate for being reason-responsive. On a reason-responsiveness account of responsibility, her talents, as forms of reason-responsiveness, may themselves be part of what makes her responsible. She may be responsible in virtue of reason-responsiveness, even if she is not responsible for being reason-responsive. It is a mistake to think that someone has to be responsible for whatever it is in virtue of which she is responsible. Where a talent is a kind of reason-responsiveness, Fiammetta may be responsible in virtue of exercising a talent, even if she is not responsible for being talented.

How does this view of Fiammetta's talents and choices in terms of reason-responsiveness leave the difference between what she produces under high marginal rates by working less and by working more? On this view, her reason-responsiveness leaves the difference at least in part immune to luck-neutralizing redistribution. However, her choice to do the extra work is not all that this argument appeals to, unlike the earlier choice-exemption argument. Choice per se is not opposed to luck, on the present view, but only choice that exercises reason-responsiveness. So the fact that the talented could choose to do more work for less does not by itself mean they would be partly responsible for their additional product if they did so choose. Only when choice that exercises talents is also choice that exercises reason-responsiveness does it exempt from redistribution. Choice that does not exercise reason-responsiveness in the required way would not have this implication.

How much consolation this is to the egalitarian luck neutralizer depends on exactly how a reason-responsiveness condition for responsibility is formulated, and how such reason-responsiveness is related to the relevant talents. If only loose responsiveness to subjective reasons is enough, nearly all choices will qualify as responsible, and the talented choice dilemma is in effect reinstated. At the other extreme, if tight responsiveness to objective reasons is required, fewer choices will qualify. But Fiammetta's choices might qualify even so. In reality, if some version of a reason-responsiveness condition for responsibility is correct, it is likely to be a version somewhere in between these two extremes—a version of intermediate reason-responsiveness—that will somewhat limit the scope of the talented choice dilemma.

Recall here (from Chapter 1) the way that certain talents and handicaps are asymmetrically related to a conception of reason-responsiveness as necessary and sufficient for responsibility. In general, having dispositions to respond to reasons tends to be more conducive to many goods than lacking such dispositions. If responsiveness to reasons is a kind of generic talent, the lack of it is a kind of generic handicap. On a conception of responsibility in terms of reason-responsiveness, people can be responsible in virtue of such generic talents, even if they are not responsible in virtue of such generic handicaps. If what you do when you act on a reason-responsive mechanism does not count as a matter of luck, then what you do when you exercise the corresponding talent does not count as a matter of luck. However, what you do as a result of being handicapped by lacking responsiveness to reasons does, on this view, count as a matter of luck.

Obviously, many independently identified handicaps, such as being deaf or having lost a leg, do not limit people's responsiveness to reasons in any way. Some, however, such as some mental handicaps, do compromise reason-responsiveness. On a reason-responsiveness view of responsibility, such reason-compromising handicaps can limit their possessors' responsibility for the position in which their action (or inaction) leaves them. Any correlation between independently identified handicaps and lack of reason-responsiveness will vary with the way reason-responsiveness is characterized: as tight or loose, in terms of subjective or objective reasons. But my point is *not* the false claim that the handicapped are not reason-responsive, and it does not turn on any such correlation. Rather, my point runs the other way around: a lack of responsiveness to reasons in itself can count as a kind of generic, responsibility-undermining handicap.

If a reason-responsiveness conception of responsibility is asymmetrical as between these generic talents and handicaps, and this conception is applied in a luck-neutralizing account to filter the currency of distributive justice, then a corresponding asymmetry will result within the currency. The choice exemption will be triggered by choices that exercise a generic talent of reason-responsiveness, but not by choices that result from a generic handicap of lack of reason-responsiveness. Positions that result from such handicaps will be matters of luck, while positions that result (at least partly) from such talents will (at least partly) not be.

Of course, using responsibility to filter the currency of distributive justice limits what is up for redistribution. As we have seen, different conceptions of responsibility filter the currency in different ways. On the reason-responsiveness conception of responsibility I've been considering, the currency limitation takes a particular, asymmetrical shape. Someone could respond by rejecting the account of responsibility that gives rise to this asymmetry. But on reflection, it is not clear that this currency limitation should be accepted even if we do think this is the right view of responsibility. What makes a view correct as a view of responsibility does not necessarily make it appropriate to use as a filter on the currency of distributive justice. This may not be the right way to give responsibility a role in distributive justice or in egalitarianism in particular.

I have just explained how a reason-responsiveness conception of responsibility factors into the luck-neutralizing conception of *what* distributive justice distributes. The exemption of the results of reason-responsive choices from redistribution yields a potential asymmetry in the currency. Recall now the arguments (in Chapters 6 and 7) that knowing *what* to redistribute does not tell us *how* to redistribute. How does a reason-responsiveness conception of responsibility factor into these arguments? I now run the argument that "you can't derive *how* from *what*" for a reason-responsiveness conception of responsibility in particular.

Recall why responsibility cannot tell us how to distribute, as opposed to what to distribute. The implications of judgments about luck and responsibility run out before they reach issues about what the pattern of distribution should be. To say that someone is or is not responsible for his position is primarily to say something about his relation to his actual position rather than about the relation between his position and someone else's position. And someone's position can be a matter of luck, even though there is no particular counterfactual position that would not be a matter of luck for him.

These points can be applied to reason-responsiveness accounts of responsibility in particular. On such accounts, judgments about responsibility relate individuals to the results of their actions, on the basis of the dispositions those actions express. Goods that do result from exercises of reason-responsiveness do not count as matters of luck for that person. Goods that do not result from exercises of reason-responsiveness do count as matters of luck for that person. But such judgments are ill suited to determine how goods should be distributed. First, these judgments about reason-responsiveness are not about the relations between the goods positions of different people, whether actual or counterfactual. Such judgments do not tell us that one person is responsible for being better off than another, or that it is a matter of luck that one is worse off than another, or that it would not be a matter of luck if the two were equally well off instead. Second, such judgments do not generally support counterfactual assignments of responsibility. Suppose someone lacks reason-responsive dispositions, and hence is not in fact responsible for his position. We can ask what would be the case, if he did not lack reason-responsive dispositions, and what he would be responsible for under this counterfactual supposition. We may want to know, for example, how someone would have chosen if he were more talented or intelligent. But there is strong reason to doubt that such questions generally have determinate answers.

Finally, we can put these points together with the asymmetry between certain generic talents and handicaps that can arise from a reason-responsiveness conception of responsibility. If a disabled person's actual goods position is a matter of luck and a talented person's is not, that does not tell us whether the relation between their positions is a matter of luck for either of them or what counterfactual relation between their positions would not be a matter of luck. The currency role of responsibility does not tell us how goods should be redistributed between such disabled and talented persons.

7. Pandora's Box Again

This chapter began by considering with Gerald Cohen how it may be inconsistent to aim to make the worst off as well off as possible while also, by choosing to demand incentives, fail to do what you can to make them as well off as possible. We found that there is also a danger of inconsistency in aiming to redistribute to the worst off only what is not down to choice while also holding that this aim requires choices to produce more so that it can be redistributed. I considered various possible responses to this point. There may be other ways to respond to the talented choice dilemma. I have not tried to canvass the possibilities thoroughly or ultimately to resolve the issues raised by the choice-exemption argument. These issues turn on the currency role of responsibility. In Chapter 9 I show how the currency role generates still further complications, and conclude that it is problematic.

However, I have shown in this chapter how these issues about incentive inequality interact with several different actual-sequence conditions of responsibility. The responses I have considered to these issues confirm that questions about responsibility cannot be avoided or bracketed or put in a black box within luck-neutralizing accounts of distributive justice. The implications of such accounts can turn on substantive questions about responsibility. This point was demonstrated by combining the currency role of responsibility with the arguments about talents and incentive inequality, for various different conceptions of responsibility. As we saw, a regressive-choice conception of responsibility nullifies the exemption from redistribution for responsible choice, but at the same time undermines the responsibility of the talented if they fail to work harder to benefit the less advantaged. A hypothetical-choice conception of responsibility exempts the results of talented choice from redistribution too easily. The impact of a reason-responsiveness conception of responsibility on these issues depends on the fine-tuning of a requirement of reason-responsiveness. However, a reason-responsiveness conception has the potential to generate an asymmetry whereby certain generic talents but not corresponding generic handicaps trigger the choice exemption from redistribution. These points should lead us, egalitarians included, to reflect again on whether the currency role is the right role to give responsibility in distributive justice.

In the following chapter I consider two further roles responsibility can play in distributive justice: the incentive-parameter role and the well-being role. I argue that these are really the most important roles for responsibility in justice, and that the currency role of responsibility is not only problematic but dispensable. We should remain open-minded about approaches to distributive justice that do not give responsibility the currency role characteristic of luck-neutralizing accounts. One such alternative, a bias-neutralizing approach, is sketched in Chapter 10, and its egalitarian potential explained.

9

The Real Roles of
Responsibility in Justice

1. Introduction and Overview

In this chapter I consider two further roles that responsibility might play in distributive justice, an incentive-parameter role and a well-being role, and argue for their importance. Along the way I also argue that the currency role of responsibility is problematic and dispensable.

First, I pursue a suggestion Gerald Cohen makes about the way alterable normative expectations might affect whether the talented can work harder for less (see also Carens 1981, chap. 3). In particular, I suggest that such normative expectations would include expectations based on the prevalent conception of responsibility and corresponding beliefs by the talented about how responsible they are for what they do. Such expectations, and hence the range of possible levels of incentive seeking, might be altered by altering conceptions of, and beliefs about, responsibility. If so, such conceptions and beliefs have a role as parameters on which the range of possible incentive-seeking behavior by the talented depends. From the perspective of a luck-neutralizing egalitarian social engineer, on what basis should such parameters be fixed? Is a consequentialist basis appropriate? How is this *incentive-parameter role* of responsibility related to its currency role? Must the same conception of responsibility play both roles?

Second, I introduce the role of responsibility and beliefs about responsibility as a part of human well-being. How should the egalitarian social engineer factor this well-being role into the incentive-parameter and currency-filter issues?

This chapter, like Chapter 8, is concerned with issues about the supposedly descriptive premise of the incentive-inequality argument (which, as Cohen suggests, turns out to embed normative issues) and the roles of responsibility in justice. In the final section of this chapter I consider how these issues look from an alternative, cognitive perspective, involving the aim to neutralize bias rather than luck. A veil of ignorance may help to address what it is possible for the talented to do, while avoiding biasing influences and a certain fallacy. An approach to distributive justice based on the aim to neutralize bias rather than luck dispenses with the currency role of responsibility, but retains the incentive-parameter and well-being roles. While responsibility has an essential position in a cognitive approach, it is a different, less demanding position, which may be better suited to the nature of responsibility and which has distinct theoretical advantages. The bias-neutralizing alternative is pursued in Chapter 10.

2. The Role of Beliefs about Responsibility as Parameters of Incentive Seeking

Recall Cohen's unwillingness to take seriously the view that the talented cannot work harder for less. This may be connected to his suggestion that normative expectations should not be uncritically permitted to underwrite views about what the talented are able to do. Even if what people are able to do depends in part on their reasons, values, and normative expectations, these may nevertheless be alterable.

In particular, I suggest, beliefs about responsibility and consequent normative expectations may affect the range of possible levels of productivity in general and of incentive seeking in particular. Prevalent beliefs about responsibility can thus operate as parameters of possible levels of incentive seeking. This role of beliefs about responsibility will be referred to for short as the *incentive-parameter role*. How should the value of this parameter be set within luck-neutralizing accounts of distributive justice? How does the incentive-parameter role of beliefs about responsibility relate to the currency role of responsibility?

I begin with two contrasting examples of beliefs about responsibility that might plausibly affect normative expectations and hence the range of possible levels of incentive seeking. I then step back from the examples to generalize and consider the methodological issues thus raised.

SCENARIO 1. Suppose first that most people, including most talented people, believe that people are at least partly responsible for doing the work their talents enable them to do and for the resulting product, even if they are not responsible for and do not deserve their talents. Suppose moreover that most people do not accept the regression principle: they do not believe that responsibility for something requires responsibility for its causes. Instead, various nonregressive conceptions of responsibility are prevalent. Since most talented people believe themselves to be in part responsible for what they produce by applying their talents in work, even if they are not responsible for their talents, they have a general normative expectation of extra reward for extra work. Extra reward for extra work is widely regarded as the rightful consequence and recognition of someone's responsibility for doing extra work. Without such recognition and extra reward, morose resentful reluctance to do extra work tends to be experienced, which operates as a drag on performance. As a result, suppose a statistical sociological law holds. Given these prevalent beliefs and normative expectations, it is not possible for general levels of incentive seeking to fall below a certain floor.

I am here supposing normative expectations based on judgments of partial responsibility for extra product, which license moderate levels of incentive seeking and make it impossible to suppress incentive seeking altogether or to reduce it to a negligible level. I am not supposing normative expectations that license unrestricted incentive seeking, or make anything other than maximal levels of incentive seeking impossible. To believe you merit some extra reward for extra productive work is not to believe you merit any reward you can extract, however exorbitant.

These suppositions are one way of spelling out Cohen's admission that "truly disabling dismay" may result from the thought of extra work at a high tax rate, if someone believes he has a right to the rewards of hard work. However, Cohen claims that such inability does not block his arguments against incentive inequality for two reasons. First, norms and ideology, along with associated habits and expectations, can change (1992, pp. 290–293). Second, someone's belief about norms should not be taken as exogenously fixed input when we are trying to determine what the right norms are:

> If the rich are unable to work as hard at 60 percent tax as they do at 40 because they believe that they should be paid more because they work harder, then the stated incapacity cannot, without bizarre circularity, figure in an argument which would justify the proposition that it is fundamentally right that they be paid more for working harder. (Cohen 1992, pp. 290–291, n. 18)

I return to these issues shortly.

SCENARIO 2. Suppose next that most people, including most talented people, believe that people are not responsible for doing the work their talents enable them to do or for the resulting product, because they are not responsible for and do not deserve their talents. Most people have a regressive conception of responsibility. As a result, the talented do not in general have a normative expectation of extra reward for extra work, nor do they experience morose resentful reluctance to do extra work because of the lack of such reward (though they may experience reluctance based on laziness or on competing leisure interests). While the lack of a sense of entitlement does not provide any positive motivation to do extra work, we can suppose that there is at least *less* strain in doing extra work without incentives with these normative expectations than with those in the first scenario. The talented can use their undeserved abilities with no sense of entitlement to the result and hence no drag from such a sense of entitlement on the extra use of their abilities without reward. As a result, suppose a different statistical sociological law holds. Given these different prevalent beliefs and normative expectations, it is possible for general levels of incentive seeking to fall to negligible levels, well below the floor on incentive seeking in the first scenario.

The second scenario may in fact be less plausible than the first. Someone's belief that he would not be responsible for the extra work he could do without incentives may act as a drag on motivation and performance just as effectively as a belief that, since he would be responsible for extra work, he should jolly well get some reward for it. Let's assume for the sake of argument that somehow the normative motivation provided by egalitarian principles can overcome or bypass this potential source of discouragement. Therefore, lower levels of incentive seeking are possible given the second set of beliefs about responsibility and normative expectations than are possible given the first.

These are relative possibilities: different levels of incentive seeking are possible relative to different beliefs about responsibility. To determine what levels of incentive seeking are possible absolutely, we need to consider in turn what beliefs about responsibility are possible. Suppose for the sake of argument that both of these two sets of beliefs about responsibility and associated normative expectations are possible. Whichever is actual could be transformed into the other through benign social engineering or education.

These specific suppositions can be generalized. There is a wide spectrum of logically possible levels of incentive seeking by the talented. Begin with some assumptions about how much work the talented would personally prefer to do for given pay. At the left, altruistic extreme of the spectrum of logical possibilities, they do additional work with no additional reward. At the right, selfish extreme, they do additional work only if the whole of their marginal product is returned to them, so that there is none left over for redistribution. In the middle range of the spectrum, they do additional work given only moderate incentives, so that part of their extra product is available for redistribution. The maximin argument for incentive inequality invokes this middle range. Which of these logical possibilities are sociologically possible depends on various parameters, including beliefs about responsibility and associated normative expectations. Relative to one set of beliefs and expectations, one portion of the incentive-seeking spectrum may be possible; relative to another set, another portion is possible. Which subset of the whole set of logical possibilities is possible absolutely and not just relatively depends on which values it is possible for the parameters, including beliefs about responsibility, to take. By altering the values of the parameters, benign social engineers could open up one or another range of possible levels of incentive seeking.

To fix ideas, let's return to the two specific pairings of beliefs about responsibility and relative possibilities of incentive seeking supposed in our two scenarios. Suppose the first set of beliefs is actual, though the second set of beliefs is also possible. If beliefs about responsibility altered from the first set to the second, the range of possible levels of incentive seeking would also shift—from the middle of the spectrum of logical possibilities toward the altruistic end of the spectrum. In particular, the undermining of normative expectations based on belief in partial responsibility for extra work would lower the floor on possible levels of incentive seeking.

On these assumptions, which value of the beliefs about responsibility that operate as parameters for incentive seeking should benign social engineers favor? In particular, consider benign social engineers who are luck-neutralizing egalitarians committed to a maximin norm. Should they favor altering beliefs about responsibility in order to lower the range of possible levels of incentive seeking? Should they, for example, encourage people to adopt regressive, highly restricted conceptions of responsibility? Cohen objects to arguments for incentive inequality underwritten by normative expectations that restrict the range of possible levels of incentive seeking. We can agree that such normative expectations can be altered. But on what basis *should* they be altered?

3. The Consequentialist-Engineering Argument: Pragmatism and Relations between the Currency and Incentive-Parameter Roles

One pragmatic suggestion is as follows. "We should encourage certain beliefs about responsibility and normative expectations rather than others directly by reference to our maximin normative principle. That is, we should aim to instill whatever beliefs about responsibility will maximize the currency position of the worst off. The set of beliefs that minimizes the floor on possible levels of incentive seeking by the same token maximizes the possible amount of extra product available for redistribution. That is, the worst off are potentially best off in terms of goods that are a matter of luck if it is possible for the talented to do extra work with little or no incentive. So, the maximin principle tells us to encourage beliefs based on a regressive choice conception of responsibility, and associated normative expectations, in preference to beliefs and expectations based on nonregressive conceptions, such as reason-responsiveness conceptions. If the latter are prevalent, we should attempt to alter them in the direction of the former."

This suggestion is pragmatic in the sense that it aims to foster beliefs on consequentialist grounds rather than in terms of cognitive values. Cohen's position is not pragmatic in this sense, so the following discussion of pragmatism is *not* directed against his view. He may be pragmatic in determining policy if justice is not possible, but that is another matter from pragmatism in determining what justice itself requires (see Cohen 1992, pp. 327–329).

I call the above pragmatic line of thought the *consequentialist-engineering argument*. It does not simply accept as given whatever beliefs about responsibility happen to be prevalent, or levels of incentive seeking that are possible relative to those prevalent beliefs. But nor does it aim to foster knowledge of the truth about responsibility, where that is lacking. Rather, it alters beliefs on consequentialist grounds. Generalized, it surveys the full spectrum of logically possible levels of incentive seeking. It asks what values are sociologically possible for parameters of incentive seeking to take, including beliefs about responsibility, and what range of possible levels of incentive seeking is therefore absolutely possible, that is, possible relative to any of the possible parameter values. It chooses among parameter values, including beliefs about responsibility, so as to enable levels of incentive seeking that maximize the currency position of the worst off.

Despite the various things wrong with this argument, there is something right about it, which may be possible to salvage. What is right is that a theory of distributive justice should not treat beliefs about responsibility and associated normative expectations as exogenously fixed external constraints. The mere fact that certain normative views are prevalent does not immunize them if they compromise the demands of justice. Egalitarians can criticize and reject the beliefs and expectations that underwrite certain levels of incentive seeking, rather than tamely accepting them and operating within the limits they impose. This point of principle applies no less to expectations of moderate incentives than to expectations of exorbitant incentives. Normative beliefs and expectations that act as parameters of incentive seeking should not be treated as exogenous to theories of distributive justice but as integral to their subject matter. Cohen's critique of the maximin argument for incentive inequality brings this correct and important point into focus.

However, unlike Cohen's argument, the consequentialist-engineering argument goes beyond this sound point and thereby becomes problematic. There are at least three difficulties with it. First, it implies a dubious pragmatism, by applying consequentialist reasoning to beliefs. Second, it raises but fails to address issues about how the currency role of responsibility relates to the incentive-parameter role of beliefs about responsibility. Third, it neglects a further role that both responsibility and beliefs about responsibility play for the worst off, along with everyone else, namely, that of elements of well-being.

These criticisms of the consequentialist-engineering argument can be thought of as negotiating a triangle whose points are each of these three roles of responsibility and beliefs about responsibility: the currency role, the incentive-parameter role, and the well-being role. To the extent responsibility plays these three roles within a theory of justice, they should be in harmony and equilibrium. To this end, the relationships between them need scrutiny.

Consider first the pragmatism of the consequentialist-engineering argument. Can it be right to advocate and encourage certain beliefs about responsibility on the basis of their consequences for the worst off, as opposed to their truth or coherence? There is something wrongheaded about the aim to engineer one or another set of beliefs about responsibility on the basis of their consequences, even if the mode of evaluation of consequences is a worthy one. This point is sometimes made against pragmatic reasons to resist or shrug off views that eliminate responsibility. For example, suppose suppression of our reactive attitudes would impoverish our lives. Galen Strawson is not comfortable giving such considerations any role in propping up those attitudes (compare P. F. Strawson 1974; Galen Strawson 1986). But the point is at least as strong applied in the other direction, against revisionism: against pragmatic reasons to adopt or encourage views that eliminate responsibility, such as their purported beneficial consequences for the worst off.

The pragmatism of the consequentialist-engineering argument presents an unattractive dilemma: either we are deluding ourselves or we are manipulating the beliefs of others, on the basis of the consequences of beliefs rather than their truth. In particular, such pragmatism is distinctly at odds with the cognitive, bias-neutralizing approach to distributive justice I sketch in Chapter 10. To preview: biases are influences on beliefs that are unrelated to their truth, influences that undermine knowledge, such as desires to believe certain things or to achieve certain consequences. Biasing desires may or may not be self-interested. On a bias-neutralizing view, we want to know how goods should be distributed, and we deliberate behind a veil of ignorance in order to remove biasing influences on our answer to this question, including the influence of various desires. If responsibility has roles in distributive justice, we should deliberate about responsibility, among other things. In doing so, we should attempt to minimize biasing influences on our beliefs about responsibility.

But to adopt certain beliefs about responsibility because these beliefs have desirable consequences, whether for ourselves or the worst off or anyone else, would be precisely to submit to biasing influences. And to encourage these beliefs in others if we do not accept them ourselves would be to propagate biasing influences on the beliefs of others and to adopt a superior, covertly manipulative stance that is itself a likely source of self-deception. It is one thing to accept the existence of biasing influences in the actual world and attempt to organize institutions so that such influences are minimized or exploited to neutralize one another in overall effect (see and cf. Hutchins 1995, chap. 5). It is another thing to engage in unmitigated propaganda. The former is compatible with a bias-neutralizing approach, but the latter is not.

However, it is not just from a bias-neutralizing perspective that the consequentialist-engineering argument is defective. Recall the currency role given to responsibility by luck-neutralizing approaches to distributive justice. The distinction between luck and responsibility determines what luck neutralizers aim to redistribute. If maximin is the rule of redistribution, then it is applied to goods that are a matter of luck and not to goods for which people are responsible. Evaluations of consequences according to how well they serve such a luck-neutralizing aim already depend on judgments about responsibility. What beliefs about responsibility should be used to determine the currency to which a maximin rule is applied? Until we know this, we have no determinate basis for evaluating the relevant consequences for the worst off. Consequentialist calculations that presuppose some currency cannot be used to determine what that currency should be. The conception of responsibility presupposed by the currency must be exogenous to consequentialist arguments that appeal to that currency. But if a conception of responsibility is important enough to define the currency of redistribution, why isn't it also good enough to set parameters of incentive seeking independently of consequentialist arguments?

A luck neutralizer who has no general commitment to cognitivist political philosophy can agree that a conception of responsibility independently regarded as coherent or correct, and beliefs about responsibility independently regarded as true, should be used to define the currency of distributive justice. Alternatively, it may be suggested that there are other exogenous sources of the currency conception of responsibility, sources that make no appeal to truth, such as views prevalent in some community (cf. Roemer 1993). The latter suggestion raises questions about how the currency role of responsibility and the incentive-parameter role of prevalent beliefs about responsibility may interact and constrain each other.

The consequentialist-engineering argument ignores these issues. It asks us to evaluate the consequences of various possible sets of beliefs about responsibility, as parameters of incentive seeking, for the currency position of the worst off. That is, it asks whether instilling one or another set of prevalent beliefs about what counts as a matter of luck makes the worst off better off with respect to what is a matter of luck. But we need first to know what currency conception of responsibility should be presupposed in this consequentialist calculation.

Consider the following *consistency argument,* which aims to rebut the consequentialist-engineering argument. We can state two versions of it, a cognitivist version and a social relativist version.

On the one hand, suppose the luck neutralizer appeals to truths about responsibility to fix the currency conception of responsibility. Then arguably whatever correct conception of responsibility occupies the currency role should also directly determine which beliefs about responsibility should be encouraged in the incentive-parameter role. No scope remains for the consequentialist-engineering argument, even from a luck-neutralizing perspective. On this view, sheer consistency between the two roles, rather than an application of maximin or any other consequentialist reasoning, should fix the occupant of the incentive parameter role of beliefs about responsibility. Otherwise, we are engaging in manipulation of beliefs contrary to acknowledged truths. It is one thing to manipulate beliefs because you are skeptical that there are any determinate truths about responsibility. It is another to rely on determinate truths as a basis for manipulating beliefs away from them. The latter is an unattractive move to place at the heart of a theory of distributive justice.

On the other hand, suppose the luck neutralizer appeals to prevalent views about responsibility in some community to fix the currency conception of responsibility. The consequentialist-engineering argument asks us to use this currency in order to determine which views about responsibility to encourage in the community. But if prevalent views about responsibility are good enough to define the very currency of redistribution, why aren't they also good enough to operate as parameters of incentive seeking? Again, sheer consistency seems to fix the occupant of the incentive-parameter role, leaving no scope for the consequentialist-engineering argument.

But perhaps this rebuttal based on sheer consistency is too swift and takes too simple a form. Perhaps the relations between the currency and incentive-parameter roles are still more complex and admit of possibilities of equilibrium.

Suppose conception A of responsibility is, for whatever reason, used in the currency role to determine what is a matter of luck and hence subject to redistribution. Suppose maximin applied to that currency is used to evaluate various sets of beliefs about responsibility as parameters of incentive seeking. If conception A is the maximin choice for the incentive-parameter role, there is no inconsistency between roles to resolve. But what if conception B is the maximin choice for the incentive parameter role, when conception A is used in the currency role? This is the problematic case.

We may be able to turn this possibility to advantage, however, by imposing an equilibrium condition on relations between the currency and incentive-parameter roles. We could require that whatever conception of responsibility occupies the currency role should, via maximin reasoning using that currency, support itself and not some other conception to occupy the incentive-parameter role. If some other conception is supported, we go back to square one and try a different view of responsibility in the currency role. This equilibrium constraint could apply, as well as whatever other reasons we may have to use one or another conception of responsibility in the currency role. This proposal is more complex than the original consequentialist-engineering proposal, but *contra* the sheer consistency argument, it does give some scope to consequentialist maximin reasoning.

This procedure is not a viable stopping point, however. This simple equilibrium constraint is still too simple. Notice the full complexity of the system of interdependencies that have accumulated among the currency and incentive-parameter roles of responsibility. It is not just that maximin reasoning about what beliefs about responsibility to engineer depends on the currency. But also the responsibility-sensitive currency in turn depends on what people believe and expect, since this affects what they can do, their dispositions and abilities. To spell this out: the currency of distributive justice depends on the distinction between what people are responsible for and what is a matter of luck. What people are responsible for depends in part on what they can do, their dispositions and abilities. The latter depend in part on their beliefs about responsibility and corresponding normative expectations. So responsibility already depends in part on people's beliefs about it,[1] and we come full circle. What a luck-neutralizing egalitarian aims to redistribute to the worst off depends in part on what people believe about responsibility. The beliefs to be engineered depend on the currency, and the currency should support itself via an engineering argument. But the currency will in turn be affected by the beliefs so engineered, so those beliefs also have to be fed back into the currency calculations before the system can settle. These genuine relations among the roles of responsibility should be respected by an equilibrium condition. But the condition needs to be formulated to avoid simply moving the currency goal post in order to win the game. It would be a delicate matter to formulate an appropriate equilibrium condition and calculate what view of responsibility should occupy these roles.

Let's take stock. Two types of problem with the consequentialist-engineering argument have been considered: its dubious pragmatism, and its

---

1. If their beliefs about responsibility amount to knowledge, then these beliefs in turn depend on the truth about responsibility, so that responsibility and beliefs about responsibility are interdependent (cf. Strawson 1986). Then knowledge of responsibility may require responsibility and beliefs about it to be in equilibrium if neither is to destabilize the other. If so, the currency of distributive justice depends on the subsystem of truths and beliefs about responsibility.

failure to address interdependencies between the currency and incentive-parameter roles of responsibility within luck-neutralizing justice. Perhaps an equilibrium condition can be imposed on any one conception of responsibility that occupies both roles. The upshot of this suggestion for incentive inequality is unclear. To return to the two scenarios we used to fix ideas, it is not obvious that the second, regressive view of responsibility would be recommended in preference to the first, less restrictive view. Some degree of incentive inequality might still, for all that has been said, emerge from the equilibrium condition. Or there might be more than one way of satisfying the equilibrium condition.

I do not pursue these issues further for present purposes. Any equilibrium condition that takes account of the complex system of interdependencies just described would count as a significant departure from the original, rather naive consequentialist-engineering argument, which is my current target. Even so, it would not yet take account of the final, well-being role of responsibility, to which I now turn.

4. The Consequentialist-Engineering Argument: The Well-Being Role of Beliefs about Responsibility

So far I have considered several ways in which prevalent views about responsibility can affect the currency of distributive justice. Because what people are responsible for may depend on their beliefs about responsibility, the placement of the responsibility / luck cut can be affected by such beliefs. Also, beliefs about responsibility can enable or drive productive activity, including levels of incentive seeking, thus affecting the total quantity of goods such as resources and well-being to which the responsibility filter is applied.

Beliefs about responsibility, however, may also be more directly related to the total quantity of goods. This is because someone's beliefs about his responsibility or lack of it contribute directly to his well-being. Indeed, on an objectivist view of well-being, not just someone's beliefs about how responsible he is but how responsible he in fact is can contribute directly to his well-being. Responsibility and beliefs about responsibility have a *well-being role*, in addition to the other roles we have considered. The direct impact of beliefs about responsibility on well-being may offset their indirect effects via incentive seeking on the overall well-being of the worst off.

When we take account of this fourth role of responsibility, we find that the system of interdependencies among the possible roles of responsibility in justice is more complex still.

How responsible you are can depend on what you can do, your dispositions and abilities, which can depend on how well off you are. But how well off you are can also depend on your beliefs about responsibility. An important source of well-being for people is their sense of responsibility for what they do, for how they use and express their abilities, for what they create by so using them. This sense of responsibility carries the potential for both praise and blame and enables people to identify in a fundamentally satisfying way with their creative products and other expressions of their abilities. A sense of responsibility contributes to well-being in this way across all levels of ability and of expression of ability. The point applies not just to the highly talented, but to children, to people who have handicaps, to people with ordinary or mediocre abilities. And it applies whether or not abilities are of high market value. The negation of this sense of responsibility is profoundly dispiriting across all levels. To be deprived of the belief that you are potentially responsible for creative expressions of whatever abilities you have would be to lose a belief in something that gives life much of its point and meaning.

We can refer to the aspect of well-being that reflects someone's responsibility and sense of responsibility as *responsibility well-being*. If well-being is included in the specification of the goods to which a responsibility filter is then applied to yield the currency of redistribution, then responsibility well-being in particular is included by that specification. Thus, to the extent responsibility well-being is not itself something for which people are responsible, so not filtered out, it would also be included within the currency of luck-neutralizing distributive justice.

Return now to the two scenarios specified earlier. The first set of beliefs about responsibility supports the sense of responsibility; the second undermines it. As a result, a shift from the first to the second scenario would reduce responsibility well-being across the board. Other things equal, this would reduce the total amount of goods to which the currency filter is applied. Even on purely consequentialist grounds and abstracting from our previous arguments against the consequentialist engineering of beliefs, such a move would be blunt and ill targeted. The goods position of the worst off will not necessarily benefit from such a change. The sense of responsibility of the talented is manipulated in order to minimize incentive seeking and so maximize the portion of their product available for redistribution to the worst off. But the sense of responsibility of everyone else is manipulated at the same time, and the effects of the manipulation are more general than these desired effects on incentive seeking by the talented. If a conception of responsibility becomes prevalent according to which responsibility is highly restricted or impossible, responsibility well-being is undermined. This hurts everyone, including the worst off.

From the point of view of the worst off, how would this loss of responsibility well-being weigh against the extra product of the talented made available by lower levels of incentive seeking? That depends on, among other things, how bad the loss of responsibility well-being is. It shouldn't be underestimated. Responsibility is something we deeply want and need and is fundamental to our well-being. Even those who believe that responsibility is impossible have waxed eloquent on the depth of the loss. For example, Galen Strawson writes:

> It seems that most people would find abandonment of the ordinary, strong notion of responsibility intolerable, not to say practically speaking impossible, from a social point of view. It would undermine the foundations of their conception of what human life is. For it is not as if one can excise one's inclination to praise and blame people while leaving all one's other attitudes to them untouched. (Strawson 1986, p. 87)

Is it clear that the extra product made available to the worst off by lower levels of incentive seeking would outweigh its cost in the loss of responsibility well-being to the worst off? The overall well-being position of the worst off might net out higher if a less restrictive conception of responsibility were prevalent, and normative expectations were such that the talented expected moderate incentives for extra work. The worst off might be best off when a smaller but still significant portion of any extra product reached them, but not at the cost of their responsibility well-being.

Moreover, it is not irrelevant here which conception of responsibility is actually correct! If responsibility is indeed impossible, trying to disguise this for the sake of delusory responsibility well-being may be unjustified. But if responsibility really is possible (as I argued in Chapter 3), depriving people of responsibility well-being by persuading them that they could not really be responsible is to do them a very serious wrong, to destroy something of very great value.

The consequences of one or another set of beliefs about responsibility for the currency position of the worst off are the result of a complex system of reciprocal feedback relations among the currency, incentive-parameter, and well-being roles of responsibility. Even if objections to pragmatism are waived, a luck-neutralizing consequentialist engineer of incentive parameters cannot bypass this triangular tangle. Luck neutralizers may be well advised to minimize these problems by forswearing the engineering of incentive parameters on maximin grounds. The best way forward for the luck neutralizer seems to be to fix a conception of responsibility on cognitive grounds to occupy all of the roles responsibility may play in distributive justice. If prevalent beliefs and expectations are to be altered, they should be altered on cognitive grounds. Whatever levels of incentive seeking are possible relative to correct beliefs about responsibility set the context for evaluating the "descriptive" premise of the maximin argument for incentive inequality.

There is thus some pressure to "go cognitive" even within a luck-neutralizing approach to distributive justice that assigns a currency role to responsibility. The question remains whether this move would resolve the various problems I have raised for the currency role given to responsibility by a luck-neutralizing approach. I do not pursue this question further here. I have shown that the currency role is at least problematic. I now argue that it is dispensable, within a more fundamentally cognitive approach to distributive justice.

5. Taking the Veil to Avoid Bias: Whose Mouth Is This, Anyway?

How do the various roles of responsibility I have distinguished look if we shift to a cognitive approach that takes the aim to neutralize bias as basic, rather than the aim to neutralize luck?

I have not yet focused on how the normative premise of the maximin argument for incentive inequality could be justified: on how the pattern rather than the currency of distribution should be arrived at. I have argued, negatively, that responsibility is ill suited to play a patterning role. It is doubtful that our conceptions of responsibility provide any determinate basis for interpersonal and counterfactual judgments about whether differences between people's positions are a matter of luck for them, or whether some other position or relative position would not be a matter of luck. In Chapter 10 I describe how the aim to neutralize bias as opposed to luck can contribute positively to arguments for a maximin rule of distribution. But that argument proceeds against the background of issues about incentive seeking and incentive inequality addressed in this chapter. How does a bias-neutralizing perspective contribute to resolving these issues?

By aiming to neutralize bias instead of luck, we eliminate a currency role as well as a patterning role for responsibility. A bias-neutralizing account does not look to considerations of luck and responsibility to provide a pattern of distribution, and it does not pass the goods it is concerned with through a responsibility filter. Cutting out the problematic currency role has desirable side effects: we bypass completely many of the problems and complexities faced by a luck-neutralizing approach. The choice-exemption argument is no longer relevant. Nor are the consistency and equilibrium arguments based on the tangled interdependencies between the currency role and the incentive-parameter role.

However, the other two roles of responsibility survive: the incentive-parameter role and the well-being role of responsibility. According to a cognitive, bias-neutralizing approach, these are the real and proper roles of responsibility in a theory of distributive justice. They provide an essential context for the bias-neutralizing argument for maximin, discussed in the following chapter. In these roles, responsibility is perhaps less central to distributive justice than in the currency role, and the judgments of responsibility needed are less detailed. Moreover, in these roles, by contrast with the patterning role, there is no need for responsibility to range over counterfactual states of affairs, so these roles are better suited to the nature of responsibility than is the patterning role. Nevertheless, responsibility plays an indispensable role in the bias-neutralizing argument by constraining acceptable levels of incentive seeking. A maximin rule is relatively empty of content in the absence of such constraints. This is the critically important message that derives from Cohen's arguments about incentive inequality. So, in this indirect, parameter-setting way, responsibility does play an essential background role in determining how goods should be distributed. But this is very different from the patterning role of determining directly how goods should be distributed.

Whether or not responsibility is used to filter the currency of distributive justice, some specification of the good is needed, as we have seen. A cognitive approach to distributive justice, like any other, requires such a specification. If the responsibility filter is rejected, how does the approach resolve currency issues?

Recall what we learned about rival currencies from the luck-neutralizing approach: many of the arguments under the "equality of what?" heading, about welfare versus resource, expensive tastes and handicaps, and so on (see Chapter 5), were inchoate luck-neutralizing arguments. These arguments reach their apex in fully articulated luck-neutralizing accounts, which have been my target. If we set this approach aside on the basis of the criticisms made and consider alternatives, we no longer aim to capture the intuitions that provide the reference points of that debate *in currency terms.* That is, we no longer aim directly to tailor what it is we are distributing so as to avoid objectionable subsidies to expensive tastes, to build in a suitable distinction between expensive tastes and handicaps, and so on. Those intuitions will have to be tested at a later point against whatever emerges from the cognitive approach.

A natural conception of the currency of distributive justice within a cognitive, bias-neutralizing approach would be an objective specification of basic goods subject to a universal-means test. On this view, distributive justice concerns goods on a list of specific basic objective goods, limited by the requirement that the goods in question are, as well as objectively good in themselves, objectively useful in the pursuit of a wide variety of further goods, goals, and lifestyles, about which people might disagree. The universal-means test requires objective instrumental value rather than merely subjective instrumental value, and in relation to a wide variety of goals, but not necessarily every conceivable goal. (It would be better called the "near-universal objective-means test," but that is a mouthful.) Such a conception of the currency would aspire to express truths about basic goods that can be identified relatively independently of controversial, potentially biased beliefs about further goods. These objective basic goods would include such goods as adequate food, shelter, clothing, good health and good quality medical care, normal mobility, a healthy natural environment, education, access to legal redress, a protected realm of free choice and speech, responsibility and a sense of responsibility, the development and exercise of capacities for excellence, friendship and / or family life, leisure and cultural opportunities, political participation, community membership, freedom from the threat of public or private violence, and so on. In some cases, the intrinsic-cum-instrumental good is the end state, such as being adequately nourished, while in others it is the opportunity or the access, as in family life or legal redress. The prevalence of these goods allows people to flourish, which is good for those who flourish, good for those who live in the midst of flourishing, and just plain good. It is objectively bad for people, both intrinsically and instrumentally, to lack these goods: bad for those who lack them, bad for those who must avert their gaze from their human surroundings or be desensitized, and just plain bad.

This rough sketch of what the currency of distributive justice might look like on a cognitive, bias-neutralizing approach is not original, and amounts to little more than the idea of primary goods adjusted to take account of the fact that various capabilities and other goods, including responsibility well-being, satisfy a universal means test. It illustrates how a specification of basic goods not subject to a responsibility filter can harmonize with a cognitive, bias-neutralizing approach. In a full-fledged cognitive theory of distributive justice, further development would obviously be needed.

Notice also that the well-being role of responsibility enters a cognitive approach via its specification of the currency, on the assumption that responsibility is not impossible. Responsibility well-being is both good in itself and useful in energizing a wide variety of productive projects. But on a cognitive approach, responsibility well-being is not assessed in purely subjective or pragmatic ways. The aim is not to foster delusions of responsibility because they make people happy or productive. Rather, what is good as well as useful is for people actually to be responsible and to have a corresponding sense of responsibility. If responsibility is impossible, so is responsibility well-being.

How would a cognitive approach address issues about the incentive-parameter role of responsibility? As already indicated, consequentialist engineering of beliefs about responsibility is clearly at odds with the general aim to neutralize bias. To engineer delusions of lack of responsibility in order to enable productive effort without incentives is no better than to engineer delusions of responsibility to make people happy. Ideally, correct beliefs about responsibility should provide parameters for incentive seeking. That is, arguments about distributive justice, such as the maximin argument for incentive inequality, should operate within that portion of the incentive-seeking spectrum that is possible relative to correct beliefs about responsibility. For example, if a regression requirement for responsibility cannot be justified (see Chapter 3), then belief in it should neither be accepted as given, if it already exists, nor, if it does not, be engineered in order to make a different portion of the incentive-seeking spectrum accessible.

Evaluating the "descriptive" premise of the maximin argument for incentive inequality involves two tasks (among others). First, we need to arrive at a view about the correct general conception of responsibility. Second, we need to arrive at a view about what is possible for the talented to do relative to normative expectations based on that conception. Only then can we consider what would be best for the worst off.

Notice that a cognitive, bias-neutralizing approach puts responsibility in a less demanding role than a luck-neutralizing approach does. A cognitive approach may seem to be more demanding, since it asks for a correct account of responsibility. But, as we have seen, this demand is properly made within a luck-neutralizing account as well. And what is needed to play the motivational role of parameter for incentive seeking are not specific judgments about what goods people are responsible for in particular cases. What is needed is only a general conception of responsibility, such as a reason-responsiveness conception or a regressive-choice conception, which licenses general background assumptions about whether people are often partly responsible for the results of their choices, or seldom, or never. Since on this approach responsibility is not supposed to operate as a currency filter or to determine a pattern of distribution, detailed judgments about people's responsibility for particular goods are not needed.

But the two tasks involved in evaluating the "descriptive" premise of the maximin argument for incentive inequality are still hard enough. They provide many openings for biasing influences. A veil of ignorance can play a role here in neutralizing bias. So far, this chapter has followed Cohen in neglecting the role of a veil of ignorance in evaluating the maximin argument for incentive inequality (but see his 1992 article, note 51). He focuses on the character of utterances of this argument in the mouths of the talented: on the incoherence between their endorsement of its normative premise and their making true its "descriptive" premise, and on their lack of community with the worst off. However, the appropriate, veiled perspective from which to consider this argument may be one that does not distinguish the mouths of the talented from the mouths of the untalented in this way. There are at least two reasons to take the veil when assessing the "descriptive" premise of the incentive-inequality argument.

First, knowledge of your own talent level is apt to distort your estimate of how hard the talented can work without incentives. Such knowledge allows desires to believe what would be better for you to influence your beliefs. The aim to neutralize bias favors evaluating the incentive argument as from a position of ignorance of such information. Even if we make no assumption about how hard it is possible for the talented to work without incentives, we can see how knowledge of your own talents could distort and bias your beliefs on this issue. You can be biased because you are talented and thus want to believe that it is not possible for the talented to do extra work that benefits the less talented without incentives, while I am also biased because I'm not talented and thus want to believe this is possible. Without prejudging the issue, we can recognize the danger of bias in both cases, since both beliefs are open to the irrational influence of desires to believe something. Anyone is more likely to reach the right answer if she can abstract from such biasing desires to believe one thing or another.

Similarly, knowledge of your own talent level is apt to distort your evaluation of rival general conceptions of responsibility, to the extent you assume that one parameter of incentive seeking may provide greater benefit to the less talented and another parameter provide greater benefit to the more talented. That is, you may favor less restrictive views of responsibility because you are relatively talented and would like normative expectations to be justified that create disabling dismay and morose resentful reluctance in many of the talented at the prospect of working harder without incentives. Or, you may favor more restrictive views of responsibility because you are relatively untalented and would like normative expectations to be justified that dissolve any such disabling dismay and enable the talented to work harder without incentives, for your benefit.

So, behind the veil we do not know whether we ourselves are talented or not. But we could still know whether the incentive argument is made by the talented, whoever they turn out to be, once the veil is lifted and the talented have access to the information that they are talented. Could this information help assess the truth of the "descriptive" premise of the incentive-inequality argument?

If the talented, knowing they are talented, make the incentive argument, they are open to biasing influences in the ways just described. Suppose we agree that the argument for incentive inequality in the mouths of the talented expresses lack of community with the untalented and various untoward motivations, some of which constitute biasing influences. This per se does not refute the argument or the "descriptive" premise on bias-neutralizing grounds. Indeed, to reject a thesis because someone who endorses it is biased or unworthy is to commit the genetic fallacy and is itself to be subject to a biasing influence. We would be better off, from a bias-neutralizing perspective, assessing the argument without knowing whose mouth it comes from. It may be true that incentives are necessary relative to a correct conception of responsibility, despite the defects of the people who hold this view. The aim of neutralizing bias is not to deny theses that are held by people affected by biasing influences. (That aim would probably lead to denying just about every interesting thesis.) Rather, it is to avoid placing reliance on judgments that are subject to biasing influences, or, more accurately, to neutralize the influence of bias in ways that do not prejudge issues.[2] We can try to avoid relying on assertions of the "descriptive" premise that are subject to biasing influences (along with any other judgments about the "descriptive" premise subject to biasing influence), while not on that basis concluding that the "descriptive" premise is false.

Notice that it is logically possible for a desire for certain goods at once to bias your belief about what it is possible for you to do and to contribute to making it true. Suppose you desire to believe that it is not possible for the talented to do extra work without large incentives, because you are talented and such incentives would leave you better off. If this desire influences your belief to this effect in the wrong way, your belief is thereby biased. But logically it could nevertheless be the case that what it is possible for you to do depends in part, via your desires, on how well off you would be as a result, hence on the incentives that are on offer. In special burden cases, working harder without extra compensation would leave the talented worse off than others as well as worse off than they would have been if they'd not done the extra work. In standard cases, working harder without extra compensation would leave the talented worse off than they would have been if they'd not done the extra work, but still better off than many others. Does what it is possible for the talented to do depend on, among other things, how well off they are as a result, either relative to how well off they might have been or to how well off others are? We need a way to assess whether abilities to work may genuinely depend on incentives, while at the same time avoiding the bias introduced by desires to believe that this dependence holds because you would be better off if it did.

Such a work-enabling role of incentives may be more plausible at the level of populations than in individual cases. In any individual case, holding other things constant, lack of incentives may make it difficult for someone to work harder, but not impossible. But that could be true even though it is not possible for all or most of the talented to work harder without incentives. Could there be lawlike sociological generalizations to this effect? There may be natural social forces that operate on choices only

---

2. The second formulation is more accurate because sometimes an institution can systematically set one bias against another in a way that does conduce to knowledge overall. The adversarial legal system may be an example. See also Hutchins 1995 on confirmation bias in individuals versus in groups.

statistically or via complex dynamics. Even if it is true of each talented person that it is possible for her to work harder for less, holding other things constant, it does not follow that it is sustainably possible for all talented people, or even most, to work harder for less. More generally, the possible situation in which some talented people work harder for less may not be the same possible situation in which other talented people work harder for less, and there may be no one possible situation in which all or most talented people work harder for less. But the latter is what is needed to make the "descriptive" premise of the incentive-inequality argument false. That is, if it is not possible for most of the talented to work harder for less, incentive inequality may still be needed to benefit the worst off, even if talented individuals can work harder for less.

The second reason why a veil of ignorance is especially suitable to evaluating the argument for incentive inequality is that a veiled perspective on this sociological issue avoids a certain danger of logical fallacy. The unveiled perspective on what is possible for the talented to do encourages us to consider the relatively easy issue of whether it is possible for individual talented persons to work harder without incentives—by allowing us information about particular talented people we know or ourselves. But what is relevant to the incentive argument is the far harder, more complex and dynamic issue of what is possible for all or most talented people to do. The unveiled perspective on the incentive-inequality argument thus lends itself to a common but fallacious inference from:

(16) for any individual it is possible to . . .

to:

(17) it is possible for all individuals to . . .

A veiled perspective, by contrast, encourages us to evaluate the relevant collective possibility of form (17) directly, by depriving us of the informational resources to assess what is possible for identified individuals considered separately, as in (16). It thus avoids the tempting fallacious inference from (16) to (17).

Assessing the maximin argument for incentive inequality requires that the relevant possibility of form (17) have been evaluated, relative to our best estimate of a correct general conception of responsibility. A veil of ignorance is appropriate to this evaluation, for the two reasons given. But *if* the maximin argument for incentive inequality is a good argument behind the veil, it doesn't become unusable because in the mouths of the talented, once the veil is lifted and they are identified as such, it expresses bias or breaches community. The full argument for incentive inequality would then not be what I have been calling the "maximin argument for incentive inequality" per se. Rather, it would be a higher-order argument to the effect that the maximin argument *would be* a good argument from behind the veil, in ignorance of identities and talents. That perspective neutralizes bias without prejudging issues.

6. Summing Up

On the basis of arguments in Part I, it seems likely that some version of a nonregressive reason-responsiveness account provides the right general conception of responsibility. For present purposes, such a view of responsibility in the incentive-parameter role would appear to land us in the middle portion of the incentive-seeking spectrum, and to support a floor on levels of incentive seeking. Since this view does not eliminate or drastically restrict responsibility, people will often correctly believe themselves at least partly responsible for the results of exercising their talents and will have corresponding normative expectations. Though they may be right or wrong in particular cases, they will not in general be wrong to have such expectations. In particular, they will not be wrong simply on the ground that they are not regressively responsible, not responsible for their natural talents and other causes of what they produce. As a result of such reasonable normative expectations, they may often experience disabling dismay if their partial responsibility is not recognized in the form of some incentive for extra work. Relative to normative expectations thus determined, various moderate levels of incentive seeking by the talented at large are possible, but there is a floor on possible levels of incentive seeking. Even if such normative expectations are alterable, if the view of responsibility that supports them is correct, they should not be altered.

Such a nonradical resolution of the incentive-parameter issues may be regarded as either disappointing or reassuring. At least it has the advantage of not being utterly revisionary of widespread everyday applications of the concept of responsibility. Moreover, the potential asymmetry I have noted between certain generic talents and handicaps on a reason-responsiveness conception of responsibility has intriguing implications in this context (see Chapter 1). The view that people can be responsible for results in virtue of certain generic talents even though they are not responsible in virtue of corresponding generic handicaps relieves some of the tension Cohen detects between the "descriptive" and normative premises of the maximin argument for incentive inequality. It has the potential to reconcile the normative expectations that underwrite moderate incentive seeking by the talented with the maximin norm that gives priority to improving the position of the worst off, among whom we can expect to find many in whom the talents of reason-responsiveness that underwrite responsibility are compromised.[3] In the following chapter I return to this suggestion briefly after examining further a bias-neutralizing argument for a maximin principle.

The topics of this section provide the background against which the next, final chapter proceeds. In particular, an objective unfiltered specification of the currency of justice, along the lines sketched here, is assumed. It is also assumed that the view of responsibility that rightly occupies the incentive-parameter role lights up the middle of the incentive-seeking spectrum. So the "descriptive" premise of the maximin argument for incentive inequality is vindicated. Chapter 10 shifts attention to the normative premise, the maximin principle itself. Perhaps surprisingly, the prospects for a bias-neutralizing justification of maximin are at least as strong, if not stronger, than those for a luck-neutralizing justification, even in the context set by assumptions about responsibility that are often associated with less egalitarian views.

---

3. See and cf. Arneson 1997, p. 343: "On the whole and on the average, individuals with poor prospects for well-being over the course of their lives (the truly disadvantaged, we might say) have lesser choice-making and choice-following abilities than others. And on the whole and on the average, impoverished people have poor prospects for well-being." See also p. 344.

10

From Ignorance to Maximin: A Bias-Neutralizing Alternative

1. A Cognitivist Approach to Distributive Justice

This chapter illustrates a cognitivist approach to distributive justice. Cognitivism in political philosophy is not a doctrine or thesis, but a category. Cognitivist accounts are cast primarily in terms of truth and knowledge rather than choice or preference. There are quite different ways of falling under this broad characterization, and cognitivist approaches can be taken to various topics in political philosophy, such as democracy and punishment, as well as distributive justice (see Hurley 2000a). But some unity can be given to a broadly cognitive approach to political philosophy by two key ideas.

A constraint on political cognitivism is that it give some basis for responding to certain worries. These worries prompt political liberals such as Rawls to deny that the search for truth can provide a shared basis for a conception of justice in a pluralistic democratic society (see Chapter 5, note 3). On this view, a pluralistic democratic state that avoids the authoritarian use of state power should be neutral about the conflicting and incommensurable conceptions of the good held by its citizens. Now Rawls is not a skeptic about ethical truth. But he still sees the absence of commitment to ethical ideals, even liberal ideals like autonomy, as essential to liberalism as a political doctrine. There is no practicable answer for political purposes to the question of the true good, since public agreement on this cannot be obtained in a nonauthoritarian, pluralistic, democratic society.[1]

---

1. Of course, people may disagree about the acceptability of Rawls's theory of justice: for example, about the normative significance of the Original Position, or about the significance for justice of those features of persons Rawls considers morally arbitrary. They may also disagree about what constitutes a biasing influence. At some level, almost any substantive theory will be open to disagreement.

How can these concerns be met within a cognitivist approach? This is where the two key ideas come into play (see and cf. Mill 1958; Cohen 1986a, 1986b; Hurley 1989). The first is that we can often know that certain biasing influences tend to undermine knowledge, even when we make no politically controversial assumptions about the truth. Moreover, we don't need to know what precise relationship between truth and belief makes for knowledge in order to know that certain factors tend to defeat knowledge. For example, even if we don't think that the notion of beliefs tracking the truth (see Nozick 1981) is all epistemology needs, we may recognize that knowledge can be defeated by influences on belief that could not possibly vary counterfactually with the truth, such as desires to believe certain things. Given lack of public agreement and the difficulty of identifying positive expertise, political cognitivism considers how we can nevertheless seek knowledge of the answers to political questions by at least avoiding the biasing influences that make knowledge impossible. Note that authoritarian power is itself a biasing influence; those who hold it tend to surround themselves with people who tell them what they want to hear. The idea of bias avoidance features in the sketch that follows of a cognitivist approach to distributive justice.

A second key idea does not feature in this chapter, but is another important aspect of political cognitivism, and links to a conception of responsibility in terms of reason-responsiveness in ways that could be pursued further. This is the idea that we should develop and use effectively certain capabilities of citizens. The cognitive capabilities of individuals to respond appropriately to relevant reasons are valuable both in their own right and to the social search for knowledge of what should be done. On a reason-responsiveness conception of responsibility, as we have seen, it is in virtue of such capabilities that people are responsible for what they do and the results of what they do. This can enhance both their productivity and their well-being. But furthermore, we can recognize that general cultivation of the cognitive, deliberative, and ethical capabilities of citizens are necessary for certain democratic procedures to avoid bias, even if we don't know the truth about the questions those procedures address.

James Griffin has expressed skepticism about the possibility that procedures and institutions can be designed that tend to lead to reliable beliefs. He writes:

> To say that we should interest ourselves only in judgements formed in the absence of conditions likely to corrupt judgment begs the impor-

tant questions. If we knew which conditions did that, and also knew we were avoiding them, we should indeed be able to isolate a class of especially reliable judgments. (Griffin 1997, 142–43)

But conditions likely to corrupt judgment can be hard to recognize; self-interest is a master of disguises.

I am less skeptical. It seems to me that these difficulties are greatest in the personal sphere, when cognitive labor cannot easily be divided. When faced by a difficult personal decision, I cannot appeal to institutions that delegate the decision to the least biased decision makers, or take a crash course in the virtues I need to make the decision well. But in the public sphere, a political distribution of cognitive labor has a distinctive contribution to make. Political institutions and procedures can be designed and adjusted to avoid overall bias and foster cognitive capabilities in the long term, while minimizing controversial political presuppositions. These two principles give a cognitive twist to the concerns that motivate political neutrality without actually being committed to neutrality. So they are well suited to play a key role in perfectionist versions of liberalism. They at once make cognitivism politically palatable in nonauthoritarian pluralist societies and give politics the potential to be of cognitive value.

2. Neutralizing Luck versus Neutralizing Bias

Theorizing about distributive justice has often made the implicit assumption that a basic aim of egalitarianism is to neutralize the effects on distribution of brute luck, understood as factors for which we are not responsible. We have seen in previous chapters how this assumption has been made explicit and clarified in important recent work by Cohen (1989, 1992) and by Roemer (1985, 1986, 1987, 1993), among others. Luck in this context is usually understood to include luck in the kind of person you are, such as genetic luck, which supposedly gives rise to what Rawls (1971) calls "morally arbitrary" differences between people. The aim to neutralize the influence of at least some such factors on distribution can be seen as having a methodological role in Rawls's theory by providing the normative significance of choices made in the Original Position. This is the case despite Rawls's official aim to avoid making issues of responsibility and desert prior to issues of justice (see and cf. Woodard 1998). By contrast, in Cohen's and Roemer's work, the role of luck neutralization or responsibility tracking is more explicit and less methodological, that of a basic substantive aim of justice.

It may be natural to assume that rejection of the aim to neutralize luck has anti-egalitarian consequences. By contrast, the view taken here is that rejection of the luck-neutralizing aim in its familiar methodological or substantive roles can strengthen rather than weaken egalitarianism.

Various negative reasons for this view have been given in previous chapters. I have considered whether the luck-neutralizing aim helps us to understand either how or what to distribute, and came to negative conclusions. Our concepts of responsibility and luck are not counterfactually determinate enough to tell us *how* we should distribute if we are to neutralize luck, or to tell us to distribute in an egalitarian way in particular. So the aim to neutralize luck cannot provide a basis for egalitarianism. When someone is not responsible for what he has, there may simply be no answer to what he is responsible for instead. Moreover, the aim to neutralize the *effects* of luck is tied to the suspect regression requirement, that in order to be responsible for something you have to be responsible for its *causes*. On plausible assumptions, this requirement makes responsibility impossible. But the supposition that no one is responsible for anything provides no basis for an egalitarian pattern of redistribution either. Furthermore, using responsibility to filter *what* we redistribute is problematic when combined with other, arguably more important roles of responsibility in distributive justice, especially the incentive-parameter role.

There are also positive reasons for an egalitarian to depart from a luck-neutralizing approach to distributive justice. Perhaps surprisingly, a stronger case for egalitarianism can be made by assuming a different fundamental aim, which displaces responsibility from center stage in theories of distributive justice in favor of knowledge. In particular, egalitarianism should give a patterning role not to the aim to neutralize *luck*, but instead to the aim to neutralize *bias*. We can admit that there is an important general connection between justice and responsibility. But this connection can be expressed in roles other than those of telling us how or what to distribute, namely, the role of setting parameters for incentive seeking and providing elements of well-being (as described in Chapters 8 and 9).

Biases are influences that distort the relationship between our beliefs about what should be done and any truths there may be about what should be done. It is antecedently unlikely that biased beliefs will constitute knowledge—unlikely, that is, antecedently to views about the truth or falsity of the beliefs in question. Biases are cognitive distortions: they distort the relationship of belief to truth in a way that prevents belief from tracking the truth or otherwise attaining the status of knowledge. For example, a personal desire to believe that something is true is a biasing influence on belief. If you believe something because you want to believe it, then even if your belief happens to be true, it isn't knowledge. Someone whose beliefs on a topic just happen to be true in this way does not have beliefs that are reliably true under relevant counterfactual suppositions. That his own beliefs on this topic are not reliable may mean that they are not a reliable general source of input to deliberation about the truth. In some institutional contexts, however, one source of bias may offset another in a way that does conduce to the truth; consider the adversarial legal system (and see Hutchins 1995). Many (but not all) desires distort the formation of beliefs and thus are biasing influences, and so does certain information that bears on how such desires can be met.

Bias is issue-relative. The same factor can be a biasing influence with regard to certain issues, but not others; love of your spouse, for example, can make for more accurate insights about his character. When a factor is biasing for one issue but not another and both are in the public domain, weighing and balancing is needed. Perhaps a degree of patriotism motivates citizens to the cognitive efforts democracy requires, for example, but too much may distort beliefs about the relationship of your own country to others.

We should distinguish two strands of thought about justice that are often run together. In Rawls's theory, for example, a Kantian, luck-neutralizing strand plays an important methodological role. It is implicitly expressed by his concern to eliminate arbitrary contingencies from the Original Position, and by his remark that the Original Position can be thought of as the point of view from which noumenal selves see the world (1971, p. 255). But there is also a distinguishable, arguably cognitivist strand that can be understood in terms of a concern to neutralize bias.

The latter, cognitivist strand can take us further toward an egalitarian account of distributive justice when detached from the former, in part because the account then does not inherit the problems about responsibility that emerge for luck-neutralizing approaches. Aiming at *knowledge* provides a reason to adopt a perspective of *ignorance* in thinking about how goods should be distributed: ignorance of ourselves would rule out many biasing influences, such as those deriving from self-interest. Egalitarianism can be supported from such a perspective in a way that does not depend on the luck-neutralizing aim.[2]

3. The Perspective of Justice: An Equal Chance of Being Anyone versus Ignorance of Who You Are, and Risk versus Uncertainty

Consider a generalization of the Rawlsian framework for thinking about distributive justice. We describe some normatively significant, fictional point of view from which principles of distribution are to be derived, under certain constraints. From such a constrained perspective, we consider the question: "What should be done about the distribution of goods?" We do not assume that the answer is necessarily to be motivated by self-interest operating within the given constraints. The general idea is that, if we specify the right, normatively significant constraints on such a point of view, principles of distribution derived from it will be principles of justice. But this could be either because, as in Rawls, the procedure determines what *count* as principles of justice, or because we think it is *likely* that principles resulting from such a procedure will yield justice—or at least more likely that they will do so than principles arrived at in other ways.

We can call such a point of view a *perspective of justice*. This counts as a *generalization* of Rawls's idea of the Original Position for two reasons: first, because it does not assume that an exercise of constrained self-interest occupies this perspective; second, because it does allow that the perspective may be a "device" in aid of the discovery of just principles rather than a way of determining what count as just principles (cf. Scanlon 1982, p. 122).

We can now further distinguish two ways of setting up the perspective of justice. One, often appealed to by utilitarians, involves assuming you have an equal chance of being anyone in society. That assumption, among others, acts as a constraint on the reasoning to principles of justice. This is the *equal chance characterization* of the perspective of justice. It assumes

---

2. The claim is not that the bias-neutralizing aim identifies a distinctively egalitarian motivation. Rather, it can be employed quite generally within a cognitive approach to political theory and its consequences for various areas can be assessed (see Hurley 2000a). The claim is that, when applied to issues of distributive justice in the way described, the bias-neutralizing aim supports egalitarianism better than the luck-neutralizing aim does.

there are known probabilities or risks. The other way of setting up the perspective of justice is Rawls's way: to assume instead a different constraint, namely, that you are radically ignorant of who and what you are. This is the *ignorance characterization* of the perspective of justice. It does not assume that risks are known, but merely assumes ignorance or uncertainty.

These assumptions are distinct so long as you do not adopt the principle that lack of information concerning different possible outcomes justifies assigning them equal probability. Some orthodox decision theorists favor this principle, but Rawls explicitly resists it. And experimental subjects tend to reject the inference from ignorance to equal probability implicitly, by reacting differently to situations involving uncertainty as opposed to known equal probabilities (an example follows). Most people are far more averse to situations of uncertainty, where risks are unknown, than they are to running known risks. And there is a flourishing school of nonexpected utility theorists who do not dismiss this tendency as irrational (see Bacharach and Hurley 1991, Introduction, secs. 2, 3, and passim, for a view of the debate; see also, for example, McClennan 1990; Gardenfors and Sahlin 1982; Hurley 1989, chap. 4 and pp. 368–382).

An example may help to see the difference between risk aversion and uncertainty aversion. As an empirical matter, most people are risk averse when they know the probabilities involved. This means that if you offer people the chance to play a game in which they have an objective 50 percent chance of winning $100, most will pay less than the game's actuarial value of $50, though risk-loving gamblers will pay more. Consider a game where someone wins $100 if she guesses correctly the color of a ball drawn from an urn known to contain 50 red and 50 black balls. It is worth something to play this game; how much? A typical answer, expressing a degree of risk aversion, might be $30. If you now change the game so that there are 100 balls, red or black, but their proportions are unknown, you are now dealing with uncertainty rather than risk. And typical offers drop dramatically, to around $5 (Raiffa 1961). This difference reflects the difference between risk aversion and uncertainty aversion. They are logically independent in that a gambler who likes to take known risks could still be averse to acting without knowledge of risks, under uncertainty.

The distinction between the equal chance and ignorance characterizations of the perspective of justice can be related to several other distinctions: to the distinction between risk aversion and uncertainty aversion, and to the distinction between the luck-neutralizing aim and the bias-neutralizing aim. On the one hand we have a set of ideas involving risk and luck: the aim to neutralize luck, the assumption that I might have an equal chance of being anyone, and the idea of risk aversion. On the other hand we have a set of cognitive ideas involving ignorance and knowledge: the aim to neutralize bias, the assumption that I am ignorant of who I am, and the idea of aversion to uncertainty. Consider how various permutations of these ideas might work in derivations of principles of distribution from a perspective of justice.

First, how does the ignorance versus equal chance issue interact with the risk aversion versus uncertainty aversion issue? While as a matter of fact most people are risk averse, Rawls does not want to assume, in the course of reasoning for his principles of justice, that the parties to his Original Position are risk averse. This is because he holds that different attitudes to risk should be respected as part of people's differing conceptions of the good, which are veiled in the Original Position. And if risks are unknown in the Original Position, risk aversion cannot get a grip anyway; only aversion to uncertainty is relevant.

By contrast, there are very general conceptual reasons to assume that, other things equal, intentional agents prefer information to lack of information, so are at least weakly averse to uncertainty. Consider the alternative: to accept uncertainty, other things equal, would be to decide how to act without making relevant information and reasons available to oneself, other things equal. That would be hard to reconcile with the minimal cognitive capabilities and rationality we require of intentional agents. So we can justify on conceptual grounds adding an assumption of weak uncertainty aversion to the ignorance characterization, even if we cannot justify adding an assumption of risk aversion to the equal chance characterization. I return to this point later.

4. The Perspective of Justice: Bias versus Luck, and Why It Is Better to Suppose Ignorance of Who You Are Rather Than an Equal Chance of Being Anyone

Second, how does the ignorance versus equal chance issue interact with the bias-neutralizing versus luck-neutralizing issue? Should the hypothetical position from which principles of justice are chosen be understood in terms of ignorance of who we are or rather of equal chances of being anyone? Rawls of course favors the ignorance assumption. But what do the aims to neutralize luck or bias have to say on this question?

The aim to neutralize bias *supports* the idea of deciding about principles of justice in a position of ignorance of your own advantages and disadvantages and your probabilities of gain or loss from various options. Knowledge of these matters might well be biasing, whatever the truth about justice. For example, how much truth is there in the view that offering large incentives to the most talented is necessary to get them to produce in a way that benefits everyone (see Cohen 1992)? We do not need already to know the answer to this hard question in order to recognize that my beliefs about this may be biased by knowledge of whether I am talented or not and my corresponding desires to believe one thing or another. You can be biased because you're talented and want very much to believe the talented need large incentives to produce in a way that benefits the less talented, while I am also biased because I'm not talented and want very much to believe the talented do not need large incentives to benefit the less talented. Anyone is more likely to reach the right answer if she can abstract from these biasing influences.

For the same reasons, the aim to neutralize bias also argues *against* the idea of deciding about justice on the basis of calculations of your chances of gain. But this point holds *even if these calculations derive from an assumption that everyone has equal chances.* Biases can distort beliefs even if they apply equally to everyone. If I didn't know for certain I was talented, but only that my chances of being talented were, say, 85 percent, the reasoning of the preceding paragraph would obviously still apply. But even if I only knew that my chances of being talented were 50 percent (and so were everyone else's), that very information would still set up the motivation for a calculation of possible payoffs in light of attitudes to risk, as opposed to the epistemic motivation to discover the truth about the incentives needed by the talented. The former does not necessarily track the latter, and when it does not, the former is potentially biasing in the cognitive sense.

To elaborate this point: The aim here is to remove information that would allow potentially biasing desires to affect deliberation about what should be done. In this sense, desires relating to your own chances of gain can be just as biasing as desires relating to your own certainty of gain. But this point is not affected by everyone's chances of gain being the same. The kind of bias in question is cognitive: a distortion of the ideal relationship between truth and belief, introduced by certain desires. *Cognitive bias* should be distinguished from *partiality*, or differential orientation to or concern for one person as opposed to another. Partiality can operate as cognitive bias, but cognitive bias doesn't necessarily involve partiality. Bias in the cognitive sense can operate when your beliefs are influenced by desires that operate via calculations of your chances of gain, even if everyone's chances of gain are the same so that impartiality obtains. The distorting influence of calculations of your chances of gain on the ideal relationship between your beliefs and the truth is not eliminated just because your chances of gain are the same as others'. Thus, the equal chance characterization can admit bias, expressed in calculations of your chances of gain, even though it excludes partiality. For these reasons the bias-neutralizing aim does not lend itself to conceptions of the perspective of justice as yielding expressions of constrained self-interest, to the extent the constraints in question still admit cognitive distortion. In this respect the position taken here has an affinity with Scanlon's criticisms of the reading of contractualism in terms of rational self-interest operating behind a veil of ignorance.[3]

---

3. Compare Scanlon's remarks about the difference between appealing to the idea of rational self-interested choice under special conditions and appealing to the idea of what no one could reasonably reject, given that people are seeking a basis for general agreement. Scanlon 1982, pp. 122–125.

Scanlon comments on the moves, first, from the idea of impartiality to the ignorance characterization of a perspective of justice, and, second, from the ignorance characterization to the equal chance characterization (p. 121). While Rawls criticizes the second move, familiar from arguments for utilitarianism, Scanlon focuses on the first move, from impartiality to ignorance (p. 124). He distinguishes a valid version of this first move from a problematic one. If I would have reason to accept a principle no matter which social position I were to occupy, "then my knowledge that I have reason to do so need not depend on my knowledge of my particular position, tastes, preferences, etc." (p. 121). This is a valid train of thought, but it does not lead to the different notion of rational self-interested choice under special conditions. Asking what I could agree to in ignorance of my true position is a "corrective device" for "considering more accurately the question of what *everyone* could reasonably agree to," and does not reduce to the quite different idea of what would be chosen by a single self-interested person ignorant of his true position (p. 122). If the first move is read in this latter, problematic way, then a mistake has already been made even before we move from the ignorance to equal chance characterizations. We should think of the interests in question as "simply those of the members of the society to whom the principles of justice are to apply" (compare the remarks in the text about people's interests engaging the Pareto preference directly), and Rawls's "reduction of the problem to the case of single person's self-interested choice should arouse our suspicion" (p. 124). (Compare Scanlon's criticisms of the first move with Sandel's remarks about

There are further reasons related to the bias-neutralizing aim that also favor an ignorance characterization of the perspective of justice over an equal chance characterization. A fundamental question here is whether we should model our attitudes to the distribution of resources across persons, all of whom are or will be actual, on our attitudes to the distribution of resources across possible states of affairs, not all of which will be actual. (Compare Scanlon 1982, p. 127.) This is what we do when we base an answer to the question of which actual people should get what on the supposition that I have an equal chance of being anyone. The analogy between people and possibilities provides a decision theoretic device for reducing interpersonal problems to individual decision problems given risk. But the formal parallel between a life being mine and a possibility being actual is disturbing in the context of thought about justice. For example, we want to say something like: "So what if the chances of it being *my* handicap are small? It's still *somebody's* real handicap; the relevance of some actual person's actual handicap to considerations of justice just doesn't depend on the chances that it might have been mine." To the extent attitudes to uncertainty do not reduce to attitudes to risk, the ignorance characterization fares better than the equal chance characterization in this respect. Imposing ignorance allows the deliberative decision maker to focus on the human reality of the handicap or other relevant circumstance, by avoiding the bias that goes with knowing that she herself is safe—or *probably safe*.

How does the aim to neutralize luck bear on the ignorance versus equal chance issue? One suggestion, which does not hold up to scrutiny, applies the luck-neutralizing aim to luck in the kind of person you are, or constitutive luck. Consider the idea of a natural lottery of constitutions, or sets of essential properties, the outcome of which is morally arbitrary. Suppose

---

"what really goes on behind the veil of ignorance" and on the way a "voluntarist interpretation of the original position gives way to a cognitive one," in Sandel 1982, pp. 122–132.)

The burden of Scanlon's criticism falls not on the assumption of a veil of ignorance, of which he admits there is a valid version, but on the reduction to the point of view of a single rational individual behind that veil. In this respect the view taken here is related to Scanlon's: it exploits the veil of ignorance as a corrective device, but without assuming an exercise of constrained self-interest. The argument here goes further by pointing out the way in which uncertainty aversion can operate, even if we do not revert to the constrained self-interest picture. The influence of attitudes to uncertainty on decision is not tied to evaluations in terms of self-interest, any more than the pointfulness of the veil of ignorance is.

that in such a lottery you have an equal chance of being anyone. This assumption might be regarded as giving a literal reading to the aim to neutralize constitutive luck. More specifically, making a decision in the ex ante position where there are equal chances of various possible constitutions might seem a way to neutralize differences that are matters of constitutive luck.

But this literal reading is in danger of incoherence, as we saw in Chapter 4. Who or what is the "I" who has an equal chance of various different sets of essential properties? We should not want to be committed to making sense of such constitutionless selves. So the luck-neutralizing aim does not support the equal chance characterization in this way. The incoherence is avoided if we restrict this reading of the equal chance characterization to nonessential properties. However, we then not only face disagreement over which properties are nonessential, but also have an account of the perspective of justice that entrenches differences in essential properties with no independent justification.

Does the luck-neutralizing aim instead support the ignorance assumption? Whether it does or not, we do not need it. The bias-neutralizing aim can support the ignorance assumption without help from the luck-neutralizing aim. Notice that the reasons why the bias-neutralizing aim supports the ignorance assumption are quite independent of the luck-neutralizing aim and of worries about the moral arbitrariness of natural advantages or disadvantages, and carry no implications about constitutionless selves. Here the negative reasons for avoiding a luck-neutralizing account are also relevant: since we don't need the luck-neutralizing aim to support the ignorance over the equal chance characterization, we might as well avoid the problems about responsibility it generates.

The net result is that the aim to neutralize bias supports the idea of deciding on principles of justice from a hypothetical position of ignorance rather than one of equal chance. To get this far with Rawls we don't need the aim to neutralize luck, with its attendant problems.

5. Maximin and the Role of Responsibility in Setting Parameters for Incentive Seeking

There are, nevertheless, important general connections between justice and responsibility. In particular, responsibility can have a parameter-setting role in a theory of distributive justice. As we saw in Chapters 8 and 9, how equally resources are distributed by a maximin principle depends critically on what assumptions we make about incentive seeking (Cohen 1992). If the most productive seek little or no incentives for being highly productive, maximin will yield a very egalitarian outcome. But if the most productive seek large incentives, maximin may, under further assumptions, allow very substantial inequalities for the sake of raising the level of the worst off a rather small amount.

What assumptions about incentive seeking should we make? Natural and sociological forces may set a range of possible incentive-seeking behaviors that are realistically feasible in modern conditions. But it is reasonable to assume that within that range, social and ethical norms influence levels of incentive seeking. In particular, norms concerning how responsible people are for the results of what they do will have an important influence on the levels of incentives that are needed to avoid demoralization and economic apathy.

Part I of this book supports the view that both the truth and popular intuition about responsibility lie between extremes. On this view, it is neither true that people are responsible for almost everything they do nor that they are responsible for almost nothing they do. Moderate incentive-seeking behavior can express a natural and widespread sense of moderate responsibility for what someone does as a result of his abilities. But this natural sense of responsibility does not license unrestricted incentive seeking. To merit praise and reward for your activities is not to merit any reward you can extract, however exorbitant. The natural sense of responsibility is vague but carries with it an unavoidable sense of proportion; it is not the view that you deserve anything you can get away with. But equally it is not the erroneous view that no one is responsible for anything they do as a result of their abilities because no one is responsible all the way back for the causes of those abilities.

It is a good thing for everyone that this erroneous regressive view is not widely held, for several reasons discussed in previous chapters. By making responsibility seem impossible this view would undercut the critically important well-being that derives from our sense of responsibility (see Strawson 1986, p. 87). Moreover—and this is an important point for egalitarians concerned with the level of well-being of the worst off—it would undermine this well-being unselectively, across all socioeconomic classes. A view that undercuts the sense of responsibility is a blunt instrument, given its universally negative consequences for the well-being that flows from our sense of responsibility.

These vague truths about responsibility set the parameters of incentive-seeking behavior within the range of feasibility: an assumption of moderate incentive seeking should be made, corresponding to the vague, moderate popular sense of responsibility. Individuals do need some significant portion of their product as incentive to produce, given this norm of responsibility. But they do not require that almost the whole of their extra product be returned to them. We should not look for more determinacy here than the vague truths about responsibility admit of. Nor do we need to, so long as we keep responsibility in this background, parameter-setting role in relation to a general assumption of moderate incentive seeking (as opposed to the more demanding patterning and currency roles). In particular, we do not need to decide in particular cases what goods someone *would* be responsible for under counterfactual circumstances, when he is not responsible for what he *actually* has. I have argued that often there is simply no determinate basis for answering such questions. By avoiding such decisions we avoid occasions for bias to outstrip truth.

Notice that despite any methodological role luck neutralizing may be given in justifying the Original Position and the assumption of ignorance, these general background issues about responsibility and incentive remain. Until the parameters of incentive seeking have been set, the implications of a maximin principle for distributive justice are indeterminate. This important point emerges from Cohen's (1992) discussion of maximin and incentive seeking. In the previous chapter I showed how responsibility plays an essential parametric role in relation to incentive seeking. The real work that responsibility must and should do in a theory of distributive justice is here in the background. But this background work does not require that the luck-neutralizing aim motivate the perspective of justice. The bias-neutralizing aim does a better job in that central methodological role.

6. How Aversion to Uncertainty Leads from Ignorance to Maximin

Where do we go from here? Rawls wishes to derive a maximin principle of distributive justice from the Original Position, which requires inequalities in primary goods to benefit the worst off groups in society. So, for example, inequalities resulting from incentives to produce given to the most talented would only be permitted if they benefited the worst off. Now one way to derive a maximin principle from a perspective of justice would be to ignore the distinction between ignorance and equal chance and to assume risk aversion. In the absence of risk aversion, an equal chance assumption will not generate egalitarian principles. Moreover, we would have to assume extreme risk aversion to get a maximin principle for resources from an equal chance assumption. Otherwise, reasoning from the equal chance assumption, I might be tempted to trade risk avoidance off against my chances of great wealth by allowing further inequalities.

But this is not Rawls's way. He does distinguish ignorance and equal chance. Risk aversion can get no grip under the ignorance characterization, since risks are unknown (and risk aversion is logically independent of uncertainty aversion). In any case, Rawls gives good reasons not to assume risk aversion, as we have seen. People's attitudes to risk vary, as well as their tastes and conceptions of the good. Their different attitudes to risk should be respected; no particular attitude to risk should be enshrined in the Original Position. But under these conditions how can the rabbit of maximin be pulled out of the hat of ignorance?

I do not discuss Rawls's attempt to do so here, which has been criticized by others. I suggest a different way, using an assumption of aversion to uncertainty instead of an assumption of risk aversion. We only need weak, not extreme, aversion to uncertainty in order to derive egalitarian principles of distributive justice from a position of ignorance—though how weak determines how egalitarian.

Isn't this just as bad as assuming risk aversion? No, for the same objections do not apply. This is not simply because uncertainty aversion is more marked and widespread than risk aversion, as an empirical matter, though that is true. As we have seen, there is a very general conceptual reason to assume that, other things equal, intentional agents prefer information to its absence. Other things equal, intentional agents make relevant information available to themselves and take account of it. Our conception of minimally rational intentional agents requires them to be weakly averse to uncertainty, even if in order to avoid bias we put such agents in a hypothetical position of ignorance to choose principles of justice. This combination of uncertainty and aversion to uncertainty yields egalitarian results. And it does so in a way that does not give a motivating role to the aim to neutralize luck or to worries about the moral arbitrariness of natural advantages or disadvantages.

A little uncertainty aversion can go a long way in generating egalitarian results. If you start with equal chance, you need extreme risk aversion to get a degree of egalitarianism that you can get instead from ignorance plus weak risk aversion. If ignorance of your identity and traits cannot be translated into known chances of gain or loss, it is not possible to trade off avoidance of uncertainty against your chances of gain. But then such trade-offs are ruled out without assuming extreme uncertainty aversion.

Recall that it was for a closely related reason that the bias-neutralizing aim favored the ignorance assumption over the equal chance assumption. Part of the point of imposing ignorance, according to the bias-neutralizing aim, is that it gives no scope to calculations of your chances of gain. But by the same token, neither does it give scope to trade-offs of chances of gain against aversion to either risk or uncertainty. So ignorance combines with even weak uncertainty aversion to preclude the influence of desires that relate to your own chances of gain.

The ignorance assumption does, however, allow certain desires to operate. First, an aversion to uncertainty may be regarded as equivalent to a desire for information about the way things actually are or will be. Unlike desires relating to your own chances of gain in particular, this desire cannot in general be regarded as biasing in the sense of cognitive distortion.

Second, we need to depend on some general conception of basic goods, in something like the way that Rawls depends on the notion of primary goods. I explained in Chapter 9 (section 5) what this might look like on a cognitive, bias-neutralizing approach. Consider then what we can call the *Pareto preference:* an impersonal and general desire that people be better off in terms of these basic goods rather than worse off, other things equal. This simply makes operational the needed specification of basic goods subject to a universal means test, which already reflects the aim to avoid bias. So the Pareto preference should not introduce bias; it if does, we have not yet got our specification of basic goods right.

Thus, uncertainty aversion and the Pareto preference are compatible with the bias-neutralizing aim in a way that concern for your own chances of gain is not. Moreover, uncertainty aversion can be assumed even though we do not assume self-interested motivation.

Consider next a perspective of justice characterized by the ignorance assumption, by weak uncertainty aversion, and by the Pareto preference relative to the assumed basic goods. In this situation, a maximin principle can be seen to be the closest you can reasonably come to avoiding uncertainty over basic goods. We can reach this conclusion in several steps, by exploiting the connection between uncertainty and the distribution of goods.[4]

---

4. It may be objected that once we reject the idea of an exercise of constrained self-interest, there is no reason to stop short of full-fledged impartial spectator theory. The argument here is indeed aiming to occupy a middle ground between these options. The role given to the Pareto preference is consistent with the perspective of an impartial spectator. But we can nevertheless use the decision-theoretic connection between uncertainty and distribution to structure the argument to maximin, in

First: Even if you have no information about your position, distributing a known fixed quantity of goods equally avoids uncertainty over those goods. You can easily calculate what everyone actually gets; there is no uncertainty about people's absolute or relative positions.

Second: If the quantity of goods for distribution is not known or fixed, it is no longer possible to avoid uncertainty about absolute positions. But distributing goods equally at least avoids uncertainty about relative positions.

Third: But now remember that uncertainty avoidance is weak, not extreme. Consider setting against it not any known chances of gain for yourself, but rather increases in basic goods for some unknown members of society, so long as the level of the worst off is kept as high as possible. Moving from equality to maximin admits uncertainty about relative as well as absolute positions, in order to satisfy the Pareto preference. But this is compatible with an assumption of only weak uncertainty aversion. You are not here trading off uncertainty avoidance for an increase in your own chances of gain. Rather, you are trading it for increases in some unknown persons' level of basic goods, increases that leave no one worse off. You judge that their improvement outweighs the additional (relative) uncertainty. This is not because you calculate that you have some chance of being them. Their improvement engages the Pareto preference directly. (Again, compare Scanlon 1982; see also Ellsberg 1961.)

There is a further question as to exactly where the compromise between uncertainty avoidance and Pareto improvements should be struck. Should weak Pareto improvements be permitted, which benefit some and make no one worse off, including of course the worst off? If so, uncertainty about who will benefit is admitted. This will result if we keep the assumption of uncertainty aversion relatively weak, so that uncertainty should be avoided only other things being equal. Or should only strong Pareto improvements be permitted, which make everyone better off—again, including the worst off? If so, at least we know that everyone will benefit. A stronger assumption of uncertainty aversion will move us in this direction, but it does not need to be extreme. The first view would admit more relative uncertainty for the sake of Pareto improvement than would the second. But neither will permit inequalities that involve anyone's being worse off than they would be if we stopped with the unknown total amount distributed equally at step two.

---

the way suggested. This connection can hold even though self-interest is not the relevant motivation. Here I am indebted to objections made by Derek Parfit.

Notice the way the ignorance constraint and the aversion to uncertainty work together in a kind of symbiotic tension. It is only in the context set by the ignorance constraint that aversion to uncertainty drives us toward equality, in order to make information available. But aversion to uncertainty itself supports the ignorance constraint, just because the constraint rules out biasing influences, cognitive distortions. So ignorance can serve knowledge. Given the ignorance constraint, we would still (other things being equal) like to avoid as much uncertainty about actual distributions of goods as possible; and by keeping everyone equal at an unknown absolute level, we do. If we allow some people to rise above this level but do not know who they are, we sacrifice some knowledge about relative levels. In particular, we do not know which people will be above this level or even the chances that particular people will be above this level. But it is precisely this knowledge about who would benefit that the ignorance constraint has denied us in the interests of avoiding cognitive distortion. The trade-off we make at step three between uncertainty avoidance and Pareto improvement is in harmony with the underlying aim of bias neutralization. Ignorance of the identity of those persons who will be above the floor of stage two is precisely the kind of ignorance that avoids cognitive distortions, such as those of self-interest or envy, that would be introduced if we considered the chances that we would be among those persons.

On the cognitivist view, the normative significance of the perspective of justice characterized by ignorance rather than equal chance is found in the aim to avoid the biasing influences that inevitably go with information, even probabilistic information, about who you are and what you are like, your talents and handicaps, your desires and chances of gain. And weak aversion to uncertainty can be justified as part of the minimal rationality required for intentional agency. By giving a cognitive slant to the perspective of justice, and dissociating it from the luck-neutralizing aim and related ideas, we can reclaim egalitarian results. In this way we can take a lead as egalitarians from Rawls even if we do not share his Kantian, luck-neutralizing sympathies. Notice that this way of developing political cognitivism has not at any point implied authoritarian power or threatened the pluralist and democratic character of liberal society.[5]

---

5. Cf. the discussion in Chapter 7 of the paternalism of Roemer's proposal and why this makes his proposal inappropriate as the basis for a general theory of distributive justice, though it may be a valuable method of implementing specific policies. Even if the dimensions of advantage in Roemer's proposal were limited to reflect basic goods that pass a universal-means test, his scheme would still base distribution on judgments

7. A Comparison with Ellsberg's View

Daniel Ellsberg discusses the maximin criterion in relation to uncertainty aversion. It may be helpful to compare his points with mine.

Ellsberg imagines an uncertainty-averse person comparing two options in terms of their expected utility, when he has little confidence in his assessment of the risks involved. Expected utility values are calculated by weighting the utility of each possible option by its probability, and maximizing the sum of these utilities. Consider the effect on this exercise of lack of confidence in one's best probability estimates. We are here distinguishing the probability judgments themselves from the weight we accord to those judgments: they may be the best we can come up with, but our evidence may be very weak. Under these conditions, perhaps one option has a higher expected value than the others. That may still not seem much of a reason for choosing it, given how little confidence this person has in his estimate of the risks the expected values are based on. So he looks for other criteria of choice. He computes expected values for his options on all the different reasonably possible probability distributions, rather than just on his best estimate of the probability distribution. He then looks at the worst outcomes each option might have. He may have much more confidence in his estimate of the lower limit of reasonable expectation than in his best estimate of the risks and hence of the expected value of the options. One option may have a higher expected value according to a very shaky estimate, while the other may have a higher security level according to a fairly solid estimate. This is not double counting of the worst possibilities, just because the person's best judgment of the risks does not itself reflect his lack of confidence in that very best judgment; probability judgments are distinct from judgments about the weight of the evidence on which those probability judgments are based. A person who gives very little weight to the evidence on which his best probability judgments are based is reasonably drawn to options whose expected value is relatively insensitive to which probability distribution turns out to be the actual one.

Ellsberg's comments on this situation are revealing, for present purposes:

> In almost no cases (excluding "complete ignorance" as unrealistic) will the only fact worth noting about a prospective action be its "se-

---

about the deservingness of people's efforts to pursue these goods, in a way that the bias-neutralizing approach I have sketched does not.

curity level": the "worst" of the expectations associated with reasonably possible probability distributions. To choose on a "maximin" criterion alone would be to ignore entirely those probability judgments for which there is evidence. But in situations of high ambiguity, such a criterion may appeal to a conservative person as deserving *some* weight. (Ellsberg 1961, pp. 662–664; cf. Raiffa 1961)

The relative weight such a person gives to the worst expectation will depend on his confidence in his estimate of the probability distribution: the less confidence he has, the more he will sacrifice expected value to increase security level.

How does Ellsberg's discussion relate to mine? Assuming that uncertainty aversion is not so extreme as to outweigh all other considerations, and that there are some probability judgments in which we have confidence, then trade-offs are possible between security level and expected value. But the implication is that if we assume either extreme uncertainty aversion or radical ignorance, then trade-offs will be excluded and maximin result. Both extreme uncertainty aversion and radical ignorance are unrealistic assumptions to make in general. Concerning the perspective of justice, moreover, I concede that the Rawlsian reasons not to assume extreme risk aversion in the face of varying attitudes to risk also apply to an assumption of extreme uncertainty aversion. My argument for maximin from uncertainty aversion does not assume that it is extreme. But it does assume radical ignorance of identity and so renders unavailable the evidence for probability judgments that provide a basis for trade-offs of expected value against security level. That such ignorance is unrealistic is irrelevant to the reasons for assuming it about the perspective of justice, which aim at bias neutralization rather than realism. Thus, my claim is implied by Ellsberg: radical ignorance renders unavailable the basis for the trade-offs that lead to a softening of maximin.

8. Loose Ends: Maximin, Sufficiency, and the Asymmetry between Talents and Handicaps

I gave a bias-neutralizing argument for maximin in section 6 above. Some may regard maximin and leximin principles, which give lexical priority to the worst off, as too extreme. They may prefer more general forms of priority view, which give some degree of priority to those in worse off positions, but without giving the worst off lexical priority. This permits trade-offs between small or few benefits to the worst off and large or more benefits to the not quite so badly off. Others may go still further and argue that what really matters is just sufficiency: whether everyone has enough (Frankfurt 1987a). Of course, the question then arises whether what counts as enough is a matter of absolute levels of goods, or at least in part a matter of interpersonally relative levels of goods. Moreover, absolute levels of some goods may depend causally on relative levels of other goods. For example, Wilkerson (1996) argues that absolute health levels depend strongly on relative levels of social and economic goods (see also Hurley (forthcoming) "Distributive Justice and Health").

Maximin, priority, and sufficiency give different answers to the "how" question, the question of what pattern of distribution of goods justice demands. It is natural to regard them as taking progressively larger steps away from strict equality. Someone with strongly egalitarian leanings might be persuaded on general Paretian grounds to adopt a maximin principle instead of strict equality, while balking at so radical a departure from egalitarian ideals as sufficiency views seem to involve.

However, we should think again about the contrast between maximin and sufficiency views (for simplicity, I will leave out of account the middle ground of priority views). Is the difference between them more notational than substantive? Each view requires certain parameters to be tweaked to yield determinate recommendations. Can we arrange to tweak them so as to keep maximin and sufficiency views in tandem? On the one hand, we need to set the range of incentive-seeking behavior for maximin to have determinate content, as we have seen in Chapters 8 and 9. Suppose we disallow incentive seeking altogether. Then maximin will support strict equality, in the way Cohen (1992) spells out. On the other hand, we need to define a threshold for sufficiency views to have determinate content, and in particular to determine whether "enough" is relative to the positions of others. Suppose we took the view that having "enough" of the relevant goods requires having the same amount as others have. Then sufficiency will also support strict equality. In this extreme case, artful parameter tweaking ties the two intuitively disparate views together.

How general is the scope for manipulating parameters to achieve convergence between sufficiency and maximum? I don't know precisely. Suppose that a small degree of incentive seeking is allowed, and that having "enough" permits a small degree of inequality: Do the views stay in tandem? I suspect not, since the sufficiency rule would give more weight to getting someone to the threshold of sufficiency than to bettering the position of someone well below the threshold, while maximin would do the reverse. Someone mathematically more adept than I could probably easily set out the general relationships between sufficiency, maximin, and their parameters, to show when convergence can be achieved by parameter tweaking and when not. But to the extent it *is* possible to tweak parameters so as to keep maximin and sufficiency views in agreement about how goods should be distributed, the difference between them is more notational than substantive. To that extent the parameter tweaking is where the action is, and the formal answer to the "how" question mere window dressing. We would do well then to endogenize our parameter tweaking—to make it the focus of normative theoretical attention, rather than treating the parameters as exogenously determined (in the way that Rawls seems to treat the parameters of incentive seeking). To the extent our parameter tweaking depends on issues about responsibility, the black box of responsibility in theories of justice is both relocated and opened.

I have argued that there are substantive issues about responsibility at stake in setting the parameters of incentive seeking: whether people are responsible for their actions and the results of what they do bears on what range of incentive-seeking behavior is defensible. I have also pointed out that certain views of responsibility generate an asymmetry between certain talents and handicaps with respect to responsibility. How would such an asymmetry bear on issues about how to set incentive-seeking parameters?

Recall the view that understands responsibility in terms of hypothetical choices. On this view, even if someone does not control or choose certain features of himself, even if they are the results of factors for which he is not responsible, he might become responsible for these features by identifying with them in a way that is reflected in his hypothetical choices—that is, in what choices he would make if he were able to, even when he is not able to in fact.

However, the ways in which people identify themselves and their corresponding hypothetical choices are likely to give rise to asymmetries. They may well be more likely to identify themselves with talents than with handicaps. If so, then on this view of responsibility, handicaps are more likely to count as bad luck for people than talents are to count as good luck.

Similarly, a reason-responsiveness conception of responsibility can yield an asymmetry between talents and handicaps. Reason-responsiveness tends to be more conducive to many goods than the lack of it, such that it counts as a kind of generic talent and the lack of it as a kind of generic handicap. If what you do when you act on a reason-responsive mechanism does not count as a matter of luck, then what you do when you exercise the corresponding generic talent does not count as a matter of luck. How-

ever, what you do as a result of being handicapped by lacking responsiveness to reasons does, on this view, count as a matter of luck. So on
this view, people handicapped by lack of reason-responsiveness may make
poor quality decisions, both to act and to omit, for which they are not responsible, even though talented, reason-responsive types are responsible
for their acts. In this sense people can be responsible in virtue of their talents even though people are not responsible in virtue of their handicaps.

Suppose the members of group *W* have a generic handicap in the form
of lack of reason-responsiveness, and that as a result the *W*s are not responsible for their goods position. Suppose the members of group *T* have
a generic talent in the form of reason-responsiveness, and that as a result
they are at least in part responsible for their goods position. Moreover, the
*T*s are better off than the *W*s. In this unrealistically simple society, the *W*s
are the worst off group, and the *T*s are, to varying degrees, better off.

Responsibility cannot in general tell us, as I have argued at length in
earlier chapters, what people should have when they are not responsible
for what they do have. Here, in particular, it cannot tell us directly what
the *W*s should have in relation to the *T*s. I have given an argument for
maximin that does not depend directly on responsibility for an answer to
the "how" question, but which does give responsibility a background role
in setting the normative parameters of incentive seeking. As we have seen,
unless assumptions about incentive seeking are made, maximin does not
have determinate content.

The argument for maximin would tell us to make the *W*s as well off as
possible. How would the asymmetry in responsibility between the *W*s and
the *T*s bear on the incentive-parameter issue? In virtue of their responsibility, the talented *T*s could have reasonable normative expectations that underwrite a degree of incentive seeking. That is, the talented *T*s could reasonably feel that they are responsible for some of the extra product that
results from the exercise of their generic talents, and could reasonably expect to operate within a moderate incentive structure that recognizes this
and rewards them differentially if they work harder and produce more. As
a result, they may need such incentives to work at their most productive,
in ways that benefit the *W*s.

However, in virtue of their lack of responsibility for their poor situations, the untalented *W*s should not have symmetrical downside normative expectations. They should not feel that they are responsible for the
relatively low value of the output that results from their relative lack of generic talents, and should not expect to be treated as if they were so responsible. Nor should the *T*s have these attitudes about the *W*s. Both *T*s and

Ws should recognize that if responsibility is asymmetrical, some people can be responsible in virtue of their talents for the goods they enjoy even though others are not responsible in virtue of their handicaps for the bads they suffer.

In this unrealistically simple society, commitment to making the worst off Ws as well off as possible is compatible with a degree of incentive seeking by the Ts. The asymmetry of responsibility could make it normatively coherent to hold that the Ws should be made as well off as possible within the context of moderate incentive seeking by the Ts. The bias-neutralizing argument for making the Ws as well off as possible does not aim to track responsibility or to neutralize luck, and leaves no opening for objections that appeal to the putative "undeserving poor." It does not use responsibility to filter goods that are redistributed, nor does it aim to reward efforts according to deservingness. Responsibility enters only when we try to answer the question: What level of incentive seeking should be assumed in the background, as compatible both with the normative motivation for maximin, to which responsibility is not directly relevant, and with reasonable background normative expectations, to which responsibility is relevant? The upward-only incentive structure combined with maximin would here reflect the general asymmetry of responsibility: the incentive and reward structure can open out upward without undermining the responsibility-free basis for maximin.

I have suggested how the asymmetry implied by certain conceptions of responsibility might, in an artificially simple society, bear on the relationship between maximin and incentive seeking. Does the suggestion have any application to realistically complex societies, without tidy groups such as the Ws and the Ts? Would the asymmetry of responsibility also bear on the question of how someone's relative position might constrain whether he has enough, whether he meets the threshold of sufficiency? How are maximin and sufficiency views related when these parametric issues are pursued? To what extent might they converge? I do not try to answer these questions here, but leave them as loose ends for further work.

9. Concluding Remarks

A central aim of this book is to open the black box of responsibility within luck-neutralizing theories of distributive justice—to display some of the ways in which arguments about responsibility interact with issues about distributive justice and constrain the roles that responsibility can play in theories of distributive justice. Different assumptions about responsibility have been made explicit and distinguished. The variety of dissociable conditions of responsibility has prompted the clarification of different senses of "luck." By distilling regressive choice or control conceptions of responsibility, we sharpen the formulation of luck-neutralizing egalitarianism and its implications, for example, concerning incentive inequality and the choices of the talented about how hard to work. If we reject such regressive conceptions, as I have argued we should, we can set aside views that implicitly trade on them, such as views that require the *effects* of luck to be neutralized. By appreciating the indeterminacy of hypothetical choice and similarly of counterfactual applications of "luck" and "responsibility," we come to recognize why these concepts cannot tell us *how* to distribute or provide a basis for egalitarian redistribution. But even so, responsibility can still play other roles. It may tell us what to distribute; it may affect the range of possible incentive-seeking behavior by the talented; and it may affect our well-being. I have considered the results of putting different conceptions of responsibility in these roles. The question whether responsibility should play a currency role and tell us *what* to distribute interacts with issues about incentive inequality and the choices of the talented, but it does so differently for different conceptions of responsibility. If we adopt, as I have urged, a reason-responsiveness conception of responsibility in preference to a regressive choice or control conception, this has implications for the range of possible levels of incentive seeking by the talented and for the well-being levels of everyone. A reason-responsiveness conception can also generate an asymmetry between certain generic talents and corresponding generic handicaps, which suggests how moderate incentive seeking can cohere with a maximin principle of redistribution. I have argued that responsibility should play incentive-parameter and well-being roles in accounts of distributive justice, rather than patterning or currency roles. In the former roles responsibility enters into an argument for a maximin principle of distribution based on the idea of neutralizing bias rather than luck.

I hope that this work will contribute to our understanding of responsibility and of distributive justice by showing why it is worthwhile for theories of distributive justice to distinguish responsibility from other values, such as deservingness or fairness, to distinguish different conceptions of responsibility, and to distinguish different roles responsibility might play in distributive justice.

Appendix

Bibliography

Index

Appendix:
Outline of the Arguments

INTRODUCTION: RESPONSIBILITY AND JUSTICE

1. Recent Advances in Two Areas (pp. 1–3)

(A) Distributive justice: understood in terms of responsibility and the aim to neutralize luck (what people are not responsible for): Cohen, Roemer, Arneson.

(B) Responsibility: following Frankfurt's challenge to the supposition that responsibility for an act requires that the agent could have done otherwise. Subsequent literature distinguishes alternate-sequence conditions of responsibility from actual-sequence conditions, and develops various reason-based accounts of responsibility: Klein, Wolf, Fischer.

Work on (A) has tended to treat responsibility as a black box and to ignore (B).

2. Opening the Black Box (pp. 3–5)

My aim: to bring (A) and (B) into contact. The black box of responsibility within luck-neutralizing approaches to distributive justice turns out to be a Pandora's box. The roles that responsibility can play in distributive justice are constrained by the way responsibility is conceived.

Distinguish different roles that responsibility might play in distributive justice. Responsibility may be able to tell us what to redistribute, but cannot tell us how to redistribute, and so cannot provide a basis for egalitarianism. Responsibility can play roles in relation to issues about incentive seeking and in our understanding of well-being. The aim to neutralize bias can do more to provide a basis for egalitarianism than the aim to neutralize luck.

3. Survey (pp. 5–12)

Abstracts of chapters.

PART I: RESPONSIBILITY

Chapter 1: Philosophical Landscape: The New Articulation of Responsibility (p. 15)

Comparison of Klein, Wolf, Fischer. Actual-sequence versus alternate-sequence requirements. Various conditions for responsibility distinguished: ability to do otherwise versus regression versus control versus choice versus hypothetical choice versus reason-responsiveness.

1. Conditional Analyses, the Distinction between Actual and Alternate Sequences, and Frankfurt Cases (pp. 16–20)

Traditional debate between compatibilists and incompatibilists about responsibility and determinism: opponents share presupposition that responsibility requires agent could have done otherwise, disagree about whether the latter compatible with determinism. Compatibilists analyzed "could have done otherwise" conditionally, as "would have done otherwise, if . . ."

Objection to conditional analyses: distinguishes outright possibility of doing otherwise, all else constant, from disposition to act otherwise under counterfactual conditions. Incompatibilists: ability to do otherwise requires the former, incompatible with determinism.

Possibility of alternate sequence of events versus dispositional features of actual sequence of events. Examples of alternate-sequence conditions of responsibility: could have done otherwise; could have avoided blame. Examples of actual-sequence conditions of responsibility: regression requirement (responsibility for *X* requires responsibility for causes of *X*); various requirements of reason-responsiveness.

Challenge to traditional presupposition: Frankfurt's denial that responsibility requires agent could have done otherwise. Responsibility turns on what actual sequence is like, not on possibility of alternate sequence. Frankfurt Cases: agent does something wrong, *X*, for her own reasons, even though there is a counterfactual intervenor (e.g., brain scientist) standing by to ensure she does *X*, should she waver . She doesn't waver, so no intervention occurs. She couldn't have done other than *X*, because in the alternate sequence there is a fail-safe device to ensure she does *X*. Yet she is responsible for doing wrong, because the actual sequence leading to *X* is such that she does *X* for her own reasons.

Different strategy of argument, which generalizes the irrelevant alternative intuition behind Frankfurt Cases: that responsibility depends on the actual sequence rather than possibility of alternate sequence. Does not depend on sci-fi counterfactual intervenors or fail-safe devices.

2. Klein on Regression and Ability to Do Otherwise (pp. 20–23)

Klein: distinguishes regression (my term, not hers) from ability-to-do-otherwise requirement. Traditional debate about compatibilism often failed to distinguish. Rejects ability-to-do-otherwise requirement for Frankfurt-type reasons. Issue shifts away from whether ability to do otherwise compatible with determinism to whether responsibility must be regressive. Klein: regression needed to explain why people not responsible in cases of brainwashing, brain tumors, emotional deprivation, etc. But determinism plus regression mean people not responsible in normal cases either. Regressive responsibility would require uncaused choice.

3. The Double Dissociability of Regression and Ability to Do Otherwise (pp. 23–24)

Causation can be statistical; hard to make sense of choice with no causes at all, even given indeterminism. Instead, regressive responsibility possible if adopt noncausal hypothetical-choice conception of responsibility. Thus, regression and ability to do otherwise are doubly dissociable. Regressive responsibility doesn't entail ability to do otherwise: hypothetical choice could extend all the way back though actual sequence in deterministic world with no alternate sequences. Ability to do otherwise doesn't require regression: possibility of alternate sequence in which agent does otherwise doesn't make agent responsible for causes of act all the way back through actual sequence.

4. Causal versus Noncausal Conceptions of Moral Responsibility, and How Regressive Responsibility Is Even Possible (pp. 24–28)

Regression requirement: responsibility for X requires responsibility for causes of X. Applies recursively, generates regress. Actual-sequence requirement. Structural requirement; can be added to various different substantive conceptions.

How regressive responsibility is possible. Klein: uncaused choice. Hurley: regressive hypothetical choice (noncausal substantive conception of responsibility compatible with regression even though causal conceptions not).

Suppose blame-licensing moral responsibility requires some kind of causal responsibility, such as choice or control (though causal responsibility not sufficient for moral responsibility). Regressive causal responsibility impossible: agent can't possibly choose or control actual causes of X, plus their causes, and so on, all the way back.

Suppose instead responsibility requires hypothetical choice: would have chosen X and its causes if could have, and wouldn't have chosen to be without them (Scanlon's believer). Not a kind of causal responsibility. Regressive noncausal responsibility is possible: agent can hypothetically choose the causes of X all the way back. Can also hypothetically choose/endorse/identify with own dispositions to hypothetical choice plus their causes, all the way back.

5. The Tame Housewife and Other Objections to Hypothetical-Choice Accounts of Responsibility (pp. 28–30)

Problems with noncausal hypothetical choice conceptions of responsibility:

(A) adaptive preferences, tame housewife. Hypothetical as well as actual choices can be adaptations to oppression, manipulation, etc.

(B) Indeterminacy, causal costlessness. Too many things people would hypothetically choose. Causal relation such as actual choice or control needed to reduce indeterminacy.

(C) Antecedents of counterfactuals about hypothetical choices may be impossible.

6. The Double Dissociability of Regression and Reason-Responsiveness (pp. 30–32)

Some actual-sequence conditions for responsibility, such as choice or control conditions, require the agent to be causally related to what he is responsible for; others, such as hypothetical-choice conditions, do not.

Regression does not entail reason-responsiveness: mentally ill agent could hypothetically choose/endorse causes of her act all the way back, though does not act on reason-responsive mechanism. Regression without reason-responsiveness not intuitively sufficient for responsibility. Reason-responsiveness does not entail regression: mechanism on which agent acts may be reason-responsive locally, even though causes all the way back are not reason-responsive.

7. Reason-Based Views of Responsibility: Wolf (pp. 32–33)

Distinction between actual and alternate sequences applied to reason-based accounts of responsibility, comparison of Wolf and Fischer.

Wolf: rejects Real Self View and Autonomy View, defends Reason View. Responsibility requires the ability to act in accordance with reason, not some other way. Asymmetry of praise and blame. Praise for acting in accordance with reason does not require alternate sequence. Blame for not acting in accordance with reason does require alternate sequence, that agent could have acted in accordance with reason.

8. Reason-Based Views of Responsibility: Fischer (pp. 38–41)

Fischer 1994: actual-sequence reason-responsiveness account of responsibility. Frankfurt Cases: agent acts on loosely reason-responsive mechanism. Mechanism as process leading to act, way it comes about in actual sequence. Reason-responsiveness as dispositional property of actual sequence. What matters for responsibility is whether actual-sequence mechanism is reason-responsive, not what might have happened in alternate sequence. Loose reason-responsiveness: mechanism on which agent acts would, in some possible worlds where there's reason to do otherwise, lead her to act on such reason, hence to do otherwise. Responsiveness to reasons compatible with determinism.

9. A Four-Point Comparison of Wolf and Fischer (pp. 41–46)

Comparison raises four issues about reason-based accounts of responsibility. Does responsibility:

(A) require dispositional property (such as reason-responsiveness) of actual sequence or does it require alternate sequence?

(B) require loose or tight link to reasons?

(C) require link to subjective or objective reasons?

(D) result in asymmetries, e.g., between praise and blame, or between acts and omissions, or between talents and handicaps? Control as requiring dispositional properties of the actual sequence, not alternate sequence.

10. Between Regression and Reason-Responsiveness (pp. 46–52)

Can a reason-responsiveness condition explain the intuitions Klein thinks require regression? Is responsibility essentially regressive? Or should we look for a condition for responsibility on middle ground between reason-responsiveness and regression?

When both reason-responsiveness and regression fail, no responsibility: some cases Klein thinks need to be explained in terms of regression could equally be explained in terms of reason-responsiveness.

Reason-responsiveness without regression: intuitions about responsibility may depend on type of reason-responsiveness: loose/tight, objective/subjective.

Switching from one type of reason-responsive mechanism to another:

bump on head case. If pre-bump reason-responsive mechanism was sufficient for responsibility despite failure of regression, and different post-bump mechanism is also reason-responsive, why should lack of responsibility for bump mean agent not responsible post-bump? Reply: appeal to normal dispositions. Does this require duration and stability; normal source; lack of manipulation? Reason-responsive dispositions could result from manipulation.

Middle-ground condition, more than reason-responsiveness, less than regression: reason-responsive dispositions must be agent's own, to avoid manipulation. Fischer and Ravizza 1998: taking responsibility requirement added to reason-responsiveness requirement. Agent must have self-perceptions as agent, as apt target for reactive attitudes in respect of actions flowing from reason-responsive mechanism (such as practical reasoning), and these self-perceptions must result from process involving agent's evidence, experience of choice and action in world, education, social and moral practices. Process element of taking responsibility supposed to prevent manipulation cases from satisfying conditions for responsibility.

Jeremiah: reason-responsive mechanism implanted by mad scientist. Not responsible if acts on it, because not his own, taking responsibility condition not satisfied. Cf. Jeremiah reasonably endorses reason-responsive mechanism implanted by therapist as on balance a good thing, even though occasionally it results in wrong acts. Takes responsibility for mechanism through appropriate process, even though implanted, so responsible for wrong acts.

Manipulation of taking responsibility itself? Process element supposed to prevent this from giving rise to responsibility, since self-perceptions would not acquired in the right sort of way, on basis of appropriate evidence, etc.

Objection: no independent account of distinction between right and wrong processes. This distinction follows, does not explain, intuitions about manipulation and responsibility in examples. Can we go objective, while admitting that people can be responsible for weak-willed or evil acts?

11. Klein, Wolf, and Fischer: How the Debate Relocates to the Actual Sequence (pp. 52–53)

Klein: addresses Frankfurt issues and issues about regression, but does not consider reason-based views of responsibility.

Wolf: develops a reason-based view and addresses issues about regression, but does not address Frankfurt issues.

Fischer 1994: develops a reason-based view and addresses Frankfurt issues, but does not address issues about regression.

Debate relocates: can a nonregressive actual sequence account of responsibility do the needed work?

Chapter 2: Why Alternate Sequences Are Irrelevant to Responsibility (p. 54)

The distinction between actual and alternate sequences and why alternate sequences are irrelevant to responsibility. How the irrelevant-alternative intuition generalizes the point of Frankfurt Cases, without his sci-fi apparatus. What matters for responsibility is whether the agent would have done otherwise, whether or not she could have.

1. The Space of Reason-Based Accounts of Responsibility (pp. 55–61)

Tight versus loose, objective versus subjective: distinctions cut across one another.

Tightly reason-responsive mechanism tracks reasons. Loosely reason-responsive mechanism follows reasons in some worlds, not all; may respond to some reasons, not others: I go to movies despite publication deadline, but wouldn't if I would lose my job by going. If tight reason-responsiveness required, weakness of will not responsible. If loose reason-responsiveness required, weakness of will can be responsible. Intermediate reason-responsiveness as more attractive than either extreme.

Responsiveness to objective versus subjective reasons. Someone with deprived upbringing may act on mechanism that tightly tracks evil subjective reasons. If only subjective reason-responsiveness required, dedicated evildoer can be responsible. If loose objective reason-responsiveness required, occasional evildoing can be responsible.

All variants of reason-responsiveness conditions are dispositional actual-sequence conditions. However, tight objective reason-responsiveness requirement very close to alternate-sequence requirement. Weaker forms of reason-responsiveness permit responsible weakness of will and evildoing. We can suppose in such cases that an agent wouldn't have done otherwise, whether or not she could have. The intuition that responsibility depends on the actual sequence then emerges.

2. A Recipe for the Irrelevant-Alternative Intuition (pp. 61–66)

Fischer: mechanism-based accounts superior to agent-based; but he does not give a full account of mechanisms. I first use the mechanism idea informally to develop generalized irrelevant-alternative intuition, then explain how it could be the case that an agent wouldn't have done otherwise, whether or not she could have.

General idea: in Frankfurt Cases, actual-sequence condition met, alternate-sequence condition not. We cannot suppose this for tight objective reason-responsiveness condition, but can suppose actual-sequence condition not met, even if alternate-sequence condition is. We can then generalize this supposition to weaker forms of reason-responsiveness: the agent wouldn't have done otherwise, whether or not she could have. Irrelevant-alternative intuition emerges: adding or subtracting the alternate sequence makes no difference to responsibility.

Virtuous Vivian: acts on an tightly objective reason-responsive mechanism, and has the ability to act in accordance with reason. Is the actual-sequence disposition or the ability doing the work in supporting judgment that Vivian is responsible?

Action on tight objective reason-responsive mechanism entails ability to do right thing; inability to do right thing entails agent does not act on tightly objective reason-responsive mechanism. *But:* ability to do right thing does not entail action on tight objective reason-responsive mechanism: Salome would not have done the right thing, even though she could have.

If neither reason-responsiveness nor ability condition met, and person not responsible, we can again ask: is actual-sequence or alternate-sequence condition doing the work? Strategy: compare case where have ability but not reason-responsiveness with case where have neither.

Frankfurt Cases: agent lacks ability to do otherwise because of fail-safe mechanism in alternate sequence, which is intuitively irrelevant since it never operates and agent acts on own reasons. Actual-sequence condition met, not alternate-sequence condition.

Cannot pry conditions apart in this way for tight objective-reason-responsiveness, since inability to do right thing entails not acting on tight objective reason-responsive mechanism, as for Virtuous Vivian. Instead, can pry conditions apart the other way around. Hold actual sequence (dispositions) constant, vary presence of alternate sequence (ability to do otherwise). Key to generalizing the irrelevant-alternative intuition.

Suppose agent was able to do right thing, but did not, so did not act on tight objective reason-responsive mechanism. Was the operative mechanism reason-responsive in a weaker way? If so and agent is responsible, is the ability or the disposition doing the work in making her responsible? If she wouldn't have done the right thing, whether or not she could have, does it make any difference if she actually can?

3. The Recipe Applied: Weakness of Will, Evil, and Medical Problems (pp. 66–70)

Why doesn't the agent do the right thing? Consider three types of case:

(A) she is weak-willed, but her act is still loosely objective-reason-responsive;

(B) she is evil, but her act is still tightly subjective-reason-responsive;

(C) she has a medical problem, so her act is not reason-responsive at all.

In each case, we ask: does it make any difference whether she could have acted rightly or, unbeknownst to her, could not have—given that either way, she would not have?

(A) Weak-willed Wilma: wouldn't do the right thing for the reasons there are, though might have for stronger reasons. Compare (A)(i): Wilma wouldn't have done the right thing even if she could have, and she could have, and (A)(ii): Wilma wouldn't have done the right thing even if she could have, and unbeknownst to her, she couldn't have. Irrelevant-alternative intuition says: difference between (A)(i) and (A)(ii) makes no difference to her responsibility. Alternate sequence in (A)(ii) is irrelevant. Intuition is conditional and comparative: *if* she is responsible in (A)(i), she is equally responsible in (A)(ii). We should blame in both cases or neither.

(B) Evil Ethel: desires to cause pain to others, her act is tightly responsive to her evil subjective reasons. Given that she wouldn't do the right thing, whether or not she could, does it matter whether in addition (B)(i) she could do the right thing, or (B)(ii) unbeknownst to her, she couldn't do the right thing. Irrelevant-alternative intuition: it makes no difference; Ethel is equally responsible in (B)(i) and (B)(ii). We should blame in both or neither.

(C) Maude has a medical problem: her act is caused by abnormal neurotransmitter fluctuations unrelated to reasons. Does it matter whether in addition (C)(i) she could do the right thing (since causation is statistical and a different mechanism might have operated), or (C)(ii) unbeknownst to her, she could not do the right thing? Irrelevant-alternative intuition: Maude is no more responsible in (C)(i) than (C)(ii).

Cf.: Alfred the willing addict.

*4. How Could It Be That the Agent Wouldn't Have Done Otherwise,
Whether or Not She Could Have? (pp. 70–76)*

My strategy elicits the irrelevant-alternative intuition, that the actual sequence is what matters for responsibility rather than the alternate sequence, while dispensing with a counterfactual intervenor in the alternate sequence who guarantees that the agent could not have done otherwise, as in Frankfurt Cases. Generalizing this intuition as above turns on the supposition that the agent wouldn't have done otherwise, whether or not she could have.

So far, this supposition has been understood intuitively, in terms of mechanisms, as in Fischer. Can it be explained further? Yes: variable realizations of a macro-level disposition.

Consider a weak-willed act X by agent A in the actual deterministic world; the agent couldn't have done otherwise. Compare the actual world with various indeterministic worlds in which there are alternate sequences (AS worlds). In the AS worlds, it is possible both that A does X and that A does not do X. In some AS worlds, A does weak-willed act X; in other AS worlds, A does otherwise.

A wouldn't have done otherwise, whether or not he could: the indeterministic AS worlds in which A does weak-willed X are closer to the actual deterministic world than are the indeterministic AS worlds in which A does otherwise.

Why closer? There could be both deterministic and indeterministic realizations of a macro-level disposition, such as control or weakness of will, which are functional equivalents.

Compare to Frankfurt: fact that he couldn't have done otherwise relevant to responsibility only if he did what he did only because he couldn't have done otherwise; if the latter is not the case, then he would have done the same thing even if he could have done otherwise.

Frankfurt Cases: what makes it impossible to do otherwise is counterfactual intervenor in alternate sequence. You don't do what you do only because you couldn't have done otherwise; you do it for your own reasons, and would have even if the fail-safe device had not been standing by.

My cases: what makes it impossible to do otherwise is determinism. But it does not follow that you do what you do only because you couldn't have done otherwise. You might have acted the same way even if the world were indeterministic and you could have done otherwise. There could be different realizations of same macro-level disposition. My way of developing the irrelevant-alternative intuition generalizes Frankfurt's claim that what matters is whether you did what you did only because you couldn't have done otherwise.

5. The Irrelevant-Alternative Intuition for Blame: Would the Agent Have Avoided Blame, Whether or Not She Could Have? (pp. 76–79)

Otsuka: replace "could have done otherwise" alternate-sequence condition for responsibility with "could have avoided blame" alternate-sequence condition. Latter resists Frankfurt style counterexamples, since in Frankfurt Cases agent could have avoided blame (by wavering and triggering intervention) even if could not have done otherwise.

But Otsuka's ability-to-avoid-blame condition is no more resistant to my strategy than is the ability-to-do-otherwise condition. Compare Frankfurt Case in which no waver actually occurs with deterministic world in which agent A could not have done otherwise and could not have avoided blame either. A acts on the same macro-dispositions and for the same reasons as in the Frankfurt Case. The actual sequence is relevantly similar in the two cases. In both cases, we can say: A wouldn't have avoided blame, whether or not he could have.

In the Frankfurt Case, A could have avoided blame; in my case, A couldn't have avoided blame. But the irrelevant-alternative intuition says: the alternate sequence makes no difference, since A wouldn't have avoided blame regardless of whether he could have or not. A is no more blameworthy in one case than the other.

Conclusion: alternate sequences not required for responsibility, so determinism does not make responsibility impossible. Next chapter: is responsibility impossible for another reason?

Chapter 3: Why Responsibility Is Not Essentially Impossible (p. 80)

The impossibility of regressive choice or control does not support eliminativism about responsibility, on either context-driven or theory-driven accounts of "responsibility." To avoid indeterminacy problems, responsibility needs a causal component that is incompatible with a regression requirement. From this we should conclude not that responsibility is impossible but that responsibility is not regressive.

1. Elimination versus Revision; Context versus Theory (pp. 80–86)

Contexts of application of concept *F* versus theoretical beliefs about *F*ness. If applications and theory mismatched, does this show applications wrong, there really are no *F*s? Or that theory should be revised, we've been wrong about what *F*s are like? Elimination versus revision: thought, qualia, persons, values.

Stich: No plausible general answer to when theory change should result in elimination of *F*s versus revision of beliefs about *F*s.

Context-driven versus theory-driven accounts of essence. Variations, combinations. This distinction cuts across elimination versus revision distinction.

Context-driven accounts tend to support revision rather than elimination (e.g., stars), which sits more easily with a theory-driven account. But this tendency should not be overstated. Elimination on context-driven view: nothing in contexts of use may do explanatory work required of essence, not even by relocating from physical to functional level of explanation; *F*s may be arbitrary hodgepodge, gruesome accidental concatenation (wizards). Revision on theory-driven view: hold onto part of theoretical role while rejecting another (triangles).

Horse versus cart: does choice between context-driven and theory-driven views influence whether we eliminate or revise, or do intuitions about whether to eliminate or revise influence former choice?

Both context-driven and theory-driven views give essences explanatory depth. Explanatory work required in relation to worldly contexts of use versus theory-internal coherence.

2. Why Impossible Essences Are Weird (pp. 86–89)

Nothing in fact has the essence of *F*ness versus nothing could possibly have the essence of *F*ness because it's impossible. G. Strawson: "true self-determination is both necessary for freedom and logically impossible" (1986, p. 56). Why impossible essences should themselves be eliminated:

Context-driven case: elimination of *F*s because arbitrary hodgepodge. No essence, not impossible essence. Impossible properties cannot do explanatory work required of essences. There are no magical powers, so having them can't be essential to wizardkind. But having magical powers is a possible essence, since there might in another world have been magical powers that were explanatory, e.g., in contexts of use of "sorcerer." But if

F is impossible, no such counterfactual about explanation makes sense. If *F* is impossible, it is not a possible essence.

Theory-driven case: subset of properties assigned to *F*s by theoretical role may best preserve coherence and point of theory, be essential in virtue of theory-internal explanatory depth. But impossible properties can't do theory-internal kind of explanatory work either.

Meaning-driven case: disagreement about whether responsibility is possible is normative and substantive, not semantic; tension between methodology of charity and attribution of incoherent essence.

3. Is Responsibility Essentially Impossible? (pp. 89–91)

The impossibility of regressive choice or control does not support eliminativism about responsibility: we can revise rather than eliminate.

4. Responsibility: Context and Theory (pp. 91–99)

(A) Contexts of use: responsibility often attributed for acts with normal causes, despite lack of regression. Not in cases of brain damage, brainwashing, hypnotism, mental illness. Disagreement over deprivation cases.

(B) Theory: various possible sets of conditions; necessary versus sufficient. Alternate-sequence conditions (ability to do otherwise, ability to avoid blame). Actual-sequence conditions: noncausal (hypothetical choice) versus causal (choice, control, reason-responsive mechanism) versus structural (regression). Hypothetical choice: necessary even though not sufficient? Causal responsibility necessary but not sufficient for moral responsibility. Animism: causal responsibility per se sufficient for moral responsibility; implausible. Choice or control as forms of causal responsibility required for moral responsibility; specified further by various forms of reason-responsiveness. Is some such refined condition also sufficient for responsibility or is more needed? Is regression required?

(C) Compatibility of various conditions: animism incompatible with regression, since causation not regressive. Rejecting regression does not support animism. Regression incompatible with choice or control, but not with hypothetical choice. Hybrid: require regressive hypothetical choice plus nonregressive choice or control.

(D) Changes: in contexts of use and theory, over time. In past: less prone to recognize regression requirement, more prone to animism.

(E) Intuitive conflict and disagreement: e.g. over regression requirement.

(F) Ethical character of disagreement: substantive and normative disagreement about regression, not semantic: Adam versus Karl. Can't settle by appeal to meaning.

5. Responsibility as Context-Driven (pp. 99–102)

Impossible-essence eliminativist may be tempted by context-driven view's tolerance of substantive disagreement about essential properties. But shouldn't be: impossible essences cannot do explanatory work. Context-driven eliminativism is not based on impossible essences, but arbitrary hodgepodge.

Context-driven views more tempting to anti-eliminativist: immunity of context-driven reference to bad theory; regressive choice/control as bad theory of responsibility, as is animism. Animism attributes responsibility too widely; regressive choice/control makes it impossible.

Need more discriminating theory of applications, which denies responsibility in brain damage, etc. cases but not ordinary cases. Should give explanatory priority to positive applications, not negative. Eliminativist needs to argue no such theory can be found. But this would be arbitrary hodgepodge eliminativism, not impossible-essence eliminativism. Impossible properties can't have explanatory depth.

6. Responsibility as Theory-Driven (pp. 102–104)

Theory-driven views make elimination easier. But essential properties still have theory-internal, coherentist explanatory role. Theory-driven essence should be a set of conditions for responsibility that have explanatory depth, are mutually coherent, exclude more controversial rather than less controversial conditions. An incoherent set of conditions such as regressive choice/control cannot play even theory-internal explanatory role.

Various possible combinations preserve coherence, e.g. nonregressive choice/control plus regressive hypothetical choice. May find nothing actually has this complex property, so that responsibility eliminated. But that would not be because responsibility is essentially impossible.

Another possibility: there is no coherent theory of responsibility; it is an unsalvageable shambles and should be abandoned. Can't mourn or regret it; not poignant, just confused. This also eliminates responsibility, but again not because it has impossible essence; rather, it has no essence.

7. Context and Theory in Reflective Equilibrium (pp. 104–105)

We are not stuck believing responsibility is essentially impossible. Probably best to combine context-driven and theory-driven views into reflective-equilibrium view, so that explanatory depth required both in relation to worldly applications and to theoretical principles.

Working hypothesis: responsibility does not require alternate sequences, does have causal actual-sequence requirements including some form of reason-responsiveness, and is not regressive overall (even if it has regressive noncausal component).

Chapter 4: Responsibility, Luck, and the "Natural Lottery" (p. 106)

The advantages of a thin concept of luck in moral and political philosophy, and why we should avoid a certain thick conception of constitutive luck, namely, the idea of a "natural lottery."

1. Terminological Tidiness: Thin Luck versus Thick Luck (pp. 107–109)
Thin luck: inverse correlate of responsibility.

Thick luck: various conceptions, e.g., lottery luck, lack of control, lack of choice, lack of regressive control.

Thick constitutive luck, e.g., "natural lottery."

Implications of thick conceptions of luck may be misleading in relation to responsibility.

2. Williams and Nagel on Moral Luck (pp. 109–114)
Williams's undifferentiated thick concept of luck:
(A) For intuitive morality, subjection of morality to luck incoherent.
(B) Aim to immunize morality against luck bound to be disappointed.
(A) might express thin luck, but (B) appears to require thick concept of luck. Williams does not specify it further.

Nagel: thick conception of luck as lack of control. Compare with thick conception of luck as lottery luck. Lack of control necessary but not sufficient for lottery luck.

Nagel requires more than control for responsibility. Control can be part of the natural world (genes, thermostats). Nagel requires regressive control: responsibility for X requires control of X and of the causes of X. Control by itself is not regressive: control of X does not require control of X's causes.

Distinguish: luck in effects, luck in causes. Constitutive luck a kind of luck in causes. Nagel's thick conception of constitutive luck: lack of control of causes of who and what you are. Cf. lack of control of effects. For X to be among the effects of luck is for X to suffer from luck in causes; to neutralize the effects of luck on X is to neutralize the influence on X of luck in X's causes.

Nagel: constitutive luck or lack of control of causes is incompatible with responsibility because responsibility requires regressive control, or control of causes. Constitutive luck compatible with responsibility if responsibility does not require regressive control.

Regression and control doubly dissociable: control does not entail regression, regression does not entail control.

3. How Thick Luck Generates an Empty Ramification of Issues, and a Proposal (pp. 114–116)

Various thick conceptions of luck: lack of control, lottery luck, lack of choice, lack of regressive control. Articulation parallels articulation of responsibility: leads to empty and redundant ramification of issues about luck. Not helpful. Luck is not an independently contested concept in moral/political philosophy, but answers to arguments about responsibility. No reason to associate luck with failure of one or another of the various distinct conditions for responsibility, and important not to run them together.

Therefore, I propose adopting thin usage of "luck" for sake of clarity. Leaves all substantive issues about responsibility open, treats issues about luck as derivative.

4. Constitutive Luck and the "Natural Lottery" (p. 117)

The thick/thin distinction applied to constitutive luck. Various thick conceptions of constitutive luck: lack of control of causes vs. the "natural lottery." Cf. thin concept: lack of responsibility for our constitutions.

The thick "natural lottery" conception of constitutive luck has implications concerning identity dependence and chance. As a result it is a misleading guide to responsibility for our constitutions. We do better to avoid the "natural lottery" metaphor and stick to thin constitutive luck.

5. Lottery Luck as Identity-Dependent (pp. 118–120)

Lottery luck requires identity of agent whose luck is in question be constant across different possible outcomes of lottery. Not all arrays of possibilities count as lotteries. Luck must be *for someone*.

Cf. identity-dependent harm, which leads to Parfit's nonidentity problem concerning policies that affect future generations: depletion policies that bring different people into existence do not harm those people. Harm must be *for someone*.

Qualification: limiting case of harm if lives are so bad as not to be worth living, so that existence counts as a harm.

Lottery luck normally a kind of luck in consequences, for which identity-dependence not problematic. Cf. luck in causes in "natural lottery" of constitutions: identity-dependence is problematic.

Is there limiting case for luck, as there is for harm, if one possibility is having a life not worth living? Can it be bad luck in a natural lottery for someone to exist at all? (A) "Not worth living" condition not met for most disabilities. (B) Identity-dependence of luck more stringent than that of harm; not clear that limiting case makes sense for luck.

Can outcome of lottery of constitutions be good or bad luck *for some-one?* If not, conception of thick constitutive luck in natural lottery incoherent.

6. The Bare Self Problem (pp. 120–123)

Strong versus weak senses of "constitution": what you are essentially, your essential properties, fix who you are versus what you are in various respects, including nonessential properties.

Bare self problem: incoherent to combine identity-dependent sense of lottery luck with strong, identity-fixing sense of "constitution." Who or what could have had different essential properties? Natural lottery conception of thick constitutive luck misleading to the extent it encourages us to think in such incoherent terms.

Avoid this incoherence if use only weak sense of "constitution."

No bare self problem or similar incoherence for lottery luck in consequences. Danger arises when try to project identity-dependent thick conception of lottery luck from luck in consequences to luck in causes, in particular, constitutive luck.

Unlike thick natural lottery conception, thin conception of constitutive luck not restricted to inessential properties.

7. Lottery Luck and Chance (pp. 123–124)

Role of chance in lotteries: outcome a matter of chance between different possible outcomes. Physical versus epistemic possibility; outcome of lottery undetermined versus unpredictable.

Lack of responsibility for one's constitution (thin constitutive luck) has no parallel implications: neither indeterminism nor unpredictability. Lottery of constitutions (thick lottery luck conception of constitutive luck) thus again a misleading guide to responsibility for one's constitution. Better to stick to thin constitutive luck.

8. Chance, Indeterminism, and Responsibility (pp. 124–126)

Lack of responsibility (thin luck) does not entail indeterminism. If it did, determinism would entail responsibility.

Cf. philosophers who hold that determinism entails lack of responsibility: they are wrong, but not perversely wrong. Mere fact of determinism does not entail responsibility.

Is lottery luck a better guide to responsibility for consequences than to responsibility for causes/constitutions? No: determinism does not entail responsibility for consequences. Fact that act determines its effects compatible both with the consequences counting as "option luck" (responsibility) and "brute luck" (lack of responsibility). Difference may turn on predictability, intervention by other agents, etc. (tort law).

So: lottery luck entails chance. Consider indeterminism reading of chance. Lack of responsibility does not entail indeterminism, either for causes or consequences.

9. Chance, Unpredictability, and Responsibility (pp. 126–127)

Lack of responsibility (thin luck) does not entail unpredictability. E.g., predictable birth defect is still bad constitutive luck.

Does unpredictability entail lack of responsibility for consequences, if not for causes? Or vice versa? Predictability is relevant to responsibility for causes. Predictability may be necessary, not sufficient, for responsibility; actual foresight may be required. Unpredictability entails lack of responsibility more securely than lack of responsibility entails unpredictability.

10. Concluding Remarks and Transition to Part II (pp. 127–129)

Natural lottery expresses thick conception of constitutive luck. It is misleading guide to responsibility for our constitutions, in respect of both identity-dependence and the relations of responsibility to chance, whether in the sense of indeterminism or unpredictability. Better to avoid these confusions by sticking to thin conception of constitutive luck, as inverse correlate of responsibility for constitution.

Why is it so intuitive to use "luck" both for lottery luck and for inverse correlate of responsibility, given that lottery luck is not inverse correlate of responsibility?

We may wrongly generalize from limited links between unpredictability and responsibility for consequences to more general links between lottery luck and responsibility. Lottery luck and responsibility have some inverse commitments in relation to predictability, control, choice. Our intuitions may not be sensitive to the distinctions between luck in consequences and luck in causes, or the double dissociability of various conditions of responsibility, including control and choice.

Review of points about responsibility from Part I that are used in Part II.

PART II: JUSTICE

Chapter 5: Philosophical Landscape: The Luck-Neutralizing Approach to Distributive Justice (p. 133)

1. Rawls as a Luck Neutralizer (pp. 133–136)

Tensions: Rawls wants to avoid making justice depend on pre-institutional concepts of responsibility or desert, but also to conceive people as responsible for their ends and conceptions of the good, and to affirm that no one is responsible for his "morally arbitrary" distribution of natural assets.

Exegetical response: distinguish earlier Kantian emphasis from later pluralist/neutralist emphasis.

Substantive point: if the judgment that no one is responsible for his natural assets is fundamental to a theory of distributive justice, then so is the concept of responsibility. Development of luck-neutralizing approach through Sen, Dworkin, Cohen, Arneson, Roemer: a longer route to a similar point.

2. Welfare and Resources, Handicaps and Expensive Tastes (pp. 136–138)

Sen on "equality of what?": distinguishes and criticizes utilitarianism, equality of welfare, equality of resources or primary goods. Proposes instead equality of basic capabilities. Dworkin: equality of resources refined to respond to Sen's points.

Well-known reference points: equality of primary goods does not compensate for handicaps; equality of welfare compensates expensive tastes as well as handicaps and ignores tame housewife and similar problems; neither compensates Tiny Tim, who is handicapped but happy.

3. Capabilities, Internalized Resources, and Dworkin's Distinctions (pp. 138–140)

Basic capabilities as universal means to varying ends (cf. primary goods). Dworkin: handicaps as internalized negative resources. Refined conception of resources should reflect distinction between people and their circumstances. Equality of resources does not aim to correct differences attributable to people themselves, such as results of different preferences between work and leisure or about taking risks. It only aims to correct differences attributable to people's circumstances, such as different natural endowments. But why identify people with their preferences, not their endowments?

4. Differences for Which People Are Not Responsible (pp. 140–144)

Cohen relocates Dworkin's cut: the fundamental distinction is not people versus circumstances or preference versus endowment, but responsibility versus luck. The fundamental motivation of egalitarianism is the aim to neutralize luck, whether luck is reflected in welfare or of resources. Luck versus choice, control, hypothetical choice.

Roemer: if someone is not responsible for her circumstances, why should she be regarded as responsible for preferences they give rise to? Tame housewife versus ascetic. Resource bundles should be measured by the degree of morally arbitrary welfare they produce. The thought that people are not responsible for their preferences if they are not responsible for their causes threatens the distinction between equality of welfare and equality of resources.

5. Luck Neutralizing: Interpretation versus Aspiration (pp. 144–145)

Luck-neutralizing view illuminating as interpretation of contemporary egalitarian debate, but still may not be best way to develop egalitarianism. We should reconsider what roles responsibility should be given in a theory of distributive justice in light of what we have learned about responsibility.

Chapter 6: Why the Aim to Neutralize Luck Cannot Provide a Basis for Egalitarianism (p. 146)

1. Introduction (pp. 146–149)

Cohen (1989): fundamental egalitarian aim is to neutralize influence of luck on distribution. Luck egalitarianism as developed by Cohen and others makes explicit a key assumption implicit in egalitarian theorizing. Nevertheless, I claim the aim to neutralize luck cannot provide a basis for egalitarianism, either in sense of *specification* or of *justification*.

Minimal constraint: to count as egalitarian, a doctrine must, for some X, favor relatively more equal patterns of distribution of X over relatively less equal distributions of X, other things equal.

Preview: distinguish what is redistributed from how it is redistributed: the currency from the pattern of distributive justice. Cannot derive how from what, or pattern from currency. Luck/responsibility can play currency role, but this does not entail an egalitarian pattern. Indeed, luck/responsibility cannot play patterning role.

2. What to Distribute versus How to Distribute (pp. 149–155)

Currency role: responsibility as filter, yielding equalisandum. We only aim to redistribute what is a matter of luck, not what people are responsible for.

Limitations of currency role:

(A) Obviously, need independent specification of good to which filter is applied, e.g., resources, welfare, both.

(B) Knowing *what* to redistribute does not tell us *how* to redistribute.

Parfit: equality (concerned with interpersonal relations) versus priority (e.g., maximin, concerned with relation between someone's actual state and other possible states he might have been in). Distinction in how-space, not what-space.

Aim to redistribute only what is a matter of luck: does not favor equality over maximin, even if maximin countenances differences that are a matter of luck. Equality may equally countenance samenesses that are a matter of luck. Nonresponsibility for difference does not entail responsibility for nondifference. Responsibility neither specifies nor justifies taking equality as default.

Egalitarian fallacy: "It is a matter of luck that a and b are unequal" does not entail "It would not be a matter of luck if a and b were equal."

Equality-default view: equality does not need to be justified; responsibility can be used to justify departures from equality. Not guilty of egalitarian fallacy. But not a counterexample to my claim. Even if it is conceded that responsibility plays a patterning role here, it does not do so in relation to aspect of the view that is egalitarian: the assumption of equality as default position. Responsibility also plays a patterning role in the inequality default view, which only permits equalities for which people are responsible and defaults to inequality.

To suggest responsibility plays only currency role, but no patterning role, is to concede that it does not provide basis for egalitarianism. Consistent with redistributing the currency in favor of inequality.

3. The Luck Neutralizer's Dilemma (pp. 155–159)

Aim to neutralize bad or good luck neither nontrivially specifies nor justifies equality as a pattern of distribution. Bad luck ambiguous, interpersonal versus counterfactual senses.

The luck neutralizer's dilemma:

Interpersonal bad luck: my situation is worse than others' situations in respect of goods that are a matter of luck. Neutralizing interpersonal bad luck specifies equal pattern of distribution of whatever is a matter of luck, but only trivially, since inequality used to identify bad luck. Provides no independent justification for favoring or defaulting to equality, for countenancing equalities that are a matter of luck but not inequalities that are a matter of luck.

Counterfactual bad luck: what I have is a matter of luck and I could have been better off. Eliminating all better possibilities for me, or putting me in best possibility for me, does not necessarily put me in same position as doing the same for you would put you. Suppose that if factors for which I'm not responsible were eliminated, it is determinate what I'd be responsible for instead and I'd be better off, and suppose the same holds for you. No reason to suppose these positions would tend to be equal either.

4. Problems of Interpersonal and Counterfactual Responsibility (pp. 159–168)

Can the aim to neutralize luck at least specify, if not justify, egalitarian pattern of distribution? No: counterfactual horn of dilemma leads to deeper problems: (A) the boring problem with responsibility for relations between people's positions; (B) the indeterminacy problem about what would not be a matter of luck when actual situation is a matter of luck.

(A) Responsibility judgments are not primarily about interpersonal relations. I may not be responsible for my income level. But this is a very different question from whether I am responsible for the relation between my income level and your income level. Not clear how responsibility could specify patterns of relations across people. What would it be for a pattern of distribution of goods not to be a matter of luck? Even when two people are both responsible for their respective levels of goods, whether unequal or equal, the relation between them is still partly a matter of luck for each of them, since neither is responsible for the other's position. Point generalizes from actual to counterfactual relations.

(B) Responsibility judgments may not extend in any determinate way to counterfactual situations. When people are not responsible for what they have, there may not be anything determinate, to be found or constructed, that they would be responsible for instead, under counterfactual conditions in which factors for which they are not responsible have been eliminated. If Sam had not had the deprived childhood that makes his current low income bad luck for him, what would he have been responsible for instead? He might have chosen to be a workaholic or a surfer, or anything in between. Choices and effort are not separable from factors that are a matter of luck. But if responsibility is not regressive, you don't have to be responsible for all the causes of your choices in order to be responsible for your choices.

Equality-default view: may be correct. But I deny that aiming to neutralize luck tells us that equality should be the default.

(B) is not merely an epistemological problem; the concept of responsibility does not extend determinately this far in many cases. Similar problem for pure hypothetical-choice accounts of responsibility: causal costlessness, indeterminacy.

(A) and (B) combine to cast doubt on whether responsibility can tell us anything about how to distribute, not just on whether it provides a basis for egalitarianism in particular.

5. Neutralizing the Effects of Luck and the Regression Requirement (pp. 168–174)

Three examples of line of thought that everything is a matter of luck:

(A) Parfit: from windfall luck through productive luck, genetic luck, to luck in ability to make effort, to make choices.

(B) Roemer: extended view of internalized resources leads to seeing all differences as matters of luck.

(C) Aim to neutralize the *effects* of luck makes operational the regression requirement, that responsibility for something requires responsibility for its *causes*. Distinguish aim to neutralize the effects of luck from aim to neutralize differences that are matters of luck. Choices are among the effects of luck. Luck-neutralizing aim does not need the "effects" formulation.

6. Rampant Luck Provides No Basis for Equality (pp. 174–175)

Under plausible assumptions, the regression requirement makes responsibility impossible. But that would not provide a basis for egalitarianism either.

(A) Danger of non sequitur: if people are not responsible for anything, it does not follow that they are all responsible for the same thing. They would be no more responsible for equality than any other distribution.

(B) Danger of incoherence: if responsibility is impossible, then it is impossible to neutralize luck, not merely indeterminate what would do so. Equality cannot be a way of doing the impossible.

7. The Lurking Bare Self (pp. 176–178)

Why autonomous, qualitatively identical bare selves don't show how eliminating responsibility could provide a basis for equality:

(A) If everything is a matter of luck, there are no such things as autonomous bare selves.

(B) Responsibility and autonomy may well be properties of selves that, to be selves at all, must also have some features that are a matter of luck.

(C) Even if stripping away luck were to leave autonomous bare selves behind, no reason to assume there would be no relevant differences between them.

8. Summary (pp. 179–180)

Importance of distinguishing aim to neutralize luck from aim to neutralize effects of luck from aim to neutralize differences that are a matter of luck.

I do not argue against egalitarianism or taking equality as default, only that responsibility provides no basis for these positions. We need to think more about what their basis could be, given that responsibility and luck cannot tell us how to distribute.

Chapter 7: Roemer on Responsibility and Equality (p. 181)

1. My Target versus Roemer's Intentions (pp. 181–182)

Can Roemer's account of luck-neutralization be used to show how the aim to neutralize luck provides a basis for egalitarianism? No. Rather, it shows how to reward people equally who make equal effort to behave in ways we regard as deserving; it can usefully be applied to specific, democratically adopted policies. But giving people what they deserve is not the same as giving them what they are responsible for; nor is equalizing what people are not responsible for the same as giving them what they are responsible for.

2. What It Would Be to Neutralize Luck: Roemer's Framework for Addressing the Problem (pp. 182–185)

All factors for which people are not responsible determine their type; society decides which these are. Within types, people make different choices, for which they are equally responsible, since all differences between people for which they are not responsible are used to sort them into types. How to redistribute between types, while respecting choice-based differences within types?

3. Why Solving the Problem Requires Judgments of Counterfactual Responsibility (pp. 185–187)

We cannot eliminate all intertype differences while leaving alone all intratype differences. Which intertype differences should be eliminated? Answers to this question will generate new intertype inequalities. The new intertype equalities and inequalities should not be a matter of luck, or we will merely have substituted one set of intertype relations that are a matter of luck for another.

4. Skepticism about Counterfactual Responsibility (pp. 187–190)

On what basis can we say what counterfactual equalities and differences between types would not be a matter of luck? We have no general basis for making such judgements of counterfactual responsibility. What people are responsible for is in many cases indeterminate when disconnected from their actual situations and the effects of their actual choices. If an untalented person in one type chooses to be a workaholic, that doesn't mean that if she were talented and so in a different type she would choose to be a workaholic; she might choose to be a surfer instead. Responsible choices not separable from talents. Indeterminacy of counterfactual responsibility cf. indeterminacy of hypothetical choice.

5. An Objection, and Why the Equality-Default View Needs to Defend Counterfactual Differences (pp. 190–191)

Equality-default view: only differences need defense, not equalities. Equality default not determined by responsibility. But we still have to substitute new differences for old differences that were regarded as a matter of luck, and these new differences require defense. If this defense must be in terms of responsibility, problematic judgments of counterfactual responsibility are still needed.

6. Equivocation Between Responsibility and Deservingness (pp. 191–195)

Judgments of deservingness instead of responsibility are really doing the needed work: for example, that people who work harder are more deserving, or prudentially "responsible." Such judgments controversial. Clear distinction needed between what people are responsible for and how deserving they are. People can be responsible for making imprudent and undeserving choices. Everyone within one Roemerian type is equally responsible for his choices, even though some are more prudent and arguably more deserving than others, e.g., because they choose to smoke less. Equalizing reward for equally deserving effort across types is not giving people what they are responsible for, but what they deserve.

7. The Paternalism of Roemer's Proposal (pp. 195–197)

Efforts to do *what* are deserving and should be rewarded? Answers controversial, need explicit scrutiny by democratic processes. Answers can play patterning role, but pattern not necessarily egalitarian.

8. A Diagnosis of the Equivocation between Responsibility and Deservingness: Monotonic Valuation (pp. 197–203)

Desert without responsibility: unsung hero gets windfall. This is luck in sense opposed to responsibility, even though deserved.

Desert as fundamental concept instead of responsibility? Desert cannot replace responsibility in Roemer's scheme, as he needs responsibility to divide people into types, even if he uses deservingness to assess choices within types.

Conflation of responsibility and deservingness natural if merit increases monotonically with behavior of a certain type, e.g., getting education, refraining from smoking. But monotonicity does not always hold, e.g., work versus leisure, number of children. For many dimensions of effort, it is objectionably illiberal/undemocratic to assume deservingness increases monotonically, in absence of specific, democratically adopted policy.

If democratic constraints satisfied, should we aim to distribute in accordance with deservingness, not responsibility? Not attractive as general basis for distributive justice, though may be useful means of implementing specific policies.

9. Summary (pp. 203–204)

When actual differences between Roemerian types are a matter of luck, what counterfactual differences would not be? Responsibility cannot answer this question. Deservingness can, but this requires us to avoid objections to paternalism by defending the needed judgments of deservingness in terms of specific, democratically adopted policies. Luck neutralizers should take care to distinguish responsibility from deservingness.

10. Concluding Thoughts (pp. 204–205)

How uncritical talk of "differences that are a matter of luck" and people being "worse off through no fault of their own" makes it natural to run together the question of what to redistribute and the question of how to redistribute.

Chapter 8: The Currency of Distributive Justice and Incentive Inequality (p. 206)

1. Introduction: Four Possible Roles of Responsibility in Justice (pp. 206–207)

(A) The patterning role: can responsibility tell us how to distribute? Chapters 7 and 8 argued: no.

(B) The currency role, distinctive of luck-neutralizing approaches to distributive justice: responsibility can help to define what we distribute, responsibility/choice act as filter on some specification of the good, what is left is a matter of luck and subject to redistribution.

(C) The incentive-parameter role: beliefs about responsibility affect expectations that influence the range of possible levels of incentive seeking.

(D) The well-being role: responsibility and beliefs about responsibility as part of well-being.

This chapter focuses on the currency role in relation to incentive inequality. Chapter 9 focuses on the incentive-parameter and well-being roles and their relations to the currency role.

2. Incentive Inequality: How Well Off Could the Worst Off Be? (pp. 207–212)

Cohen on the maximin argument for incentive inequality: normative maximin premise versus "descriptive" trickle-down premise. Are inequalities absolutely necessary for maximin or only necessary relative to the choices of the talented to demand incentives? Incoherence between endorsement of maximin and choice to demand incentives.

Cohen: factual question of what can be done without incentives downplayed. Special burden cases versus standard cases. Ambiguity in difference principle: strict versus lax. Another view: no ambiguity, just different resolutions of factual issue.

3. The Choice-Exemption Argument and the Talented Choice Dilemma (pp. 212–216)

How does the choice by the talented to work harder for less relate to the use of responsibility/choice as a filter on the currency of distributive justice?

Danger of self-defeatingness. Choice-exemption argument. Why isn't extra product resulting from choice to work harder for less by talented at least in part filtered out of currency of redistribution (and so returned at least in part to the talented)? First horn of a dilemma.

Talented choice dilemma: if the talented can choose to work harder for less, not all their extra product within currency of distributive justice. If the talented cannot choose to work harder for less, original incentive inequality argument stands.

First horn of dilemma: choice exemption justified in terms of reward rather than incentives. Second horn is incentive inequality argument proper.

But rewards can operate as incentives even if not justified in terms of incentives, and separation of rewards and incentives artificial, static. More realistic dynamic perspective of a temporally extended agent sees rewards and incentives as two sides of same coin: incentives work partly because the provide rewards and rewards provide incentives.

4. Responses to the Choice-Exemption Argument: Lack of Responsibility for Talents, and Regression (pp. 216–219)

Consider how different conceptions of responsibility affect this argument.

First response to dilemma: nonresponsibility for talents. Intermingling of choice and talent in producing results.

More radical response: regression requirement and aim to neutralize the effects of luck, e.g., Fiammetta. Choice does not exempt from redistribution after all.

5. Talents and Regressive Responsibility: Actual Choice or Control versus Hypothetical Choice (pp. 219–224)

Alternate- versus actual-sequence conditions and talented choice: e.g., Fiammetta.

Consider various actual sequence conditions of responsibility:

Regressive choice or control: makes responsibility impossible, e.g.,

Fiammetta. Effect of regressive choice/control requirement on talented choice dilemma? Blocks first horn, choice-exemption argument, while avoiding second horn, leaving it possible for the talented to choose to work harder for less. But still unsatisfactory:

(A) If the talented could work harder for less, though they would not be responsible even in part for what they produce as a result, should they do so? Responsibility as presupposition of normative commitments/obligations? Equivocation between different conceptions of responsibility: not responsible for choices because not regressively responsible, yet could have done otherwise and therefore should have.

(B) Impossibility of responsibility a high price to pay; doubtful such an account can be independently justified.

Regressive hypothetical choice, e.g., Fiammetta. Responsibility for results of talents now not impossible, but too easy.

6. Talents and Responsibility as Reason-Responsiveness (pp. 224–229)

Consider actual-sequence reason-responsiveness conditions, with no regression requirement. Review: reason-responsiveness as kind of control that operates through choice. Control requires dispositional properties of actual sequence, not alternate sequences; control not regressive. Varieties of reason-responsiveness: objective versus subjective reasons, tight versus loose responsiveness; yield different judgements on responsibility of weak willed, evil.

How does this approach to responsibility bear on choice-exemption argument? Talent and reason-responsiveness: Fiammetta. Effect on incentive-inequality argument depends on specification of reason-responsiveness.

Asymmetry of certain talents and handicaps under reason-responsiveness. Reason-responsiveness as generic talent, lack of it as generic handicap. Responsibility in virtue of such talents plus nonresponsibility in virtue of such handicaps. Effect on currency, if responsibility given currency role.

Reason-responsiveness and the how versus what distinction.

7. Pandora's Box Again (pp. 230–231)

Issues about of currency role, choice exemption, and choices about how much to produce: interact with different conceptions of responsibility. Responsibility should not be treated as a black box in luck-neutralizing accounts of justice. Regressive conception nullifies choice exemption, undermines responsibility for choices of how much to produce. Hypothetical-choice conception exempts results of talented choice from redistribution too easily. Reason-responsiveness conception may generate asymmetry between talents and handicaps, reflected in choice exemption and currency.

Next chapter: can a theory of distributive justice do without currency role for responsibility while retaining incentive-parameter and well-being roles?

Chapter 9: The Real Roles of Responsibility in Justice (p. 232)

1. Introduction and Overview (pp. 232–233)

(A) More on the "descriptive" premise of the incentive-inequality argument: can the talented work harder for less? The parametric role of normative expectations and beliefs about responsibility. On what basis should these be engineered? Relations of incentive-parameter role to currency role of responsibility?

(B) Responsibility and beliefs about responsibility as parts of well-being. Relations of well-being role to incentive-parameter and currency roles of responsibility?

(C) The "descriptive" premise from a bias-neutralizing perspective: the role of a veil of ignorance. Dispensing with the currency role while retaining the incentive-parameter and well-being roles.

2. The Role of Beliefs about Responsibility as Parameters of Incentive Seeking (pp. 233–236)

Cohen: normative expectations that are parametric in relation to how hard the talented can work for less: should not be taken as given/exogenous to theories of justice. May be alterable.

Beliefs about responsibility as parameters of need for incentives: *incentive-parameter role.*

Scenario 1: Prevalent beliefs: people are partly responsible for what their talents enable them to do even if not for their talents. Responsibility not regarded as regressive. May experience morose reluctance/disabling dismay if denied some reward for extra work. Resulting sociological generalization: a certain floor on possible levels of incentive seeking.

Scenario 2: Prevalent beliefs: responsibility is regressive, people not responsible for what their talents enable them to do because not responsible for their talents. No morose reluctance, no sense of entitlement to some reward for extra work. Resulting sociological generalization: a lower floor on possible levels of incentive seeking. Query: would lack of responsibility itself act as a drag on extra work?

Different levels of incentive seeking are possible relative to different prevalent beliefs about responsibility. Generalize to a spectrum of possible beliefs and associated possible levels of incentive seeking, from left extreme (demanding no reward for extra work) to right extreme (demanding all the extra product). Maximin argument for incentive inequality invokes middle of spectrum.

If prevalent beliefs are alterable, which set of possible beliefs should be engineered? On what basis?

3. The Consequentialist-Engineering Argument: Pragmatism and Relations between the Currency and Incentive-Parameter Roles (pp. 237–243)

Pragmatic suggestion: engineer the beliefs that make possible levels of incentive seeking that maximin the currency position of the worst off: the left extreme. Consequentialist-engineering argument (not attributed to Cohen).

Objections: (A) Ignores truth of beliefs, purely consequentialist. (B) Fails to consider how currency role relates to incentive-parameter role of responsibility. (C) Ignores well-being role (next section). Harmony needed between these three roles.

(A) Wrong to engineer beliefs about responsibility on basis of their consequences, irrespective of their truth: applies to engineering beliefs that responsibility is impossible as much as to engineering beliefs that responsibility is possible. Either self-deceptive or manipulative. Incompatible with aim to neutralize biasing influences on our beliefs about responsibility and justice.

(B) Responsibility already used to filter the currency to which maximin applied; consequentialist maximin calculations thus presuppose some conception of responsibility. Shouldn't the same one be used to set parameters of incentive seeking? If a conception of responsibility is good enough for the currency role, isn't it also good enough to set parameters?

Consistency argument: Whatever views about responsibility (whether truths or prevalent views in community) are used in the currency role should also be used in the incentive-parameter role.

Too simple: can require equilibrium between conception of responsibility in currency role and upshot of consequentialist maximin calculations used to fix conception of responsibility for incentive-parameter role.

Still too simple: evaluation of consequences depends on currency, but also currency depends on beliefs about responsibility, since these affect dispositions and abilities and hence what people are responsible for. Beliefs to be engineered depend on currency, currency should support itself via an engineering argument, but currency will in turn be affected by beliefs so engineered, so these must be fed back into currency calculations before system can settle.

Upshot of these complex interdependencies for engineering question unclear.

4. The Consequentialist-Engineering Argument: The Well-Being Role of Beliefs about Responsibility (pp. 243–246)

(C) Beliefs and truths about responsibility constitutive of well-being at all levels of ability: *well-being role*. Direct impact of beliefs about responsibility on well-being of worst off. Shift from Scenario 1 to Scenario 2 would reduce responsibility well-being of worst off, along with others'. How would this balance against gain to worst off from lower levels of incentive seeking? Relevance of truth of beliefs about responsibility: depriving people of sense of responsibility if responsibility is not impossible deprives them of something of very great value.

Triangular tangle of interdependencies among currency, incentive-parameter, and well-being roles. Response: avoid consequentialist engineering of beliefs about responsibility; go cognitive, encourage true beliefs about responsibility. Pressure to go cognitive even within luck-neutralizing approaches, where responsibility given a currency role. Or, drop problematic currency role, adopt bias-neutralizing rather than luck-neutralizing aim?

5. Taking the Veil to Avoid Bias: Whose Mouth Is This, Anyway? (pp. 246–254)

How do these issues look from a cognitivist, bias-neutralizing perspective, if we drop the currency role but retain the other two as the real roles of responsibility in justice? Avoids much of the above tangle of interdependencies. Responsibility still plays essential roles in well-being and in constraining acceptable levels of incentive seeking; maximin empty in absence of such constraints.

Currency: objective specification of the good subject to a universal means test, with no responsibility filter. Unoriginal. Includes responsibility well-being. Harmonizes with cognitive, bias-neutralizing approach.

Correct beliefs about responsibility should be used as parameters of incentive seeking. So need first to arrive at correct view of responsibility, and then to determine what is possible for the talented to do relative to normative expectations based on that conception. Responsibility here is in a less demanding role than in luck-neutralizing accounts; does not require detailed case-by-case judgments of responsibility to filter currency, just general account and its general implications.

Veil of ignorance as neutralizing bias re: how hard the talented can work for less. Cohen ignores role of veil; he distinguishes the mouths of the talented from the mouths of others, in assessing utterances of the incentive inequality argument. Two reasons to veil this difference:

(A) Knowledge of own talent level apt to bias your assessment of how hard the talented can work for less, and of rival general conceptions of responsibility. We are cognitively better off assessing arguments on these issues without knowing whether they come from the mouths of the talented or not: avoids biasing influences.

(B) Need to assess work-enabling role of incentives at level of populations, not individuals. "For each talented person, it is possible for her to work harder for less" does not entail "It is possible for all/most talented people to work harder for less." Veiled perspective avoids this fallacious inference by depriving us of information about ourselves and other individuals, forcing us to confront the relevant collective issue directly.

If the maximin argument for incentive inequality is a good argument behind the veil, it doesn't become a bad argument once the veil is lifted and we know whose mouth is uttering it.

6. Summing Up (pp. 254–255)

Nonregressive reason-responsiveness view of responsibility would land us in middle of spectrum of levels of incentive seeking.

Recall the potential asymmetry between talents and handicaps on reason-responsiveness conception: can be responsible in virtue of certain generic talents even if not responsible in virtue of corresponding handicaps. This could relieve some of the tension between "descriptive" and normative premises of incentive-inequality argument by reconciling normative expectations that underwrite moderate levels of incentive seeking with priority to improving position of worst off (with no responsibility filter applied to currency).

This chapter has shown how "descriptive" premise of argument for incentive inequality could be vindicated, taking account of Cohen's points. Next chapter turns to normative maximin principle.

Chapter 10: From Ignorance to Maximin: A Bias-Neutralizing Alternative (p. 256)

1. A Cognitivist Approach to Distributive Justice (pp. 256–258)

Cognitivist political philosophy: gives truth and knowledge central roles. Constraint: respond to worries that prompt political liberals to commit to neutrality about the true good, given pluralism and disagreement.

Two key ideas: (A) Can often identify and avoid bias without making controversial assumptions about the truth. Cognitive biases distort relation of belief to truth needed for knowledge. (B) Can foster and use effectively cognitive capabilities, reason-responsiveness, of citizens without making controversial assumptions about the truth.

Difficulties of recognizing bias greatest in personal sphere, reduced for an institutional division of cognitive labor.

Perfectionist liberalism can in this way respect concerns that motivate commitment to neutrality, but without such commitment.

2. Neutralizing Luck versus Neutralizing Bias (pp. 258–261)

Luck-neutralizing aim implicit in Rawls's motivations for Original Position, explicit in luck egalitarianism. Often assumed that rejection of it is anti-egalitarian. By contrast, I argue rejection of it can strengthen a broadly egalitarian position.

Negative reason: luck-neutralizing aim cannot do patterning work. Positive reason: bias-neutralizing aim may do better on this score, while responsibility still plays important background roles, i.e., incentive-parameter and well-being roles.

Biases as cognitive distortions. Antecedently unlikely that biased beliefs constitute knowledge—i.e., antecedent to views about their truth; they are not reliable inputs to deliberation. E.g., personal desires to believe something, information about how certain desires can be met. Bias is issue relative.

Distinguish Kantian, luck-neutralizing strand in Rawls from cognitive, bias-neutralizing strand. Latter goes further when detached from former. Aiming at knowledge provides reason to adopt perspective of ignorance.

3. The Perspective of Justice: An Equal Chance of Being Anyone versus Ignorance of Who You Are, and Risk versus Uncertainty (pp. 261–263)

Perspective of justice: generalization of Rawlsian framework: significant fictional point of view, from which we ask: what should be done about distribution? Does not assume exercise of constrained self-interest involved. Allows this may be a device that helps discover principles of justice rather than a way of determining what counts as principles of justice.

Two ways of characterizing the perspective of justice: you have an equal chance of being anyone (as in Harsanyian utilitarianism) versus you are radically ignorant of who you are and what you are like, your situation, etc.

Equal-chance and ignorance assumptions distinct so long as reject orthodox claim that lack of information about possible outcomes justifies assigning them equal probabilities. Rawls rejects this claim, as do experimental subjects (implicitly) and various nonexpected utility theorists.

Example: Game 1: guess color of ball drawn from urn known to contain 50 red, 50 black balls, win $100 if guess correctly. How much would you pay to play it once? Actuarial value: $50. Typical answer reflects risk aversion: $30. Compare Game 2: guess color of ball drawn from urn with 100 balls, with unknown proportions of red and black. Typical offers drop dramatically, to around $5. The difference reflects difference between risk aversion and uncertainty aversion.

Relations among: (A) aim to neutralize luck, equal-chance assumption, risk aversion, and (B) aim to neutralize bias, ignorance assumption, uncertainty aversion?

How does equal chance versus ignorance issue relate to risk aversion versus uncertainty aversion distinction? Risk aversion rightly veiled by Rawls as part of conception of good. If risks unknown in Original Position, risk aversion irrelevant, cannot get grip. So neither equal chance nor ignorance should admit risk aversion. By contrast, general conceptual reasons to assume intentional agents weakly prefer information to lack of it, are weakly averse to uncertainty. So can justify assumption of uncertainty aversion even if not risk aversion.

4. The Perspective of Justice: Bias versus Luck, and Why It Is Better to Suppose Ignorance of Who You Are Rather Than an Equal Chance of Being Anyone (pp. 263–267)

How does equal chance versus ignorance issue relate to luck-neutralizing versus bias-neutralizing distinction?

Bias neutralization supports ignorance assumption: e.g., ignorance of my talent levels avoids bias.

Bias neutralization opposes deciding about justice on basis of calculations of chances of gain—even if these are equal for all. (A) Cognitive bias can operate even if there is no partiality because everyone's chances are the same. Affinity with Scanlon's rejection of contractualism understood as involving an exercise of constrained self-interest. (B) Reject analogy between people and possibilities. A circumstance or a handicap being mine as opposed to someone else's is not like a possibility being actual instead of merely possible. Ignorance assumption avoids decision-theoretic reduction of interpersonal issues to risk for one person.

Luck neutralization applied to essential properties might support assumption that you have an equal chance of being anyone, but this involves dubious constitutionless selves.

Luck neutralization not needed to support ignorance assumption, as bias neutralization does the work, and avoids the problems about responsibility.

5. Maximin and the Role of Responsibility in Setting Parameters for Incentive Seeking (pp. 267–269)

Background from last chapter: truth about responsibility lies between extremes, supports moderate levels of incentive seeking. Responsibility here in an undemanding role, don't need specific judgments about who is responsible for what in particular cases, or what they would be responsible for under different conditions. But until the parameters of incentive seeking have been set, the implications of a maximin principle for distributive justice are indeterminate, and responsibility plays an essential parametric role in relation to incentive seeking.

6. How Aversion to Uncertainty Leads from Ignorance to Maximin (pp. 269–273)

Risk aversion: risk attitudes should remain veiled, and anyway risk aversion no help in getting to maximin if risks are unknown. Can we get there instead from uncertainty aversion? Same objections don't apply: weak aversion to uncertainty part of minimal rationality of intentional agent. Other things equal, intentional agents make relevant information available to themselves and take account of it.

Don't need extreme uncertainty aversion, given ignorance. Need extreme risk aversion to rule out trading off against chances of gain, under equal chance assumption. But if no chances of gain are known, no such trade-offs against uncertainty aversion are possible.

Ignorance does allow general weak desire for information (equivalent to weak uncertainty aversion) plus Pareto preference: impersonal, general desire that people be better off in terms of basic goods, other things equal.

Perspective of justice: ignorance, weak uncertainty aversion, Pareto preference for basic goods.

(A) Known fixed quantity of goods: equality avoids uncertainty about absolute and relative positions

(B) Unknown or unfixed quantity of goods: equality avoids uncertainty about relative if not absolute position

(C) Uncertainty aversion only weak, so can set it against Pareto preference to allow inequalities that benefit some so long as worst off are as well off as possible. This admits uncertainty about relative positions also. Permitting weak Pareto improvements to some admits uncertainty about who will benefit. Permitting only strong Pareto improvements to all does not.

Ignorance and aversion to ignorance work together: aversion to ignorance/bias supports ignorance assumption, which combined with aversion to ignorance drives toward equality.

Cognitivist view: normative significance of perspective of justice with assumption of ignorance is in avoidance of bias. Can reclaim egalitarian results by dissociating bias-neutralizing aim from luck-neutralizing aim. No threat of authoritarianism or threat to pluralistic democratic values here.

7. A Comparison with Ellsberg's View (pp. 274–275)

Ellsberg: distinguish probability of outcome from degree of confidence in estimate of probability. Comparison of options by expected utility, where have little confidence in assessment of risks and averse to uncertainty, may not give strong reason for choice. Other choice criteria? Maximin. May have more confidence in estimates of worst outcomes of each option.

May be reasonable to give some weight to both expected utility and maximin criteria, relative weight depending on confidence in estimates of probabilities. Trade-offs between security level and expected utility. Maximin alone almost never called for, excluding complete ignorance of probabilities as unrealistic.

Implication: complete ignorance of probabilities excludes such trade-offs, maximin results.

8. Loose Ends: Maximin, Sufficiency, and the Asymmetry between Talents and Handicaps (pp. 275–279)

How to distribute: maximin, priority, sufficiency. Notational versus substantive differences? Need for parameter tweaking to yield determinate results: e.g., parameters of incentive seeking for maximin, and threshold and absolute/relative issues for sufficiency. By tweaking parameters, can we get these views to coincide in general?

Parameters are where the action is, and importantly depend on responsibility:

(A) Beliefs about responsibility influence possible levels of incentive seeking.

(B) Certain conceptions of responsibility (hypothetical choice/self-identification, reason-responsiveness) support asymmetry between certain talents and handicaps.

Toy example of (B): *W*s lack reason-responsiveness and are worst off, *T*s are reason-responsive hence generically talented and better off. Maximin principle: make the *W*s as well off as possible. Context: levels of incentive seeking reflect asymmetry in responsibility between *W*s and *T*s. *T*s feel partly responsible for their extra product when they do extra work, and seek moderate incentives, but do not regard *W*s as responsible for being worst off; nor do *W*s see themselves this way. Reconciles moderate incentive seeking with maximin, without currency role.

Loose ends: how does asymmetry bear on threshold for sufficiency, and on whether relative as well as absolute position affects sufficiency? Do maximin and sufficiency views converge when these parametric issues are pursued?

9. Concluding Remarks (pp. 279–280)

This book has aimed to show some of the ways in which issues about responsibility interact with issues about distributive justice and with the roles responsibility can play in distributive justice. Work on distributive justice should distinguish responsibility from other values, such as desert or fairness; different conceptions of responsibility; and different roles responsibility might play in distributive justice.

Bibliography

Adams, Robert Merrihew (1985). "Involutary Sins," *Philosophical Review* 94:1, 3–31.

Andenaes, Johannes (1974). *Punishment and Deterrence*. Ann Arbor: University of Michigan Press.

Anderson, Elizabeth (1999). "What Is the Point of Equality?" *Ethics* 109, 287–337.

Anscombe, Elizabeth (1993). "Causality and Determination," in *Causation,* ed. Ernest Sosa and Michael Tooley, 88–104. Oxford: Oxford University Press.

Arneson, Richard (1989). "Equality and Equal Opportunity for Welfare," *Philosophical Studies* 56, 77–93.

——— (1990). "Liberalism, Distributive Subjectivism, and Equal Opportunity for Welfare," *Philosophy and Public Affairs* 19, 159–194.

——— (1997). "Egalitarianism and the Undeserving Poor," *Journal of Political Philosophy* 5:4, 327–350.

——— (forthcoming). "Rawls, Responsibility, and Distributive Justice," in *Justice, Political Liberalism, and Utilitarianism: Themes from Harsanyi and Rawls,* ed. Maurice Salles and John A. Weymark. Cambridge, England: Cambridge University Press.

Arrow, Kenneth J. (1963). *Social Choice and Individual Values,* 2nd ed. New Haven: Yale University Press.

Ashby, W. Ross (1956). *An Introduction to Cybernetics*. London: Methuen.

Audi, Robert (1991). "Responsible Action and Virtuous Character," *Ethics* 101, 301–321.

Bacharach, Michael, and Susan Hurley, eds. (1991). *Foundations of Decision Theory: Issues and Advances*. Oxford: Blackwell.

Barry, Brian (1989). *Theories of Justice*. London: Harvester Wheatsheaf.

——— (forthcoming). "Rationality and Want-Satisfaction," in *Justice, Political Liberalism, and Utilitarianism: Themes from Harsanyi and Rawls,* ed. Maurice Salles and John A. Weymark. Cambridge, England: Cambridge University Press.

Boden, Margaret (1996). "Autonomy and Artificiality," in *The Philosophy of Artificial Life,* ed. Margaret A. Boden, 95–108. Oxford: Oxford University Press.

Broome, John (1993). "A Cause of Preference Is Not an Object of Preference," *Social Choice and Welfare* 10, 57–68.

—— (1998). "Extended Preferences," in *Preferences,* Christoph Fehige and Ulla Wessels, de Gruyter, 279–296. Reprinted in John Broome, *Ethics out of Economics* (Cambridge, England: Cambridge University Press, 1999), 29–43.

—— (forthcoming). "Can There Be a Preference-Based Utilitarianism?" in *Justice, Political Liberalism, and Utilitarianism: Themes from Harsanyi and Rawls,* ed. Maurice Salles and John A. Weymark. Cambridge, England: Cambridge University Press.

Campbell, C. A. (1967). "In Defence of Free Will," in *In Defence of Free Will,* ed. C. A. Campbell, 35–55. London: Allen and Unwin.

Carens, Joseph H. (1981). *Equality, Moral Incentives, and the Market.* Chicago: University of Chicago Press.

Cheverie, Paul (n.d.). "The XYY Syndrome and the Judicial System," *North Carolina Central Law Journal,* 66–80.

Churchland, Paul M. (1993). "Evaluating our Self-Conception," *Mind and Language* 8, 211–222.

Clarke, Randolph (1995). "Indeterminism and Control," *American Philosophical Quarterly* 32:2, 125–137.

Cohen, Gerald A. (1989). "On the Currency of Egalitarian Justice," *Ethics* 99:4, 906–944.

—— (1992). "Incentives, Inequality and Community," in *The Tanner Lectures on Human Values,* vol. 13, ed. Grethe Petersen, 263–329. Salt Lake City: University of Utah Press.

—— (1995). "The Pareto Argument for Inequality," *Social Philosophy and Policy* 12:1, 160–185.

—— (1997). "Where the Action Is: On the Site of Distributive Justice," *Philosophy and Public Affairs* 26, 3–30.

Cohen, Joshua (1986a). "An Epistemic Conception of Democracy," *Ethics* 97, 26–38.

—— (1986b). "Reflections on Rousseau: Autonomy and Democracy," *Philosophy and Public Affairs* 15, 273–297.

Cussins, Adrian (1993). "Nonconceptual Content and the Elimination of Misconceived Composites!" *Mind and Language* 8:2, 234–252.

Dennett, Daniel C. (1984). *Elbow Room.* Oxford: Clarendon Press.

—— (1988). "Quining Qualia," in *Consciousness in Contemporary Science,* ed. A. J. Marcel and E. Bisiach, 42–77. Oxford: Clarendon Press.

Dworkin, Ronald. (1981a), "What Is Equality? Part 1: Equality of Welfare," *Philosophy and Public Affairs* 10, 185–246.

—— (1981b). "What Is Equality? Part 2: Equality of Resources," *Philosophy and Public Affairs* 10, 283–345.

Ellsberg, Daniel (1961). "Risk, Ambiguity, and the Savage Axioms," *Quarterly Journal of Economics,* 643–669.

Elster, Jon (1983). *Sour Grapes.* Cambridge, England: Cambridge University Press.

Fischer, John Martin (1982). "Responsibility and Control," *Journal of Philosophy* 79:1, 24–40.

——— (1983). "Incompatibilism," *Philosophical Studies* 43, 127–137.

——— (1987). "Responsiveness and Moral Responsibility," in *Responsibility, Character, and the Emotions,* ed. Ferdinand Schoeman, 81–106. Cambridge, England: Cambridge University Press.

——— (1994). *The Metaphysics of Free Will: An Essay on Control.* Oxford: Blackwell.

Fischer, John Martin, and Mark Ravizza, (1991). "Responsibility and Inevitability," *Ethics* 101, 258–278.

——— (1992). "The Inevitable," *Australasian Journal of Philosophy* 70, 388–404.

——— (1998). *Responsibility and Control: A Theory of Moral Responsibility.* Cambridge, England: Cambridge University Press.

Frankfurt, Harry G. (1969). "Alternate Possibilities and Moral Responsibility," *Journal of Philosophy* 66, 23.

——— (1971). "Freedom of the Will and the Concept of a Person," *Journal of Philosophy* 67:1, 5–20.

——— (1973). "Coercion and Moral Responsibility," in *Essays on Freedom of Action,* ed. Ted Honderich, 65–86. London: Routledge and Kegan Paul.

——— (1976). "Identification and Externality," in *The Identities of Persons,* ed. Amelie Rorty, 239–251. Berkeley: University of California Press.

——— (1987a). "Equality as a Moral Ideal," *Ethics* 98, 21–43.

——— (1987b). "Identification and Wholeheartedness," in *Responsibility, Character, and the Emotions,* ed. Ferdinand Schoeman, 27–45. Cambridge, England: Cambridge University Press.

Gardenfors, Peter, and Nils-Eric Sahlin (1982). "Unreliable Probabilities, Risk Taking, and Decision Making," *Synthese* 53, 361–386.

Glover, Jonathan (1988). *I: The Philosophy and Psychology of Personal Identity.* London: Allen Lane, Penguin Press.

Goldsmith, Robert W., and Nils-Eric Sahlin (1983). "The Role of Second-Order Probabilities in Decision-Making," in *Analysing and Aiding Decision Processes,* ed. P. C. Humphreys, O. Svenson, and A. Vari. Amsterdam: North-Holland.

Griffin, James (1997). *Value Judgements.* Oxford: Oxford University Press.

Hampton, Jean (1984). "The Moral Education Theory of Punishment," *Philosophy and Public Affairs* 13, 208–238.

Hannan, Barbara (1993). "Don't Stop Believing: The Case against Eliminativist Materialism," *Mind and Language* 8:2, 165–179.

Harsanyi, John C. (1976). *Essays on Ethics, Social Behavior, and Scientific Explanation.* Dordrecht: Reidel.

——— (1977), *Rational Behavior and Bargaining Equilibrium in Games and Social Situations.* Cambridge, England: Cambridge University Press.

———— (1998). "John Rawls' Theory of Justice: Some Critical Comments," in *Justice, Political Liberalism, and Utilitarianism: Themes from Harsanyi and Rawls*, ed. Maurice Salles and John A. Weymark. Cambridge, England: Cambridge University Press.

Hobart, R. E. (1934). "Free Will as Involving Determinism and Inconceivable without it," *Mind* 43, 1–27.

Honderich, Ted (1993). *How Free Are You? The Determinism Problem*. Oxford: Oxford University Press.

Honderich, Ted, ed. (1973). *Essays on Freedom of Action*. London: Routledge and Kegan Paul.

Honoré, Tony (1988). "Responsibility and Luck," *Law Quarterly Review* 104, 530–553.

Hooker, C. A., H. B. Penfold, and R. J. Evans (1992). "Control, Connectionism and Cognition: Towards a New Regulatory Paradigm," *British Journal of Philosophy of Science* 43, 517–536.

Horgan, Terence (1993). "The Austere Ideology of Folk Psychology," *Mind and Language* 8, 282–297.

Hornsby, Jennifer (1980). *Actions*. London: Routledge and Kegan Paul.

Hurley, S. L. (1989). *Natural Reasons*. New York: Oxford University Press.

———— (1993). "Justice without Constitutive Luck," in *Ethics, Royal Institute of Philosophy Supplement*, vol. 35, ed. A. Phillips Griffiths, 179–212. Cambridge, England: Cambridge University Press.

———— (1995). "Troubles with Responsibility," *Boston Review* 20:2, 12–3.

———— (1998). *Consciousness in Action*. Cambridge, Mass.: Harvard University Press.

———— (2000a). "Cognitivism in Political Philosophy," in *Morality and Well-Being: Essays in Honour of James Griffin*, ed. Roger Crisp and Brad Hooker, 177–208. Oxford: Oxford University Press.

———— (2000b). "Is Responsibility Essentially Impossible?" *Philosophical Studies* 99, 229–268.

———— (2000c). "Responsibility, Reason, and Irrelevant Alternatives," *Philosophy and Public Affairs* 28, 205–241.

———— (2001). "Luck and Equality," with response by Richard Arneson, *Proceedings of the Aristotelian Society*, supp. vol. 75, 51–72.

———— (forthcoming). "Distributive Justice and Health," commissioned by the World Health Organization for *Fairness and Goodness: Ethical Dimensions of Health Resource Allocation*, ed. Daniel Wikler and Christopher Murray. World Health Organization.

———— (2002a). "Luck, Responsibility, and the 'Natural Lottery,'" *Journal of Political Philosophy* 10:1, 79–94.

———— (2002b). "Roemer on Responsibility and Equality," *Law and Philosophy* 21, 39–64.

Hutchins, Edwin (1995). *Cognition in the Wild*. Cambridge, Mass.: MIT Press.

Jackson, Frank, and Phillip Pettit (1983). "Folk Belief and Commonplace Belief," *Mind and Language* 8, 298–305.

Kenny, Anthony (1978). *Freewill and Responsibility*. London: Routledge and Kegan Paul.

Klein, Martha (1990). *Determinism, Blameworthiness and Deprivation*. Oxford: Clarendon Press.

Levine, Andrew (1974). "Rawls' Kantianism," *Social Theory and Practice* 3, 47–63.

Lewis, David (1970). "How to Define Theoretical Terms," *Journal of Philosophy* 67, 427–446.

——— (1986). "Causation," in *Philosophical Papers,* vol. 2, 159–213. New York: Oxford University Press.

Luhrmann, T. (1989). *Persuasions of the Witch's Craft*. Cambridge, Mass.: Harvard University Press.

Lyons, David (1972). "Rawls vs. Utilitarianism," *Journal of Philosophy* 69:18, 535–545.

Mackie, J. L. (1977). *Ethics: Inventing Right and Wrong*. Harmondsworth, Middlesex: Penguin.

Marken, Richard S. (1986). "Perceptual Organization of Behavior: A Hierarchical Control Model of Coordinated Action," *Journal of Experimental Psychology: Human Perception and Performance* 12:3, 267–276.

McClennan, Edward F. (1974). "Review of Barry, The Liberal Theory of Justice," *Social Theory and Practice* 3, 117–122.

——— (1990). *Rationality and Dynamic Choice*. Cambridge, England: Cambridge University Press.

Mill, John Stuart (1958). *Considerations of Representative Government*. New York: Liberal Arts Press.

Moon, J. Donald (1988). "The Moral Basis of the Welfare State," in *Democracy and the Welfare State,* ed. Amy Gutman, 27–52. Princeton: Princeton University Press.

Moore, G. E. (1952). "Reply to My Critics," in *The Philosophy of G. E. Moore,* 2nd ed., ed. P. Schilpp, 535–687. New York: Tudor.

Moore, Michael S. (1987). "The Moral Worth of Retribution," in *Responsibility, Character, and the Emotions,* ed. Ferdinand Schoeman, 179–219. Cambridge, England: Cambridge University Press.

Nagel, Thomas (1979). *Mortal Questions*. Cambridge, England: Cambridge University Press.

——— (1986). *The View from Nowhere*. Oxford: Oxford University Press.

Nozick, Robert (1974). *Anarchy, State and Utopia*. New York: Basic Books.

——— (1981). *Philosophical Explanations*. Cambridge, Mass.: Harvard University Press.

Otsuka, Michael (1998). "Incompatibilism and the Avoidance of Blame," *Ethics* 108, 685–701.

Owens, David (1992). *Causes and Coincidences.* Cambridge, England: Cambridge University Press.

Papineau, David (1996). "Theory-Dependent Terms," *Philosophy of Science* 63, 1–20.

Parfit, Derek (1984). *Reasons and Persons.* Oxford: Oxford University Press.

——— (1995). "Equality or Priority?" Lindley Lecture, 1991, Dept. of Philosophy, University of Kansas, reprinted in *Some Questions for Egalitarians,* ed. Matthew Clayton and Andrew Williams, 81–125. London: Macmillan, 2000.

Potter, Beatrix (1909). *The Tale of Ginger and Pickles.* London: Penguin.

Powers, William T. (1973). *Behavior: The Control of Perception.* Chicago: Aldine.

Putnam, Hilary (1975). "The Meaning of 'Meaning,'" in *Mind, Language, and Reality,* 215–271. Cambridge, England: Cambridge University Press.

Raiffa, Howard (1961). "Risk, Ambiguity, and the Savage Axioms: Comment," *Quarterly Journal of Economics* 75, 690–694.

Ramsey, William, Stephen Stich, and Joseph Garon (1991). "Connectionism, Eliminativism and the Future of Folk Psychology," in *The Future of Folk Psychology: Intentionality and Cognitive Science,* ed. John D. Greenwood, 93–119. Cambridge, England: Cambridge University Press. Also in *Philosophical Perspectives,* vol. 4, 499–533, in James E. Tomberlin, ed., *Action Theory and Philosophy of Mind.* Atascadero, Calif.: Ridgeview.

Rawls, John (1971). *A Theory of Justice.* Cambridge, Mass.: Harvard University Press.

——— (1982). "Social Unity and Primary Goods," in *Utilitarianism and Beyond,* ed. Amartya Sen and Bernard Williams, 159–185. Cambridge, England: Cambridge University Press.

——— (1985). "Justice as Fairness: Political not Metaphysical," *Philosophy and Public Affairs* 14, 223–251.

——— (1993). *Political Liberalism.* New York: Columbia University Press.

——— (2001). *Justice as Fairness: A Restatement,* ed. Erin Kelley. Cambridge, Mass.: Harvard University Press.

Raz, Joseph (1986). *The Morality of Freedom.* Oxford: Clarendon Press.

——— (1989). "Liberalism, Skepticism, and Democracy," *Iowa Law Review* 74, 761–786.

Ripstein, Arthur (1994). "Equality, Luck, and Responsibility," *Philosophy and Public Affairs* 23, 1–23.

Roemer, John E. (1985). "Equality of Talent," *Economics and Philosophy* 1, 151–187.

——— (1986). "Equality of Resources Implies Equality of Welfare," *Quarterly Journal of Economics,* 751–784.

——— (1987). "Egalitarianism, Responsibility and Information," *Economics and Philosophy* 3, 215–244.

——— (1993). "A Pragmatic Theory of Responsibility for the Egalitarian Planner," *Philosophy and Public Affairs* 22, 146–166.

——— (1995). "Equality and Responsibility," *Boston Review* 20:2, 3–7, 15–16.

——— (1996). *Theories of Distributive Justice.* Cambridge: Harvard University Press.

——— (1998). *Equality of Opportunity.* Cambridge, Mass.: Harvard University Press.

Sabini, John, and Maury Silver (1987). "Emotions, Responsibility, and Character," in *Responsibility, Character, and the Emotions,* ed. Ferdinand Schoeman, 165–178. Cambridge, England: Cambridge University Press.

Salmon, Nathan (1982). *Reference and Essence.* Oxford: Blackwell.

Salmon, Wesley C. (1993). "Probabilistic Causality," in Ernest Sosa and Michael Tooley, eds., *Causation* (Oxford: Oxford University Press), 137–153. Reprinted from *Pacific Philosophical Quarterly* 61 (1980), 50–74.

Sandel, Michael J. (1982). *Liberalism and the Limits of Justice.* Cambridge, England: Cambridge University Press.

Scanlon, T. M. (1975). "Preference and Urgency," *Journal of Philosophy* 72:19, 655–669.

——— (1982). "Contractualism and Utilitarianism," in *Utilitarianism and Beyond,* ed. Amartya Sen and Bernard Williams, 103–128. Cambridge, England: Cambridge University Press.

——— (1986). "Equality of Resources and Equality of Welfare: A Forced Marriage?" *Ethics* 97, 111–118.

——— (1988). "The Significance of Choice," in *The Tanner Lectures on Human Values,* vol. 8, ed. S. MacMurrin, 151–216. Salt Lake City: University of Utah Press.

——— (1998). *What We Owe to Each Other.* Cambridge, Mass.: Harvard University Press.

Scheffler, Samuel (1992). "Responsibility, Reactive Attitudes, and Liberalism in Philosophy and Politics," *Philosophy and Public Affairs* 21:4, 299–323.

Schoeman, Ferdinand (1987). "Statistical Norms and Moral Attributions," in *Responsibility, Character, and the Emotions,* ed. Ferdinand Schoeman, 287–315. Cambridge, England: Cambridge University Press.

Sen, Amartya K. (1970). *Collective Choice and Social Welfare.* San Francisco: Holden-Day.

——— (1973). *On Economic Inequality.* Oxford: Clarendon Press.

——— (1979). "Utilitarianism and Welfarism," *Journal of Philosophy* 76:9, 463–489.

——— (1980). "Equality of What?" in *The Tanner Lectures on Human Values,* ed. S. McMurrin, 197–220. Salt Lake City: University of Utah Press.

——— (1987). *The Standard of Living.* Cambridge, England: Cambridge University Press.

——— (1990). "Justice: Means vs. Freedoms," *Philosophy and Public Affairs* 19:2, 111–121.

——— (1992). *Inequality Reexamined.* Cambridge, Mass.: Harvard University Press.

Shatz, David (1986). "Free Will and the Structure of Motivation," in *Midwest*

Studies in Philosophy: Studies in the Philosophy of Mind, vol. 10, ed. Peter French, Theodore E. Uehling Jr., and Howard K. Wettstein, 451–482. Minneapolis: University of Minnesota Press.

Slitt, Wayne (1971). "The XYY Chromosome Abnormality and Criminal Behavior," *Connecticut Law Review* 3, 484–510.

Sloman, Aaron (1993). "The Mind as a Control System," in *Philosophy and Cognitive Science, Royal Institute of Philosophy Supplement: 34,* ed. Christopher Hookway and Donald Petersen, 69–110. Cambridge, England: Cambridge University Press.

Slote, Michael (1985). "Book Review: Peter van Inwagen: 'An Essay on Free Will,'" *Journal of Philosophy* 72:6, 327–330.

Sorabji, Richard, ed. (1980). *Necessity, Cause and Blame: Perspectives on Aristotle's Theory.* London: Duckworth.

Steiner, Hillel (1994). *An Essay on Rights.* Oxford: Blackwell.

—— (1997). "Choice and Circumstance," *Ratio* 10:3, 298–312.

Stich, Stephen P. (1991). "Radical Ascent: Do True Believers Exist?" *Proceedings of the Aristotelian Society,* supp. 65, 229–244.

—— (1996). *Deconstructing the Mind.* New York: Oxford University Press, 1996.

Strawson, Galen (1986). *Freedom and Belief.* London: Methuen.

—— (1989). "Consciousness, Free Will, and the Unimportance of Determinism," *Inquiry* 32, 3–27.

—— (1991). *Freedom and Belief,* 2nd ed. Oxford: Clarendon Press.

—— (1994). "The Impossibility of Moral Responsibility," *Philosophical Studies* 75, 5–24.

Strawson, P. F. (1974). "Freedom and Resentment," in *Freedom and Resentment and Other Essays,* 1–25. London: Methuen.

Taylor, Charles (1985). *Philosophy and the Human Sciences.* Cambridge, England: Cambridge University Press.

Temkin, Larry S. (1986). "Inequality," *Philosophy and Public Affairs* 15, 99–121.

—— (1993). *Inequality* (New York: Oxford University Press).

Van Inwagen, Peter, ed. (1983). *An Essay on Free Will.* Oxford: Clarendon Press.

Van Parijs, Philippe (1995). *Real Freedom for All.* Oxford: Clarendon Press.

Vandenbroucke, Frank (1999). *Social Justice and Individual Ethics in an Open Society.* Ph.D. diss., Oxford University.

Wallace, R. Jay (1996). *Responsibility and the Moral Sentiments.* Cambridge, Mass.: Harvard University Press.

Walzer, Michael (1983). *Spheres of Justice.* New York: Basic Books.

Watson, Gary, ed. (1982). *Free Will.* New York: Oxford University Press.

—— (1987). "Responsibility and the Limits of Evil: Variations on a Strawsonian Theme," in *Responsibility, Character, and the Emotions,* ed. Ferdinand Schoeman, 256–286. Cambridge, England: Cambridge University Press.

Wiggins, David (1973). "Towards a Reasonable Libertarianism," in *Essays on Free-*

dom of Action, ed. Ted Honderich, 49–50. London: Routledge and Kegan Paul.

Williams, Bernard (1973). "Imagination and the Self," in *Problems of the Self.* Cambridge, England: Cambridge University Press, 40–45.

——— (1981). *Moral Luck.* Cambridge, England: Cambridge University Press.

Wilkerson, Richard G. (1996). *Unhealthy Societies: the Afflictions of Inequality.* London: Routledge.

Wolf, Susan (1980). "Asymmetrical Freedom," *Journal of Philosophy* 77:3, 151–166.

——— (1987). "Sanity and the Metaphysics of Responsibility," in *Responsibility, Character, and the Emotions,* ed. Ferdinand Schoeman, 46–62. Cambridge, England: Cambridge University Press.

——— (1990). *Freedom within Reason.* New York: Oxford University Press.

Wood, Allen W. (1984). *Self and Nature in Kant's Philosophy.* Ithaca: Cornell University Press.

Woodard, Christopher (1998). "Egalitarianism, Responsibility, and Desert," *Imprints* 3:1, 25–448.

Index

ability claim, 62
ability to act in accordance with reason, 33, 36, 41
ability-to-avoid-blame requirements, 17, 76, 77, 79
ability-to-do-otherwise requirements, 16–19, 79, 221, 222; alternate-sequence, 32; embarrassed, 76; regression and, 20–23, 24, 25, 28, 30, 103; threatening, 53
abuse, 182, 183
accident, 47, 48
accountability, 44n, 92n; moral, 107
acting otherwise, 16, 17, 18
acts, 42, 43, 45; bad, 36; evil, 58–59; praiseworthy, 60; right, 37; wrong, 37
actual choice, 95, 142, 168, 189; causal responsibility and, 24, 26, 27, 28, 29, 80, 92, 93; hypothetical choice versus, 30, 31, 219–224
actual control, 24, 28, 30, 31, 80, 92, 93, 168, 189, 219–224; causal, 25, 26, 27, 29, 42
actual-sequence conditions/requirements, 17, 19, 41, 43, 48, 60, 69, 92, 219–222; ability to act in accordance with reason, 33; ability-to-do-otherwise and, 18; alternate-sequence confused with, 44, 102; Autonomy View, 34; blame, 64, 70; causal, 71, 105; counterfactual characterizations in, 55; determinism and, 40; dispositional, 20; distinction between alternate-sequence and, 35, 52, 53, 61, 62; hypothetical choice and, 31; middle-ground account, 49, 51; Real Self View, 34, 35; regression, 32, 52, 79
Adams, R. M., 31n
addiction, 69–70

advantages, 150, 154, 196, 264; access to, 141; natural, 117, 267, 270
agency, 111, 113, 119n
alternate sequence conditions/ requirements, 20, 24, 33, 41, 105, 220–222; ability-to-do-otherwise requirement, 32, 219; actual-sequence confused with, 44, 102; counterfactual-intervention, 39; distinction between actual-sequence and, 35, 52, 53, 61, 62; hypothetical choice and, 31; incompatible with determinism, 103; indeterminism, 91, 171n; irrelevant to responsibility, 19, 46, 54–79; misunderstanding of control and, 42; outright possibility, 16, 17, 18; possible, 36, 37, 38, 40, 45
ambiguity, 20, 275
ambitions, 142, 143, 170
Andenaes, J., 215n
Anderson, E., 205n
animism, 92, 93–95, 96, 101–102, 103
Anscombe, E., 72n
antecedents, 95, 113; causal, 173
applications, 81, 82, 100, 103, 104; negative, 135; positive, 101
arbitrary hodge-podge scenario, 83, 84n, 86, 87, 100, 102, 104
Arneson, R., 134, 136, 141n, 144n, 147, 167, 176n, 255n
Arrow, K. J., 82
Ashby, W. R., 43n
aspiration, 144–145
asymmetry, 228; acts and omissions, 45; praise and blame, 33, 35, 36, 40, 42; talents and handicaps, 45, 46, 275–279

331